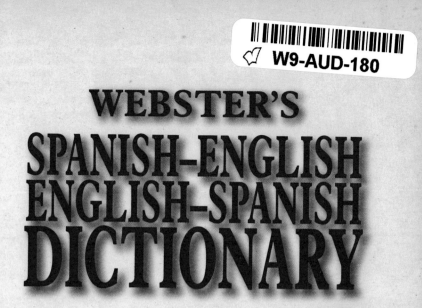

WEBSTER'S
SPANISH–ENGLISH
ENGLISH–SPANISH
DICTIONARY

**GEDDES &
GROSSET**

Published 2004 by Geddes & Grosset,
David Dale House, New Lanark, ML11 9DJ, Scotland

ISBN 1 84205 434 1

Printed and bound in Poland

Spanish–English Dictionary

A

a *prep* to; in; at; according to; on; by; for; of.
abadía *f* abbey.
abajo *adv* under, underneath; below.
abalanzarse *vr* to rush forward.
abandonado/da *adj* derelict; abandoned; neglected.
abandonar *vt* to abandon; to leave: —~**se** *vr* ~ **a** to give oneself up to.
abarcar *vt* to include; to monopolize.
abarrotado/da *adj* packed.
abarrotar *vt* to tie down; *(mar)* to stow.
abastecer *vt* to purvey.
abatido/da *adj* dejected, low-spirited; abject.
abatimiento *m* low spirits *pl*, depression.
abatir *vt* to knock down; to humble.
abdicar *vt* to abdicate.
abdomen *m* abdomen.
abdominal *adj* abdominal.
abecedario *m* alphabet; spelling book, primer.
abeja *f* bee.
aberración *f* aberration.
abertura *f* aperture, chink, opening.
abeto *m* fir tree.
abierto/ta *adj* open; sincere; frank.
abismal *adj* abysmal.
abismo *m* abyss; gulf; hell.
ablandar *vt* , *vi* to soften.
abnegado/da *adj* selfless.
abogacía *f* legal profession.
abogado/a *m/f* lawyer; barrister.
abogar *vi* to intercede: —— **por** to advocate.
abolir *vt* to abolish.
abollar *vt* to dent.
abonado/da *adj* paid-up: —*m/f* subscriber.
abonar *vt* to settle; to fertilize.
abono *m* payment; subscription; dung, manure.
aborrecer *vt* to hate, abhor.
abortar *vi* to miscarry; to have an abortion.
aborto *m* abortion; monster.
abotonar *vt* to button.
abovedado/da *adj* vaulted.
abrasar *vt* to burn; to parch: ——**se** *vr* to burn oneself.
abrazar *vt* to embrace; to surround; to contain.
abrazo *m* embrace.
abrebotellas *m invar* bottle opener.
abrelatas *m invar* can opener.
abreviar *vt* to abridge, cut short.
abridor *m* opener.
abrigar *vt* to shelter; to protect.
abrigo *m* shelter; protection; aid.
abril *m* April.
abrillantar *vt* to polish.
abrir *vt* to open; to unlock.
abrochar *vt* to button; to do up.
abrumar *vt* to overwhelm.
absolución *f* forgiveness, absolution.
absoluto/ta *adj* absolute.
absorber *vt* to absorb.
absorción *f* absorption; takeover.
absorto *adj* engrossed.

abstemio *adj* teetotal.
abstracción *f* abstraction.
abstracto/ta *adj* abstract.
abstraer *vt* to abstract: ——**se** *vr* to be absorbed.
absuelto/ta *adj* absolved.
absurdo *adj* absurd.
abuela *f* grandmother.
abuelo *m* grandfather.
abulia *f* lethargy.
abultado/da *adj* bulky, large, massive.
abultar *vt* to increase, enlarge: —*vi* to be bulky.
abundante *adj* abundant, copious.
aburrido/da *adj* boring, bored.
aburrir *vt* to bore, weary.
abusar *vt* to abuse.
acá *adv* here.
acabado/da *adj* perfect, accomplished; old.
acabar *vt* to finish, complete; to achieve: ——**se** *vr* to finish, expire.
academia *f* academy; literary society.
acaecer *vi* to happen.
acallar *vt* to quiet, hush; to soften, appease.
acalorado/da *adj* heated.
acampar *vt (mil)* to encamp.
acanalado/da *adj* grooved; fluted.
acaparar *vt* to monopolize; to hoard.
acariciar *vt* to fondle, caress.
acarrear *vt* to transport; to occasion.
acaso *m* chance: —*adv* perhaps.
acatarrarse *vr* to catch cold.
acceder *vi* to agree: —~ **a** to have access to.
accesible *adj* attainable; accessible.
acceso *m* access; fit.
accidentado/da *adj* uneven; hilly; eventful.
accidental *adj* accidental; casual.
accidente *m* accident.
acción *f* action, operation; share.
accionar *vt* to work.
accionista *m* shareholder.
acebo *m* holly tree.
acechar *vt* to lie in ambush for; to spy on.
aceite *m* oil.
aceituna *f* olive.
aceitunado/da *adj* olive-green.
aceleración *f* acceleration.
aceleradamente *adv* swiftly, hastily.
acelerar *vt* to accelerate; to hurry.
acento *m* accent.
aceptar *vt* to accept, admit.
acera *f* sidewalk.
acerca *prep* about, relating to.
acercar *vt* to move nearer: —~**se** *vr*~ **a** to approach.
acero *m* steel.
acertar *vt* to hit; to guess right.
acertijo *m* riddle.
achacar *vt* to impute.
achaque *m* ailment; excuse; subject, matter.
achicar *vt* to diminish; to humiliate; to bale (out).
achicharrar *vt* to scorch; to overheat.
aciago/ga *adj* unlucky; ominous.

ácido *m* acid: —~/da *adj* acid, sour.
acierto *m* success; solution; dexterity.
aclamar *vt* to applaud, acclaim.
aclaración *f* clarification.
aclarar *vt* to clear; to brighten; to explain; to clarify.
acobardar *vt* to intimidate.
acodarse *vr* to lean.
acoger *vt* to receive; to welcome; to harbor: —~se *vr* to take refuge.
acogida *f* reception; asylum.
acometida *f* attack, assault.
acomodar *vt* to accommodate, arrange: —~se *vr* to comply.
acompañar *vt* to accompany; to join; *(mus)* to accompany.
acompasado/da *adj* measured; wellproportioned.
acondicionar *vt* to arrange; to condition.
acongojar *vt* to distress.
aconsejar *vt* to advise: —~se *vr* to take advice.
acontecer *vi* to happen.
acontecimiento *m* event, incident.
acoplar *vt* to couple; to fit; to connect.
acordar *vt* to agree; to remind: —~se *vr* to agree; to remember.
acorde *adj* harmonious: —*m* chord.
acordeón *m* accordion.
acorralar *vt* to round up; to intimidate.
acortar *vt* to abridge, shorten: —~se *vr* to become shorter.
acostar *vt* to put to bed; to lay down: —~se *vr* to go to bed; to lie down.
acostumbrar *vi* to be used to: —*vt* to accustom: —~se *vr* ~ **a** to become used to.
acotar *vt* to set bounds to; to annotate.
ácrata *m/f* anarchist.
acreditar *vt* to guarantee; to assure; to authorize.
acreedor *m* creditor.
acribillar *vt* to riddle with bullets; to molest, torment.
acta *f* act: —~s *fpl* records *pl.*
actitud *f* attitude; posture.
actividad *f* activity; liveliness.
activo/va *adj* active; diligent.
acto *m* act, action; act of a play; ceremony.
actor *m* actor; plaintiff.
actriz *f* actress.
actuación *f* action; behavior; proceedings *pl.*
actual *adj* actual, present.
actualizar *vt* to update.
actuar *vt* to work; to operate: —*vi* to work; to act.
acuarela *f* watercolor.
acudir *vi* to go to; to attend; to assist.
acuerdo *m* agreement: —**de** ~ OK.
acumular *vt* to accumulate, collect.
acurrucarse *vr* to squat; to huddle up.
adelantado/da *adj* advanced; fast.
adelantar *vt , vi* to advance, accelerate; to pass.
adelante *adv* forward(s): —*excl* come in!
adelanto *m* advance; progress; improvement.
adelgazar *vt* to make thin or slender; to discuss with subtlety.
además *adv* moreover, besides: —~**de** besides.
adentro *adv* in; inside.
aderezar *vt* to dress, adorn; to prepare; to season.
adeudar *vt* to owe: —~se *vr* to run into debt.
adherir *vi:* —~ **a** to adhere to; to espouse.
adiestrar *vt* to guide; to teach, to instruct.
adiós *excl* goodbye; hello.

adivinar *vt* to foretell; to guess.
admirar *vt* to admire; to surprise: —~se *vr* to be surprised.
admitir *vt* to admit; to let in; to concede; to permit.
admonición *f* warning.
adobar *vt* to dress; to season.
adobe *m* adobe, sun-dried brick.
adobo *m* dressing; pickle sauce.
adolecer *vi* to suffer from.
adolescencia *f* adolescence.
adónde *adv* where.
adoptar *vt* to adopt.
adoquín *m* paving stone.
adorar *vt* to adore; to love.
adormecer *vt* to put to sleep: —~se *vr* to fall asleep.
adornar *vt* to embellish, adorn.
adosado/da *adj* semi-detached.
adquirir *vt* to acquire.
adrede *adv* on purpose.
aduana *f* customs *pl.*
adueñarse *vr:* —~ **de** to take possession of.
adular *vt* to flatter.
adulterio *m* adultery.
adulto/ta *adj , m/f* adult, grown-up.
advenedizo *m* upstart.
advenimiento *m* arrival; accession.
adversidad *f* adversity; setback.
advertencia *f* warning, foreword.
advertir *vt* to notice; to warn.
aerodeslizador *m* hovercraft.
aeronave *f* spaceship.
aeropuerto *m* airport.
afán *m* hard work; desire.
afanar *vt* to harass; *(col)* to pinch: —~se *vr* to strive.
afear *vt* to deform, misshape.
afección *f* affection; fondness, attachment; disease.
afectar *vt* to affect, feign.
afectuoso/sa *adj* affectionate; moving; tender.
afeitar *vt :* —~se *vr* to shave.
aferrar *vt* to grapple, grasp, seize.
afianzar *vt* to strengthen; to prop up.
aficionado/da *adj* keen: —*m/f* lover, devotee; amateur.
afilado *adj* sharp.
afilar *vt* to sharpen, grind.
afín *m* related; similar.
afinar *vt* to tune; to refine.
afincarse *vr* to settle.
afirmar *vt* to secure, fasten; to affirm, assure.
aflicción *f* affliction, grief.
aflictivo/va *adj* distressing.
aflojar *vt* to loosen, slacken, relax.
aflorar *vi* to emerge.
afluente *adj* flowing: —*m* tributary.
afónico/ca *adj* hoarse; voiceless.
afortunado/da *adj* fortunate, lucky.
afrenta *f* outrage; insult.
afrontar *vt* to confront; to bring face to face.
afuera *adv* out, outside.
agacharse *vr* to stoop, squat.
agarradero *m* handle.
agarrar *vt* to grasp, seize: —~se *vr* to hold on tightly.
agasajar *vt* to receive and treat kindly; to regale.
agenciarse *vr* to obtain.
agenda *f* diary.
agente *m* agent; policeman.

ágil *adj* agile.

agilidad *f* agility, nimbleness.

agitar *vt* to wave; to move: —~se *vr* to become excited; to become worried.

aglomeración *f* crowd; jam.

agobiar *vt* to weigh down; to oppress; to burden.

agolparse *vr* to assemble in crowds.

agonía *f* agony.

agorar *vt* to predict.

agostar *vt* to parch.

agosto *m* August.

agotado/da *adj* exhausted; finished; sold out.

agotar *vt* to exhaust; to drain; to misspend.

agradable *adj* pleasant; lovely.

agradar *vt* to please, gratify.

agradecer *vt* to be grateful for; to thank.

agradecido/da *adj* thankful.

agrandar *vt* to enlarge; to exaggerate.

agrario/ria *adj* agrarian; agricultural.

agravante *f* further difficulty.

agraviar *vt* to wrong; to offend: —~se *vr* to be aggrieved; to be piqued.

agredir *vt* to attack.

agregar *vt* to aggregate, heap together; to collate; to appoint.

agreste *adj* rustic, rural.

agrícola *adj* farming *compd*.

agricultor/ra *m/f* farmer.

agrietarse *vr* to crack.

agrimensor *m* surveyor.

agrio *adj* sour, acrid; rough, craggy; sharp, rude, unpleasant.

agrupar *vt* to group, cluster; to crowd.

agua *f* water.

aguacate *m* avocado pear.

aguacero *m* cloudburst, downpour.

aguado/da *adj* watery.

aguafuerte *m* etching.

aguamarina *f* aquamarine (gem stone).

aguanieve *f* sleet.

aguantar *vt* to bear, suffer; to hold up.

aguardar *vt* to wait for.

aguarrás *f* turpentine.

agudo/da *adj* sharp; keen-edged; smart; fine; acute; witty; brisk.

aguijón *m* sting of a bee, wasp, etc; stimulation.

águila *f* eagle; genius.

aguileño/ña *adj* aquiline; sharpfeatured.

aguja *f* needle; spire; hand; magnetic needle; (*ferro*) points *pl*.

agujerear *vt* to pierce, bore.

agujero *m* hole.

ahí *adv* there.

ahijada *f* goddaughter.

ahijado *m* godson.

ahínco *m* earnestness; eagerness.

ahogar *vt* to smother; to drown; to suffocate; to oppress; to quench.

ahora *adv* now, at present; just now.

ahorrar *vt* to save; to avoid.

ahumar *vt* to smoke, cure (in smoke): —~se *vr* to fill with smoke.

ahuyentar *vt* to drive off; to dispel.

aire *m* air; wind; aspect; musical composition.

aislar *vt* to insulate; to isolate.

ajardinado/da *adj* landscaped.

ajedrez *m* chess.

ajedrezado/da *adj* chequered.

ajeno/na *adj* someone else's; foreign; ignorant; improper.

ajetreo *m* activity; bustling.

ajo *m* garlic.

ajorca *f* bracelet.

ajustar *vt* to regulate, adjust; to settle (a balance); to fit.

al = a el.

ala *f* wing; aisle; row, file; brim: —*m/f* winger.

alabar *vt* to praise; to applaud.

alacena *f* cupboard, closet.

alacrán *m* scorpion.

alambre *m* wire.

alameda *f* avenue; poplar grove.

álamo *m* poplar.

alargar *vt* to lengthen; to extend.

alarido *m* outcry, shout: —dar ~s to howl.

alarma *f* alarm.

alba *f* dawn.

albañil *m* mason, bricklayer.

albarán *m* invoice.

albaricoque *m* apricot.

albedrío *m* free will.

albergue *m* shelter: —~ de juventud youth hostel.

albóndiga *f* meatball.

albornoz *m* burnous: —~ de bañio bath robe.

alboroto *m* noise; disturbance, riot.

alborozo *m* joy.

albricias *fpl* good news *pl*.

albufera *f* lagoon.

álbum *m* album.

alcachofa *f* artichoke.

alcalde *m* mayor.

alcaldesa *f* mayoress.

alcantarilla *m* sewer; gutter.

alcanzar *vt* to reach; to get, obtain; to hit.

alcaparra *f* caper.

alcayata *f* hook.

alcázar *m* castle, fortress.

alcornoque *m* cork tree.

aldea *f* village.

aleatorio/ria *adj* random.

aleccionar *vt* to instruct; to train.

alegar *vt* to allege; to quote.

alegrar *vt* to cheer; to poke; to liven up: —~se *vr* to get merry.

alegre *adj* happy; merry, joyful; content.

alegría *f* happiness; merriment.

alejar *vt* to remove; to estrange: —~se *vr* to go away.

alemán/ana *adj* , *m/f* German: —*m* German language.

alentar *vt* to encourage.

alergia *f* allergy.

alero *m* gable-end; eaves *pl*.

alertar *vt* to alert.

aleta *f* fin; wing; flipper; fender.

alfabeto *m* alphabet.

alfarería *f* pottery.

alféizar *m* window sill.

alfiler *m* pin; clip; clothes pin.

alfombra *f* carpet; rug.

alga *f* (*bot*) seaweed.

algo *pn* something; anything: —*adv* somewhat.

algodón *m* cotton; cotton plant; cotton wool.

alguien *pn* someone, somebody; anyone, anybody.

alguno/na *adj* some; any; no: —*pn* someone, somebody.

alhaja f jewel.
aliado/da adj allied.
alianza f alliance, league; wedding ring.
alicates mpl pincers pl, nippers pl.
aliciente m attraction; incitement.
aliento m breath; respiration.
aligerar vt to lighten; to alleviate; to hasten; to ease.
alijo m lightening of a ship; alleviation; cache.
alimentar vt to feed, nourish: —se vr to feed.
aliñar vt to adorn; to season.
alinear vt to arrange in line: —se vr to line up.
alisar vt to plane; to polish; to smooth.
aliviar vt to lighten; to ease; to relieve, mollify.
allá adv there; over there; then.
allanar vt to level, flatten; to subdue; to burgle.
allí adv there, in that place.
alma f soul; human being.
almacén m warehouse, store; magazine.
almacenar vt to store (up).
almeja f clam.
almena f battlement.
almendra f almond.
almíbar m syrup.
almirez m mortar.
almizcle m musk.
almohada f pillow; cushion.
almorranas fpl hemorrhoids pl.
almuerzo m lunch.
alocado/da adj crazy; foolish; inconsiderate.
alojamiento m lodgings, rooming house; housing.
alpargata f rope-soled shoe.
alpinismo m mountaineering.
alquilar vt to rent; to hire.
alquitrán m tar, liquid pitch.
alrededor adv around.
alta f (mil) discharge from hospital.
altanero/ra adj haughty, arrogant, vain, proud.
altavoz m loudspeaker, amplifier.
alterar vt to alter, change; to disturb.
altercado m altercation, controversy; quarrel.
alterno/na adj alternate; alternating.
Alteza f Highness (title).
altibajos mpl ups and downs pl.
altitud f height; altitude.
altivo/va adj haughty, proud, highflown.
alto/ta adj high; tall: —m height; story; highland; (mil) halt; (mus) alto: —¡~!/ ¡~ ahí! interj stop!
altura f height; depth; mountain summit; altitude.
alubia f kidney bean.
alucinar vt to blind, deceive: —vi to hallucinate.
alumbrado m lighting; illumination.
alumbrar vt to light: —vi to give birth.
alumno/na m/f student, pupil.
alza f rise; sight.
alzar vt to raise, lift up: —se vr to get up; to rise in rebellion.
ama f mistress, owner; housewife; foster mother.
amable adj kind, nice.
amagar vt to threaten; to shake one's fist at: —vi to feint.
amamantar vt to suckle.
amanecer vi to dawn: —al ~ at daybreak.
amanerado/da adj affected.
amansar vt to tame; to soften; to subdue: —se vr to calm down.
amante m/f lover.
amapola f (bot) poppy.

amar vt to love.
amargo/ga adj bitter, acrid; painful: — m bitterness.
amarillo/lla adj yellow: —m yellow.
amarrar vt to moor; to tie, fasten.
amasar vt to knead; (fig) to arrange, settle; to prepare.
ámbar m amber.
ambiente m atmosphere; environment.
ambiguo/gua adj ambiguous; doubtful, equivocal.
ámbito m circuit, circumference; field; scope.
ambos/bas adj , pn both.
ambulante adj traveling.
ambulatorio m state-run clinic.
amenazar vt to threaten.
ameno/na adj pleasant; delicious; flowery (of language).
América f America: —~ del Norte/del Sur North/ South America.
amianto m asbestos.
amiga f (female) friend.
amigo m friend; comrade; lover: —~/ga adj friendly.
aminorar vt to diminish; to reduce.
amistad f friendship.
amistoso/sa adj friendly, cordial.
amo m owner; boss.
amoldar vt to mold; to adapt: —se vr to adapt oneself.
amor m love; fancy; lover: —~ mio my love: —por ~ de Dios for God's sake: —~ propio self-love.
amortiguador m shock absorber.
amortizar vt to redeem, pay, liquidate, discharge (a debt).
amperio m amp.
ampliar vt to amplify, enlarge; to extend; to expand.
amplificador m amplifier.
amplio/lia adj ample, extensive.
ampolla f blister; ampoule.
amueblar vt to furnish.
anacoreta m anchorite, hermit.
anacronismo m anachronism.
añadir vt to add.
analfabeto/ta adj illiterate.
analgésico m painkiller.
análisis m analysis.
anaranjado/da adj orange-colored.
anarquía f anarchy.
ancho/cha adj broad, wide, large: —m breadth, width.
anchoa f anchovy.
anchura f width, breadth.
anciano/na adj old: —m/f old man/ woman.
ancla f anchor.
anclaje m anchorage.
andamiaje m scaffolding.
andar vi to go, walk; to fare; to act, proceed.
andén m sidewalk; (ferro) platform; quayside.
andrajo m rag.
anegar vt to inundate, submerge; .
añejo/ja adj old; stale, musty.
anexión f annexation.
anfibio/bia adj amphibious.
anfitrión/ona m/f host(ess).
ángel m angel.
angosto/ta adj narrow, close.
anguila f eel.
angula f elver.

angular *adj* angular: —**piedra ~** *f* cornerstone.
ángulo *m* angle, corner.
angustia *f* anguish; heartache.
anhelar *vi* to gasp: —*vt* to long for.
anidar *vi* to nestle, make a nest; to dwell, inhabit.
añil *m* indigo plant; indigo.
anillo *m* ring.
ánima *f* soul.
animación *f* liveliness; activity.
animado/da *adj* lively.
animal *adj , m* animal.
animar *vt* to animate, liven up; to comfort; to revive: —**~se** *vr* to cheer up.
ánimo *m* soul; courage; mind; intention: —*excl* come on!
anís *m* aniseed; anisette.
aniversario/ria *adj* annual: —*m* anniversary.
ano *m* anus.
año *m* year.
anoche *adv* last night.
anochecer *vi* to grow dark: —*m* nightfall.
anónimo/ma *adj* anonymous.
añoranza *f* longing.
anormal *adj* abnormal.
anotar *vt* to comment, note.
anquilosamiento *m* paralysis.
ánsar *m* goose.
ansiar *vt* to desire.
ansiedad *f* anxiety.
antagónico/ca *adj* antagonistic; opposed.
antaño *adv* formerly.
ante *m* suede: —*prep* before; in the presence of; faced with.
anteanoche *adv* the night before last.
anteayer *adv* the day before yesterday.
antebrazo *m* forearm.
antelación *f*: —**con ~** in advance.
antemano *adv* : —**de ~** beforehand.
antena *f* feeler, antenna; aerial.
antepasado/da *adj* passed, elapsed: —**~s** *mpl* ancestors *pl*.
anterior *adj* preceding; former.
antes *prep, adv* before: —*conj* before.
antibiótico *m* antibiotic.
anticiclón *m* anticyclone.
anticipar *vt* to anticipate; to forestall; to advance.
anticonceptivo *m* contraceptive. ·
anticongelante *m* antifreeze.
anticuado/da *adj* antiquated.
anticuerpo *m* antibody.
antiestético/ca *adj* unsightly.
antifaz *m* mask.
antiguamente *adv* in ancient times, of old.
antiguo/gua *adj* antique, old, ancient.
antipático/ca *adj* unpleasant.
antojo *m* whim, fancy; longing.
antorcha *f* torch; taper.
antro *m* (*poet*) cavern, den, grotto.
antropófago *m* cannibal.
antropología *f* anthropology.
anual *adj* annual.
anudar *vt* to knot; to join: —**~se** *vr* to get into knots.
anular *vt* to annul; to revoke; to cancel: —*adj* annular.
anunciar *vt* to announce; to advertise.
anuncio *m* advertisement.

anzuelo *m* hook; allurement.
apacible *adj* affable; gentle; placid, quiet.
apaciguar *vt* to appease; to pacify, calm.
apagar *vt* to put out; to turn off; to quench, extinguish.
apañar *vt* to grasp; to pick up; to patch: —**~se** *vr* to manage.
aparador *m* sideboard; store window.
aparato *m* apparatus; machine; radio or television set; ostentation, show; (*med*) bandage, dressing.
aparcamiento *m* parking lot.
aparcar *vt , vi* to park.
aparecer *vi* to appear: —**~se** *vr* to appear.
aparentar *vt* to look; to pretend; to deceive.
apariencia *f* outward appearance.
apartamento *m* flat, apartment.
apartar *vt* to separate, divide; to remove; to sort; .
aparte *m* aside; new paragraph: —*adv* apart, separately; besides; aside.
apasionado/da *adj* passionate; devoted; fond; biased.
apeadero *m* halt, stopping place; station.
apearse *vr* to dismount; to get down/out/off.
apechugar *vt* to face up to.
apego *m* attachment, fondness.
apelar *vi* (*jur*) to appeal: —**~ a** to have recourse to.
apellido *m* surname; family name; epithet.
apenar *vt* to grieve; to embarrass: —**~se** *vr* to grieve; to be embarrassed.
apenas *adv* scarcely, hardly: —*conj* assoon as.
apéndice *m* appendix, supplement.
apercibirse *vr* to notice.
aperitivo *m* aperitif; appetizer.
apero *m* agricultural implement.
apesadumbrar *vt* to sadden.
apestar *vt* to infect: —*vi* **~ a** to stink of.
apetito *m* appetite.
apiadarse *vr* to take pity.
apilar *vt* to pile up: —**~se** *vr* to pile up.
apiñado/da *adj* crowded; pyramidal; pine-shaped.
apio *m* (*bot*) celery.
apisonadora *f* steamroller.
aplacar *vt* to appease, pacify: —**~se** *vr* to calm down.
aplastar *vt* to flatten, crush.
aplatanarse *vr* to get weary.
aplaudir *vt* to applaud; to extol.
aplauso *m* applause; approbation, praise.
aplazar *vt* to postpone.
aplicado/da *adj* studious; industrious.
aplicar *vt* to apply; to clasp; to attribute: —**~se** *vr* **~ a** to devote oneself to.
aplique *m* wall light.
aplomo *m* self-assurance.
apocado/da *adj* timid.
apoderado/da *adj* powerful: —*m* proxy, attorney; agent.
apodo *m* nickname, sobriquet.
apogeo *m* peak.
apósito *m* (*med*) external dressing.
aposta *adv* on purpose.
apostar *vt* to bet, wager; to post soldiers: —*vi* to bet.
apóstol *m* apostle.
apoteosis *f* apotheosis.
apoyar *vt* to rest; to favor, patronize, support: —**~se** *vr* to lean.
apreciar *vt* to appreciate; to estimate, value.

aprecio *m* appreciation; esteem.

apremiante *adj* urgent.

aprender *vt* to learn: —~ **de memoria** to learn by heart.

aprensión *f* apprehension.

apresar *vt* to seize, grasp.

apresurar *vt* to accelerate, hasten, expedite: —~**se** *vr* to hurry.

apretar *vt* to compress, tighten; to constrain: —*vi* to be too tight.

aprisa *adv* quickly, swiftly; promptly.

aprobar *vt* to approve; to pass: —*vi* to pass.

apropiado/da *adj* appropriate.

aprovechar *vt* to use; to exploit; to profit from; to take advantage of: —*vi* to be useful; to progress: —~**se** *vr* ~**de** to use; to take advantage of.

aproximar *vt* to approach: —~**se** *vr* to approach.

aptitud *f* aptitude, fitness, ability.

apto/ta *adj* apt; fit, able; clever.

apuesta *f* bet, wager.

apuñalar *vt* to stab.

apuntar *vt* to aim; to level, point at; to mark: —*vi* to begin to appear or show itself; to prompt (theater): —~**se** *vr* to score; to enrol.

apurado/da *adj* poor, destitute of means; exhausted; hurried.

aquél/~ la *pn* that (one): —~ **los/~las** *pl* those (ones).

aquel/~la *adj* that: —~**los/~las** *pl* those.

aquello *pn* that.

aquí *adv* here; now.

árabe *adj , m/f , m (ling)* Arab, Arabic.

arado *m* plough.

araña *f* spider; chandelier.

arañar *vt* to scratch; to scrape; to corrode.

arancel *m* tariff.

arandela *f* washer.

arar *vt* to plough.

árbitro *m* arbitrator; referee; umpire.

árbol *m* tree; *(mar)* mast; shaft.

arbolado/da *adj* forested; wooded: — *m* woodland.

arbusto *m* shrub.

arca *f* chest, wooden box.

arcada *f* arch; arcade: —~**s** *fpl* retching.

arce *m* maple tree.

archivar *vt* to file.

arcilla *f* clay.

arco *m* arc; arch; fiddle bow; hoop: — ~**iris** rainbow.

arder *vi* to burn, blaze.

ardilla *f* squirrel.

área *f* area.

arena *f* sand; grit; arena.

arenque *m* herring: —~ **ahumado** red herring.

argolla *f* large ring.

argucia *f* subtlety.

argumentar *vt , vi* to argue, dispute; to conclude.

árido/da *adj* dry; barren.

arisco/ca *adj* fierce; rude; intractable.

arlequín *m* harlequin, buffoon.

arma *f* weapon, arms.

armado/da *adj* armed; reinforced.

armador *m* shipowner; privateer; jacket, jerkin.

armar *vt* to man; to arm; to fit: —~**la** to kick up a fuss.

armario *m* wardrobe; cupboard.

armazón *f* chassis; skeleton; frame.

armonía *f* harmony.

armonizar *vt* to harmonize; to reconcile.

arnés *m* harness: —~**eses** *mpl* gear, trappings *pl*.

aro *m* ring; earring.

aroma *m* aroma, fragrance.

arpa *f* harp.

arpía *f (poet)* harpy, shrew.

arpillera *f* sackcloth.

arpón *m* harpoon.

arqueado/da *adj* arched, vaulted.

arquero *m* archer.

arquitectónico/ca *adj* architectural.

arrabal *m* suburb; slum.

arraigado/da *adj* deep-rooted; established.

arraigar *vi* to root; to establish: —*vt* to establish .

arrancar *vt* to pull up by the roots; to pull out: —*vi* to start; to move.

arrasar *vt* to demolish, destroy.

arrastrar *vt* to drag: —*vi* to creep, crawl; to lead a trump at cards: —~**se** *vr* to crawl; to grovel.

arrebatar *vt* to carry off, snatch; to enrapture.

arrebato *m* fury; rapture.

arrecife *m* reef.

arreglar *vt* to regulate; to tidy; to adjust: —~**se** *vr* to come to an understanding.

arrellanarse *vr* to sit at ease; to make oneself comfortable.

arrendar *vt* to rent, let out, lease.

arrendatario/ria *m/f* tenant.

arrepentirse *vr* to repent.

arrestar *vt* to arrest; to imprison.

arriate *m* flowerbed; causeway.

arriba *adv* above, over, up; high, on high, overhead; aloft.

arribista *m/f* upstart.

arriendo *m* lease; farm rent.

arriesgado *adj* risky, dangerous; daring.

arriesgar *vt* to risk, hazard; to expose to danger: —~**se** *vr* to take a chance.

arrimar *vt* to approach, draw near; *(mar)* to stow (cargo): —~**se** *vr* to sidle up; to lean.

arrinconar *vt* to put in a corner; to lay aside.

arrodillarse *vr* to kneel down.

arrogante *adj* arrogant; haughty, proud; stout.

arrojar *vt* to throw, fling; to dash; to emit; to shoot, sprout: —~**se** *vr* to hurl oneself.

arrollar *vt* to run over; to defeat heavily.

arropar *vt* to clothe, dress: —~**se** *vr* to wrap up.

arroyo *m* stream; gutter.

arroz *m* rice.

arrozal *m* ricefield.

arrugar *vt* to wrinkle; to rumple; to fold: —~ **la frente** to frown: —~**se** *vr* to shrivel.

arruinar *vt* to demolish; to ruin: — ~**se** *vr* to go bankrupt.

arrullar *vt* to lull: —*vi* to coo.

artesanía *f* craftsmanship.

ártico/ca *adj* arctic, northern: —*m* el A~ the Arctic.

articular *vt* to articulate; to joint.

artículo *m* article; clause; point; *(gr)* article; condition.

artífice *m* artisan; artist.

artificio *m* workmanship, craft; artifice, cunning trick.

artimaña *f* trap; cunning.

artista *m* artist; craftsman.

arzobispo *m* archbishop.

as *m* ace.
asa *f* handle; lever.
asado *m* roast meat; barbecue.
asaltar *vt* to assault; to storm (a position); to assail.
asamblea *f* assembly, meeting.
asar *vt* to roast.
ascender *vi* to be promoted; to rise: —*vt* to promote.
ascenso *m* promotion; ascent.
ascensor *m* elevator.
asco *m* nausea; loathing.
ascua *f* red-hot coal.
asear *vt* to clean; to tidy.
asedio *m* siege.
asegurar *vt* to secure; to insure; to affirm; to bail: —~se *vr* to make sure.
asentar *vt* to sit down; to affirm, assure; to note: —*vi* to suit.
asentir *vi* to acquiesce, concede.
aseo *m* cleanliness; neatness: —~s *mpl* rest room.
aséptico/ca *adj* germ-free.
asequible *adj* attainable; obtainable.
aserrar *vt* to saw.
aserrín *m* sawdust.
asesinar *vt* to assassinate; to murder.
asesorar *vt* to advise; to act as consultant: —~se *vr* to consult.
asfalto *m* asphalt.
asfixiar *vt* to suffocate: —~se *vr* to suffocate.
así *adv* so, thus, in this manner; like this; therefore; so that; also: —~ que so that; therefore: —**así/así** so-so; middling.
asiento *m* chair; bench, stool; seat; contract; entry; residence.
asignar *vt* to assign, attribute.
asignatura *f* subject; course.
asilo *m* asylum, refuge.
asimismo *adv* similarly, in the same manner.
asir *vt* to grasp, seize; to hold, grip: —*vi* to take root.
asistencia *f* audience; presence; assistance, help.
asistir *vi* to be present; to assist: —*vt* to help.
asma *f* asthma.
asno *m* ass.
asociación *f* association; partnership.
asolear *vt* to expose to the sun: —~se *vr* to sunbathe.
asomar *vi* to appear: —~se *vr* to appear, show up.
asombrar *vt* to amaze; to astonish: —~se *vr* to be amazed; to get a fright.
aspa *f* cross; sail.
aspecto *m* appearance; aspect.
áspero/ra *adj* rough, rugged; craggy, knotty; horrid; harsh, hard; severe, austere; gruff.
aspiración *f* breath; pause.
asqueroso/sa *adj* disgusting.
asta *f* lance; horn; handle.
astilla *f* chip (of wood), splinter.
astillero *m* dockyard.
astral *adj* astral.
astro *m* star.
astrología *m* astrology.
astronomía *f* astronomy.
astucia *f* cunning, slyness.
astuto/ta *adj* cunning, sly; astute.
asumir *vt* to assume.
asunto *m* subject, matter; affair, business.
asustar *vt* to frighten: —~se *vr* to be frightened.

atacar *vt* to attack.
atajo *m* short cut.
atañer *vi:* —~ a to concern.
atar *vt* to tie; to fasten.
atardecer *vi* to get dark: —*m* dusk; evening.
atascar *vt* to jam; to hinder: —~se *vr* to become bogged down.
ataúd *m* coffin.
atemorizar *vt* to frighten: —~se *vr* to get scared.
atención *f* attention, heedfulness; civility; observance, consideration.
atender *vi* to be attentive: —*vt* to attend to; to heed, expect, wait for; to look at.
atenerse *vr:* —~ a to adhere to.
atentamente *adv :* —le saluda ~yours faithfully.
atento/ta *adj* attentive; heedful; observing; mindful; polite, courteous, mannerly.
atenuar *vt* to diminish; to lessen.
ateo/a *adj , m/f* atheist.
aterciopelado/da *adj* velvety.
aterrar *vt* to terrify: —~se *vr* to be terrified.
aterrizar *vi* to land.
aterrorizar *vt* to frighten, terrify.
atesorar *vt* to treasure *or* hoard up(riches).
atestado/da *adj* packed: —*m* affidavit.
atestiguar *vt* to witness, attest.
atiborrar *vt* to stuff: —~se *vr* to stuff oneself.
ático *m* attic.
atinado/da *adj* wise; correct.
atizar *vt* to stir (the fire) with a poker; to stir up.
atlántico/ca *adj* atlantic.
atleta *m* athlete.
atletismo *m* athletics.
atomizador *m* spray.
átomo *m* atom.
atónito/ta *adj* astonished, amazed.
atontado/da *adj* stunned; silly.
atornillar *vt* to screw on; to screw down.
atosigar *vt* to poison; to harass; to oppress.
atracar *vt* to moor; to rob: —~se *vr* ~(de) to stuff oneself (with).
atractivo/va *adj* attractive; magnetic: —*m* charm.
atraer *vt* to attract, allure.
atragantarse *vr* to stick in the throat, choke.
atrapar *vt* to trap; to nab; to deceive.
atrás *adv* backward(s); behind; previously: —hacia ~ backward(s).
atrasar *vi* to be slow: —*vt* to postpone: —~ el reloj to put back a watch: —~se *vr* to stay behind; to be late.
atravesado/da *adj* oblique; cross; perverse; mongrel; degenerate.
atravesar *vt* to cross; to pass over; to pierce; to go through: —~se *vr* to get in the way; to meddle.
atreverse *vr* to dare, venture.
atribuir *vt* to attribute, ascribe; to impute.
atril *m* lectern; bookrest.
atrio *m* porch; portico.
atrocidad *f* atrocity.
atropellar *vt* to trample; to run down; to hurry; to insult: —~se *vr* to hurry.
atroz *adj* atrocious, heinous; cruel.
atuendo *m* attire.
atún *m* tuna (fish).
aturdir *vt* to stun, confuse; to stupefy.
audaz *adj* audacious, bold.
audiencia *f* audience.

auge *m* boom; climax.
augurio *m* omen.
aula *f* lecture room.
aullar *vi* to howl.
aumentar *vt* to augment, increase; to magnify; to put up: —*vi* to increase; to grow larger.
aún *adv* even: —~ **asi** even so.
aunque *adv* though, although.
auricular *m* receiver: —~**es** *mpl* headphones *pl*.
aurora *f* dawn.
ausencia *f* absence.
ausente *adj* absent.
auspicio *m* auspice; prediction; protection.
austero/ra *adj* austere, severe.
auténtico/ca *adj* authentic.
autoadhesivo/va *adj* self-adhesive.
autobús *m* bus.
autocar *m* bus, coach.
autóctono/na *adj* native.
autodefensa *f* self-defense.
autodeterminación *f* self-determination.
autoescuela *f* driving school.
automovilismo *m* motoring; motor racing.
autónomo/ma *adj* autonomous.
autopista *f* motorway.
autopsia *f* post mortem, autopsy.
autor/ra *m/f* author; maker; writer.
autoridad *f* authority.
autorizar *vt* to authorize.
autorretrato *m* self-portrait.
autoservicio *m* self-service store; restaurant.
autostop *m* hitch-hiking.
autosuficiencia *f* self-sufficiency.
autovía *f* state highway.
auxiliar *vt* to aid, help, assist; to attend: —*adj* auxiliary.
aval *m* guarantee; guarantor.
avanzar *vt* , *vi* to advance.
avaricia *f* avarice.
avaro/ra *adj* miserly: —*m/f* miser.
ave *f* bird; fowl.

avecinarse *vr* to approach.
avellana *f* hazelnut.
avena *f* oats *pl*.
avenida *f* avenue.
aventajar *vt* to surpass, excel.
aventura *f* adventure; event, incident.
avergonzar *vt* to shame, abash: —~**se** *vr* to be ashamed.
avería *f* breakdown.
averiado/da *adj* broken down; out of order.
averiguar *vt* to find out; to inquire into; to investigate.
avestruz *m* ostrich.
aviación *f* aviation; air force.
avicultura *f* poultry farming.
avidez *f* covetousness.
avinagrado/da *adj* sour.
avión *m* airplane.
avioneta *f* light aircraft.
avisar *vt* to inform; to warn; to advise.
aviso *m* notice; warning; hint.
avispa *f* wasp.
avispado/da *adj* lively, brisk; vivacious.
¡ay! *excl* alas!; ow!: —¡~ **de mi!** alas! poor me!
ayer *adv* yesterday.
ayuda *f* help, aid; support: —*m* deputy, assistant.
ayudar *vt* to help, assist; to further.
ayunar *vi* to fast, abstain from food.
ayuntamiento *m* town/city hall.
azabache *m* jet.
azafata *f* air hostess.
azafrán *m* saffron.
azahar *m* orange or lemon blossom.
azar *m* fate: —**por** ~ by chance: —**al**~ at random.
azotar *vt* to whip, lash.
azotea *f* flat roof of a house.
azúcar *m* sugar.
azufre *m* sulfur, brimstone.
azul *adj* blue: —~ **celeste** sky blue.
azulejo *m* tile.

B

baba *f* dribble, spittle.
babero *m* bib.
babia *f*: —**estar en** ~ to be absentminded *or* dreaming.
baca *f (auto)* luggage rack.
bacalao *m* cod.
bache *m* pothole.
bachillerato *m* baccalaureate.
bahía *f* bay.
bailar *vi* to dance.
bailarín/ina *m/f* dancer.
baja *f* fall; casualty.
bajada *f* descent; inclination; slope; ebb.
bajamar *f* low tide.
bajar *vt* to lower, let down; to lessen; to humble; to go/come down.
bajo/ja *adj* low; abject, despicable; common; humble: —*prep* under, underneath, below: —*adv* softly; quietly: —*m (mus)* bass; low place.
bala *f* bullet.
balance *m* hesitation; balance sheet; balance; rolling (of a ship).

balanza *f* scale; balance; judgement.
balar *vi* to bleat.
balcón *m* balcony.
balde *m* bucket: —**de** ~ *adv* gratis, for nothing: —**en** ~ in vain.
baldío/dia *adj* waste; uncultivated.
baldosa *f* floor; tile; flagstone.
ballena *f* whale; whalebone.
balneario *m* spa.
baloncesto *m* basketball.
balonmano *m* handball.
balonvolea *m* volleyball.
balsa *f* balsa wood; pool; raft, float; ferry.
bañador *m* swimsuit.
bañar *vt* to bathe; to dip; to coat (with varnish): —~**se** *vr* to bathe; to swim.
bancarrota *f* bankruptcy.
banco *m* bench; work bench; bank.
banda *f* band; sash; ribbon; troop; party; gang; to uchline.
bandada *f* flock; shoal.

bandeja *f* tray, salver.
bandera *f* banner, standard; flag.
bando *m* faction, party; edict.
bandolero *m* bandit.
bañera *f* bath (tub).
baño *m* bath; dip; bathtub; varnish; crust of sugar; coating.
banqueta *f* three-legged stool; sidewalk.
banquete *m* banquet; formal dinner.
banquillo *m* dock.
bar *m* bar.
baraja *f* deck of cards.
barandilla *f* small balustrade, small railing.
barato/ta *adj* cheap: —**de** ~ gratis: — *m* cheapness; bargain sale.
barba *f* chin; beard: —~ **a** ~ face to face.
barbaridad *f* barbarity, barbarism; outrage.
bárbaro/ra *adj* barbarous; cruel; rude; rough.
barbecho *m* first ploughing, fallow land.
barbero *m* barber.
barbilampiño/ña *adj* clean-shaven; *(fig)* inexperienced.
barbilla *f* chin.
barca *f* boat.
barco *m* boat; ship.
barnis *m* varnish; glaze.
barómetro *m* barometer.
barquillo *m* wafer; cornet, cone.
barra *m* bar; rod; lever; French loaf; sandbank.
barraca *f* hut.
barranco *m* gully, ravine; *(fig)* great difficulty.
barrenar *vt* to drill, bore; *(fig)* to frustrate.
barrendero *m* sweeper, garbage man.
barrer *vt* to sweep.
barrera *f* barrier; turnpike, claypit.
barriga *f* abdomen; belly.
barril *m* barrel; cask.
barrio *m* area, district.
barro *m* clay, mud.
barrote *m* ironwork of doors, windows, tables; crosspiece.
barruntar *vt* to guess; to foresee; to conjecture.
bártulos *mpl* gear, belongings *pl*.
barullo *m* uproar.
basar *vt* to base: —**se** *vr* ~ **en** to be based on.
báscula *f* scales *pl*.
base *f* base, basis.
básico/ca *adj* basic.
bastante *adj* sufficient, enough: —*adv* quite.
bastar *vi* to be sufficient, be enough.
bastidor *m* embroidery frame: —**es** *mpl* scenery (on stage).
basto/ta *adj* coarse, rude, unpolished.
bastón *m* cane, stick; nightstick; *(fig)* command.
bastos *mpl* clubs *pl* (one of the four suits at cards).
basura *f* trash, garbage.
bata *f* bathrobe; overall; laboratory coat.
batalla *f* battle, combat; fight.
batata *f* sweet potato.
batería *m* battery; percussion.
batir *vt* to beat; to whisk; to dash; to demolish; to defeat.
baúl *m* trunk.
bautisar *vt* to baptize, christen.
baza *f* card-trick.
bazo *m* spleen.
beato/ta *adj* happy; blessed; devout: —*m* lay brother: —*m/f* pious person.

bebé *m/f* baby.
beber *vt* to drink.
bebida *f* drink, beverage.
beca *f* fellowship; grant, bursary, scholarship; sash; hood.
bedel *m* head porter; uniformed employee.
belén *m* nativity scene.
bélico/ca *adj* warlike, martial.
belladona *f* *(bot)* deadly nightshade.
belleza *f* beauty.
bello/lla *adj* beautiful; handsome; lovely; fine.
bellota *f* acorn.
bemol *m* *(mus)* flat.
bendecir *vt* to bless; to consecrate; to praise.
bendito/ta *adj* saintly; blessed; simple; happy.
beneficiar *vt* to benefit; to be of benefit to.
beneficio *m* benefit, advantage; profit; benefit night.
beneficioso/sa *adj* beneficial.
beneplácito *m* consent, approbation.
benévolo/la *adj* benevolent, kindhearted.
benigno/na *adj* benign; kind; mild.
berberecho *m* cockle.
berenjena *f* eggplant.
bergantín *m* *(mar)* brig.
berrear *vi* to low, bellow.
berrinche *m* anger, rage, tantrum (applied to children).
berrinchudo/da *adj* bad-tempered.
berro *m* watercress.
berza *f* cabbage.
besar *vt* to kiss: —**se** *vr* to kiss.
bestia *f* beast, animal; idiot.
besugo *m* sea bream.
betún *m* shoe polish.
biberón *m* feeding bottle.
bibliófilo/la *m/f* book-lover, bookworm.
bibliografía *f* bibliography.
biblioteca *f* library.
bicarbonato *m* bicarbonate.
bicho *m* small animal; bug: —**mal** ~ villain.
bici *f* *(fam)* bike.
bicicleta *f* bicycle.
bidé *m* bidet.
bien *m* good, benefit; profit: —**es** *mpl* goods *pl*, property; wealth: —*adv* well, right; very; willingly; easily: —~ **que** *conj* although: —**está** ~ very well.
bienestar *m* well-being.
bienhechor/ra *m/f* benefactor.
bienvenida *f* welcome.
bifurcación *f* fork.
bigote *m* mustache; whiskers *pl*.
bilingüe *adj* bilingual.
bilis *f* bile.
billar *m* billiards *pl*.
billete *m* note, bill; ticket; *(ferro)* ticket: —~ **sencillo** single ticket: —~ **de ida y vuelta** return ticket.
biografía *f* biography.
biología *f* biology.
biombo *m* screen.
birlar *vt* to knock down at one blow; to pinch *(fam)*.
bis *excl* encore.
bisabuela *f* great-grandmother.
bisabuelo *m* great-grandfather.
bisagra *f* hinge.
bisiesto *adj* : —**año** ~ leap year.
bisnieto/ta *m/f* great-grandson/ daughter.

bistec *m* steak.

bisturí *m* scalpel.

bisutería *f* costume jewelry.

bisco/ca *adj* cross-eyed.

biscocho *m* sponge cake; biscuit; ship's biscuit.

blanco/ca *adj* white; blank: —*m* whiteness; white person; blank, blank space; target (to shoot at).

blando/da *adj* soft, smooth; mild, gentle; *(fam)* cowardly.

blanquear *vt* to bleach; to whitewash; to launder (money).

blasfemar *vi* to blaspheme.

bledo *m*: —**no me importa un ~** I don't give a damn *(sl)*.

blindado/da *adj* armor-plated; bulletproof.

bloc *m* writing pad.

bloque *m* block.

bloquear *vt* to block; to blockade.

blusa *f* blouse.

bobada *f* folly, foolishness.

bobina *f* bobbin.

bobo/ba *m/f* idiot, fool; clown, funny man: —*adj* stupid, silly.

boca *f* mouth; entrance, opening; mouth of a river: —~ **en** ~ *adv* by word of mouth: —**a pedir de** ~ to one's heart's content.

bocacalle *f* entrance to a street.

bocadillo *m* sandwich, roll.

bocado *m* mouthful.

bocazas *m invar* big-mouth.

boceto *m* sketch; design; mock-up.

bochorno *m* sultry weather, scorching heat; blush.

bocina *f (mus)* trumpet; *(auto)* horn.

bocinar *vi* to sound a horn, hoot.

boda *f* wedding.

bodega *f* wine cellar; warehouse; bar.

bofetada *f* slap (in the face).

boina *f* beret.

boj *m* box, box tree.

bola *f* ball; marble; globe; *(fam)* lie, fib.

bolera *f* bowling alley.

bolero *m* bolero jacket; bolero dance.

boletín *m* bulletin; journal, review.

boleto *m* ticket.

boliche *m* jack at bowls; bowls, bowling alley; dragnet.

bolígrafo *m* (ballpoint) pen.

bollo *m* bread roll; lump.

bolo *m* ninepin; (large) pill.

bolsa *f* purse; bag; pocket; sac; stock exchange.

bolsillo *m* pocket; purse.

bomba *f* pump; bomb; surprise: —**dara la** ~ to pump: —~ **de gaso- lina**gas pump.

bombero *m* fireman.

bombilla *f* light bulb.

bombo *m* large drum.

bombón *m* chocolate.

bondad *f* goodness, kindness; courtesy.

bondadoso/sa *adj* good, kind.

boñiga *f* cow pat.

bonito *adj* pretty, nice-looking; pretty good, passable: —*m* tuna (fish).

boquerón *m* anchovy; large hole.

boquilla *f* mouthpiece of a musical instrument; nozzle.

borde *m* border; margin; *(mar)*board.

bordear *vi (mar)* to tack: —*vt* to go along the edge of; to flank.

bordillo *m* curb.

bordo *m (mar)* board of a ship.

boreal *adj* boreal, northern.

borracho/cha *adj* drunk, intoxicated; blind with passion: —*m/f* drunk, drunkard.

borrador *m* first draft; scribbling pad; eraser.

borrar *vt* to erase, rub out; to blur; to obscure.

borrasca *f* storm; violent squall of wind; hazard; danger.

borrico/ca *m/f* donkey, ass; blockhead.

borrón *m* blot, blur.

bosque *m* forest; wood.

bosquejo *m* sketch (of a painting); unfinished work.

bostezar *vi* to yawn; to gape.

bota *f* leather wine-bag; boot.

botánica *f* botany.

bote *m* bounce; thrust; tin, can; boat.

botella *f* bottle.

botijo *m* earthenware pitcher.

botín *m* high boot, half-boot; gaiter; booty.

botiquín *m* medicine chest.

botón *m* button; knob (of a radio etc); *(bot)* bud.

bóveda *f* arch; vault, crypt.

boxeo *m* boxing.

boya *f (mar)* buoy.

boyante *adj* buoyant, floating; *(fig)* fortunate, successful.

bozo *m* down (on the upper lip or chin); headstall (of a horse).

braga *f* sling, rope; nappy, diaper: —~s *fpl* breeches *pl;* panties *pl.*

bragueta *f* fly, flies *pl* (of pants/trousers).

brasa *f* live coal: —**estar hecho una~** to be very flushed.

bravío/vía *adj* ferocious, savage, wild; coarse.

bravo/va *adj* brave, valiant; bullying; savage, fierce; rough; sumptuous; excellent, fine: —*excl* well done!

braza *f* fathom.

brazo *m* arm; branch (of a tree); enterprise; courage: —**luchar a ~par-tido** to fight hand-to-hand.

brea *f* pitch; tar.

brebaje *m* potion.

brecha *f (mil)* breach; gap, opening.

breva *f* early fig; early large acorn.

breve *m* papal brief: —*f (mus)* breve: —*adj* brief, short: —**en** ~ shortly.

brezo *m (bot)* heather.

bribón/ona *adj* dishonest, rascally.

bricolaje *m* do-it-yourself.

brida *f* bridle; clamp, flange.

brigada *f* brigade; squad, gang.

brillante *adj* brilliant; bright, shining: —*m* diamond.

brillar *vi* to shine; to sparkle, glisten; to shine, be outstanding.

brincar *vi* to skip; to leap, jump; to gambol; to fly into a passion.

brindis *m invar* toast.

brío *m* spirit, dash.

brisca *f* card game.

broca *f* reel; drill; shoemaker's tack.

brocado *m* gold or silver brocade: —~/**da** *adj* embroidered, like brocade.

brocha *f* large brush: —~ **de afeitar** shaving brush.

broche *m* clasp; brooch; cufflink.

broma *f* joke.

bromear *vi* to joke.
bronca *f* row.
bronceado/da *adj* tanned: —*m* bronzing, suntan.
brotar *vi (bot)* to bud, germinate; to gush, rush out; *(med)* to break out.
bruces *adv* : —**a** ~/**de** ~ face downward(s).
bruja *f* witch.
brújula *f* compass.
bruma *f* mist; *(mar)* sea mist.
bruñir *vt* to polish; to put rouge on.
brusco/ca *adj* rude; sudden; brusque.
brutal *adj* brutal, brutish: —*m* brute.
bruto *m* brute, beast: —~/ **ta** *adj* stupid; gross; brutish.
bucal *adj* oral.
bucear *vi* to dive.
bucle *m* curl.
buen *adj (before m nouns)* good.
bueno/na *adj* good, perfect; fair; fit, proper; good-looking: —**¡buenos días!** good morning!: —**¡buenas tardes!** good afternoon: —**¡buenas noches!** good night!: —**¡~!** right!
buey *m* ox, bullock.
bufanda *f* scarf.
bufete *m* desk, writing-table; lawyer's office.
bufo/fa *adj* comic: —**opera ~a** *f* comic opera.
buhardilla *f* attic.

búho *m* owl; unsocial person.
buitre *m* vulture.
bujía *f* candle; spark plug.
bullicio *m* bustle; uproar.
bulto *m* bulk; tumor, swelling; bust; baggage.
buñuelo *m* doughnut; fritter.
buque *m* vessel, ship, tonnage, capacity (of a ship); hull (of a ship).
burbuja *f* bubble.
burdel *m* brothel.
burguesía *f* bourgeoisie.
burlar *vt* to hoax; to defeat; to play tricks on, deceive; to frustrate: —**~se** *vr* to joke, laugh at.
burro *m* ass, donkey; idiot; sawhorse.
bursátil *adj* stock exchange *compd.*
buscar *vt* to seek, search for; to look for; to hunt after: —*vi* to look, search, seek.
busilis *m* difficulty, snag.
busto *m* bust.
butaca *f* armchair; seat.
butano *m* butane.
butifarra *f* Catalan sausage.
butrón *m* burglary.
buzo *m* diver.
buzón *m* mailbox; conduit, canal; cover of a jar.

C

cabalgar *vi* to ride, go riding.
cabalgata *f* procession.
caballa *f* mackerel.
caballería *f* mount, steed; cavalry; cavalry horse; chivalry; knighthood.
caballero *m* knight; gentleman; rider, horseman.
caballete *m* ridge of a roof; painter's easel; trestle; bridge (of the nose).
caballo *m* horse; (at chess) knight; queen (in cards): —**a** ~ on horseback.
cabecera *f* headboard; head; far end; pillow; head-line; vignette.
cabecilla *m* ringleader.
cabello *m* hair.
caber *vi* to fit.
cabeza *f* head; chief, leader; main town, chief center.
cabida *f* room, capacity.
cabildo *m* chapter (of church); meeting of a chapter; corporation of a town.
cabina *f* cabin; telephone booth.
cabizbajo/ja, cabizcaido/da *adj* crestfallen; pensive, thoughtful.
cable *m* cable, lead, wire.
cabo *m* end, extremity; cape, headland; *(mar)* cable, rope.
cabra *f* goat.
cabrón *m* cuckold: —**¡~!** *(fam)* bastard! *(sl).*
cacahuete *m* peanut.
cacao *m (bot)* cacao tree; cocoa.
cacarear *vi* to crow; to brag, boast.
cacerola *f* pan, saucepan; casserole.
cachalote *m* sperm whale.
cacharro *m* pot.

cachivache *m* pot; piece of junk.
cachondo/da *adj* randy; funny.
cachorro/ra *m/f* puppy; cub.
caco *m* pickpocket; coward.
cada *adj invar* each; every.
cadáver *m* corpse, cadaver.
cadena *f* chain; series, link; radio or TV network.
cadera *f* hip.
caducar *vi* to become senile; to expire, lapse; to deteriorate.
caer *vi* to fall; to tumble down; to lapse; to happen; to die: —**~se** *vr* to fall down.
café *m* coffee; cafe, coffee house.
cafetera *f* coffee pot.
cagar *vi (fam)* to have a shit *(sl).*
caimán *m* caiman, alligator.
caja *f* box, case; casket; cashbox; cash desk; super-market check-out: —**~de ahorros** savings bank: —**~ decambios** gearbox.
cajón *m* bureau; locker.
cal *f* lime: —**~ viva** quick lime.
calabacín *m* small marrow, zucchini.
calabaza *f* pumpkin, squash.
calamar *m* squid.
calar *vt* to soak, drench; to penetrate, pierce; to see through; to lower: —**~se** *vr* to stall (of a car).
calavera *f* skull; madcap.
calcar *vt* to trace, copy.
calcetín *m* sock.
calcio *m* calcium.
calcomanía *f* transfer.
calculadora *f* calculator.
calcular *vt* to calculate, reckon; to compute.
caldear *vt* to weld; to warm, heat up.

calderada *f* stew.
calderilla *f* small change.
caldo *m* stock; broth.
calefacción *f* heating.
calendario *m* calendar.
calentar *vt* to warm up, heat up: —**se** *vr* to grow hot; to dispute.
calidad *f* grade, quality, condition; kind.
cálido/da *adj* hot; *(fig)* warm.
caliente *adj* hot; fiery: —**en** ~ in the heat of the moment.
callado/da *adj* silent, quiet.
callar *vi*, ~**se** *vr* to be silent, keep quiet.
calle *f* street; road.
callejear *vi* to loiter about the streets.
callejón *m* alley.
callo *m* corn; callus: —**s** *mpl* tripe.
calmante *m (med)* sedative.
calmar *vt* to calm, quiet, pacify: —*vi* to become calm.
calor *m* heat, warmth; ardor, passion.
calumnia *f* calumny, slander.
calvo/va *adj* bald; bare, barren.
calzado *m* footwear.
calzoncillos *mpl* underpants, shorts *pl*.
cama *f* bed: —**hacer la** ~ to make the bed.
cámara *f* hall; chamber; room; camera; cine camera.
camarada *m/f* comrade, companion.
camarera *f* waitress.
camarero *m* waiter.
camarón *m* shrimp, prawn.
camarote *m* berth, cabin.
cambalache *m* exchange, swap.
cambiar *vt* to exchange; to change: — *vi* to change, alter: —~**se** *vr* to move house.
cambio *m* change, exchange; rate of exchange; bureau de change.
camelar *vt* to flirt with.
camello *m* camel; drug dealer.
camilla *f* couch; cot; stretcher.
caminar *vi* to travel; to walk, go.
camino *m* road; way.
camión *m* truck.
camisa *f* shirt; chemise.
camisería *f* dry goods store.
camiseta *f* T-shirt; undershirt.
camisón *m* nightgown.
campamento *m (mil)* encampment.
campana *f* bell.
campanario *m* belfry.
campeón/ona *m/f* champion.
campesino/na, campestre *adj* rural.
campo *m* country; field; camp; ground; pitch.
caña *f* cane, reed; stalk; shinbone; glass of beer: —~ **dulce** sugar cane.
cañada *f* gully; glen; sheep-walk.
canal *m* channel, canal.
canalla *f* mob, rabble.
cáñamo *m* hemp.
canas *fpl* gray hair: —**peinar** ~ to grow old.
cañaveral *m* reedbed.
cancelar *vt* to cancel; to write off.
cancha *f* (tennis) court.
canción *f* song.
candado *m* padlock.
candilejas *fpl* footlights *pl*.
canela *f* cinnamon.

cangrejo *m* crab; crayfish.
canica *f* marble.
canilla *f* shinbone; arm-bone; tap of a cask; spool.
canjear *vt* to exchange.
cano/na *adj* gray-haired; white-haired.
canoso/sa *adj* gray-haired; white-haired.
cansancio *m* tiredness, fatigue.
cansar *vt* to tire, tire out; to bore: —~**se** *vr* to get tired, grow weary.
cantante *m/f* singer.
cantar *m* song: —*vt* to sing; to chant: —*vi* to sing; to chirp.
cántaro *m* pitcher; jug: —**llover a** ~**s** to rain heavily, pour.
cantera *f* quarry.
cantidad *f* quantity, amount; number.
cantina *f* buffet, refreshment room; canteen; cellar; snack bar; bar.
canto *m* stone; singing; song; edge.
canuto *m (fam)* joint *(sl)*, marijuana cigarette.
caño *m* tube, pipe; sewer.
cañón *m* tube, pipe; barrel; gun; canyon.
caoba *f* mahogany.
caos *m* chaos; confusion.
capa *f* cloak; cape; layer, stratum; cover; pretext.
capacidad *f* capacity; extent; talent.
capataz *m* foreman, overseer.
capaz *adj* capable; capacious, spacious, roomy.
capeo *m* challenging of a bull with a cloak.
caperuza *f* hood.
capirote *m* hood.
capital *m* capital; capital sum: —*f* capital, capital city: —*adj* capital; principal.
capítulo *m* chapter of a cathedral; chapter (of a book).
capó *m (auto)* hood.
capote *m* greatcoat; bullfighter's cloak.
capricho *m* caprice, whim, fancy.
captar *vt* to captivate; to understand; *(rad)* to tune in to, receive.
capturar *vt* to capture.
capucha *f* cap, cowl, hood of a cloak.
capullo *m* cocoon of a silkworm; rosebud.
cara *f* face; appearance: —~ **a** ~ face to face.
cárabe *m* amber.
caracol *m* snail; seashell; spiral.
carácter *m* character; quality; condition; hand-writing.
característico/ca *adj* characteristic.
caradura *m/f* : —**es un** ~ he's got a nerve.
caramba *excl* well!
carámbano *m* icicle.
carambola *f* cannon (at billiards); trick.
caravana *f* trailer; queue; tailback(traffic).
carbón *m* coal; charcoal; carbon; carbon paper.
carboncillo *m* charcoal.
carbono *m (quim)* carbon.
carburador *m* carburettor.
carcajada *f* (loud) laugh.
cárcel *f* prison, penitentiary; jail.
carcoma *f* deathwatch beetle; woodworm; anxious concern.
cardenal *m* cardinal; cardinal bird; *(med)* bruise, weal.
cardo *m* thistle.
carecer *vi*: —~ **de** to want, lack.
cargar *vt* to load, burden; to charge: —*vi* to charge; to load (up); to lean.

cargo *m* burden, loading; employment, post; office; charge, care; obligation; accusation.

carguero *m* freighter.

caricia *f* caress.

caridad *f* charity.

caries *f (med)* tooth decay, caries.

cariño *m* fondness, tenderness; love.

carmesí *adj , m* crimson.

carmín *m* carmine; rouge; lipstick.

carne *f* flesh; meat; pulp (of fruit).

carné, carnet *m* driver's license: ──de identidad identity card.

carnicería *f* butcher's (store); carnage, slaughter.

caro/ra *adj* dear; affectionate; dear, expensive: ─*adv* dearly.

carpa *f* carp (fish); tent.

carpeta *f* table cover; folder, file, portfolio.

carpintero *m* carpenter.

carraca *f* carrack (ship); rattle.

carrera *f* career; course; race; run, running; route; journey: ─**a ~ abierta**, at full speed.

carrete *m* reel, spool, bobbin.

carretera *f* highway.

carril *m* lane (of road); furrow.

carrillo *m* cheek; pulley.

carro *m* cart; car.

carrocería *f* bodywork, coachwork.

carta *f* letter; map; document; playing card; menu: ──**~ blanca** carte blanche: ──**~ credencial** *o* **de creencia** credentials *pl:* ──**~ certificada** registered letter: ──**~ de crédito** credit card: ──**~ verde** green card.

cartabón *m* square (tool).

cartel *m* placard; poster; wall chart; cartel.

cartera *f* satchel; purse, handbag; briefcase.

carterista *m/f* pickpocket.

cartero *m* mailman.

cartón *m* cardboard, pasteboard; cartoon.

casa *f* house; home; firm, company: ── **~ de campo** country house: ──**~ de moneda** mint: ──**~ de huéspedes** boarding house, rooming house.

casar *vt* to marry; to couple; to abrogate; to annul: ─**~se** *vr* to marry, get married.

cascabel *m* small bell; rattlesnake.

cascada *f* cascade, waterfall.

cascanueces *m invar* nutcracker.

cascar *vt* to crack, break into pieces; *(fam)* to beat: ─**~se** *vr* to be broken open.

cáscara *f* rind, peel; husk, shell; bark.

casco *m* skull; helmet; fragment; shard; hulk (of a ship); crown (of a hat); hoof; empty bottle, returnable bottle.

cascote *m* rubble, fragment of material used in building.

caserío *m* country house; hamlet.

casero *m* landlord; janitor: ──**~/ra**, *adj* domestic; household *compd;* homemade.

caset(t)e *m* cassette: ─*f* cassette player.

casi *adv* almost, nearly: ──**~ nada** next to nothing: ──**~ nunca** hardly ever, almost never.

caso *m* case; occurrence; event; hap, casuality; occasion; *(gr)* case: ──**enese ~** in that case: ──**en todo ~** in any case: ──**~ que** in case.

caspa *f* dandruff; scurf.

castaño *m* chestnut tree: ──**~/ na** *adj* chestnut(-colored), brown.

castañuela *f* castanet.

castellano *m* Castilian, Spanish.

castigar *vt* to castigate, punish; to afflict.

castillo *m* castle.

castizo/za *adj* pure, thoroughbred.

casto/ta *adj* pure, chaste.

castor *m* beaver.

castrar *vt* to geld, castrate; to prune; to cut the honeycombs out of(beehives).

casualidad *f* chance, accident.

cataplasma *f* poultice.

catar *vt* to taste; to inspect, examine; to look at; to esteem.

catarata *f (med)* cataract; waterfall.

catarro *m* catarrh; cold.

cátedra *f* professor's chair.

categoría *f* category; rank.

católico/ca *adj , m/f* catholic.

catorce *adj , m* fourteen.

catre *m* cot.

cauce *m* riverbed; *(fig)* channel.

caucho *m* rubber; tire.

caudal *m* volume, flow; property, wealth; plenty.

causa *f* cause; motive, reason; lawsuit: ──**a ~ de** considering, because of.

causar *vt* to cause; to produce; to occasion.

cautela *f* caution, cautiousness.

cautivar *vt* to take prisoner in war; to captivate, charm.

cauto/ta *adj* cautious, wary.

cavar *vt* to dig up, excavate: ─*vi* to dig, delve; to think profoundly.

caverna *f* cavern, cave.

cavidad *f* cavity, hollow.

cavilar *vt* to ponder, consider carefully.

cazador/ra *m/f* hunter; *m* huntsman: ──**~ furtivo** poacher.

cazar *vt* to chase, hunt; to catch.

cazo *m* saucepan; ladle.

cazuela *f* casserole; pan.

cebada *f* barley.

cebar *vt* to feed (animals), fatten.

cebo *m* feed, food; bait, lure; priming.

cebolla *f* onion; bulb.

cebra *f* zebra.

cedazo *m* sieve, strainer.

ceder *vt* to hand over; to transfer, make over; to yield, give up: ─*vi* to submit, comply, give in; to diminish, grow less.

cedro *m* cedar.

cédula *f* certificate; document; slip of paper; bill: ──**~ de cambio** bill of exchange.

cegar *vi* to grow blind: ─*vt* to blind; to block up.

ceja *f* eyebrow.

cejar *vi* to go backward(s); to slacken, give in.

celebrar *vt* to celebrate; to praise: ── **~ misa** to say mass.

célebre *adj* famous, renowned; witty, funny.

celeste *adj* heavenly; sky-blue.

celestial *adj* heavenly; delightful.

celo *m* zeal; rut (in animals): ──**~s** *mpl* jealousy.

celoso/sa *adj* zealous; jealous.

célula *f* cell.

cementerio *m* graveyard.

cena *f* supper.

cenar *vt* to have for dinner: ─*vi* to have supper, have dinner.

cenegal *m* quagmire.

cenicero m ashtray.
ceniza f ashes pl: —**miércoles de** ~Ash Wednesday.
censo m census; tax; ground rent: —~ **electoral** electoral roll.
censurar vt to review, criticize; to censure, blame.
centella f lightning; spark.
centenar m hundred.
centeno m rye.
centésimo/ma adj hundredth: —mhundredth.
centígrado m centigrade.
centímetro m centimeter.
céntimo m cent.
centinela f sentry, guard.
central adj central: —f head office, headquarters; (telephone) exchange.
centro m center: —~ **comercial** shopping center.
centuplicar vt to increase a hundredfold.
ceñido/da adj tight-fitting; sparing, frugal.
ceñudo/da adj frowning, grim.
cepa f stock (of a vine); origin (of a family).
cepillo m brush; plane (tool).
cepo m branch, bough; trap; snare; poorbox.
cera f wax: —~s fpl honeycomb.
cerámica f pottery.
cerca f enclosure; fence: —~s mpl objects pl in the foreground of a painting: —adv near, at hand, close by: —~ **de** close, near.
cercano/na adj near, close by; neighboring, adjoining.
cerciorar vt to assure, ascertain, affirm: —~se vr to find out.
cerdo m pig, hog.
cerebro m brain.
cereza f cherry.
cerilla f wax taper; ear wax: —~s fpl matches, safety matches pl.
cero m nothing, zero.
cerrado/da adj closed, shut; locked; overcast, cloudy; broad (of accent).
cerrajero m locksmith.
cerrar vt to close, shut; to block up; to lock: —~ **la cuenta** to close an account: —~se vr to close; to heal; to cloud over: —vi to close, shut; to lock.
cerro m hill; neck (of an animal); backbone; combed flax or hemp: —**en** ~ bareback.
cerrojo m bolt (of a door).
certamen m competition, contest.
certero adj accurate; well-aimed.
certeza, certidumbre f certainty.
certificado m certificate: —~/ **da** adj registered (of a letter).
cerveza f beer.
cesar vt to cease, stop; to fire (sl); to remove from office: —vi to cease, stop; to retire.
cese m suspension; dismissal.
cesión f cession; transfer.
césped m grass; lawn.
cesta f basket, pannier.
chabola f shack.
chal m shawl.
chalado/da adj crazy.
chale(t) m detached house.
chaleco m vest.
champán m champagne.
champiñón m mushroom.
champú m shampoo.

chamuscar vt to singe, scorch.
chantaje m blackmail.
chapa f metal plate; panel; (auto)license plate.
chaparrón m heavy shower (of rain).
chapuza f badly done job.
chaqueta f jacket.
charco m pool, puddle.
charcutería f store selling pork meat products.
charlar vi to chat.
charlatán/ana m/f chatterbox.
charol m varnish; patent leather.
chasco m disappointment; joke, jest.
chasis m invar (auto) chassis.
chasquido m crack; click.
chatarra f scrap.
chato/ta adj flat, flattish; snub-nosed.
chaval/la m/f lad/lass.
chicle m chewing gum.
chico/ca adj little, small: —m/f boy/girl.
chiflado/da adj crazy.
chile m chilli pepper.
chillar vi to scream, shriek; to howl; to creak.
chimenea f chimney; fireplace.
china f pebble; porcelain, chinaware; China silk.
chincheta f thumbtack.
chino/na adj , m/f Chinese: —m Chinese language.
chirriar vi to hiss; to creak; to chirp.
chisme m tale; thingummyjig.
chispa f spark; sparkle; wit; drop (of rain); drunkenness.
chiste m funny story, joke.
chivo/va m/f billy/nanny goat.
chocar vi to strike, knock; to crash: — vt to shock.
chochear vi to dodder, be senile; to dote.
chocolate m chocolate.
chófer m driver.
chopo m (bot) black poplar.
chorizo m pork sausage.
chorro m gush; jet; stream: —**a** ~s abundantly.
chuchería f trinket.
chulear vi to brag.
chuleta f chop.
chulo m rascal; pimp.
chupar vt to suck; to absorb.
churro m fritter.
ciática f sciatica.
cicatriz f scar.
cicatrizar vt to heal.
ciclista m/f cyclist.
ciclo m cycle.
cicuta f (bot) hemlock.
ciego/ga adj blind.
cielo m sky; heaven; atmosphere; climate.
ciempiés m invar centipede.
cien adj , m a hundred.
ciénaga f swamp.
ciencia f science.
cieno m mud; mire.
cierto/ta adj certain, sure; right, correct: —**por** ~ certainly.
ciervo m deer, hart, stag: —~ **volante** stag beetle.
cierzo m cold northerly wind.
cifra f number, numeral; quantity; cipher; abbreviation.
cigarra f cicada.
cigarro m cigar; cigarette.
cigüeña f stork; crank (of a bell).

cilindro *m* cylinder.
cima *f* summit; peak; to p.
cimiento *m* foundation, groundwork; basis, origin.
cinc *m* zinc.
cincelar *vt* to chisel, engrave.
cinco *adj*, *m* five.
cincuenta *adj*, *m* fifty.
cine *m* cinema.
cínico/ca *adj* cynical.
cinta *f* band, ribbon; reel.
cintura *f* waist.
cinturón *m* belt, girdle; (*fig*) zone: —~ **de seguridad** seatbelt.
ciprés *m* cypress tree.
circo *m* circus.
circuito *m* circuit; circumference.
circular *adj* circular; circulatory: —*vt* to circulate: —*vi (auto)* to drive.
círculo *m* circle; (*fig*) scope, compass.
circunspecto/ta *adj* circumspect, cautious.
circunstancia *f* circumstance.
circunvalacion *f*: —**carretera de** ~bypass.
cirio *m* wax candle.
ciruela *f* plum: —~ **pasa** prune.
cirugía *f* surgery.
cisne *m* swan.
citar *vt* to make an appointment with; to quote; (*jur*) to summon.
ciudad *f* city; to wn.
ciudadano/na *m/f* citizen: —*adj* civic.
clamor *m* clamor, outcry; peal of bells.
clandestino/na *adj* clandestine, secret, concealed.
clara *f* egg-white.
claraboya *f* skylight.
clarear *vi* to dawn: —~**se** *vr* to be transparent.
clarín *m* bugle; bugler.
clarinete *m* clarinet: —*m/f* clarinetist.
claro/ra *adj* clear, bright; evident, manifest: —*m* opening; clearing (in a wood).
clase *f* class; rank; order.
clasificar *vt* to classify.
claudicar *vi* to limp; to act deceitfully; to back down.
claustro *m* cloister; faculty (of a university).
cláusula *f* clause.
clavar *vt* to nail.
clave *f* key; (*mus*) clef: —*m* harpsichord.
clavel *m (bot)* carnation.
clavicordio *m* clavichord.
clavícula *f* clavicle, collar bone.
clavija *f* pin, peg.
clavo *m* nail; corn (on the feet); clove.
clemente *adj* clement, merciful.
clérigo *m* priest; clergyman.
cliente *m/f* client.
clima *m* climate.
climatizado/da *adj* air-conditioned.
clínica *f* clinic; private hospital.
clip *m* paper clip.
cloaca *f* sewer.
coacción *f* coercion, compulsion.
coagular *vt*, ~**se** *vr* to coagulate; to curdle.
coartada *f (jur)* alibi.
coartar *vt* to limit, restrict, restrain.
cobalto *m* cobalt.
cobarde *adj* cowardly, timid.
cobaya *f* guinea pig.

cobertizo *m* small shed; shelter.
cobijar *vt* to cover; to shelter.
cobrar *vt* to recover: —~**se** *vr (med)*to come to.
cobre *m* copper; kitchen utensils *pl; (mus)* brass.
cocear *vt* to kick; (*fig*) to resist.
cocer *vt* to boil; to bake (bricks): —*vi* to boil; to ferment: —~**se** *vr* to suffer intense pain.
cochambroso/sa *adj* nasty; filthy, stinking.
coche *m* car; coach, carriage; pram, baby carriage: —(*ferro*) ~ **cama** sleeping car: —~ **restaurante** restaurant car.
cochino/na *adj* dirty, filthy; nasty: —*m*pig, hog.
cocina *f* kitchen; stove; cookery.
cocinero/ra *m/f* cook.
coco *m* coconut; bogeyman.
cocodrilo *m* crocodile.
codazo *m* blow given with the elbow.
codear *vt*, *vi* to elbow: —~**se** *vr* ~**secon** to rub shoulders with.
codiciar *vt* to covet, desire.
código *m* code; law; set of rules.
codillo *m* knee of a four-legged animal; angle; (*tec*) elbow (joint).
codo *m* elbow.
codorniz *f* quail.
coetáneo/nea *adj* contemporary.
coexistir *vi* to coexist.
cofia *f* (nurse's) cap.
cofradía *f* brotherhood, fraternity.
cofre *m* trunk.
coger *vt* to catch, take hold of; to occupy, take up: —~**se** *vr* to catch.
cogollo *m* heart of a lettuce or cabbage; shoot of a plant.
cogote *m* back of the neck.
cohecho *m* bribery.
coherencia *f* coherence.
cohete *m* rocket.
cohibido/da *adj* shy.
coincidir *vi* to coincide.
coito *m* intercourse, coitus.
cojear *vi* to limp, hobble; (*fig*) to go astray.
cojín *m* cushion.
cojo/ja *adj* lame, crippled.
col *f* cabbage.
cola *f* tail; queue; last place; glue.
colaborar *vi* to collaborate.
colada *f* wash, washing; (*quím*) bleach; sheep run.
colador *m* sieve.
colar *vt* to strain, filter: —*vi* to ooze: —~**se en** to get into without paying.
colcha *f* bedspread, counterpane.
colchón *m* mattress.
coleccionar *vt* to collect.
colecta *f* collection (for charity).
colectivo/va *adj* collective.
colega *m/f* colleague.
colegial *m* schoolboy.
colegiala *f* schoolgirl.
colegio *m* college; school.
colegir *vt* to collect; to deduce, infer.
cólera *f* bile; anger; fury, rage; cholera.
coleta *f* pigtail.
colgar *vt* to hang; to suspend; to decorate with tapestry: —*vi* to be suspended.
colibrí *m* hummingbird.
coliflor *m* cauliflower.

colina f hill.
colisión f collision; friction.
colmar vt to heap up: —vi to fulfill, realize.
colmena f hive, beehive.
colmillo m eyetooth; tusk.
colmo m height, summit; extreme: **—a ~** plentifully.
colocar vt to arrange; to place; to provide with a job: **—~se** vr to get a job.
collar m necklace; (dog) collar.
colono m colonist; farmer.
coloquio m conversation; conference.
color m color, hue; dye; rouge; suit (of cards).
colorado/da adj ruddy; red.
colorete m rouge.
columna f column.
columpio m swing, seesaw.
colza f (bot) rape; rape seed.
coma f (gr) comma: **—m (med)** coma.
comadreja f weasel.
comandante m commander.
comarca f territory, district.
combatir vt to combat, fight; to attack: —vi to fight.
combinar vi to combine.
combustible adj combustible: **—m**fuel.
comedia f comedy; play, drama.
comedido/da adj moderate, restrained.
comedor/ra m/f glutton: —m dining room.
comentar vt to comment on, expound.
comentario m comment, remark; commentary.
comenzar vi to commence, begin.
comer vt to eat; to take (a piece at chess): —vi to have lunch.
comercial adj commercial.
comercio m trade, commerce; business.
comestible adj eatable: **—mpl ~s**food, foodstuffs pl.
cometa m comet: —f kite.
cometer vt to commit, charge; to entrust.
cómico/ca adj comic, comical.
comida f food; eating; meal; lunch.
comillas fpl quotation marks pl.
comino m cumin (plant or seed).
comisaría f police station; commissariat.
como adv as; like; such as.
cómo adv how?; why?: —excl what? **cómoda** f bureau.
cómodo/da adj convenient; comfortable.
compacto/ta adj compact; close, dense.
compadecer vt to pity: **—~se** vr to agree with each other.
compaginar vt to arrange, put in order: **—~se** vr to tally.
compañero/ra m/f companion, friend; comrade; partner.
compañía f company.
comparar vt to compare.
compartimento m compartment.
compartir vt to share.
compás m compass; pair of compasses; (mus) measure, beat.
compatible adj : **—~ con** compatible with, consistent with.
compensar vt to compensate; to recompense.
competencia f competition, rivalry; competence.
competente adj competent; adequate.
compilar vt to compile.
compinche m pal, mate (sl).
complacencia f pleasure; indulgence.

complacer vt to please: **—~se** vr to be pleased with.
complejo m complex: **—~/ ja** adj complex.
complementario/ria adj complementary.
complemento m complement.
completar vt to complete.
completo/ta adj complete; perfect.
complicar vt to complicate.
cómplice m/f accomplice.
complot m plot.
componer vt to compose; to constitute; to mend, repair; to strengthen, restore; to compose, calm: **—~se vr se de** to consist of.
comportamiento m behavior.
compostura f composition, composure; mending, repairing; discretion; modesty, demureness.
compota f stewed fruit.
comprar vt to buy, purchase.
comprender vt to include, contain; to comprehend, understand.
compresa f sanitary napkin.
comprimido m pill.
comprimir vt to compress; to repress, restrain.
comprobar vt to verify, confirm; to prove.
comprometer vt to compromise; to embarrass; to implicate; to put in danger: **—~se** vr to compromise oneself.
compuerta f hatch; sluice.
compuesto m compound: **—~/ta** adj composed; made up of.
compulsar vt to collate, compare; to make an authentic copy.
compungirse vr to feel remorseful.
comulgar vt to administer communion to: —vi to receive communion.
común adj common, usual, general: — m community; public: **—en ~** in common.
comunicar vt to communicate: **—~se** vr to communicate (with each other).
comunidad f community.
con prep with; by: **—~ que** so then, providing that.
coñac m brandy, cognac.
cóncavo/va adj concave.
concebir vt to conceive: —vi to become pregnant.
conceder vt to give; to grant; to concede, allow.
concejal/la m/f member of a council.
concentrar vt : **—~se** vr to concentrate.
concepto m conceit, thought; judgement, opinion.
concernir v imp to regard, concern.
concertar vt to coordinate; to settle; to adjust; to agree; to arrange, fix up: —vi (mus) to harmonize, be in tune.
concesión f concession.
concha f shell; tortoise-shell.
conciencia f conscience.
concienciar vt to make aware: **—~se** vr to become aware.
concierto m concert; agreement; concerto: **—de ~** in agreement, in concert.
conciliar vt to reconcile: —adj conciliar, council.
conciso/sa adj concise, brief.
concluir vt to conclude, end, complete; to infer, deduce: **—~se** vr to conclude.
concordar vt to reconcile, makeagree: —vi to agree, correspond.
concordia f conformity, agreement.
concretar vt to make concrete; to specify.
concubina f concubine.

concurrido/da *adj* busy.
concursante *m/f* competitor.
concurso *m* crowd; competition; help, cooperation.
conde *m* earl, count.
condenable *adj* culpable.
condenar *vt* to condemn; to find *f* preparation; clothing
condensar *vt* to condense.
condescender *vi* to acquiesce, comply.
condición *f* condition, state; quality; status; rank; stipulation.
condimentar *vt* to flavor, season.
condolerse *vr* to sympathize.
condón *m* condom.
conducir *vt* to convey, conduct; to drive; to manage: —*vi* to drive: —~(a) to lead (to): —~se *vr* to conduct oneself.
conducta *f* conduct, behavior; management.
conducto *m* conduit, pipe; drain; (*fig*)channel.
conductor/ra *m/f* conductor, guide; (*ferro*) guard; driver.
conectar *vt* to connect.
conejo *m* rabbit.
conexión *f* connection; plug; relationship.
confección *f* preparation; clothing industry.
conferencia *f* conference; telephone call.
confesar *vt* to confess; to admit.
confianza *f* trust; confidence; conceit; familiarity: —en ~ confidential.
confiar *vt* to confide, entrust: —*vi* to trust.
configurar *vt* to shape, form.
confinar *vt* to confine: —*vi* ~ con to border upon.
confirmar *vt* to confirm; to corroborate.
confiscar *vt* to confiscate.
confitería *f* sweet store.
confitura *f* preserve; jam.
conflicto *m* conflict.
conformar *vt* to shape; to adjust, guilty: —~se *vr* to blame oneself; to adapt: —*vi* to agree: —~se *vr* to
conconfess (one's guilt).
form; to resign oneself.
conforme *adj* alike, similar; agreed: — *prep* according to.
confortar *vt* to comfort; to strengthen; to console.
confundir *vt* to confound, jumble; to confuse: —~se *vr* to make a mistake.
confusión *f* confusion.
congelado/da *adj* frozen: —*mpl* ~s frozen food.
congelar *vt* to freeze: —~se *vr* to congeal.
congeniar *vi* to get on well.
congoja *f* anguish, distress, grief.
congraciarse *vr* to ingratiate oneself.
congregar(se) *vt (vr)* to assemble, meet, collect.
conjetura *f* conjecture, guess.
conjugar *vt (gr)* to conjugate; to combine.
conjunto/ta *adj* united, joint: —*m*whole; (*mus*) ensemble, band; team.
conjurar *vt* to exorcize: —*vi* to conspire, plot.
conmemorar *vt* to commemorate.
conmigo *pn* with me.
conmover *vt* to move; to disturb.
conmutador *m* switch.
conmutar *vt (jur)* to commute; to exchange.
connotar *vt* to imply.
cono *m* cone.
conocer *vt* to know, understand: —~se *vr* to know one another.

conocimiento *m* knowledge, understanding; (*med*) consciousness; acquaintance; (*mar*) bill of lading.
conquistar *vt* to conquer.
consabido/da *adj* well-known; abovementioned.
consagrar *vt* to consecrate.
consanguíneo/nea *adj* related by blood.
consecuencia *f* consequence; conclusion; consistency: —por ~ therefore.
consecuente *adj* consistent.
conseguir *vt* to attain; to get, obtain.
consejo *m* advice; council.
consentir *vt* to consent to; to allow; to admit; to spoil (a child).
conserje *m* doorman; janitor.
conservar *vt* to conserve; to keep; to preserve (fruit).
conservas *fpl* canned food.
conservatorio *m (mus)* conservatoire.
consideración *f* consideration; respect.
considerar *vt* to consider.
consigna *f (mil)* watchword; order, instruction; (*ferro*) left-luggage office.
consignar *vt* to consign, dispatch; to assign; to record, register.
consigo *pn (m)* with him; (*f*) with her; (*vd*) with you; (*refl*) with oneself.
consiguiente *adj* consequent.
consistente *adj* consistent; firm, solid.
consistir *vi:* —~ en to consist of; to be due to.
consola *f* control panel.
consolar *vt* to console, comfort, cheer.
consolidar *vt* to consolidate.
consonante *m* rhyme: —*f (gr)* consonant: —*adj* consonant, harmonious.
consorcio *m* partnership.
consorte *m/f* consort, companion, partner; accomplice.
conspirar *vi* to conspire, plot.
constante *adj* constant; firm.
constar *vt* to be evident, be certain; to be composed of, consist of.
constatar *vt* to note; to check.
consternar *vt* to dismay; to shock.
constipado/da *adj :* —estar ~ to have a cold.
constituir *vt* to constitute; to establish; to appoint.
construir *vt* to form; to build, construct; to construe.
consuegro/gra *m/f* father-in-law/ mother-in-law of one's son or daughter.
consuelo *m* consolation, comfort.
cónsul *m* consul.
consultar *vt* to consult, ask for advice.
consultor/ra *m/f* adviser, consultant.
consultorio *m (med)* consulting room, doctor's rooms.
consumar *vt* to consummate, finish; to carry out.
consumir *vt* to consume; to burn, use; to waste, exhaust: —~se *vr* to waste away, be consumed.
contabilidad *f* accounting; bookkeeping.
contacto *m* contact; (*auto*) ignition.
contado/da *adj :* —~s scarce, few: — *m* pagar al ~ to pay (in) cash.
contador *m* meter; counter in a cafe: — ~/~a *m/f* accountant.
contagiar *vt* to infect: —~se *vr* to get infected.
contaminar *vt* to contaminate; to pollute; to corrupt.
contar *vt* to count, reckon; to tell: —*vi* to count: —~ con to rely upon.

contemplar *vt* to look at; to contemplate, consider; to meditate.

contemporáneo/nea *adj* contemporary.

contenedor *m* container.

contener *vt* to contain, hold; to holdback; to repress: —**~se** *vr* to controloneself.

contentar *vt* to content, satisfy; to please: —**~se** *vr* to be pleased or satisfied.

contento/ta *adj* glad; pleased; content: —*m* contentment; *(jur)*release.

contestador *m*: —**~ automatico** answering machine.

contestar *vt* to answer, reply; to prove, corroborate.

contienda *f* contest, dispute.

contigo *pn* with you.

contiguo/gua *adj* contiguous, close.

continente *m* continent, mainland: — *adj* continent.

contingencia *f* risk; contingency.

continuar *vt , vi* to continue.

continuo/nua *adj* continuous.

contorno *m* environs *pl;* contour, outline: —**en ~** round about.

contra *prep* against; contrary to; opposite.

contrabajo *m (mus)* double bass; bass guitar; low bass.

contrabando *m* contraband; smuggling.

contrachapado *m* plywood.

contradecir *vt* to contradict.

contraer *vt* to contract, shrink; to make (a bargain): —**~se** *vr* to shrink, contract.

contrahecho/cha *adj* deformed; hunchbacked; counterfeit, fake, false.

contralto *m (mus)* contralto.

contrapartida *f (com)* balancing entry.

contrapelo *adv :* —**a ~** against the grain.

contrapeso *m* counterpoise; counterweight.

contraproducente *adj* counterproductive.

contrariar *vt* to contradict, oppose; to vex.

contrariedad *f* opposition; setback; annoyance.

contrario/ria *m/f* opponent: —*adj* contrary, opposite: —**por el ~** on the contrary.

contrarrestar *vt* to return a ball; *(fig)* to counteract.

contraseña *f* countersign; *(mil)* watch word.

contrasentido *m* contradiction.

contrastar *vt* to resist; to contradict; to assay (metals); to verify (measures and weights): —*vi* to contrast.

contratar *vt* to contract; to hire, engage.

contratiempo *m* setback; accident.

contrato *m* contract, agreement.

contravenir *vi* to contravene, transgress; to violate.

contraventana *f* shutter.

contribución *f* contribution; tax.

contribuir *vt , vi* to contribute.

contrincante *m* competitor.

controlar *vt* to control; to check.

contumaz *adj* obstinate, stubborn; *(jur)* guilty of contempt of court.

contundente *adj* overwhelming; blunt.

contusión *f* bruise.

convalecer *vi* to recover from sickness, convalesce.

convencer *vt* to convince.

conveniencia *f* suitability; usefulness; agreement: —**~s** *fpl* property.

convenir *vi* to agree, suit.

convento *m* convent, nunnery; monastery.

conversar *vi* to talk, converse.

convicto/ta *adj* convicted (found guilty).

convidar *vt* to invite.

convocar *vt* to convoke, assemble.

convocatoria *f* summons; notice of a meeting.

conyugal *adj* conjugal, married.

cónyuge *m/f* spouse.

cooperar *vi* to cooperate.

coordinar *vt* to arrange, coordinate.

copa *f* cup; glass; to p of a tree; crown of a hat: —**~s** *fpl* hearts *pl* (at cards).

copiar *vt* to copy; to imitate.

copla *f* verse; *(mus)* popular song, folksong.

copo *m* small bundle; flake of snow.

coquetear *vi* to flirt.

coraje *m* courage; anger, passion.

coral *m* coral; choir: —*adj* choral.

corazón *m* heart; core: —**de ~** willingly.

corazonada *f* inspiration; quick decision; presentiment.

corbata *f* tie.

corchete *m* clasp; hook and eye.

corcho *m* cork; float (for fishing); cork bark.

cordel *m* cord, rope; *(mar)* line.

cordero *m* lamb; lambskin; meek, gentle person.

cordial *adj* cordial, affectionate: —*m* cordial.

cordillera *f* range of mountains.

cordón *m* cord, string; lace; cordon.

cornada *f* thrust with a bull's horn.

coro *m* choir; chorus.

corona *f* crown; coronet; top of the head; crown (of a tooth); tonsure; halo.

coronilla *f* crown of the head.

corpiño *m* bodice.

corporal *adj* corporal.

corpulento/ta *adj* corpulent, bulky.

corral *m* yard; farmyard; corral; playpen.

correa *f* leather strap, thong; flexibility.

correcto/ta *adj* exact, correct.

corregir *vt* to correct, amend; to reprehend: —**~se** *vr* to reform.

correo *m* post, mail; courier; mailman: —**a vuelta de ~** by return of post: —**~s** *mpl* post office.

correr *vt* to run; to flow; to travel over; to pull (a drape): —*vi* to run, rush; to flow; to blow (applied to the wind): —**~se** *vr* to be ashamed; to slide, move; to run (of colors).

correspondencia *f* correspondence; communication; agreement.

corresponder *vi* to correspond; to answer; to be suitable; to belong; to concern: —**~se** *vr* to love one another.

corresponsal *m/f* correspondent.

corriente *f* current; course, progression; (electric) current: —*adj* current; common, ordinary, general; fluent; flowing, running.

corro *m* circle of people.

corroer *vt* to corrode, erode.

corromper *vt* to corrupt; to rot; to turn bad; to seduce; to bribe: —**~se** *vr* to rot; to become corrupted: —*vi* to stink.

cortacesped *m* lawn mower.

cortado *m* coffee with a little milk: — **~/ da** *adj* cut; sour; embarrassed.

cortar *vt* to cut; to cut off, curtail; to intersect; to carve; to chop; to cut (at cards); to interrupt: —**~se** *vr* to be ashamed or embarrassed; to curdle.

corte *m* cutting; cut; section; length (of cloth); style:

—*f* (royal) court; capital (city): —**C~s** *fpl* Spanish Parliament.

cortejo *m* entourage; courtship; procession; lover.

cortés/esa *adj* courteous, polite.

cortesía *f* courtesy, good manners *pl.*

corteza *f* bark; peel; crust; *(fig)* outward appearance.

cortina *f* curtain.

corto/ta *adj* short; scanty, small; stupid; bashful: —**a la ~a** *o* **a la larga** sooner or later.

corzo/za *m/f* roe deer, fallow deer.

cosa *f* thing; matter, affair: —**no haytal ~** nothing of the sort!

cosecha *f* harvest; harvest time: —**desu ~** of one's own invention.

coser *vt* to sew; to join.

cosquillas *fpl* tickling; *(fig)* agitation.

costa *f* cost, price; charge, expense; coast, shore: —**a toda ~** at all events.

costado *m* side; *(mil)* flank; side of a ship.

costal *m* sack, large bag.

costar *vt* to cost; to need.

coste *m* cost, expense.

costero/ra *adj* coastal; *(mar)* coasting.

costilla *f* rib; cutlet: —**~s** *fpl* back, shoulders *pl.*

costra *f* crust; *(med)* scab.

costumbre *f* custom, habit.

cotejar *vt* to compare.

cotidiano/na *adj* daily.

cotilla *m/f* gossip.

cotizar *vt* to quote: —**~se** *vr* ~ **a** to sell at; to be quoted at.

coto *m* enclosure; reserve; boundary stone.

cotorra *f* small parrot; *(col)* chatterbox.

covacha *f* small cave, grotto.

coyuntura *f* joint, articulation; juncture.

coz *f* kick; recoil (of a gun); ebbing (of a flood); *(fig)* insult.

cráneo *m* skull.

crear *vt* to create, make; to establish.

crecer *vi* to grow, increase; to rise.

crecida *f* swell (of rivers).

creciente *f* crescent (moon); *(mar)*flood tide: —*adj* growing; crescent.

crecimiento *m* increase; growth.

crédito *m* credit; belief, faith; reputation.

creer *vt , vi* to believe; to think; to consider.

crema *f* cream; custard.

cremallera *f* zipper.

crepúsculo *m* twilight.

cresta *f* crest (of birds).

creyente *m/f* believer.

cría *f* breeding; young.

criadero *m (bot)* nursery; breeding place.

criadilla *f* testicle; small loaf; truffle.

crianza *f* breeding, rearing.

criar *vt* to create, produce; to breed; to breast-feed; to bring up.

criatura *f* creature; child.

crimen *m* crime.

criminal *adj , m/f* criminal.

crin *f* mane; horsehair.

crío/a *m/f (fam)* kid.

cripta *f* crypt.

crisis *f invar* crisis.

crisol *m* crucible; melting pot.

crispar *vt* to set on edge; to tense up.

cristal *m* crystal; glass; pane; lens.

cristalino/na *adj* crystalline.

cristalizar *vt* to crystallize.

cristiano/na *adj , m/f* Christian.

criterio *m* criterion.

crítica *m/f* criticism.

criticar *vt* to criticize.

croar *vi* to croak.

cromo *m* chrome.

crónica *f* chronicle; news report; feature.

crónico/ca *adj* chronic.

cronista *m/f* chronicler; reporter, columnist.

cronómetro *m* stopwatch.

cruce *m* crossing; crossroads.

crucero *m* cruiser; cruise; transept; crossing.

crucifijo *m* crucifix.

crucigrama *m* crossword.

crudo/da *adj* raw; green, unripe; crude; cruel; hard to digest.

cruel *adj* cruel.

crueldad *f* cruelty.

crujiente *adj* crunchy.

crujir *vi* to crackle; to rustle.

crustáceo *m* crustacean.

cruz *f* cross; tails (of a coin).

cruzar *vt* to cross; *(mar)* to cruise: —**~se** *vr* to cross; to passeach other.

cuaderno *m* notebook; exercise book; logbook.

cuadra *f* block; stable.

cuadrado/da *adj , m* square.

cuadrante *m* quadrant; dial.

cuadrar *vt , vi* to square; to fit, suit, correspond.

cuadrilátero/ra *adj , m* quadrilateral.

cuadrilla *f* party, group; gang, crew.

cuadro *m* square; picture, painting; window frame; scene; chart.

cuadrúpedo/da *adj* quadruped.

cuajar *vt* to coagulate; to thicken; to adorn; to set: —**~se** *vr* to coagulate, curdle; to set; to fill up.

cual *pn* which; who; whom: —*adv* as; like: —*adj* such as.

cuál *pn* which (one).

cualidad *f* quality.

cualquier *adj* any.

cualquiera *adj* anyone, anybody; someone, somebody; whoever; whichever.

cuando *adv* when; if; even: —*conj* since: —**de ~ en ~** from time to time: —**~ más/~ mucho** at most, at best: —**~ menos** at least.

cuándo *adv* when: —**¿de cuándo acá?** since when?

cuánto *adj* what a lot of; how much?: —**¿~s?** how many?: —*pn* , *adv* how; how much; how many.

cuanto/ta *adj* as many as; as much as; all; whatever: —*adv* **en ~** as soon as: —**en ~ a** as regards: —**~ más** moreover, the more as.

cuarenta *adj , m* forty.

cuaresma *f* Lent.

cuarto *m* fourth part; quarter; room, apartment; span: —**~s** *mpl* cash, money: —**~/ ta** *adj* fourth.

cuarzo *m* quartz.

cuatro *adj , m* four.

cuatrocientos/tas *adj* four hundred.

cuba *f* cask; tub; *(fig)* drunkard.

cubierta *f* cover; deck of a ship; *(auto)*hood; tire; pretext.

cubierto *m* cover; shelter; place at table; meal at a fixed charge: —**~s** *mpl* cutlery, silverware.

cubo *m* cube; bucket; can: —~**de la basura** garbage can.

cubrir *vt* to cover; to disguise; to protect; to roof a building: —~**se** *vr* to become overcast.

cucaracha *f* cockroach.

cuchara *f* spoon.

cucharada *f* spoonful; ladleful.

cucharadita *f* teaspoonful.

cuchichear *vi* to whisper.

cuchillo *m* knife.

cuclillas *adv* : —**en** ~ squatting.

cuclillo *m* cuckoo; (*fig*) cuckold.

cuello *m* neck; collar.

cuenca *m* bowl, deep valley; hollow; socket of the eye.

cuenta *f* calculation; account; check, bill (in a restaurant); count, counting; bead; importance.

cuento *m* tale, story, narrative.

cuerda *f* rope; string; spring.

cuerdo/da *adj* sane; prudent, judicious.

cuerno *m* horn.

cuero *m* hide, skin, leather.

cuerpo *m* body; cadaver, corpse.

cuesta *f* slope, hill; incline: —**ir** ~**abajo** to go down-hill: —~ **arriba** uphill.

cuestión *f* question, matter; dispute; quarrel; problem.

cueva *f* cave; cellar.

cuidado *m* care, worry, concern; charge.

cuidar *vt* to care for; to mind, look after.

culebra *f* snake.

culo *m* backside; bum (*sl*); bottom.

culpa *f* fault, blame; guilt.

culpable *adj* culpable; guilty: —*m/f* culprit.

cultivar *vt* to cultivate.

culto/ta *adj* cultivated, cultured; refined, civilized: —*m* culture; worship.

cumbre *f* top, summit.

cumplir *vt* to carry out, fulfil; to serve (a prison sentence); to carry out (death penalty); to attain, reach (a certain age): —~**se** *vr* to be fulfilled; to expire, be up.

cuna *f* cradle.

cuña *f* wedge.

cuñado/da *m/f* brother/sister-inlaw.

cura *m* priest: —*f* cure; treatment.

curar *vt* to cure; to treat, dress (a wound); to salt; to dress; to tan.

curioso/sa *adj* curious: —*m/f* bystander.

currar *vi* (*fam*) to work.

curso *m* course, direction; year (at university); subject.

curtir *vt* to tan leather: —~**se** *vr* to become sun-burned; to become inured.

curva *f* curve, bend.

custodia *f* custody, safekeeping, care; monstrance.

cutis *m* skin.

cutre *adj* (*fam*) mean, grotty.

cuyo/ya *pn* whose, of which, of whom.

D

dado *m* die (*pl* dice).

daga *f* dagger.

dama *f* lady, gentlewoman; mistress; queen; actress of principal parts.

damnificar *vt* to hurt, injure, damage.

dañar *vt* to hurt, injure; to damage.

dañino/na *adj* harmful; noxious; mischievous.

danza *f* dance.

dar *vt* to give; to supply, administer, afford; to deliver.

dátil *m* (*bot*) date.

dato *m* fact.

de *prep* of; from; for; by; on; to ; with.

debajo *adv* under, underneath, below.

debatir *vt* to debate, argue, discuss.

debe *m* (*com*) debit: —~ **y haber** debit and credit.

deber *m* obligation, duty; debt: —*vt* to owe; to be obliged to: —*vi* **debe (de)** it must, it should.

debidamente *adv* justly, duly; exactly, perfectly.

débil *adj* feeble, weak; sickly; frail.

debilitar *vt* to debilitate, weaken.

decadencia *f* decay, decline.

decena *f* ten.

decencia *f* decency.

decepción *f* disappointment.

decidir *vt* to decide, determine.

décimo/ma *adj* , *m* tenth.

decir *vt* to say; to tell; to speak; to name.

decisión *f* decision; determination, resolution; sentence.

declamar *vi* to declaim; to harangue.

declarar *vt* to declare; to manifest; to expound; to explain; (*jur*) to decide: —~**se** *vr* to declare one's opinion: —*vi* to testify.

declinar *vi* to decline; to decay, degenerate: —*vt* (*gr*) to decline.

declive *m* slope; decline.

decorar *vt* to decorate, adorn; to illustrate.

decrecer *vi* to decrease.

decrépito/ta *adj* decrepit, worn out with age.

decretar *vt* to decree, determine.

dedal *m* thimble; very small drinking glass.

dedicar *vt* to dedicate, devote; to consecrate: —~**se** *vr* to apply one-self to.

dedo *m* finger; to e; small bit: —~ **meñique** little finger: —~ **pulgar** thumb: —~ **del corazón** middle finger: —~ **anular** ring finger.

deducir *vt* to deduce, infer; to allege in pleading; to subtract.

defecto *m* defect; defectiveness.

defectuoso/sa *adj* defective, imper-fect, faulty.

defender *vt* to defend, protect; to justify, assert; to resist, oppose.

defensor/ra *m/f* defender, protector; lawyer, defense counsel.

deferir *vi* to defer; to yield (to another's opinion): —*vt* to commun-icate.

deficiente *adj* defective.

definir *vt* to define, describe, explain; to decide.

definitivo/va *adj* definitive; positive.

deformar *vt* to deform: —~**se** *vr* to become de-formed.

deforme *adj* deformed; ugly.
defraudar *vt* to defraud, cheat; to usurp; to disturb.
defunción *f* death; funeral.
degenerar *vi* to degenerate.
degollar *vt* to behead; to destroy, ruin.
degradar *vt* to degrade: —~se *vr* to degrade or demean oneself.
degustar *vt* to taste.
dehesa *f* pasture.
dejadez *f* slovenliness, neglect.
dejar *vt* to leave, quit; to omit; to let; to permit, allow; to forsake; to bequeath; to pardon: —~ **de** to stop; to fail to: —~se *vr* to abandon oneself.
del *adj* of the (contraction of *de* and *el*).
delantal *m* apron.
delante *adv* in front; opposite; ahead: —~ **de** in front of; before.
delantero/ra *adj* front: —*m* forward.
delegar *vt* to delegate; to substitute.
deleitar *vt* to delight.
deletrear *vt* to spell; to examine; to conjecture.
delfín *m* dolphin; dauphin.
delgado/da *adj* thin; delicate, fine; light; slender, lean.
deliberadamente *adv* deliberately.
deliberar *vi* to consider, deliberate: — *vt* to debate; to consult.
delicado/da *adj* delicate, tender; faint; exquisite; delicious, dainty; slender, subtle.
delicioso/sa *adj* delicious; delightful.
delincuencia *f* delinquency.
delineante *m/f* draftsman/woman.
delirar *vi* to rave; to talk nonsense.
delito *m* offence; crime.
demacrado/da *adj* pale and drawn.
demandar *vt* to demand; to ask; to claim; to sue.
demarcar *vt* to mark out (limits).
demás *adj* other; remaining: —*pn* **los/las** ~ the others, the rest: —**estar** ~ to be over and above; to be useless or superfluous: —**por** ~in vain.
demasiado/da *adj* too; excessive: — *adv* too, too much.
demencia *f* madness.
demoler *vt* to demolish; to destroy.
demonio *m* demon.
demorar *vt* to delay: —~se *vr* to be delayed: —*vi* to linger.
demostrar *vt* to prove, demonstrate; to manifest.
denegar *vt* to deny; to refuse.
denigrar *vt* to blacken; to insult.
denominar *vt* to name; to designate.
denotar *vt* to denote; to express.
denso/sa *adj* dense, thick; compact.
dentado/da *adj* toothed; indented.
dentadura *f* set of teeth.
dentífrico *m* toothpaste.
dentista *m/f* dentist.
dentro *adv* within: —*pn* ~ **de** in, inside.
denunciar *vt* to advise; to denounce; to report.
depender *vi:* —~ **de** to depend on, be dependent on.
dependiente *m* sales clerk: —*adj* dependent.
depilatorio *m* hair remover.
deponer *vt* to depose; to declare; to displace; to deposit.
deportar *vt* to deport.
deporte *m* sport.
deportista *m/f* sportsman/woman.

depositar *vt* to deposit; to confide; to put away for safekeeping.
depravación *f* depravity.
deprimir *vt* to depress: —~se *vr* to become depressed.
deprisa *adv* quickly.
depurar *vt* to cleanse, purify; to filter.
derecho/cha *adj* right; straight; just; perfect; certain: —*m* right, justice; law; just claim; tax, duty; fee: —*adv* straight.
derivar *vt , vi* to derive; *(mar)* to drift.
derogar *vt* to derogate, abolish; to reform.
derramar *vt* to drain off (water); to spread; to spill, scatter; to waste, shed: —~se *vr* to pour out.
derretir *vt* to melt; to consume; to thaw: —~se *vr* to melt.
derribar *vt* to demolish; to flatten.
derrochar *vt* to dissipate; to squander.
derrotar *vt* to destroy; to defeat.
derruir *vt* to demolish.
derrumbar *vt* to throw down: —~se *vr* to collapse.
desabrido/da *adj* tasteless, insipid; rude; unpleasant.
desacato *m* disrespect, incivility.
desacertado/da *adj* mistaken; unwise; inconsiderate.
desaconsejar *vt* to advise against.
desacostumbrado/da *adj* unusual.
desacuerdo *m* blunder; disagreement; forgetfulness.
desafiar *vt* to challenge; to defy.
desafinar *vi* to be out of tune.
desafuero *m* outrage; excess.
desagradable *adj* disagreeable, unpleasant.
desagradecido/da *adj* ungrateful.
desagüe *m* channel, drain; drainpipe; drainage.
desahogar *vt* to ease; to vent: —~se *vr* to recover; to relax.
desahuciar *vt* to cause to despair; to give up; to evict.
desajustar *vt* to make uneven; to unbalance: —~se *vr* to get out of order.
desalentar *vt* to put out of breath; to discourage.
desaliño *m* slovenliness; carelessness.
desalmado/da *adj* cruel, inhuman.
desalojar *vt* to eject; to move out: —*vi* to move out.
desamparar *vt* to forsake, abandon; to relinquish.
desangrar *vt* to bleed; to drain (a pond); *(fig)* to exhaust (one's means): —~se *vr* to lose a lot of blood.
desanimar *vt* to discourage: —~se *vr* to lose heart.
desaparecer *vi* to disappear.
desapercibido/da *adj* unnoticed.
desaprobar *vt* to disapprove; to condemn; to reject.
desaprovechado/da *adj* useless; unprofitable; backward; slack.
desaprovechar *vt* to waste, turn to a bad use.
desarmar *vt* to disarm; to disband (troops); to dismantle; *(fig)* to pacify.
desarraigar *vt* to uproot; to root out; to extirpate.
desarrollar *vt* to develop; to unroll; to unfold: —~se *vr* to develop; to be unfolded; to open.
desasosiego *m* restlessness; anxiety.
desastre *m* disaster; misfortune.
desatar *vt* to untie, loose; to separate; to solve: —~se *vr* to come undone; to break.
desatascar *vt* to unblock; to clear.
desatender *vt* to pay no attention to; to disregard.

desatinar *vi* to talk nonsense; to reel, stagger.
desatornillar *vt* to unscrew.
desayunar *vt* to have for breakfast: —~se *vr* to breakfast: —*vi* to have breakfast.
desazón *f* disgust; uneasiness; annoy-ance.
desbarrar *vi* to talk nonsense.
desbordar *vt* to exceed: —~se *vr* to overflow.
descalabrado/da *adj* wounded on the head; imprudent.
descalificar *vt* to disqualify; to discredit.
descalzo/za *adj* barefooted; *(fig)* destitute.
descaminado/da *adj (fig)* misguided.
descansar *vt* to rest; —*vi* to rest; to lie down.
descansillo *m* landing.
descapotable *m* convertible.
descarado/da *adj* cheeky, barefaced.
descargar *vt* to unload, discharge: —~se *vr* to unburden oneself.
descarriar *vt* to lead astray; to misdirect: —~se *vr* to lose one's way; to stray; to err.
descarrilar *vi (ferro)* to leave or runoff the rails.
descartar *vt* to discard; to dismiss; to rule out.
descendencia *f* descent, offspring.
descender *vt* to take down: —*vi* to descend, walk down; to flow; to fall: —~ **de** to be derived from.
descenso *m* descent; drop.
descifrar *vt* to decipher; to unravel.
descollar *vi* to excel.
descolorido/da *adj* pale, colorless.
descomunal *adj* uncommon; huge.
desconcertar *vt* to disturb; to confound; to disconcert: —~se *vr* to be bewildered; to be upset.
desconectar *vt* to disconnect.
desconfiar *vi:* —~ **de** to mistrust, suspect.
descongelar *vt* to defrost.
desconocer *vt* to disown, disavow; to be totally ignorant of (a thing); not to know (a person); not to acknowledge (a favor received).
desconsuelo *m* distress; trouble; despair.
descontar *vt* to discount; to deduct.
descontento *m* dissatisfaction; dis-gust.
descortés/esa *adj* impolite, rude.
descoser *vt* to unseam; to separate: —~se *vr* to come apart at the seams.
descreído/da *adj* incredulous.
descremado/da *adj* skimmed.
describir *vt* to describe; to draw, delineate.
descuartizar *vt* to quarter; to carve.
descubrir *vt* to discover, disclose; to uncover; to reveal; to show: —~se *vr* to reveal oneself; to take off one's hat; to confess.
descuento *m* discount; decrease.
descuidado/da *adj* careless, negligent.
descuidar *vt* to neglect: —*vi* ~se *vr* to be careless.
desde *prep* since; after; from: —~ **luego** of course: —~ **entonces** since then.
desdén *m* disdain, scorn.
desdeñar *vt* to disdain, scorn: —~se *vr* to be disdainful.
desdentado/da *adj* toothless.
desdicha *f* misfortune, calamity; great poverty.
desdoblar *vt* to unfold, spread open.
desear *vt* to desire, wish; to require, demand.
desecar *vt* to dry up.
desechar *vt* to depreciate; to reject; to refuse; to throw away.
desecho *m* residue: —~s *mpl* trash.

desembarcar *vt* to unload, disembark: —*vi* to disembark, land.
desembolsar *vt* to pay out.
desempatar *vi* to hold a play-off.
desempeñar *vt* to redeem; to extricate from debt; to fulfil (any duty or promise); to acquit: —~se *vr* to get out of debt.
desempleo *m* unemployment.
desencadenar *vt* to unchain: —~se *vr* to break loose; to burst.
desencajar *vt* to disjoint; to dislocate; to disconnect.
desencanto *m* disenchantment.
desenchufar *vt* to unplug.
desenfado *m* ease; facility; calmness, relaxation.
desenfocado/da *adj* out of focus.
desenfreno *m* wildness; lack of self-control.
desengañar *vt* to disillusion: —~se *vr* to become disillusioned.
desenganchar *vt* to unhook; to uncouple.
desengrasar *vt* to take the grease off.
desenlace *m* climax; outcome.
desenredar *vt* to disentangle.
desenroscar *vt* to untwist; to unroll.
desentenderse *vr* to feign not to understand; to pass by without noticing.
desenterrar *vt* to exhume; to dig up.
desentonar *vi* to be out of tune; to clash.
desenvolver *vt* to unfold; to unroll; to decipher, unravel; to develop: —~se *vr* to develop; to cope.
deseo *m* desire, wish.
desequilibrado/da *adj* unbalanced.
desertar *vt* to desert; *(jur)* to abandon (a cause).
desesperar *vi,* ~se *vr* to despair: —*vt* to make desperate.
desestabilizar *vt* to destabilize.
desfachatez *f* impudence.
desfalco *m* embezzlement.
desfallecer *vi* to get weak; to faint.
desfasado/da *adj* old-fashioned.
desfavorable *adj* unfavorable.
desfiladero *m* gorge.
desfilar *vi (mil)* to parade.
desfogarse *vr* to give vent to one's passion or anger.
desgana *f* disgust; loss of appetite; aversion, reluctance.
desgañitarse *vr* to scream, bawl.
desgarrar *vt* to tear; to shatter.
desgaste *m* wear (and tear).
desgracia *f* misfortune; disgrace; accident; setback.
desgreñado/da *adj* disheveled.
deshabitado/da *adj* deserted, unin-habited; desolate.
deshacer *vt* to undo, destroy; to can-cel, efface; to rout (an army); to solve; to melt; to break up, divide; to dissolve in a liquid; to violate (a treaty); to diminish; to disband (troops): —~se *vr* to melt; to come apart.
deshelar *vt* to thaw: —~se *vr* to thaw, melt.
desheredar *vt* to disinherit.
deshidratar *vt* to dehydrate.
deshinchar *vt* to deflate: —~se *vr* to go flat, go down.
deshonesto/ta *adj* indecent.
deshonrar *vt* to affront, insult, defame; to dishonor.
deshuesar *vt* to rid of bones; to stone.
desidia *f* idleness, indolence.
desierto/ta *adj* deserted; solitary: —*m* desert; wilderness.

designar *vt* to design; to intend; to appoint; to express, name.

desigual *adj* unequal, unlike; uneven, craggy, cliffy.

desilusionar *vt* to disappoint: —~se *vr* to become disillusioned.

desinfectar *vt* to disinfect.

desinflar *vt* to deflate.

desinteresado/da *adj* disinterested; unselfish.

desistir *vi* to desist, cease.

desleal *adj* disloyal; unfair.

desleír *vt* to dilute; to dissolve.

deslenguado/da *adj* foul-mouthed.

desligar *vt* to untie; to separate.

deslizar *vt* to slip, slide; to let slip (a comment): —~se *vr* to slip; to skid; to flow softly; to creep in.

deslumbrar *vt* to dazzle; to puzzle.

desmayar *vi* to be dispirited or fainthearted: —~se *vr* to faint.

desmedido/da *adj* disproportionate.

desmemoriado/da *adj* forgetful.

desmentir *vt* to give the lie to: —~se *vr* to contradict oneself.

desmenuzar *vt* to crumble; to chip at; to fritter away; to examine minutely.

desmesurado/da *adj* excessive; huge; immeasurable.

desmoralizar *vt* to demoralize.

desnatado/da *adj* skimmed.

desnivel *m* unevenness of the ground.

desnudar *vt* to undress; to strip; to discover, reveal: —~se *vr* to undress.

desnutrido/da *adj* undernourished.

desobedecer *vt , vi* to disobey.

desocupar *vt* to vacate; to empty: —~se *vr* to retire from a business; to withdraw from an arrangement.

desodorante *m* deodorant.

desolado/da *adj* desolate, disconsolate.

desordenar *vt* to disorder; to untidy: —~se *vr* to get out of order.

desorganizar *vt* to disorganize.

desorientar *vt* to mislead; to confuse: —~se *vr* to lose one's way.

desovar *vi* to spawn.

despabilado/da *adj* watchful, vigilant; wide-awake.

despacho *m* dispatch, expedition; cabinet; office; commission; war-rant, patent; expedient; smart answer.

despachurrar *vt* to squash, crush; to mangle.

despacio *adv* slowly, leisurely; little by little: —¡~! softly!, gently!

desparramar *vt* to disseminate, spread; to spill; to squander, lavish: —~se *vr* to be dissipated.

despavorido *adj* frightened.

despecho *m* indignation; displeasure; spite; dismay, despair; deceit; deri-sion, scorn: —a ~ de in spite of.

despectivo/va *adj* pejorative, deroga-tory.

despedir *vt* to discharge; to dismiss (from office); to see off: —~se *vr ~ de* to say goodbye to.

despegar *vt* to unglue; to take off: — ~se *vr* to come loose.

despegue *m* take-off.

despeinar *vt* to ruffle.

despejado/da *adj* sprightly, quick; clear.

despellejar *vt* to skin.

despensa *f* pantry, larder; provisions *pl.*

desperdiciar *vt* to squander.

desperdigar *vt* to separate; to scatter.

desperfecto *m* slight damage; flaw.

despertador *m* alarm clock.

despertar *vt* to wake up, rouse from sleep; to excite: —*vi* to wake up; to grow lively or sprightly: —~se *vr* to wake up.

despiadado/da *adj* heartless; merciless.

despido *m* dismissal.

despierto/ta *adj* awake; vigilant; fierce; brisk, sprightly.

despistar *vt* to mislead; to throw off the track: —~se *vr* to take the wrong way; to become confused.

desplazar *vt* to move; to scroll: —~se *vr* to travel.

desplegar *vt* to unfold, display; to explain, elucidate; *(mar)* to unfurl: —~se *vr* to open out; to travel.

desplomarse *vr* to fall to the ground; to collapse.

despoblar *vt* to depopulate; to desolate: —~se *vr* to become depopulated.

despojar *vt : —~ (de)* to strip (of); to deprive (of): —~se *vr* to undress.

desposar *vt* to marry, betroth: —~se *vr* to be betrothed or married.

desposeer *vt* to dispossess.

déspota *m* despot.

despreciar *vt* to offend; to despise.

desprender *vt* to unfasten, loosen; to separate: —~se *vr* to give way; to fall down; to extricate oneself.

despreocupado/da *adj* careless; unworried.

desprevenido/da *adj* unawares, unprepared.

desproporcionado/da *adj* disproportionate.

desprovisto/ta *adj* unprovided.

después *adv* after, afterwards; next.

despuntar *vt* to blunt: —*vi* to sprout; to dawn: —**al ~ del día** at break of day.

desquiciar *vt* to upset; to discompose; to disorder.

desquite *m* recovery of a loss; revenge, retaliation.

destacamento *m (mil)* detachment.

destacar *vt* to emphasize; *(mil)* to detach (a body of troops): —~se *vr* to stand out.

destajo *m* piecework.

destapar *vt* to uncover; to open: —~se *vr* to be uncovered.

destartalado/da *adj* untidy.

destello *m* signal light; sparkle.

desteñir *vt* to discolor: —~se *vr* to fade.

desternillarse *vr: —~ de risa* to roar with laughter.

desterrar *vt* to banish; to expel, drive away.

destetar *vt* to wean.

destilar *vt , vi* to distil.

destinar *vt* to destine for, intend for.

destinatario/a *m/f* addressee.

destino *m* destiny; fate, doom; destination; office.

destornillador *m* screwdriver.

destreza *f* dexterity, cleverness, cun-ning, expert-ness, skill.

destrozar *vt* to destroy, break into pieces; *(mil)* to defeat.

destruir *vt* to destroy.

desvalido/da *adj* helpless; destitute.

desvalijar *vt* to rob; to burgle.

desván *m* garret.

desvanecer *vt* to dispel: —~se *vr* to grow vapid, become insipid; to vanish; to be affected with giddiness.

desvarío *m* delirium; giddiness; inconstancy, caprice; extravagance.

desvelar *vt* to keep awake: —**se** *vr* to stay awake.
desventaja *f* disadvantage; damage.
desventura *f* misfortune; calamity.
desvergüenza *f* impudence; shamelessness.
desvestir *vt* : —**se** *vr* to undress.
desviar *vt* to divert; to dissuade; to parry (at fencing): —**se** *vr* to go off course.
detallar *vt* to detail, relate minutely.
detener *vt* to stop, detain; to arrest; to keep back; to reserve; to withhold: —**se** *vr* to stop; to stay.
detenidamente *adv* carefully.
detergente *m* detergent.
deteriorar *vt* to damage.
determinar *vt* to determine: —**se** *vr* to decide.
detestar *vt* to detest, abhor.
detonar *vi* to detonate.
detrás *adv* behind; at the back, in the back.
deuda *f* debt; fault; offence.
devanar *vt* to reel; to wrap up.
devastar *vt* to devastate.
devengar *vt* to accrue.
devoción *f* devotion, piety; strong affection; ardent love.
devolver *vt* to return; to send back; to refund: —*vi* to be sick.
devorar *vt* to devour, swallow up.
día *m* day.
diablo *m* devil.
diablura *f* prank.
diana *f (mil)* reveille; bull's-eye.
diapositiva *f* transparency, slide.
diario *m* journal, diary; daily newspaper; daily expenses *pl*: —/ ria *adj* daily.
diarrea *f* diarrhea.
dibujar *vt* to draw, design.
diccionario *m* dictionary.
dicha *f* happiness, good fortune: —**por**~ by chance.
diciembre *m* December.
dictamen *m* opinion, notion; sugges-tion; judgement.
dictar *vt* to dictate.
diecinueve *adj* , *m* nineteen.
dieciocho *adj* , *m* eighteen.
dieciséis *adj* , *m* sixteen.
diecisiete *adj* , *m* seventeen.
diente *m* tooth; fang; tusk.
diestro/tra *adj* right; dexterous, skillful, clever; sagacious, prudent; sly, cunning: —*m* skillful fencer; halter; bridle.
dieta *f* diet, regimen; diet, assembly; daily salary of judges.
diez *adj* , *m* ten.
diezmar *vt* to decimate.
difamar *vt* to defame, libel.
diferencia *f* difference.
diferenciar *vt* to differentiate, distin-guish: —**se** *vr* to differ, distinguish oneself.
diferente *adj* different, unlike.
diferido/da *adj* recorded.
difícil *adj* difficult.
dificultad *f* difficulty.
difundir *vt* to diffuse, spread; to divulge: —**se** *vr* to spread (out).
difunto/ta *adj* dead, deceased; late.
digerir *vt* to digest; to bear with patience; to adjust, arrange.
dignarse *vr* to condescend, deign.

digno/na *adj* worthy; suitable.
dilatado/da *adj* large; numerous; prolix; spacious, extensive.
dilatar *vt* to dilate, expand; to spread out; to defer, protract.
dilema *m* dilemma.
diligencia *f* diligence; affair, business; call of nature; stage coach.
dilucidar *vt* to elucidate, explain.
diluir *vt* to dilute.
diluviar *vi* to rain in torrents.
diminuto/ta *adj* minute, small.
dimitir *vt* to give up: —*vi* to resign.
dinamita *f* dynamite.
dinamo *f* dynamo.
dineral *m* large sum of money.
dinero *m* money.
dios *m* god.
diosa *f* goddess.
diplomado/da *adj* qualified.
dique *m* dam.
dirección *f* direction, guidance; administration; steering.
directo/ta *adj* direct, straight; apparent, evident; live.
director/ra *m/f* director; conductor; president; manager.
dirigir *vt* to direct; to conduct; to regulate, govern: —**se** *vr* to go towards; to address oneself to.
discernir *vt* to discern, distinguish.
discípulo *m* disciple; scholar.
disco *m* disc; record; discus; light; face (of the sun or moon); lens (of a telescope).
díscolo/la *adj* ungovernable; peevish.
discordante *adj* dissonant, discordant.
discreción *f* discretion; acuteness of mind.
discrepar *vi* to differ.
discreto/ta *adj* discreet; ingenious; witty, eloquent.
disculpar *vt* to exculpate, excuse; to acquit, absolve: —**se** *vr* to apologize; to excuse oneself.
discurrir *vi* to ramble about; to run to and fro; to discourse (on a subject): —*vt* to invent, contrive; to meditate.
discurso *m* speech; conversation; dissertation; space of time.
discutir *vt* , *vi* to discuss.
disecar *vt* to dissect; to stuff.
diseminar *vt* to scatter; to dissemi-nate, propagate.
diseñar *vt* to draw; to design.
disentir *vi* to dissent, disagree.
disfrazar *vt* to disguise, conceal; to cloak, dissemble: —**se** *vr* to disguise oneself as.
disfrutar *vt* to enjoy: —**se** *vr* to enjoy oneself.
disgustar *vt* to disgust; to offend: —**se** *vr* to be displeased; to fall out.
disidente *adj* dissident: —*m/f* dissident, dissenter.
disimular *vt* to hide; to tolerate.
disipar *vt* to dissipate, disperse, scat-ter; to lavish.
dislocarse *vr* to be dislocated or out of joint.
disminuir *vt* to diminish; to decrease.
disolver *vt* to loosen, untie; to dis-solve; to disunite; to melt, liquefy; to interrupt.
disparar *vt* to shoot, discharge, fire; to let off; to throw with violence: —*vi* to shoot, fire.
disparate *m* nonsense, absurdity, extravagance.
displicencia *f* displeasure; dislike.
disponer *vt* to arrange, prepare; to dispose.

disponible *adj* available; disposable.
dispositivo *m* device.
disputar *vt* to dispute, controvert, question: —*vi* to debate, argue.
disquete *m* floppy disk.
distancia *f* distance; interval; differ-ence.
distante *adj* distant, far off.
distinguido/da *adj* distinguished, con-spicuous.
distinguir *vt* to distinguish; to discern: —~se *vr* to distinguish oneself.
distinto/ta *adj* distinct, different; clear.
distraer *vt* to distract: —~se *vr* to be absent-minded, be inattentive.
distraído/da *adj* absent-minded, inattentive.
distribuir *vt* to distribute.
distrito *m* district; territory.
disturbio *m* riot; disturbance, interruption.
disuadir *vt* to dissuade.
diurno/na *adj* daily.
diva *f* prima donna.
divagar *vt* to digress.
divergencia *f* divergence.
diversidad *f* diversity; variety of things.
diversificar *vt* to diversify; to vary.
diversión *f* diversion; sport; amusement; *(mil)* diversion.
divertir *vt* to divert (the attention); to amuse, enter-tain; *(mil)* to draw off: —~se *vr* to amuse oneself.
dividir *vt* to divide; to disunite; to separate; to share out.
divieso *m (med)* boil.
divino/na *adj* divine, heavenly; excellent.
divorcio *m* divorce; separation, disunion.
divulgar *vt* to publish, divulge.
dobladillo *m* hem; turn-up.
doblar *vt* to double; to fold; to bend: —*vi* to turn; to toll: —~se *vr* to bend, bow, submit.
doble *adj* double; dual; deceitful: —al~ doubly: —*m* double.
doblegar *vt* to bend: —~se *vr* to yield.
doblez *m* crease; fold; turn-up: —*f* duplicity.
doce *adj* , *m* twelve.
docena *f* dozen.
dócil *adj* docile, tractable.
doctor/ra *m/f* doctor.
documento *m* document; record.

dogma *m* dogma.
dólar *m* dollar.
doler *vt* , *vi* to feel pain; to ache: —~se *vr* to feel for the sufferings of others; to complain.
dolor *m* pain; aching, ache; affliction.
domar *vt* to tame; to subdue, master.
domesticar *vt* to domesticate.
domicilio *m* domicile; home, abode.
dominar *vt* to dominate; to be fluent in: —~se *vr* to moderate one's passions.
domingo *m* Sunday; (Christian) Sab-bath.
donar *vt* to donate; to bestow.
donativo *m* contribution.
doncella *f* virgin, maiden; lady's maid.
donde *relative adv* where ¿dónde? *interrogative adv* where?: —¿de dónde? from where? dondequie-ra *adv* wherever.
dorado/da *adj* gilt *compd;* golden: —*m* gilding.
dormir *vi* to sleep: —~se *vr* to fall asleep.
dos *adj* , *m* two.
doscientos/tas *adj pl* two hundred.
dosis *f invar* dose.
dotado/da *adj* gifted.
drama *m* drama.
dramatizar *vt* to dramatize.
droga *f* drug; stratagem; artifice, deceit.
droguería *f* hardware store.
ducha *f* shower; *(med)* douche.
ducho/cha *adj* skilled, experienced.
dudar *vt* to doubt.
duelo *m* grief, affliction; mourning.
duende *m* elf, hobgoblin.
dueño/ña *m/f* owner; landlord/lady; employer.
dulce *adj* sweet; mild, gentle, meek; soft: —*m* sweet, candy.
dúo *m (mus)* duo, duet.
duodécimo/ma *adj* twelfth.
duplicar *vt* to duplicate; to repeat.
duradero/ra *adj* lasting, durable.
durante *adv* during.
durar *vi* to last, continue.
durazno *m* peach; peach tree.
dureza *f* hardness; harshness: —~ deoido hardness of hearing.
duro/ra *adj* hard; cruel; harsh, rough: —*m* five peseta coin: —*adv* hard.

E

e *conj* and (before words starting with *i* and *hi).*
ébano *m* ebony.
ebrio/ia *adj* drunk.
ebullición *f* boiling.
echar *vt* to throw; to add; to pour out; to mail: —~se *vr* to lie down.
eco *m* echo.
económico/ca *adj* economic; cheap; thrifty; finan-cial; avaricious.
ecuánime *adj* level-headed.
ecuménico/ca *adj* ecumenical; uni-versal.
edad *f* age.
edición *f* edition; publication.
edificar *vt* to build, construct; to edify.
edificio *m* building; structure.

editar *vt* to edit; to publish.
educación *f* education; upbringing; (good) man-ners *pl.*
educar *vt* to educate, instruct; to bring up.
efectivamente *adv* exactly; really; in fact.
efecto *m* effect; consequence; pur-pose: —~s *mpl* effects *pl,* goods *pl*: —en ~ in fact, really.
efectuar *vt* to effect, carry out.
eficaz *adj* efficient; effective.
eficiente *adj* efficient.
egoísta *m/f* self-seeker: —*adj* selfish.
eje *m* axle; axis.
ejecutar *vt* to execute, perform; to put to death; *(jur)* to distrain, seize.
ejecutivo/va *adj* executive: —*m/f* executive.

ejemplar *m* specimen; copy; exam-ple: —*adj* exemplary.

ejemplo *m* example: —**por** ~ for example, for instance.

ejercer *vt* to exercise; *vi* to apply one-self to the functions of an office.

ejercicio *m* exercise.

ejercitar *vt* to exercise.

ejército *m* army.

el *art, m* the.

él *pn* he, it.

elaborar *vt* to elaborate.

elástico/ca *adj* elastic.

elección *f* election; choice.

eléctrico/ca *adj* electric, electrical.

electrocutar *vt* to electrocute.

electrodomesticos *mpl* (electrical)household appliances *pl*.

electrotecnia *f* electrical engineering.

elefante *m* elephant.

elegante *adj* elegant, fine.

elegir *vt* to choose, elect.

elemento *m* element: —**s** *mpl* elements, rudiments, first principles *pl*.

elevar *vt* to raise; to elevate: —**~se** *vr* to rise; to be enraptured; to be conceited.

eliminar *vt* to eliminate, remove.

eliminatoria *f* preliminary (round).

ella *pn* she; it.

ello *pn* it.

elogiar *vt* to praise, eulogize.

eludir *vt* to elude, escape.

emanar *vi* to emanate.

embadurnar *vt* to smear, bedaub.

embalaje *m* packing, package.

embaldosar *vt* to pave with tiles.

embalse *m* reservoir.

embarazada *f* pregnant woman: —*adj* pregnant.

embarazoso/sa *adj* difficult; intricate, entangled.

embarcación *f* embarkation; any vessel or ship.

embarcar *vt* to embark: —**~se** *vr* to go on board; *(fig)* to get involved (in a matter).

embargo *m* embargo: —**sin** ~ still, however.

embarque *m* embarkation.

embaucar *vt* to deceive; to trick.

embeber *vt* to soak; to saturate: —*vi* to shrink: —**~se** *vr* to be enraptured; to be absorbed.

embeleso *m* amazement, enchantment.

embellecer *vt* to embellish, beautify.

embestir *vt* to assault, attack.

emblanquecer *vt* to whiten: —**~se** *vr* to grow white; to bleach.

embobado/da *adj* amazed; fascinated.

émbolo *m* plunger; piston.

embolsar *vt* to put money into (a purse); to pocket.

emborrachar *vt* to intoxicate, inebriate: —**~se** *vr* to get drunk.

emboscada *f* (mil) ambush.

embotar *vt* to blunt: —**~se** *vr* to go numb.

embotellamiento *m* traffic jam.

embotellar *vt* to bottle (wine).

embozar *vt* to muffle (the face); *(fig)*to cloak, conceal.

embrague *m* clutch.

embriagar *vt* to intoxicate, inebriate; to transport, enrapture.

embrión *m* embryo.

embrollo *m* muddle.

embromar *vt* to tease; to cajole, wheedle.

embrujar *vt* to bewitch.

embrutecer *vt* to brutalize: —**~se** *vr* to become depraved.

embudo *m* funnel.

embustero/ra *m/f* impostor, cheat; liar: —*adj* deceitful.

embutido *m* sausage; inlay.

emerger *vi* to emerge, appear.

emigrar *vi* to emigrate.

eminente *adj* eminent, high; excel-lent, conspicuous.

emisora *f* broadcasting station.

emitir *vt* to emit; to issue; to broad-cast.

emoción *f* emotion; feeling; excite-ment.

emocionar *vt* to excite; to move, touch.

emotivo/va *adj* emotional.

empacho *m* (med) indigestion.

empalagoso/sa *adj* cloying; tiresome.

empalmar *vt* to join.

empanada *f* (meat) pie.

empanar *vt* to cover with breadcrumbs.

empantanarse *vr* to get swamped; to get bogged down.

empapar *vt* to soak; to soak up: —**~se** *vr* to soak.

empapelar *vt* to paper.

empaquetar *vt* to pack, parcel up.

emparedado *m* sandwich.

emparrado *m* vine arbor.

empastar *vt* to paste; to fill (a tooth).

empatar *vi* to draw.

empedernido/da *adj* inveterate; heartless.

empedrado *m* paving.

empeine *m* instep.

empellón *m* push; heavy blow.

empeñar *vt* to pawn, pledge: —**~se** *vr* to pledge oneself to pay debts; to get into debt: —**~se en algo** to insist on something.

empeorar *vt* to make worse: —*vi* **~se** *vr* to grow worse.

empequeñecer *vt* to dwarf; *(fig)* to be little.

empezar *vt* to begin, start.

emplazamiento *m* summons; location.

empleado/da *m/f* official; employee.

emplear *vt* to employ; to occupy; to commission.

empobrecer *vt* to reduce to poverty: —*vi* to become poor.

empollar *vt* to incubate; to hatch; *(fam)* to swot (up).

empolvar *vt* to powder; to sprinkle powder upon.

empotrado/da *adj* built-in.

emprender *vt* to embark on; to tackle; to undertake.

empresa *f* (com) company; enterprise, undertaking.

empujar *vt* to push; to press forward.

empujón *m* push; impulse: —**a ~ones** in fits and starts.

emular *vt* to emulate, rival.

en *prep* in; for; on, upon.

enaguas *fpl* petticoat.

enamorado/da *adj* in love, lovesick.

enamorar *vt* to inspire love in: —**~se** *vr* to fall in love.

enano/na *adj* dwarfish: —*m* dwarf.

enardecer *vt* to fire with passion, inflame.

enarenar *vt* to fill with sand.

encabezar *vt* to head; to put a heading to; to lead.

encadenar *vt* to chain, link together; to connect, unite.

encajar *vt* to insert; to drive in; to encase; to intrude: —*vi* to fit (well).

encaje *m* lace.

encalar *vt* to whitewash.

encallar *vi (mar)* to run aground.

encaminar *vt* to guide, show the way: —~**se** *vr* ~ **a** to take the road to.

encandilar *vt* to dazzle.

encanecer *vi* to grow gray; to grow old.

encantado/da *adj* bewitched; delighted; pleased.

encantador/ra *adj* charming: —*m/f* magician.

encantar *vt* to enchant, charm; (*fig*) to delight.

encarcelar *vt* to imprison.

encarecimiento *m* price increase: — **con** ~ insistently.

encargado/da *adj* in charge: —*m/f* representative; person in charge.

encargar *vt* to charge; to commission.

encariñarse *vr*: —~ **con** to grow fond of.

encarnar *vt* to embody, personify.

encasillar *vt* to pigeonhole; to typecast.

encastillarse *vr* to refuse to yield.

encausar *vt* to prosecute.

encauzar *vt* to channel.

encebollado *m* casseroled beef or lamb and onions, seasoned with spice.

encenagado/da *adj* muddy, mud-stained.

encendedor *m* lighter.

encender *vt* to kindle, light, set on fire; to inflame, incite; to switch on, to turn on: —~**se** *vr* to catch fire; to flare up.

encerado *m* blackboard.

encerar *vt* to wax; to polish.

encerrar *vt* to shut up, confine; to contain: —~**se** *vr* to withdraw from the world.

enchufar *vt* to plug in; to connect.

enchufe *m* plug; outlet, socket; connection; (*fam*) contact, connection.

encía *f* gum (of the teeth).

encierro *m* confinement; enclosure; prison, penitentiary; bull-pen; penning (of bulls).

encima *adv* above; over; at the top; besides: —~ **de** *prep* above; over; at the top of; besides.

encina *f* evergreen oak.

encinta *adj* pregnant.

enclenque *adj* weak, sickly: —*m* weakling.

encoger *vt* to contract, shorten; to shrink; to discourage: —~**se** *vr* to shrink; (*fig*) to cringe.

encolar *vt* to glue.

encolerizar *vt* to provoke, irritate: —~**se** *vr* to get angry.

encomendar *vt* to recommend; to entrust: —~**se** *vr* ~ **a** to entrust oneself to; to put one's trust in.

encontrar *vt* to meet, encounter: —*vr* ~**se con** to run into: —*vi* to assem-ble, come together.

encrucijada *f* four way stop, intersec-tion; junction.

encuadernar *vt* to bind (books).

encubierto/ta *adj* hidden, concealed.

encubrir *vt* to hide, conceal.

encuesta *f* inquiry; opinion poll.

encurtir *vt* to pickle.

endeble *adj* feeble, weak.

endemoniado/da *adj* possessed with the devil; devilish.

enderezar *vt* to straighten out; to set right: —~**se** *vr* to stand upright.

endeudarse *vr* to get into debt.

endosar *vt* to endorse.

endrino *m* blackthorn, sloe.

endulzar *vt* to sweeten; to soften.

endurecer *vt* to harden, toughen: —~**se** *vr* to become cruel; to grow hard.

enebro *m* (*bot*) juniper.

enemistar *vt* to make an enemy: —~**se** *vr* to become enemies; to fall out.

energía *f* energy, power, drive; strength of will.

energúmeno/na *m/f* (*fam*) madman/ woman.

enero *m* January.

enfadar *vt* to anger, irritate; to trou-ble: —~**se** *vr* to become angry.

énfasis *m* emphasis.

enfermar *vi* to fall ill: —*vt* to make sick; to weaken.

enfermedad *f* illness.

enfermero/ra *m/f* nurse.

enfermo/ma *adj* sick, ill: —*m/f* invalid, sick person; patient.

enfocar *vt* to focus; to consider (a problem).

enfoque *m* focus.

enfrentar *vt* to confront; to put face to face: —~**se** *vr* to face each other; to meet (two teams).

enfrente *adv* over against, opposite; in front.

enfriar *vt* to cool; to refrigerate: —~**se** *vr* to cool down; (*med*) to catch a cold.

enfurecer *vt* to madden, enrage: —~**se** *vr* to get rough (of the wind and sea); to become furious or enraged.

enfurruñarse *vr* to get sulky; to frown.

engañar *vt* to deceive, cheat: —~**se** *vr* to be deceived; to make a mistake.

enganchar *vt* to hook, hang up; to hitch up; to couple, connect; to recruit into military service: —~**se** *vr(mil)* to enlist.

engañoso/sa *adj* deceitful, artful, false.

engastar *vt* to set, mount.

engatusar *vt* to coax.

engendrar *vt* to beget, engender; to produce.

englobar *vt* to include.

engordar *vt* to fatten: —*vi* to grow fat; to put on weight.

engorroso/sa *adj* troublesome, cumbersome.

engranaje *m* gear; gearing.

engrasar *vt* to grease, lubricate.

engreído/da *adj* conceited, vain.

engullir *vt* to swallow; to gobble, devour.

enharinar *vt* to cover or sprinkle with flour.

enhebrar *vt* to thread.

enhorabuena *f* congratulations *pl*: — *adv* all right; well and good.

enhoramala *interj* good riddance!

enjalbegar *vt* to whitewash.

enjambre *m* swarm of bees; crowd, multitude.

enjuagar *vt* to rinse out; to wash out.

enjuiciar *vt* to prosecute, try; to pass judgement on, judge.

enlace *m* connection, link; relation-ship.

enladrillar *vt* to pave with bricks.

enlazar *vt* to join, unite; to tie.

enlodar *vt* to cover in mud; (*fig*) to stain.

enloquecer *vt* to madden, drive crazy: —*vi* to go mad.

enmarañar *vt* to entangle; to compli-cate; to confuse: —~**se** *vr* to become entangled; to get confused.

enmendar *vt* to correct; to reform; to repair, compensate for; to amend: — **~se** *vr* to mend one's ways.

enmohecer *vt* to make moldy; to rust: —**~se** *vr* to grow moldy or musty; to rust.

enmudecer(se) *vt* to silence: —**~se** *vr* to grow dumb; to be silent.

ennegrecer *vt* to blacken; to darken; to obscure.

enojar *vt* to irritate, make angry; to annoy; to upset; to offend: —**~se** *vr* to get angry.

enorgullecerse *vr:* —**~ (de)** to be proud (of).

enorme *adj* enormous, vast, huge; horrible.

enredadera *f* climbing plant; bind-weed.

enredar *vt* to entangle, ensnare, con-found, perplex; to puzzle; to sow discord among: —**~se** *vr* to get entangled; to get complicated; to get embroiled.

enrejado *m* trelliswork.

enrevesado/da *adj* complicated.

enriquecer *vt* to enrich; to adorn: —**~se** *vr* to grow rich.

enrojecer *vt* to redden: —*vi* to blush.

enrolar *vt* to recruit: —**~se** *vr (mil)* to join up.

enrollar *vt* to roll (up).

enroscar *vt* to twist: —**~se** *vr* to curl or roll up.

ensalada *f* salad.

ensalmo *m* enchantment, spell.

ensalzar *vt* to exalt, aggrandize; to exaggerate.

ensamblar *vt* to assemble.

ensañar *vt* to irritate, enrage: —**~secon** *vr* to treat brutally.

ensanchar *vt* to widen; to extend; to enlarge: —**~se** *vr* to expand; to assume an air of importance.

ensangrentar *vt* to stain with blood.

ensartar *vt* to string (beads, etc).

ensayar *vt* to test; to rehearse.

ensayo *m* test, trial; rehearsal of a play; essay.

enseñar *vt* to teach, instruct; to show.

ensimismarse *vr* to be or become lost in thought.

ensordecer *vt* to deafen: —*vi* to grow deaf.

ensuciar *vt* to stain, soil; to defile: —**~se** *vr* to wet oneself; to dirty oneself.

ensueño *m* fantasy; daydream; illusion.

entablar *vt* to board (up); to strike up (conversation).

entablillar *vt (med)* to put in a splint.

entallar *vt* to tailor (a suit): —*vi* to fit.

ente *m* organization; entity, being; *(fam)* odd character.

entender *vt , vi* to understand, compre-hend; to re-mark, take notice (of); to reason, think: —**a mi ~** in my opinion: —**~se** *vr* to understand each other.

enterar *vt* to inform; to instruct: — **~se** *vr* to find out.

enternecer *vt* to soften; to move (to pity): —**~se** *vr* to be moved.

entero/ra *adj* entire, complete; per-fect; honest; resolute: —**por ~** entirely, completely.

enterrar *vt* to inter, bury.

entidad *f* entity; company; body; soci-ety.

entierro *m* burial; funeral.

entonar *vt* to tune, intonate; to intone; to tone: —*vi* to be in tune: —**~se** *vr* to give oneself airs.

entonces *adv* then, at that time.

entornar *vt* to half close.

entorpecer *vt* to dull; to make lethar-gic; to hinder; to delay.

entrada *f* entrance, entry; *(com)* receipts *pl;* entree; ticket (for cin-ema, theater, etc).

entrampar *vt* to trap, snare; to mess up; to burden with debts: —**~se** *vr* get into debt.

entrañable *adj* intimate; affectionate.

entrañas *fpl* entrails *pl,* intestines *pl.*

entrar *vi* to enter, go in; to commence.

entre *prep* between; among(st); in: — **~ manos** in hand.

entrecejo *m* space between the eye-brows; frown.

entredicho *m (jur)* injunction: —**estar en ~** to be banned: —**poner en ~** to cast doubt on.

entregar *vt* to deliver; to hand over: —**~se** *vr* to surrender; to devote oneself.

entremeses *mpl* hors d'oeuvres.

entrenarse *vr* to train.

entrepierna *f* crotch.

entresuelo *m* entresol; mezzanine.

entretanto *adv* meanwhile.

entretejer *vt* to interweave.

entretela *f* interfacing, stiffening, interlining.

entretener *vt* to amuse; to entertain, divert; to hold up; to maintain: —**~se** *vr* to amuse oneself; to linger.

entrever *vt* to have a glimpse of.

entrevistar *vt* to interview: —**~se** *vr* to have an interview.

entristecer *vt* to sadden.

entrometer *vt* to put (one thing)between (others): —**~se** *vr* to interfere.

entumecido/da *adj* numb, stiff.

enturbiar *vt* to make cloudy; to obscure, confound: —**~se** *vr* to become cloudy; *(fig)* to get confused.

entusiasmar *vt* to excite, fill with enthusiasm; to delight.

enumerar *vt* to enumerate.

envalentonar *vt* to give courage to: —**~se** *vr* to boast.

envanecer *vt* to make vain; to swell with pride: —**~se** *vr* to become proud.

envaramiento *m* stiffness; numbness.

envasar *vt* to pack; to bottle; to can.

envase *m* packing; bottling; canning; container; package; bottle; can.

envejecer *vt* to make old: —*vi* **~se** *vr* to grow old.

envenenar *vt* to poison; to embitter.

envés *m* wrong side (of material).

enviar *vt* to send, transmit, convey, dispatch.

enviciar *vt* to vitiate, corrupt: —**~se** *vr* to get corrupted.

envidia *f* envy; jealousy.

envidiar *vt* to envy; to grudge; to be jealous of.

envilecer *vt* to vilify, debase: —**~se** *vr* to degrade oneself.

envío *m (com)* dispatch, remittance of goods; consignment.

enviudar *vi* to become a widower or widow.

envolver *vt* to involve; to wrap up.

enyesar *vt* to plaster; *(med)* to put in a plaster cast.

enzarzarse *vr* to get involved in a dispute; to get oneself into trouble.

épico/ca *adj* epic.

epígrafe *f* epigraph, inscription; motto; headline.

episodio *m* episode, installment.

época *f* epoch; period, time.

epopeya *f* epic.

equidad *f* equity, honesty; impartial-ity, justice.

equilibrar *vt* to balance; to poise.

equilibrio *m* balance, equilibrium.

equipaje *m* luggage; equipment.
equipar *vt* to fit out, equip, furnish.
equipararse *vr:* —~ **con** to be on a level with.
equipo *m* equipment; team; shift.
equitación *f* horsemanship; riding.
equitativo/va *adj* equitable; just.
equivaler *vi* to be of equal value.
equivocación *f* mistake, error; misunderstanding.
equivocar *vt* to mistake: —~**se** *vr* to make a mistake, be wrong.
equívoco/ca *adj* equivocal, ambiguous: —*m* equivocation; quibble.
era *f* era, age; threshing floor.
erario *m* treasury, public funds *pl.*
erguir *vt* to erect, raise up straight: —~**se** *vr* to straighten up.
erial *m* fallow land.
erigir *vt* to erect, raise, build; to establish.
erizarse *vr* to bristle; to stand on end.
erizo *m* hedgehog: —~ **de mar** sea urchin.
ermita *f* hermitage.
erotismo *m* eroticism.
errar *vi* to be mistaken; to wander.
errata *f* misprint.
erre: —~ **que** ~ *adv* obstinately.
error *m* error, mistake, fault.
eructar *vi* to belch, burp.
esbelto/ta *adj* slim, slender.
esbirro *m* bailiff; henchman; killer.
esbozo *m* outline.
escabeche *m* pickle; pickled fish.
escabroso/sa *adj* rough, uneven; craggy; rude, risqué, blue.
escabullirse *vr* to escape, evade; to slip through one's fingers.
escafandra *f* diving suit; space suit.
escala *f* ladder; *(mus)* scale; stopover.
escalar *vt* to climb.
escalera *f* staircase; ladder.
escalfar *vt* to poach (eggs).
escalofriante *adj* chilling.
escalón *m* step of a stair; rung.
escama *f* (fish) scale.
escamar *vt* to scale, take off scales: —~**se** *vr* to flake off; to become suspicious.
escamotear *vt* to swipe; to make disappear.
escampar *vi* to stop raining.
escándalo *m* scandal; uproar.
escaño *m* bench with a back; seat (par-liament).
escapar *vi* to escape: —~**se** *vr* to getaway; to leak (water), etc).
escaparate *m* store window; wardrobe.
escape *m* escape, flight; leak; exhaust (of motor).
escarabajo *m* beetle.
escaramuza *f* skirmish; dispute, quarrel.
escarbar *vt* to scratch (the earth as hens do); to inquire into.
escarcha *f* white frost.
escarlata *adj* scarlet.
escarlatina *f* scarlet fever.
escarmentar *vi* to learn one's lesson: —*vt* to punish severely.
escarola *f* (bot) endive.
escarpado/da *adj* sloped; craggy.
escaso/sa *adj* small, short, little; spar-ing; scarce; scanty.
escenario *m* stage; set.

escéptico/ca *adj* sceptic, sceptical.
esclarecer *vt* to lighten; to illuminate; to illustrate; to shed light on (problem, etc).
esclavo/va *m/f* slave; captive.
esclusa *f* sluice, floodgate.
escoba *f* broom, brush.
escocer *vt* to sting; to burn: —~**se** *vr* to chafe.
escoger *vt* to choose, select.
escolar *m/f* schoolboy/girl: —*adj* scho-lastic.
escollo *m* reef, rock.
escoltar *vt* to escort.
escombros *mpl* trash; debris.
esconder *vt* to hide, conceal: —~**se** *vr* to be hidden.
escondite *m* hiding place: —**juego de** ~ hide-and-seek.
escoplo *m* chisel.
escorbuto *m* scurvy.
escote *m* low neck (of a dress).
escribir *vt* to write; to spell.
escrito *m* document; manuscript, text.
escritor/ra *m/f* writer, author.
escritorio *m* writing desk; office, study.
escrúpulo *m* doubt, scruple, scrupulousness.
escuchar *vt* to listen to, heed.
escudilla *f* bowl.
escudo *m* shield.
escudriñar *vt* to search, examine; to pry into.
escuela *f* school.
esculpir *vt* to sculpt.
escupir *vt* to spit.
escurreplatos *m invar* plate rack.
escurrir *vt* to drain; to drip: —~**se** *vr* to slip away; to slip, slide: —*vi* to wring out.
ese/esa *adj* that: —**esos/as** *pl* those.
ése/ésa *pn* that (one): —**ésos/as** *pl* those (ones).
esencial *adj* essential; principal.
esfera *f* sphere; globe.
esforzarse *vr* to exert oneself, make an effort.
esfuerzo *m* effort.
esfumarse *vr* to fade away.
esgrima *f* fencing.
esguince *m* (med) sprain.
eslabón *m* link of a chain; steel; shackle.
esmalte *m* enamel.
esmerado/da *adj* careful, neat.
esmeralda *m* emerald.
esmero *m* careful attention, great care.
eso *pn* that.
esos/as; ésos/as *pl* of **ese/a; ése/a.**
espabilar *vt* to wake up: —~**se** *vr* to wake up; *(fig)* to get a move on.
espaciar *vt* to spread out; to space (out).
espacio *m* space; (radio or TV) pro-gram.
espada *f* sword; ace of spades.
espalda *f* back, back-part: —~**s** *fpl* shoulders *pl.*
español/la *adj* Spanish: —*m/f* Spaniard: —*m* Spanish language.
espantajo *m* scarecrow; bogeyman.
espantar *vt* to frighten; to chase or drive away.
esparadrapo *m* adhesive tape.
esparcir *vt* to scatter; to divulge: —~**se** *vr* to amuse oneself.
espárrago *m* asparagus.
espátula *f* spatula.
especia *f* spice.
especial *adj* special; particular: —**en** ~ especially.
especie *f* species; kind, sort; matter.

especificar *vt* to specify.

espectáculo *m* spectacle; show.

espectador/ra *m/f* spectator.

especular *vt* to speculate.

espejismo *m* mirage.

espejo *m* mirror.

espeluznante *adj* horrifying.

esperanza *f* hope.

esperar *vt* to hope; to expect, wait for.

esperma *f* sperm.

espeso/sa *adj* thick, dense.

espesor *m* thickness.

espía *m/f* spy.

espiga *f* ear (of corn).

espigón *m* ear of corn; sting; *(mar)* breakwater.

espina *f* thorn; fishbone.

espinaca *f (bot)* spinach.

espinilla *f* shinbone.

espino *m* hawthorn.

espiral *adj* , *f* spiral.

espirar *vt* to exhale.

espíritu *m* spirit, soul; mind; intelligence: **—el E~ Santo** the Holy Ghost: **—~s** *pl* demons, hobgoblins *pl*.

espléndido/da *adj* splendid.

espliego *m (bot)* lavender.

espolón *m* spur (of a cock); spur (of a mountain range); sea wall; jetty; *(mar)* buttress.

espolvorear *vt* to sprinkle.

esponja *f* sponge.

espontáneo/nea *adj* spontaneous.

esposa *f* wife.

esposas *fpl* handcuffs *pl*.

esposo *m* husband.

espuma *f* froth, foam.

espumar *vt* to skim, take the scum off.

espumoso/sa *adj* frothy, foamy; sparkling (wine).

esputo *m* spit, saliva.

esqueje *m* cutting (of plant).

esquela *f* note, slip of paper.

esqueleto *m* skeleton.

esquema *m* scheme; diagram; plan.

esquí *m* ski; skiing.

esquina *f* corner, angle.

esquirol *m* blackleg.

esquivar *vt* to shun, avoid, evade.

esta *adj f* this: **—~s** *pl* these.

ésta *pn f* this: **—~s** *pl* these.

estable *adj* stable.

establecer *vt* to establish.

establo *m* stable.

estaca *f* stake; stick; post.

estación *f* season (of the year); station; railroad station, terminus: **—~ deautobuses** bus station: **—~ de servicio** service station.

estacionar *vt* to park; *(mil)* to station.

estadio *m* phase; stadium.

estado *m* state, condition.

Estados Unidos *mpl* United States (of America).

estafar *vt* to deceive, defraud.

estallar *vi* to crack; to burst; to break out.

estambre *m* stamen.

estamento *m* estate; body; layer; class.

estampa *f* print; engraving; appear-ance.

estampar *vt* to print.

estancar *vt* to check (a current); to monopolize; to prohibit, suspend: **— ~se** *vr* to stagnate.

estancia *f* stay; bedroom; ranch; *(poet)* stanza.

estanco *m* tobacconist's (store): **—~/ ca** *adj* watertight.

estándar *adj* , *m* standard.

estaño *m* tin.

estanque *m* pond, pool; reservoir.

estantería *f* shelves *pl*, shelving.

estar *vi* to be; to be (in a place).

estatua *f* statue.

este[1] *m* east; este[2]/ta *adj* this: **—estos/tas** *pl* these.

estera *f* mat.

estéreo *adj invar*, *m* stereo.

estereotipo *m* stereotype.

estéril *adj* sterile, infertile.

esterlina *adj* : **—libra ~** pound sterling.

estético/ca *adj* esthetic: **—f** esthetics.

estiércol *m* dung; manure.

estilo *m* style; fashion; stroke (swimming).

estima *f* esteem.

estimar *vt* to estimate, value; to esteem; to judge; to think.

estimular *vt* to stimulate, excite; to goad.

estío *m* summer.

estipular *vt* to stipulate.

estirar *vt* to stretch out.

esto *pn* this.

estofado *m* stew.

estómago *m* stomach.

estopa *f* tow.

estorbar *vt* to hinder; *(fig)* to bother: **—vi** to be in the way.

estornudar *vi* to sneeze.

estos/as, éstos/tas *pl* of este/ta, éste/ta.

estrado *m* drawing room; stage, platform.

estrafalario/ria *adj* slovenly; eccentric.

estrago *m* ruin, destruction; havoc.

estrangular *vt* to strangle; *(med)* to strangulate.

estraperlo *m* black market.

estratagema *f* stratagem, trick.

estrato *m* stratum, layer.

estraza *f* rag: **—papel de ~** brown paper.

estrechar *vt* to tighten; to contract, constrain; to compress: **—~se** *vr* to grow narrow; to embrace: **—~ lamano** to shake hands.

estrecho *m* straits *pl*: **—~/ cha** *adj* narrow, close; tight; intimate; rigid, austere; short (of money).

estrella *f* star.

estrellar *vt* to dash to pieces: **—~se** *vr* to smash; to crash; to fail.

estremecer *vt* to shake, make tremble: **—~se** *vr* to shake, tremble.

estrenar *vt* to wear for the first time; to move into (a house); to show (a movie) for the first time: **—~se** *vr* to make one's debut.

estreñido/da *adj* constipated.

estrépito *m* noise, racket; fuss.

estribillo *m* chorus.

estribo *m* buttress; stirrup; running board: **—perder los ~s** to fly off the handle *(fam)*.

estribor *m (mar)* starboard.

estricto/ta *adj* strict; severe.

estrofa *f (poet)* verse, strophe.

estropajo *m* scourer.

estropear *vt* to spoil; to damage: **— ~se** *vr* to get damaged.

estructura *f* structure.

estruendo *m* clamor, noise; confusion, uproar; pomp, ostentation.
estuche *m* case (for scissors, etc); sheath.
estudiar *vt* to study.
estufa *f* heater, fire.
estupefaciente *m* narcotic.
estupefacto *adj* speechless; thunder-struck.
estupendo/da *adj* terrific, marvel-ous.
estúpido *adj* stupid.
etapa *f* stage; stopping place; (*fig*) phase.
etcétera *adv* etcetera, and so on.
eterno/na *adj* eternal.
ético/ca *adj* ethical, moral.
etiqueta *f* etiquette; label.
evacuar *vt* to evacuate, empty.
evadir *vt* to evade, escape.
evaluar *vt* to evaluate.
evaporar *vt* to evaporate: —~se *vr* to vanish.
eventual *adj* possible; temporary, casual (worker).
evidente *adj* evident, clear.
evitar *vt* to avoid.
evolucionar *vi* to evolve.
ex *adj* ex.
ex profeso *adv* on purpose.
exacerbar *vt* to exacerbate; to irritate.
exacto/ta *adj* exact; punctual; accurate.
exagerar *vt* to exaggerate.
exaltar *vt* to exalt, elevate; to praise, extol: —~se *vr* to get excited.
examen *m* exam, examination, test, inquiry.
examinar *vt* to examine.
exasperar *vt* to exasperate, irritate.
excavar *vt* to excavate, dig out.
exceder *vt* to exceed, surpass, excel, outdo.
excelente *adj* excellent.
excéntrico/ca *adj* eccentric.
excepto *adv* excepting, except (for).
exceso *m* excess.
excitar *vt* to excite: —~se *vr* to get excited.
exclamar *vt* to exclaim, cry out.
excluir *vt* to exclude.
excremento *m* excrement.
excursión *f* excursion, trip.
excusa *f* excuse, apology.
excusado *m* bathroom.
excusar *vt* to excuse; to avoid: —~ de to exempt from: —~se *vr* to apologize.
exento/ta *adj* exempt, free.
exhalar *vt* to exhale; to give off; to heave (a sigh).
exhausto/ta *adj* exhausted.
exhibir *vt* to exhibit.
exhortar *vt* to exhort.
exhumar *vt* to disinter, exhume.
exigir *vt* to demand, require.
exiliado/da *adj* exiled: —*m/f* exile.
existir *vi* to exist, be.
éxito *m* outcome; success; (*mus, etc*)hit: —**tener ~**

to be successful.
exorbitante *adj* exhorbitant, excessive.
exótico/ca *adj* exotic.
expandir *vt* to expand.
expatriarse *vr* to emigrate; to go into exile.
expectativa *f* expectation; prospect.
expedición *f* expedition.
expediente *m* expedient; means; (*jur*)proceedings *pl*; dossier, file.
expedir *vt* to send, forward, dispatch.
expensas *fpl*: —**a ~ de** at the expense of.
experimentar *vt* to experience: —*vi*~ **con** to experiment with.
experto/ta *adj* expert; experienced.
expiar *vt* to atone for; to purify.
expirar *vi* to expire.
explayarse *vr* to speak at length.
explicar *vt* to explain, expound: —~se *vr* to explain oneself.
explorar *vt* to explore.
explotar *vt* to exploit; to run: —*vi* to explode.
exponer *vt* to expose; to explain.
exportar *vt* to export.
exposición *f* exposure; exhibition; explanation; account.
expresar *vt* to express.
expreso/sa *adj* express, clear, specific; fast (train).
exprimir *vt* to squeeze out.
expropiar *vt* to expropriate.
expulsar *vt* to expel, drive out.
éxtasis *m* ecstasy, enthusiasm.
extender *vt* to extend, stretch out: —~se *vr* to extend; to spread.
extenso/sa *adj* extensive.
extenuar *vt* to exhaust, debilitate.
exterior *adj* exterior, external: —*m* exterior, outward appearance.
exterminar *vt* to exterminate.
externo/na *adj* external, outer: —*m/f* day pupil.
extinguir *vt* to wipe out; to extinguish.
extintor *m* (fire) extinguisher.
extra *adj invar* extra; good quality: — *m/f* extra: —*m* bonus.
extraer *vt* to extract.
extrañar *vt* to find strange; to miss: —~se *vr* to be surprised; to grow apart.
extranjero/ra *m/f* stranger; foreigner: —*adj* foreign, alien.
extraño/ña *adj* foreign; rare; singular, strange, odd.
extraviar *vt* to mislead: —~se *vr* to lose one's way.
extremidad *f* extremity; brim; tip: —~**es** *fpl* extremities *pl*.
extremo/ma *adj* extreme, last: —*m* extreme, highest degree: —**en ~/por ~** extremely.
extrovertido/da *adj* , *m/f* extrovert.
exuberancia *f* exuberance; luxuriance.

F

fábrica *f* factory.
fabricar *vt* to build, construct; to manufacture; (*fig*) to fabricate.
fábula *f* fable; fiction; rumor, common

fabuloso/sa *adj* fabulous, fictitious.
facción *f* (political) faction; feature.
fachada *f* facade, face, front.
fácil *adj* facile, easy.

facilitar *vt* to facilitate.
fácilmente *adv* easily.
factor *m (mat)* factor; *(com)* factor, agent.
factura *f* invoice.
facultativo/va *adj* optional: —*m/f* doc-tor, practitioner.
faena *f* task, job; hard work.
faisán *m* pheasant.
fajo *m* bundle; wad.
falaz *adj* deceitful, fraudulent; falla-cious.
falda *f* skirt; lap; flap; train; slope, hill-side.
fallar *vt (jur)* to pronounce sentence on, judge: —*vi* to fail.
fallecer *vi* to die.
falso/sa *adj* false, untrue; deceitful; fake.
falta *f* fault, defect; want; flaw, mis-take; *(dep)* foul.
faltar *vi* to be wanting; to fail; not to fulfil one's promise; to need; to be missing.
fama *f* fame; reputation, name.
familia *f* family.
familiar *adj* familiar; homely, domes-tic: —*m/f* relative, relation.
famoso/sa *adj* famous.
fanfarrón *m* bully, braggart.
fango *m* mire, mud.
fantasía *f* fancy; fantasy; caprice; pre-sumption.
fantasma *f* phantom, ghost.
fardo *m* bale, parcel.
farmacia *f* drugstore.
faro *m (mar)* lighthouse; *(auto)* head-lamp; flood-light.
farola *f* street light.
fascículo *m* part, installment.
fascinar *vt* to fascinate; to enchant.
fase *f* phase.
fastidiar *vt* to annoy; to offend; to spoil.
fatal *adj* fatal; mortal; awful.
fatiga *f* weariness, fatigue.
fatuo/tua *adj* fatuous, stupid, foolish; conceited.
fauces *fpl* jaws *pl,* gullet.
favor *m* favor; protection; good turn.
favorecer *vt* to favor, protect.
fe *f* faith, belief.
febrero *m* February.
fecha *f* date (of a letter etc).
fecundar *vt* to fertilize.
felicitar *vt* to congratulate.
feliz *adj* happy, fortunate.
felpa *f* plush; toweling.
felpudo *m* doormat.
femenino/na *adj* feminine; female.
feo/ea *adj* ugly; bad, nasty.
feria *f* fair, rest day; village market.
fermentar *vi* to ferment.
feroz *adj* ferocious, savage; cruel.
ferretería *f* hardware store.
ferrocarril *m* railway.
fértil *adj* fertile, fruitful.
festejo *m* courtship; feast.
festivo/va *adj* festive, merry; witty: —**dia** ~ holiday.
feto *m* fetus.
fiable *adj* trustworthy; reliable.
fiambre *m* cold meat.
fianza *f (jur)* surety.
fiar *vt* to entrust, confide; to bail; to sell on credit: —**~se** *vr* to trust.

fibra *f* fibre.
ficha *f* token, counter (at games); (index) card.
fidelidad *f* fidelity; loyalty.
fideos *mpl* noodles *pl.*
fiebre *f* fever.
fiel *adj* faithful, loyal: —*mpl* **los ~es** the faithful *pl.*
fieltro *m* felt.
fiera *f* wild beast.
fiesta *f* party; festivity: —**~s** *fpl* vaca-tions *pl.*
figura *f* figure, shape.
figurar *vt* to figure: —**~se** *vr* to fancy, imagine.
fijar *vt* to fix, fasten: —**~se** *vr* to become fixed: —**~se en** to notice.
fijo/ja *adj* fixed, firm; settled, permanent.
fila *f* row, line; *(mil)* rank: —**en ~** in a line, in a row.
filete *m* fillet; fillet steak.
filmar *vt* to film.
filo *m* edge, blade.
filosofía *f* philosophy.
filtro *m* filter.
fin *m* end; termination, conclusion; aim, purpose: —**al ~** at last: —**en ~** *(fig)* well then: —**por ~** finally, lastly.
finalmente *adv* finally, at last.
financiar *vt* to finance.
finca *f* land, property, real estate; country house; farm.
fingir *vt* to feign, fake: —**~se** *vr* to pretend to be: —*vi* to pretend.
fino/na *adj* fine, pure; slender; polite; acute; dry (of sherry).
firma *f* signature; *(com)* company.
firmamento *m* firmament, sky, heaven.
firme *adj* firm, stable, strong, secure; constant; reso-lute: —*m* road surface.
fiscal *adj* fiscal: —*m/f* district attorney.
fisco *m* treasury, exchequer.
fisgar *vt* to pry into.
física *f* physics.
flaco/ca *adj* lean, skinny; feeble.
flan *m* crème caramel.
flauta *f (mus)* flute.
flecha *f* arrow.
flequillo *m* fringe (of hair).
flete *m (mar)* freight; charter.
flexible *adj* flexible; compliant; docile.
flojo/ja *adj* loose; flexible; slack; lazy.
flor *f* flower.
florecer *vi* to blossom.
florero *m* vase.
flotador *m* float; rubber ring.
flotar *vi* to float.
fluctuar *vi* to fluctuate; to waver.
fluir *vi* to flow.
foco *m* focus; center; source; floodlight; (light)bulb.
fogón *m* stove; hearth.
fogoso/sa *adj* fiery; ardent, fervent; impetuous, boisterous.
folleto *m* pamphlet; folder, brochure.
follón *m (fam)* mess; fuss.
fomentar *vt* to encourage; to promote.
fondo *m* bottom; back; background; space: —**~s** *mpl* stock, funds *pl,* capital: —**a ~** perfectly, com-pletely.
fontanero/ra *m/f* plumber.
forjar *vt* to forge; to frame; to invent.
forma *f* form, shape; pattern; *(med)* fitness; *(dep)*

form; means, method: **—de ~ que** in such a manner that.
formación *f* formation; form, figure; education; training.
formar *vt* to form, shape.
fornido/da *adj* well-built.
forro *m* lining; book jacket.
fortuna *f* fortune; wealth.
forzar *vt* to force.
forzoso/sa *adj* indispensable, necessary.
mpl **fosa** *f* grave; pit.
fósforo *m* phosphorus: **—s matches** *pl.*
fotocopia *f* photocopy.
fotografía *f* photography; photo-graph.
fracasar *vi* to fail.
frágil *adj* fragile, frail.
fraguar *vt* to forge; to contrive: **—vi** to solidify, harden.
fraile *m* friar, monk.
frambuesa *f* raspberry.
francés/sa *adj* French: **—m** French language: **—m/f** Frenchman/woman.
frasco *m* flask.
frase *f* phrase.
fraternal *adj* fraternal, brotherly.
fraude *m* fraud, deceit; cheat.
frazada *f* blanket.
frecuencia *f* frequency.
fregar *vt* to scrub; to wash up.
freír *vt* to fry.
frenar *vt* to brake; *(fig)* to check.
frenesí *m* frenzy.
freno *m* bit; brake; *(fig)* check.
frente *f* front; face: **—~ a ~** face to face: **—en ~** opposite; *(mil)* front: **— m** forehead.
fresa *f* strawberry.
fresco/ca *adj* fresh; cool; new; ruddy; **—m** fresh air: **—m/f** *(fam)* shameless or impudent person.
fresno *m* ash tree.
frigorífico *m* fridge.
frijol *m* kidney bean.
frío/fría *adj* cold; indifferent: **—m** cold; indifference.

friso *m* frieze; wainscot.
frito/ta *adj* fried.
frívolo/la *adj* frivolous.
frondoso/sa *adj* leafy.
frontera *f* frontier.
frontón *m* *(dep)* pelota court; pelota.
frotar *vi* to rub.
fructificar *vi* to bear fruit; to come to fruition.
frugal *adj* frugal, sparing.
fruncir *vt* to pleat; to knit; to contract: **—~ las cejas** to knit the eyebrows.
frustrar *vt* to frustrate.
fruta *f* fruit: **—~ del tiempo** seasonal fruit.
frutal *m* fruit tree.
frutilla *f* strawberry.
fuego *m* fire.
fuente *f* fountain; spring; source; large dish.
fuera *adv* out(side); away: **—~ de** *prep* outside: **—¡~!** out of the way!
fuerte *m* *(mil)* fortification, fort; forte: **—adj** vigorous, tough; strong; loud; heavy: **—adv** strongly; hard.
fuerza *f* force, strength; *(elec)* power; violence: **—a ~ de** by dint of: **—s** *mpl* troops *pl.*
fugarse *vr* to escape, flee.
fugaz *adj* fleeting.
fullero *m* cardsharper, cheat.
fumar *vt* , *vi* to smoke.
función *f* function; duties *pl;* show, performance.
funcionar *vi* to function; to work (of a machine).
funcionario/ria *m/f* official; civil servant.
funda *f* case, sheath: **—~ de almohada** pillowcase.
fundar *vt* to found; to establish; to ground.
fundir *vt* to fuse; to melt; to smelt; *(com)* to merge; to bankrupt; *(elec)* to fuse, blow.
fúnebre *adj* mournful, sad; funereal.
furgoneta *f* pick-up (truck).
furioso/sa *adj* furious.
furtivo/va *adj* furtive.
fusible *m* fuse.
fusión *f* fusion; *(com)* merger.
fútbol *m* soccer.
futuro/ra *adj* , *m* future.

G

gabardina *f* gabardine; raincoat.
gabinete *m* *(pol)* cabinet, study; office (of solicitors, etc).
gafas *fpl* glasses *pl,* spectacles *pl.*
gafe *m* jinx.
gai *(fam) adj invar, m* gay *(sl),* homo-sexual.
gajo *m* segment (of orange).
galápago *m* tortoise.
galardón *m* reward, prize.
galbana *f* laziness, idleness.
galera *f* *(mar)* galley; wagon; galley (of type).
galería *f* gallery.
galgo *m* greyhound.
gallardo/da *adj* graceful, elegant; brave, daring.
galleta *f* biscuit.
gallina *f* hen: **—m/f** *(fig)* coward: **—~ ciega** blindman's buff.
gallo *m* cock.

gama *f* *(mus)* scale; *(fig)* range, gamut; doe.
gamba *f* shrimp.
gamberro/rra *m/f* hooligan.
gamuza *f* chamois.
gana *f* desire, wish; appetite; will, longing: **—de buena ~** with plea-sure, voluntarily: **—de mala ~** unwillingly, with reluctance.
ganado *m* livestock, cattle *pl:* **—~mayor** horses and mules *pl:* **—~menor** sheep, goats and hogs *pl.*
ganar *vt* to gain; to win; to earn: **—vi** to win.
gancho *m* hook; crook.
gandul *adj* , *m/f* layabout.
ganga *f* bargain.
ganso/sa *m/f* gander; goose; *(fam)* idiot.
garabatear *vi* , *vt* to scrawl, scribble.
garaje *m* garage.
garantía *f* warranty, guarantee.
garbanzo *m* chickpea, garbanzo.

garbo *m* gracefulness, elegance; stylishness; generosity.

garganta *f* throat, gullet; instep; neck (of a bottle); narrow pass between mountains or rivers.

gárgara *f* gargling, gargle.

garra *f* claw; talon; paw.

garrafa *f* carafe; (gas) cylinder.

garrafal *adj* great, vast, huge.

garrotillo *m (med)* croup.

garrucha *f* pulley.

garza *f* heron.

gasa *f* gauze.

gaseoso/sa *adj* fizzy: —*f* lemonade.

gasoil *m* diesel (oil).

gasolina *f* gas.

gasolinera *f* gas station.

gastar *vt* to spend; to expend; to waste; to wear away; to use up: —~se *vr* to wear out; to waste.

gata *f* she-cat: —**a ~s** on all fours.

gato *m* cat; jack.

gavilán *m* sparrow hawk.

gavilla *f* sheaf of corn.

gaviota *f* seagull.

gazpacho *m* Spanish cold tomato soup.

gelatina *f* jelly; gelatine.

gemelo/la *m/f* twin.

gemir *vi* to groan, moan.

generación *f* generation; progeny, race.

general *m* general: —*adj* general: —**en ~** generally, in general.

género *m* genus; kind, type; gender; cloth, material: —~**s** *mpl* goods, commodities *pl.*

generoso/sa *adj* noble, generous.

genio *m* nature, character; genius.

genital *adj* genital: —*mpl* ~**es** genitals *pl.*

gente *f* people; nation; family.

gentileza *f* grace; charm; politeness.

genuino/na *adj* genuine; pure.

geografía *f* geography.

geología *f* geology.

geometría *f* geometry.

geranio *m (bot)* geranium.

gerente *m/f* manager; director.

germinar *vi* to germinate, bud.

gestión *f* management; negotiation.

gesto *m* face; grimace; gesture.

gigante *m* giant: —*adj* gigantic.

gilipollas *adj invar (fam)* stupid: —*m/f invar* wimp *(sl).*

gimnasia *f* gymnastics.

ginebra *f* gin.

ginecólogo/ga *m/f* gynecologist.

gira *f* trip, tour.

girar *vt* to turn around; to swivel: —*vi* to go round, revolve.

girasol *m* sunflower.

gitano/na *m/f* Gipsy.

glacial *adj* icy.

glándula *f* gland.

globo *m* globe; sphere; orb; balloon: —~ **aerostatico** air balloon.

glorieta *f* bower, arbor; traffic circle.

glosar *vt* to gloss; to comment on.

glotón/ona *m/f* glutton.

gobierno *m* government.

goce *m* enjoyment.

gol *m* goal.

golondrina *f* swallow.

golosina *f* dainty, titbit; sweet.

golpe *m* blow, stroke, hit; knock; clash; coup: —**de ~** suddenly.

goma *f* gum; rubber; elastic.

gordo/da *adj* fat, plump, big-bellied; first, main; *(fam)* enormous.

gorjear *vi* to twitter, chirp.

gorrión *m* sparrow.

gorro *m* cap; bonnet.

gorrón/ona *m/f* scrounger.

gota *f* drop; *(med)* gout.

gotera *f* leak.

gozar *vt* to enjoy, have, possess: —~**se** *vr* to enjoy oneself, rejoice.

gozne *m* hinge.

gozo *m* joy, pleasure.

grabado *m* engraving.

grabar *vt* to engrave; to record.

gracia *f* grace, gracefulness; wit: —¡**(muchas) ~s!** thanks (very much): —**tener ~** to be funny.

gracioso/sa *adj* graceful; beautiful; funny; pleasing: —*m* comic character.

grada *f* step of a staircase; tier, row: —~**s** *fpl* seats *pl* of stadium or theater.

grado *m* step; degree: —**de buen ~** willingly.

gráfico/ca *adj* graphic: —*m* diagram: —*f* graph.

grajo *m* rook.

gramo *m* gram(me).

gran *adj* = **grande.**

granada *f* pomegranate.

granate *m* garnet (precious stone).

grande *adj* great; big; tall; grand: —*m/f* adult.

grandioso/sa *adj* grand, magnificent.

granel *adv* : —**a ~** in bulk.

granizado *m* iced drink.

granizo *m* hail.

granja *f* farm.

grano *m* grain.

granuja *m/f* rogue; urchin.

grapa *f* staple; clamp.

grasa *f* suet, fat; grease.

gratis *adj* free.

grato/ta *adj* pleasant, agreeable.

gravamen *m* charge, obligation; nui-sance; tax.

grave *adj* weighty, heavy; grave, important; serious.

gravilla *f* gravel.

gravoso/sa *adj* onerous, burden-some; costly.

graznar *vi* to croak; to cackle; to quack.

gremio *m* union, guild; society; com-pany, corporation.

greña *f* tangle; shock of hair.

gresca *f* clatter; outcry; confusion; wrangle, quarrel.

grieta *f* crevice, crack, chink.

grifo *m* faucet, tap; gas station.

grillo *m* cricket; bud, shoot.

gripe *f* flu, influenza.

gris *adj* gray.

gritar *vi* to cry out, shout, yell.

grosella *f* redcurrant: —~ **negra** blackcurrant.

grosero/ra *adj* coarse; rude, bad-mannered.

grúa *f* crane (machine); derrick.

grueso/sa *adj* thick; bulky; large; coarse: —*m* bulk.

grulla *f* crane (bird).

gruñir *vi* to grunt; to grumble; to creak (of hinges, etc).

grupo *m* group.

gruta *f* grotto.
guadaña *f* scythe.
guante *m* glove.
guapo/pa *adj* good-looking; handsome; smart.
guardabosque *m* gamekeeper; ranger.
guardacostas *m invar* coastguard vessel.
guardaespaldas *m/f invar* bodyguard.
guardar *vt* to keep, preserve; to save (money); to guard: —~se *vr* to be on one's guard: —~se de to avoid, abstain from.
guardarropa *f* wardrobe; cloakroom.
guardia *f* guard; (mar) watch; care, custody: —m/f guard; police officer: —m (mil) guardsman.
guarecer *vt* to protect; to shelter: —~se *vr* to take refuge.
guarnecer *vt* to provide, equip; to reinforce; to garnish, set (in gold, etc); to adorn.

guasa *f* joke.
gubernativo/va *adj* governmental.
guía *m/f* guide: —f guidebook.
guiar *vt* to guide; (auto) to steer.
guijarro *m* pebble.
guiñar *vt* to wink.
guinda *f* cherry.
guindilla *f* chilli pepper.
guión *m* hyphen; script (of movie).
guisante *m (bot)* pea.
guisar *vt* to cook.
guitarra *f* guitar.
gula *f* gluttony.
gusano *m* maggot, worm.
gustar *vt* to taste; to sample: —vi to please, be pleasing: **—me gusta...**I like...

H

haba *f* bean.
haber *vt* to get, lay hands on; to occur: — v imp **hay** there is, there are: —v aux to have: —~se *vr* **habérselas con uno** to have it out with somebody: —m income, salary; assets pl; (com) credit.
hábil *adj* able, clever, skillful, dexter-ous, apt.
habitación *f* habitation, abode, rooming house, dwelling, residence; room.
habitar *vt* to inhabit, live in.
hábito *m* dress; habit, custom.
habitual *adj* habitual, customary.
hablar *vt , vi* to speak; to talk.
hacendoso/sa *adj* industrious.
hacer *vt* to make; to do; to put into practice; to perform; to effect; to prepare; to imagine; to force; (mat)to amount to, make: —vi to act, behave: —~se *vr* to become.
hacha *f* torch; ax, hatchet.
hacia *adv* toward(s); about: —~ **arriba/abajo** up(wards)/ down(wards).
hada *f* fairy.
halagar *vt* to cajole, flatter.
halcón *m* falcon.
hallar *vt* to find; to meet with; to discover: —~se *vr* to find oneself; to be.
hambre *f* hunger; famine; longing.
harina *f* flour.
harto/ta *adj* full; fed up: —adv enough.
hasta *prep* up to; down to; until, as far as: —adv even.
haya *f* beech tree.
hazaña *f* exploit, achievement.
hebilla *f* buckle.
hebra *f* thread; vein of minerals or metals; grain of wood.
hebreo/ea *m/f , adj* Hebrew; Israeli: — m Hebrew language.
hechizar *vt* to bewitch, enchant; to charm.
hecho/cha *adj* made; done; mature; ready-to-wear; cooked: —m action; act; fact; matter; event.
hectárea *f* hectare.
helado/da *adj* frozen; glacial, icy; astonished; astounded: —m ice cream.
helar *vt* to freeze; to congeal; to astonish, amaze:

—~se *vr* to be frozen; to turn into ice; to congeal: —vi to freeze; to congeal.
helecho *m* fern.
hélice *f* helix; propeller.
hembra *f* female.
heno *m* hay.
heredar *vt* to inherit.
hereje *m/f* heretic.
herir *vt* to wound, hurt; to beat, strike; to affect, touch, move; to offend.
hermana *f* sister.
hermano *m* brother: —~/na adj matched; resembling.
hermético/ca *adj* hermetic, airtight.
hermoso/sa *adj* beautiful, handsome, lovely; large, robust.
héroe *m* hero.
herradura *f* horseshoe.
herrero *m* smith.
hervir *vt* to boil; to cook: —vi to boil; to bubble; to seethe.
hiedra *f* ivy.
hiel *f* gall, bile.
hielo *m* frost; ice.
hierba *f* grass; herb.
hierro *m* iron.
hígado *m* liver; (fig) courage, pluck.
higiene *f* hygiene.
higo *m* fig.
hijo/ja *m/f* son/daughter; child; off-spring.
hilera *f* row, line, file.
hilo *m* thread; wire.
hincar *vt* to thrust in, drive in.
hinchar *vt* to swell; to inflate; (fig) to exaggerate: —~se *vr* to swell; to become vain.
hinojo *m (bot)* fennel.
hipo *m* hiccups pl.
hipócrita *adj* hypocritical: —m/f hypo-crite.
hipódromo *m* racetrack.
hipoteca *f* mortgage.
historia *f* history; tale, story.
historieta *f* short story; short novel; comic strip.
hocico *m* snout: —**meter el ~ entodo** to meddle in everything.

hogar *m* hearth, fireplace; (*fig*) house, home; family life.
hogaza *f* large loaf of bread.
hoguera *f* bonfire; blaze.
hoja *f* leaf; petal; sheet of paper; blade.
hojalata *f* tin (plate).
hojaldre *f* puff pastry.
hojear *vt* to turn the pages of.
hola *excl* hello!
holgado/da *adj* loose, wide, baggy; at leisure; idle, unoccupied; well-off.
hollín *m* soot.
hombre *m* man; human being.
hombro *m* shoulder.
homenaje *m* homage.
homicidio *m* murder.
hondo/da *adj* deep, profound.
honesto/ta *adj* honest; modest.
hongo *m* mushroom; fungus.
honor *m* honor.
honorario/ria *adj* honorary: —~s *mpl* fees *pl*.
honra *f* honor, reverence; self-esteem; reputation; integrity: —~sfunebres *pl* funeral honors *pl*.
hora *f* hour; time.
horario/ria *adj* hourly, hour *compd*: — *m* schedule.
horchata *f* tiger-nut milk.
horma *f* mold, form.
hormiga *f* ant.
hormigón *m* concrete.
horno *m* oven; furnace.
horquilla *f* pitchfork; hairpin.
hórreo *m* granary.
horrible *adj* horrid, horrible.
horror *m* horror, fright; atrocity.
hortaliza *f* vegetable.
hospedar *vt* to put up, lodge; to entertain.

hospicio *m* orphanage; hospice.
hospital *m* hospital.
hostal *m* small hotel.
hostelería *f* hotel business or trade.
hostia *f* host; wafer; (*fam*) whack *(sl)*, punch.
hostil *adj* hostile; adverse.
hotel *m* hotel.
hoy *adv* today; now, nowadays: **—de ~ en adelante** from now on, hence-forward.
hoyo *m* hole, pit; excavation.
hoz *f* sickle; gorge.
hucha *f* money-box.
hueco/ca *adj* hollow, concave; empty; vain, ostentatious: —*m* interval; gap, hole; vacancy.
huelga *f* strike.
huella *f* track, footstep.
huérfano/na *adj* , *m/f* orphan.
huerta *f* market garden; irrigated region.
hueso *m* bone; stone, core.
huésped/da *m/f* guest, lodger, roomer; inn-keeper.
huevo *m* egg.
huir *vi* to flee, escape.
humano/na *adj* human; humane, kind.
húmedo/da *adj* humid; wet; damp.
humilde *adj* humble.
humillar *vt* to humble; to subdue: —~**se** *vr* to humble oneself.
humo *m* smoke; fumes *pl*.
humor *m* mood, temper; humor.
hundir *vt* to submerge; to sink; to ruin: —~**se** *vr* to sink, go to the bottom; to collapse; to be ruined.
huraño/ña *adj* shy; unsociable.
hurtadillas *adv* : **—a ~** by stealth.
hurtar *vt* to steal, rob.
husmear *vt* to scent; to pry into.

I

ictericia *f* jaundice.
ida *f* departure, going: **—(viaje de) ~** outward journey: **—~ y vuelta** round trip: **—~s y venidas** comings and goings *pl*.
idea *f* idea; scheme.
ídem *pn* ditto.
idéntico/ca *adj* identical.
idioma *m* language.
idiota *m/f* idiot.
idóneo/nea *adj* suitable, fit.
iglesia *f* church.
ignorar *vt* to be ignorant of, not to know.
igual *adj* equal; similar; the same: **—al ~** equally.
ilegal *adj* illegal, unlawful.
ileso/sa *adj* unhurt.
ilimitado/da *adj* unlimited.
iluminar *vt* to illumine, illuminate, enlighten.
ilusión *f* illusion; hope: **—hacerse~ones** to build up one's hopes.
ilustre *adj* illustrious, famous.
imagen *f* image.
imaginar *vt* to imagine; to think up: — *vi* ~**se** *vr* to imagine.
imán *m* magnet.
imitar *vt* to imitate, copy; to counterfeit.

impaciente *adj* impatient.
impar *adj* odd.
imparcial *adj* impartial.
impedir *vt* to impede, hinder; to prevent.
impeler *vt* to drive, propel; to impel; to incite, stimulate.
impenetrable *adj* impenetrable, impervious; incomprehensible.
impenitente *adj* impenitent.
imperdible *m* safety pin.
imperdonable *adj* unforgivable.
imperfecto/ta *adj* imperfect.
impermeable *adj* waterproof: —*m* raincoat.
imperturbable *adj* imperturbable; unruffled.
implacable *adj* implacable, inexorable.
implicar *vt* to implicate, involve.
imponer *vt* to impose; to command: —~**se** *vr* to assert oneself; to prevail.
impopular *adj* unpopular.
importante *adj* important, considerable.
importar *vi* to be important, matter: —*vt* to import; to be worth.
importe *m* amount, cost.
importunar *vt* to bother, pester.
imposible *adj* impossible; extremely difficult; slovenly.

impostor/ra *m/f* impostor, fraud.
impotencia *f* impotence.
impracticable *adj* impracticable, unworkable.
impreciso/sa *adj* imprecise, vague.
imprenta *f* printing; press; printing office.
imprescindible *adj* essential.
impresión *f* impression; stamp; print; edition.
impresionar *vt* to move; to impress: —**se** *vr* to be impressed; to be moved.
imprevisto/ta *adj* unforeseen, unexpected.
imprimir *vt* to print; to imprint; to stamp.
improbable *adj* improbable, unlikely.
improvisar *vt* to extemporize; to improvise.
improviso/sa *adj* : —**de** ~unexpectedly.
imprudente *adj* imprudent; indiscreet; unwise.
impúdico/ca *adj* shameless; lecherous.
impuesto/ta *adj* imposed: —*m* tax, duty.
impulso *m* impulse; thrust; *(fig)*impulse.
impune *adj* unpunished.
impuro/ra *adj* impure; foul.
inaccesible *adj* inaccessible.
inadvertido/da *adj* unnoticed.
inagotable *adj* inexhaustible.
inaguantable *adj* unbearable, intolerable.
inalterable *adj* unalterable.
inapreciable *adj* imperceptible; invaluable.
inaudito/ta *adj* unheard-of.
inaugurar *vt* to inaugurate.
incalculable *adj* incalculable.
incansable *adj* untiring, tireless.
incapaz *adj* incapable, unable.
incauto/ta *adj* incautious, unwary.
incendio *m* fire.
incentivo *m* incentive.
incertidumbre *f* doubt, uncertainty.
incierto/ta *adj* uncertain, doubtful.
incineración *f* incineration; cremation.
incitar *vt* to incite, excite.
inclemencia *f* inclemency, severity; inclemency (of the weather).
inclinar *vt* to incline; to nod, bow (the head): —**se** *vr* to bow; to stoop.
incluir *vt* to include, comprise; to incorporate; to enclose.
incluso/sa *adj* included: —*adv* inclusively; even.
incógnito/ta *adj* unknown: —**de** ~incognito.
incombustible *adj* incombustible, fireproof.
incómodo/da *adj* uncomfortable; annoying; inconvenient.
incomparable *adj* incomparable, matchless.
incompasivo *adj* unsympathetic.
incompleto/ta *adj* incomplete.
incomunicado/da *adj* isolated, cut off; in solitary confinement.
inconcebible *adj* inconceivable.
incondicional *adj* unconditional; whole-hearted; staunch.
inconfundible *adj* unmistakable.
inconsciente *adj* unconscious; thoughtless.
inconstante *adj* inconstant, variable, fickle.
incorporar *vt* to incorporate: —**se** *vr* to sit up; to join (an organization), become incorporated.
incorrecto/ta *adj* incorrect.
incrédulo/la *adj* incredulous.
increíble *adj* incredible.
incremento *m* increment, increase; growth; rise.
inculcar *vt* to inculcate.

inculto/ta *adj* uncultivated; uneducated; uncouth.
incumbencia *f* obligation; duty.
incurable *adj* incurable; irremediable.
indagar *vt* to inquire into.
indebido/da *adj* undue; illegal, unlawful.
indeciso/sa *adj* hesitant; undecided.
indefenso/sa *adj* defenseless.
indemnizar *vt* to indemnify, compensate.
independiente *adj* independent.
indeterminado/da *adj* indeterminate; indefinite.
indicador *m* indicator; gage.
indicar *vt* to indicate.
índice *m* ratio, rate; hand (of a watch or clock); index, table of contents; catalog; forefinger, index finger.
indicio *m* indication, mark; sign, token; clue.
indiferencia *f* indifference, apathy.
indígena *adj* indigenous, native: —*m/f* native.
indignar *vt* to irritate; to provoke, tease: —**se** *vr* ~**por** to get indignant about.
indigno/na *adj* unworthy, contemptible, low.
indirecta *f* innuendo, hint.
indiscreción *f* indiscretion, tactlessness; gaffe.
individual *adj* individual; single (of a room): —*m (dep)* singles.
individuo *m* individual.
índole *f* disposition, nature, character; soft, kind.
indolente *adj* indolent, lazy.
indómito/ta *adj* untamed, ungoverned.
inducir *vt* to induce, persuade.
indudable *adj* undoubted; unquestionable.
indultar *vt* to pardon; to exempt.
industria *f* industry; skill.
inédito/ta *adj* unpublished; *(fig)* new.
ineficaz *adj* ineffective; inefficient.
inepto/ta *adj* inept, unfit, useless.
inercia *f* inertia, inactivity.
inerte *adj* inert; dull; sluggish, motionless.
inesperado/da *adj* unexpected, unforeseen.
inevitable *adj* unavoidable.
inexacto/ta *adj* inaccurate, untrue.
inexperto/ta *adj* inexperienced.
infame *adj* infamous.
infancia *f* infancy, childhood.
infantil *adj* infantile; childlike; children's.
infarto *m* heart attack.
infatigable *adj* tireless, untiring.
infectar *vt* to infect.
infeliz *adj* unhappy, unfortunate.
inferior *adj* inferior.
infernal *adj* infernal, hellish.
infiel *adj* unfaithful; disloyal; inaccurate.
infierno *m* hell.
infiltrarse *vr* to infiltrate.
ínfimo/ma *adj* lowest; of very poor quality.
infinidad *f* infinity; immensity.
infinito/ta *adj* infinite; immense.
inflamable *adj* inflammable.
inflar *vt* to inflate, blow up; *(fig)* to exaggerate.
inflexible *adj* inflexible.
influir *vt* to influence.
información *f* information; news; *(mil)* intelligence; investigation, judicial inquiry.
informal *adj* irregular, incorrect; untrustworthy; informal.
informar *vt* to inform; to reveal, make known: —**se** *vr* to find out: —*vi* to report; *(jur)* to plead; to inform.

informática *f* computer science, information technology.

informe *m* report, statement; piece of information, account: —*adj* shape-less, formless.

infortunio *m* misfortune, ill luck.

infracción *f* infraction; breach, infringement.

infructuoso/sa *adj* fruitless, unpro-ductive, unprofitable.

infundado/da *adj* groundless.

ingeniero/ra *m/f* engineer.

ingenio *m* talent; wit; ingenuity; engine: —~ **de azúcar** sugar mill.

ingenuo/nua *adj* naive.

ingerir *vt* to ingest; to swallow; to con-sume.

ingle *f* groin.

inglés/esa *adj* English: —*m* English language: —*m/f* Englishman/woman.

ingrato/ta *adj* ungrateful, thankless; disagreeable.

ingresar *vt* to deposit: —*vi* to come in.

inhabilitar *vt* to disqualify, disable.

inhabitable *adj* uninhabitable.

inhibir *vt* to inhibit; to restrain.

iniciar *vt* to initiate; to begin.

ininteligible *adj* unintelligible.

injertar *vt* to graft.

injuriar *vt* to insult, wrong.

injusto/ta *adj* unjust.

inmediaciones *fpl* neighborhood.

inmediatamente *adv* immediately, at once.

inmobiliario/ria *adj* real-estate *compd:* —*f* estate agency.

inmortal *adj* immortal.

inmóvil *adj* immovable, still.

inmueble *m* property: —*adj* **bienes~s** real estate.

inmundo/da *adj* filthy, dirty; nasty.

inmune *adj (med)* immune; free, exempt.

innato/ta *adj* inborn, innate.

innecesario/ria *adj* unnecessary.

innegable *adj* undeniable.

innumerable *adj* innumerable, countless.

inocente *adj* innocent.

inodoro *m* washroom: —~/ra *adj* odorless, without smell.

inofensivo/va *adj* harmless.

inolvidable *adj* unforgettable.

inoxidable *adj* : —**acero ~** stainless steel.

inquietar *vt* to worry, disturb: —~se *vr* to worry, get worried.

inquilino/na *m/f* tenant; roomer, lodger.

inquirir *vt* to inquire into, investigate.

inscribir *vt* to inscribe; to list, register.

insecto *m* insect.

insensato/ta *adj* senseless, stupid; mad.

insensible *adj* insensitive; impercepti-ble; numb.

inseparable *adj* inseparable.

insertar *vt* to insert.

inservible *adj* useless.

insignia *f* badge: —~s *fpl* insignia *pl.*

insinuar *vt* to insinuate: —~se *vr* ~ **en** to worm one's way into.

insípido/da *adj* insipid.

insistir *vi* to insist.

insolación *f (med)* sunstroke.

insolencia *f* insolence, rudeness, effrontery.

insólito/ta *adj* unusual.

insolvente *adj* insolvent.

insomnio *m* insomnia.

insondable *adj* unfathomable; inscru-table.

insoportable *adj* unbearable.

inspeccionar *vt* to inspect; to supervize.

inspector/ra *m/f* inspector; superintendent.

inspirar *vt* to inspire; *(med)* to inhale.

instalar *vt* to install.

instantáneo/nea *adj* instantaneous: —*f* snap(shot): —**café** ~ instant coffee.

instante *m* instant: —**al** ~ immediately, instantly.

instigar *vt* to instigate.

instinto *m* instinct.

instructivo/va *adj* instructive; educa-tional.

instrumento *m* instrument; tool, implement.

insuficiente *adj* insufficient, inadequate.

insulso/sa *adj* insipid; dull.

insultar *vt* to insult.

insuperable *adj* insuperable, insur-mountable.

intacto/ta *adj* untouched; entire; intact.

integral *adj* integral, whole: —**pan** ~ wholewheat bread.

intemperie *f*: —**a la** ~ out in the open.

intencionado/da *adj* meaningful; deliberate.

intenso/sa *adj* intense, strong; deep.

intentar *vt* to try, attempt.

intercalar *vt* to insert.

intercambio *m* exchange, swap.

interés *m* interest; share, part; concern, advantage; profit.

interesar *vt* to be of interest to, interest: —~se *vr* ~ **en** *o* **por** to take an interest in: —*vi* to be of interest.

interferir *vt* to interfere with; to jam (a telephone): —*vi* to interfere.

interfono *m* intercom.

interino/na *adj* provisional, temporary: —*m/f* temporary holder of a post; stand-in.

interior *adj* interior, internal: —*m* interior, inside.

intermedio/dia *adj* intermediate: —*m* interval.

interminable *adj* interminable, endless.

intermitente *adj* intermittent; *m(auto)* indicator.

internado *m* boarding school.

interno/na *adj* interior, internal: —*m/f* boarder.

interpretar *vt* to interpret, explain; *(teat)* to perform; to translate.

interrogación *f* interrogation; question mark.

interrogatorio *m* questioning; *(jur)* examination; questionnaire.

interrumpir *vt* to interrupt.

interruptor *m* switch.

intervenir *vt* to control, supervise; *(com)* to audit; *(med)* to operate on: —*vi* to participate; to in-tervene.

intestino/na *adj* internal, interior: —*m* intestine.

íntimo/ma *adj* internal, innermost; intimate, private.

intranquilo/la *adj* worried.

intransitable *adj* impassable.

intrépido/da *adj* intrepid, daring.

intrigar *vt* , *vi* to intrigue.

introducir *vt* to introduce; to insert.

introvertido/da *adj* , *m/f* introvert.

intruso/sa *adj* intrusive: —*m/f* intruder.

inundar *vt* to inundate, overflow; to flood.

inusitado/da *adj* unusual.

inútil *adj* useless.

inválido/da *adj* invalid, null and void: —*m/f* in-valid.

invencible *adj* invincible.

invernadero *m* greenhouse.
inverosímil *adj* unlikely, improbable.
inverso/sa *adj* inverse; inverted; contrary.
invertir *vt (com)* to invest; to invert.
investigar *vt* to investigate; to do research into.
invierno *m* winter.
invitar *vt* to invite; to entice; to pay for.
invocar *vt* to invoke.
ir *vi* to go; to walk; to travel: —~**se** *vr* to go away, depart.
ira *f* anger, wrath.
iris *m* iris (eye): —**arco** ~ rainbow.
ironía *f* irony.
irracional *adj* irrational.
irreal *adj* unreal.
irreflexión *f* rashness, thoughtlessness.
irregular *adj* irregular; abnormal.
irremediable *adj* irremediable; incurable.
irresistible *adj* irresistible.
irreverente *adj* irreverent; disrespectful.
irrisorio/ria *adj* derisory, ridiculous.
irritar *vt* to irritate, exasperate; to stir up; to inflame.
isla *f* island, isle.
istmo *m* isthmus.
italiano/na *adj* Italian: —*m* Italian language: —*m/f* Italian.
itinerario *m* itinerary.
izquierdo/da *adj* left; left-handed: —*f* left; left(-wing).
jamón *m* ham: —~ **de York** cooked ham: —~ **serrano** cured ham.
jaque *m* check (at game of chess): —~**mate** checkmate.
jaqueca *f* migraine.
jarabe *m* syrup.
jardín *m* garden.
jarra *f* jug, jar, pitcher: —**en** ~**s, de**~**s** with hands to the sides.
jaula *f* cage; cell for mad people.
jazmín *m* jasmin.
jefe *m* chief, head, leader: —*(ferro)* ~ **de tren** guard, conductor.
jerarquía *f* hierarchy.
jerigonza *f* jargon, gibberish.
jeringa *f* syringe.

jeroglífico/ca *adj* hieroglyphic: —*m* hieroglyph, hieroglyphic.
jersey *m* sweater, pullover.
jilguero *m* goldfinch.
jinete/ta *m/f* horseman/woman, rider.
jipijapa *m* straw hat.
jirón *m* rag, shred.
jornada *f* journey; day's journey; working day.
jornal *m* day's wage.
jornalero *m* (day) laborer.
joroba *f* hump: —*m/f* hunchback.
jota *f* jot, iota; Spanish dance.
joven *adj* young: —*m/f* youth; young woman.
jovial *adj* jovial, cheerful.
joya *f* jewel: —**s** *fpl* jewelry.
juanete *m* (med) bunion.
jubilar *vt* to pension off; to superannu-ate; to discard: —~**se** *vr* to retire.
júbilo *m* joy, rejoicing.
judía *f* bean: —~ **verde** French bean.
judicial *adj* judicial.
judío/día *adj* Jewish: —*m/f* Jewish man/woman.
juego *m* play; amusement; sport; game; gambling.
jueves *m invar* Thursday.
juez *m/f* judge.
jugar *vt , vi* to play, sport, gamble.
jugo *m* sap, juice.
juguete *m* toy, plaything.
juicio *m* judgement, reason; sanity; opinion.
julio *m* July.
junco *m (bot)* rush; junk (Chinese ship).
junio *m* June.
junta *f* meeting; assembly; congress; council.
juntar *vt* to join; to unite: —~**se** *vr* to meet, assemble; to draw closer.
junto/ta *adj* joined; united; near; adjacent: —~**s** together: —*adv* **todo** ~all at once.
jurar *vt , vi* to swear.
jurídico/ca *adj* lawful, legal; juridical.
justicia *f* justice; equity.
justificante *m* voucher; receipt.
justo/ta *adj* just; fair, right; exact, correct; tight: —*adv* exactly, precisely; just in time.
juventud *f* youthfulness, youth; young people *pl*.
juzgado *m* tribunal; court.

K

kilogramo *m* kilogram(me).
kilómetro *m* kilometer.

kiosco *m* kiosk.

L

la *art f* the: —*pn* her; you; it.
labio *m* lip; edge.
labor *f* labor, task; needlework; farm-work; ploughing.
laborioso/sa *adj* laborious; hard-working.
labrar *vt* to work; to carve; to farm; *(fig)* to bring about.
laca *f* lacquer; hairspray.
lacio/cia *adj* faded, withered; languid; lank (hair).

lacrar *vt* to seal (with sealing wax).
lactancia *f* lactation; breast-feeding.
lácteo/tea *adj* : —**productos** ~**s** dairy products.
ladera *f* slope.
ladino/na *adj* cunning, crafty.
lado *m* side; faction, party; favor, protection; *(mil)* flank: —**al** ~ **de** beside: —**poner a un** ~ to put aside: —**por todos** ~**s** on all sides.

ladrar *vt* to bark.
ladrillo *m* brick.
ladrón/ona *m/f* thief, robber.
lagar *m* wine press.
lagartija *f* (small) lizard.
lagarto *m* lizard.
lago *m* lake.
lágrima *f* tear.
laguna *f* lake; lagoon; gap.
laico/ca *adj* lay.
lamentar *vt* to be sorry about; to lament, regret: —*vi* ~**se** *vr* to lament, complain; to mourn.
lamer *vt* to lick, lap.
lámina *f* plate, sheet of metal; engraving.
lámpara *f* lamp.
lana *f* wool.
lancha *f* barge, lighter; launch.
langosta *f* locust; lobster.
lanzar *vt* to throw; *(dep)* to bowl, pitch; to launch, fling; *(jur)* to evict.
lápida *f* flat stone, tablet.
lápiz *m* pencil; mechanical pencil.
largamente *adv* for a long time.
largo/ga *adj* long; lengthy, generous; copious: —**a la** ~**a** in the end, eventually.
las *art fpl* the: —*pn* them; you.
lascivo/va *adj* lascivious; lewd.
láser *m* laser.
lástima *f* compassion, pity; shame.
lastimar *vt* to hurt; to wound; to feel pity for: —~**se** *vr* to hurt oneself.
lastre *m* ballast.
lata *f* tin; tin can; *(fam)* nuisance.
latido *m* (heart)beat.
latifundio *m* large estate.
latir *vi* to beat, palpitate.
latitud *f* latitude.
latón *m* brass.
latoso/sa *adj* annoying; boring.
laúd *f* lute (musical instrument).
laudable *adj* laudable, praiseworthy.
laurel *m (bot)* laurel; reward.
lavabo *m* washbasin; washroom.
lavadora *f* washing machine.
lavanda *f* lavender.
lavar *vt* to wash; to wipe away: —~**se** *vr* to wash oneself.
laxante *m (med)* laxative.
lazarillo *m:* —**perro** ~ guide dog.
letra *f* letter; handwriting; printing type; draft of a song; bill, draft: —**s** *fpl* letters *pl,* learning.
letrero *m* sign; label.
leucemia *f* leukemia.
elevate; to hearten, cheer up: —~**se** *vr* to get up; to stand up.
levante *m* Levant; east; east wind.
levantisco *adj* turbulent, restless.
leve *adj* light; trivial.
léxico *m* vocabulary.
ley *f* law; standard (for metal).
leyenda *f* legend.
liar *vt* to tie, bind; to confuse.
libélula *f* dragonfly.
liberal *adj* liberal, generous: —*m/f* liberal.
libertad *f* liberty, freedom.
libra *f* pound: —~ **esterlina** pound sterling.
libre *adj* free; exempt; vacant.

librería *f* book store.
libreta *f* notebook: —~ **de ahorros** savings book.
libro *m* book.
licencia *f* license; licentiousness.
licenciado/da *adj* licensed: —*m/f* graduate.
lícito/ta *adj* lawful, fair; permissible.
líder *m/f* leader.
liebre *f* hare.
lienzo *f* linen; canvas; face or front of a building.
liga *f* suspender; birdlime; league; coalition; alloy.
ligar *vt* to tie, bind, fasten: —~**se** *vr* to commit oneself: —*vi* to mix, blend; *(fam)* to pick up.
ligero/ra *adj* light, swift; agile; superficial.
lazo *m* knot; bow; snare, trap; tie; bond.
le *pn* him; you; *(dativo)* to him; to her; to it; to you.
leal *adj* loyal; faithful.
lebrel *m* greyhound.
levadura *f* yeast; brewer's yeast.
lección *f* reading; lesson; lecture; class.
levantar *vt* to raise, lift up; to build; to **leche** *f* milk.
lecho *m* bed; layer.
lechón *m* sucking pig.
lechuga *f* lettuce.
lechuza *f* owl.
leer *vt* , *vi* to read.
legado *m* bequest, legacy; legate.
legal *adj* legal; trustworthy.
legaña *f* sleep (in eyes).
legislar *vt* to legislate.
legítimo/ma *adj* legitimate, lawful; authentic.
legumbres *fpl* pulses *pl.*
lejano/na *adj* distant, remote; far.
lejía *f* bleach.
lejos *adv* at a great distance, far off.
lelo/la *adj* stupid, ignorant: —*m/f* idiot.
lema *m* motto; slogan.
leña *f* firewood, kindling.
lencería *f* linen, drapery.
lengua *f* tongue; language.
lenguado *m* sole.
lenguaje *m* language.
lente *m/f* lens.
lenteja *f* lentil.
lentilla *f* contact lens.
lento/ta *adj* slow.
león *m* lion.
leopardo *m* leopard.
leotardos *mpl* tights, pantihose.
lesión *f* wound; injury; damage.
letal *adj* mortal, deadly.
letanía *f* litany.
letargo *m* lethargy.
liguero *m* suspender belt.
lijar *vt* to smooth, sandpaper.
lima *f* file.
límite *m* limit, boundary.
limón *m* lemon.
limosna *f* alms *pl,* charity.
limpiar *vt* to clean; to cleanse; to purify; to polish; *(fig)* to clean up.
linaza *f* linseed.
lince *m* lynx.
lindar *vi* to be adjacent.
lindo/da *adj* pretty; lovely.
línea *f* line; cable; outline.
lino *m* flax.
linterna *f* lantern, lamp; torch.

lío *m* bundle, parcel; *(fam)* muddle, mess.
liquidar *vt* to liquidate; to settle (accounts).
líquido/da *adj* liquid.
lirio *m (bot)* iris.
lirón *m* dormouse; *(fig)* sleepy-head.
liso/sa *adj* plain, even, flat, smooth.
lisonja *f* adulation, flattery.
lista *f* list; register; catalog; menu.
listo/ta *adj* ready; smart, clever.
litera *f* berth; bunk, bunk bed.
litigio *m* lawsuit.
litoral *adj* coastal: —*m* coast.
litro *m* liter (measure).
liviano/na *adj* light; fickle; trivial.
llama *f* flame; llama (animal).
llamar *vt* to call; to name; to summon; to ring up, telephone: —*vi* to knock at the door; to ring up, telephone: —~se *vr* to be named.
llano/na *adj* plain; even, level, smooth; clear, evident: —*m* plain.
llanta *f* (wheel) rim; tire; inner (tube).
llanura *f* evenness, flatness; plain, prairie.
llave *f* key: —~ **maestra** master key.
llegar *vi* to arrive: —~ **a** to reach: —~se *vr* to come near, approach.
llenar *vt* to fill; to cover; to fill out (a form); to satisfy, fulfil: —~se *vr* to gorge oneself.
llevar *vt* to take; to wear; to carry; to convey, transport; to drive; to lead; to bear: —~se *vr* to carry off, takeaway.
llorar *vt*, *vi* to weep, cry.
llover *vi* to rain.
lluvia *f* rain.
lo *pn* it; him; you: —*art* the.
lobo *m* wolf.
lóbulo *m* lobe.
local *adj* local: —*m* place, site.

loco/ca *adj* mad: —*m/f* mad person.
locutor/ra *m/f (rad)* announcer; *(TV)* newsreader.
lodo *m* mud, mire.
lograr *vt* to achieve; to gain, obtain.
lombarda *f* red cabbage.
lombriz *f* worm.
lomo *m* loin; back (of an animal); spine (of a book): —**llevar** *o* **traer a** ~ to carry on the back.
lona *f* canvas.
loncha *f* slice; rasher.
longaniza *f* pork sausage.
longitud *f* length; longitude.
loro *m* parrot.
los *art mpl* the: —*pn* them; you.
losa *f* flagstone.
lote *m* lot; portion.
loza *f* crockery.
lucero *m* morning star, bright star.
luchar *vi* to struggle; to wrestle.
luciérnaga *f* glowworm.
lucir *vt* to light (up); to show off: —*vi* to shine: —~se *vr* to make a fool of oneself.
luego *adv* next; afterward(s): —**desde** ~ of course.
lugar *m* place, spot; village; reason: —**en** ~ **de** instead of, in lieu of.
lúgubre *adj* lugubrious; sad, gloomy.
lujo *m* luxury; abundance.
lujuria *f* lust.
lumbre *f* fire; light.
luna *f* moon; glass plate for mirrors; lens.
lunar *m* mole, spot: —*adj* lunar.
lunes *m invar* Monday.
lupa *f* magnifying glass.
lupanar *m* brothel.
luto *m* mourning (dress); grief.
luz *f* light.

M

maceta *f* flowerpot.
machacar *vt* to pound, crush: —*vi* to insist, go on.
macho *adj* male; *(fig)* virile: —*m* male; *(fig)* he-man.
macizo/za *adj* massive; solid: —*m* mass, chunk.
madera *f* wood; lumber.
madrastra *f* stepmother.
madre *f* mother; womb.
madreselva *f* honeysuckle.
madriguera *f* burrow; den.
madrugar *vi* to get up early; to get ahead.
maduro/ra *adj* ripe, mature.
maestro *m* master; teacher: —~/**tra** *adj* masterly, skilled; principal.
magia *f* magic.
magisterio *m* teaching; teaching profession; teachers *pl*.
magnetofón, magnetófono *m* tape recorder.
magnífico/ca *adj* magnificent, splendid.
mago/ga *m/f* magician.
magullar *vt* to bruise; to damage; to bash *(sl)*.
mahometano/na *m/f*, *adj* Muslim.
maíz *m* maize, Indian corn.
majadero/ra *adj* dull; silly, stupid: —*m* idiot.

majo/ja *adj* nice; attractive; smart.
majuelo *m* vine newly planted; hawthorn.
mal *m* evil; hurt; harm, damage; misfortune; illness: —*adj* (before masculine nouns) bad.
malcriado/da *adj* rude, ill-behaved; naughty; spoiled.
maldad *f* wickedness.
maldecir *vt* to curse.
maldito/ta *adj* wicked; damned, cursed.
malecón *m* pier.
maleducado/da *adj* bad-mannered, rude.
malestar *m* discomfort; *(fig)* uneasiness; unrest.
maleta *f* suitcase; *(auto)* trunk.
maleza *f* weeds *pl*; thicket.
malgastar *vt* to waste, ruin.
malhablado/da *adj* foul-mouthed.
malhechor/ra *m/f* malefactor; criminal.
malhumorado/da *adj* cross, bad-tempered.
malla *f* mesh, network: —**s** *fpl* leotard.
malo/la *adj* bad; ill; wicked: —*m/f* villain.
maltratar *vt* to ill-treat, abuse, mis-treat.
malva *f (bot)* mallow.
malvado/da *adj* wicked, villainous.
mama *f* teat; breast.

mamá f (fam) mum, mummy.
mamar vt , vi to suck.
mamífero m mammal.
manada f flock, herd; pack; crowd.
manantial m source, spring; origin.
manchar vt to stain, soil.
manco/ca adj one-armed; one-handed; maimed; faulty.
mancomunidad f union, fellowship; community; (jur) joint responsibility.
mandar vt to command, order; to bequeath; to send.
mandarina f tangerine.
mandíbula f jaw.
mandil m apron.
manera f manner, way; fashion; kind.
manga f sleeve; hose.
mango m handle; mango.
manguera f hose; pipe.
maní m peanut.
manifestación f manifestation; show; demonstration; mass meeting.
manifestar vt to manifest, declare.
maniobrar vt to maneuvre; to handle.
manipular vt to manipulate.
maniquí m dummy: —m/f model.
manivela f crank.
mano f hand; hand (of clock, etc); foot, paw (of animal); coat (of paint); lot, series; hand (at game): —a ~ by hand: —a ~s llenas liberally, gener-ously.
manojo m handful, bunch.
manopla f wash cloth; mitten; gaunt-let.
manosear vt to handle; to mess up.
manso/sa adj tame; gentle, soft.
manta f blanket.
manteca f fat: —~ de cerdo lard.
mantel m tablecloth.
mantener vt to maintain, support; to nourish; to keep: —~se vr to hold one's ground; to support oneself.
mantequilla f butter.
manzana f apple.
manzanilla f camomile; camomile tea; manzanilla sherry.
maña f handiness, dexterity, cleverness, cunning; habit, custom; trick.
mañana f morning: —adv tomorrow.
mapa m map.
maquillar vt to make up: —~se vr to put on make-up.
máquina f machine; (ferro) engine; camera; (fig) machinery; plan, project.
maquinilla f: —~ de afeitar razor.
maquinista m (ferro) train driver; operator; (mar) engineer.
mar m/f sea.
maravilla f wonder.
marca f mark; stamp; make, brand.
marcar vt to mark; to dial; to score; to record; to set (hair): —vi to score; to dial.
marchar vi to go; to work: —~se vr to go away.
marco m frame; framework; (dep) goalposts pl.
marea f tide.
marear vt (mar) to sail, navigate; to annoy, upset: —~se vr to feel sick; to feel faint; to feel dizzy.
marfil m ivory.
margarita f daisy.

margen m margin; border: —f bank (of river).
marido m husband.
marinero/ra adj sea compd; seawor-thy: —m sailor.
marioneta f puppet.
mariposa f butterfly.
mariquita f ladybird.
marisco m shellfish pl.
mármol m marble.
marrano m hog, boar.
marrón adj brown.
martes m invar Tuesday.
martillo m hammer.
marzo m March.
mas adv but, yet.
más adv more; most; besides, moreover: —a ~ tardar at latest: —sin ~ni ~ without more ado.
masa f dough, paste; mortar; mass.
mascar vt to chew.
máscara m/f masked person: —f mask.
mascullar vt to mumble, mutter.
mástil m (mar) mast.
mastín m mastiff.
mata f shrub; sprig, blade; grove, group of trees; mop of hair.
matadero m slaughterhouse.
matar vt to kill; to execute; to murder: —~se vr to kill oneself, commit suicide.
matasellos m invar postmark.
mate m checkmate: —adj matt.
material adj material, physical: —m equipment, materials pl.
maternidad f motherhood.
matinal adj morning compd.
matiz m shade of color; shading.
matrícula f register, list; (auto) registration number; license plate.
matrimonio m marriage, matrimony.
matriz f matrix; womb; mold, form.
maullar vi to mew.
mayo m May.
mayor adj main, chief; (mus) major; biggest; eldest; greater, larger; elderly: —m chief, boss; adult: —al por ~ wholesale: —es mpl forefathers.
mayoría f majority, greater part: —~de edad coming of age.
mayúsculo/la adj (fig) tremendous: —f capital letter.
mazo m bunch; club, mallet; bat.
mazorca f ear of corn.
me pn me; to me.
mear vi (fam) to pee, piss (sl).
mecanógrafo/fa m/f typist.
mecer vt to rock; to dandle (a child).
mechar vt to lard; to stuff.
mechón m lock of hair; large bundle of threads or fibres.
media f stocking; sock; average.
medianoche f midnight.
mediante prep by means of.
mediar vi to intervene; to mediate.
medicamento m medicine.
médico/ca adj medical: —m/f doctor.
medida f measure.
medio/dia adj half: —a medias partly: —m middle; average; way, means; medium.
mediodía m noon, midday.
medir vt to measure: —~se vr to be moderate.

medrar *vi* to grow, thrive, prosper; to improve.
fpl/**médula** *f* marrow; essence, substance; pith.
medusa *f* jellyfish.
mejilla *f* cheek.
mejillón *m* mussel.
mejor *adj , adv* better; best.
mejorar *vt* to improve, ameliorate; to enhance: —*vi*
   to improve; *(med)* to recover, get better: —**~se** *vr*
   to improve, get better.
melenudo/da *adj* long-haired.
melindroso/sa *adj* prudish, finicky.
mella *f* notch in edged tools; gap.
mellizo/za *adj , m/f* twin.
melocotón *m* peach.
meloso/sa *adj* honeyed; mellow.
membrete *m* letter head.
membrillo *m* quince; quince tree.
memoria *f* memory; report; record: —**s** *fpl* mem-
   oirs *pl.*
mendigar *vt* to beg.
menear *vt* to move from place to place; *(fig)* to
   handle: —**~se** *vr* to move; to shake; to sway.
menguante *f* waning.
meñique *m* little finger.
menor *m/f* young person, juvenile: — *adj* less;
   smaller; minor: —**al por ~** retail.
menos *adv* less; least: —**a lo ~ o por lo ~** at least:
   —*prep* except; minus.
menospreciar *vt* to undervalue; to despise, scorn.
mensaje *m* message.
mensual *adj* monthly.
menta *f* mint.
mente *f* mind; understanding.
mentecato/ta *adj* silly, stupid: —*m/f* idiot.
mentir *vt* to feign; to pretend: —*vi* to lie.
mentira *f* lie, falsehood.
menudo/da *adj* small; minute; petty, insignificant:
   —**a ~** frequently, often.
mercader *m* dealer, trader.
mercado *m* market; marketplace.
mercancía *f* commodity: —**s** goods *pl,* merchandise.
mercurio *m* mercury.
merecer *vt* to deserve, merit.
meridional *adj* southern.
merienda *f* (light) tea; afternoon snack; picnic.
merluza *f* hake.
mermelada *f* jam.
mero *m* pollack (fish): —**~/ra** *adj* mere, pure.
mes *m* month.
mesa *f* table; desk; plateau: —**~redonda** round table.
mestizo/za *adj* of mixed race; crossbred: —*m/f*
   half-caste.
meta *f* goal; finish.
metal *m* metal; *(mus)* brass; timbre (of voice).
meter *vt* to place, put; to insert, put in; to involve; to
   make, cause: —**~se** *vr* to meddle, interfere.
método *m* method.
metro *m* meter; subway.
mezclar *vt* to mix: —**~se** *vr* to mix; to mingle.
mezquino/na *adj* mean; small-minded, petty;
   wretched.
mezquita *f* mosque.
mi *adj* my.
mí *pn* me; myself.
miedo *m* fear, dread.
miel *f* honey.

miembro *m* member.
mientras *adv* meanwhile: —*conj* while; as long as.
miércoles *m invar* Wednesday.
mierda *f (fam)* shit *(sl).*
miga *f* crumb: —**s** *fpl* fried bread-crumbs *pl.*
mijo *m (bot)* millet.
mil *m* one thousand.
milagro *m* miracle, wonder.
milésimo/ma *adj , m* thousandth.
milímetro *m* millimeter.
milla *f* mile.
millón *m* million.
mimar *vt* to spoil, pamper.
mimbre *m* wicker.
mimo *m* caress; spoiling; mime.
mina *f* mine; underground passage.
minero/ra *m/f* miner.
minifalda *f* miniskirt.
mínimo/ma *adj* minimum.
minoría *f* minority.
minucioso/sa *adj* meticulous; very detailed.
minúsculo/la *adj* minute: —*f* small letter.
minusválido/da *adj* (physically)handicapped: —*m/f*
   (physically)handicapped person.
minuto *m* minute.
mío/mía *adj* mine.
miope *adj* short-sighted.
mirar *vt* to look at; to observe; to consider: —*vi* to
   look: —**~se** *vr* to look at oneself; to look at one
   another.
mirlo *m* blackbird.
misa *f* mass: —**~ del gallo** midnight mass.
miserable *adj* miserable; mean; squalid (place);
   (fam) despicable: —*m/f* rotter.
misericordia *f* mercy.
mismo/ma *adj* same; very.
mitad *f* half; middle.
mitin *m* (political) rally.
mixto/ta *adj* mixed.
mobiliario *m* furniture.
mochila *f* backpack.
mochuelo *m* red owl.
moco *m* snot *(sl),* mucus.
moda *f* fashion, style.
modales *mpl* manners *pl.*
modelo *m* model, pattern.
módico/ca *adj* moderate.
modificar *vt* to modify.
modisto/ta *m/f* dressmaker.
modo *m* mode, method, manner.
modorra *f* drowsiness.
mofarse *vr:* —**~ de** to mock, scoff at.
moflete *m* fat cheek.
moho *m* rust; mold, mildew.
mojar *vt* to wet, moisten: —**~se** *vr* to get wet.
mojón *m* landmark.
molde *m* mold; pattern; model.
moler *vt* to grind, pound; to tire out; to annoy, bore.
molestar *vt* to annoy, bother; to trouble: —*vi* to be
   a nuisance.
molino *m* mill.
momentáneo/nea *adj* momentary.
momento *m* moment.
momia *f* mummy.
mondadientes *m invar* toothpick.
mondar *vt* to clean; to cleanse; to peel: —**~se** *vr* **~ de**
   risa *(fam)* to split one's sides laughing.

mondo/da *adj* clean; pure: —~ **ylirondo** bare, plain; pure and simple.

moneda *f* money; currency; coin.

monja *f* nun.

mono/na *adj* lovely; pretty; nice: —*m/f* monkey; ape: —*mpl* dungarees *pl;* overalls *pl.*

monstruo *m* monster.

montaje *m* assembly; decor (of theater); montage.

montaña *f* mountain.

montar *vt* to mount, get on (a bicycle, horse, etc); to assemble, put together; to overlap; to set up (a business); to beat, whip (in cooking): —*vi* to mount; to ride: —~ **a** to amount to.

monte *m* mountain; woodland: —~ **alto** forest: —~ **bajo** scrub.

montón *m* heap, pile; mass: —**a ~ones,** abundantly, by the score.

montura *f* mount; saddle.

monzón *m* monsoon.

mora *f* blackberry.

morado/da *adj* violet, purple.

morcilla *f* blood sausage.

mordaz *adj* biting, scathing; pungent.

mordaza *f* gag; clamp.

morder *vt* to bite; to nibble; to cor-rode, eat away.

moreno/na *adj* brown; swarthy; dark-skinned.

morir *vi* to die; to expire; to die down: —~**se** *vr* to die; (*fig*) to be dying.

morisco/ca *adj* Moorish.

moroso/sa *adj* slow, sluggish; (*com*) slow to pay up.

morral *m* haversack.

morro *m* snout; nose (of plane, etc).

morsa *f* walrus.

mortal *adj* mortal; fatal, deadly.

mosca *f* fly.

mosquearse *vr* (*fam*) to get cross; (*fam*) to take offence.

mosquitero *m* mosquito net.

mosquito *m* gnat, mosquito.

mostaza *f* mustard.

mosto *m* must, grape juice.

mostrador *m* counter.

mostrar *vt* to show, exhibit; to explain: —~**se** *vr* to appear, show oneself.

mote *m* nickname.

motivo *m* motive, cause, reason.

moto *(fam),* **motocicleta** *f* motorcycle.

motor *m* engine, motor.

mover *vt* to move; to shake; to drive; (*fig*) to cause: —~**se** *vr* to move; (*fig)*to get a move on.

móvil *adj* mobile, movable; moving: — *m* motive.

mozo/za *adj* young: —*m/f* youth, young man/girl; waiter/waitress.

muchacho/a *m/f* boy/girl: —*f* maid, maidservant.

mucho/cha *adj* a lot of, much: —*adv* much, a lot; long.

mudar *vt* to change; to shed: —~**se** *vr* to change one's clothes; to change house: —*vi* to change; **mudo/da** *adj* dumb; silent, mute.

mueble *m* piece of furniture: —~**s** *mpl* furniture.

mueca *f* grimace, funny face.

muela *f* tooth, molar.

muelle *m* spring; regulator; quay.

muérdago *m (bot)* mistletoe.

muerte *f* death.

mujer *f* woman.

mulato *adj* mulatto.

muleta *f* crutch.

mullido/da *adj* soft; springy.

mulo/la *m/f* mule.

multa *f* fine, penalty.

mundial *adj* worldwide; world *compd.*

mundo *m* world.

muñeca *f* wrist; child's doll.

municipio *m* town council; municipality.

murciélago *m* bat.

murmullo *m* murmur, mutter.

murmurar *vi* to murmur; to gossip.

muro *m* wall.

músculo *m* muscle.

museo *m* museum.

musgo *m* moss.

música *f* music.

muslo *m* thigh.

mutuo/tua *adj* mutual, reciprocal.

mustio/tia *adj* parched, withered; sad, sorrowful.

muy *adv* very; to o; greatly: —~ **ilustre** most il-lustrious.

N

nabo *m* turnip.

nácar *m* mother-of-pearl, nacre.

nacer *vi* to be born; to bud, shoot (of plants); to rise; to grow.

nacimiento *m* birth; nativity.

nada *f* nothing: —*adv* no way, not at all, by no means.

nadar *vi* to swim.

nadie *pn* nobody, no one.

nafta *f* gas.

nalgas *fpl* buttocks *pl.*

naranja *f* orange.

nariz *f* nose.

narrar *vt* to narrate, tell.

nata *f* cream.

natillas *fpl* custard.

naturaleza *f* nature.

naufragar *vi* to be shipwrecked; to suffer ruin in one's affairs.

náutica *f* navigation.

navaja *f* penknife; razor.

nave *f* ship; nave; warehouse.

navegar *vt , vi* to navigate; to sail; to fly.

Navidad *f* Christmas.

nebuloso/sa *adj* misty; cloudy; nebulous; foggy; hazy; drizzling: —*f* nebula.

neceser *m* toilet bag; holdall.

necesitar *vt* to need: —*vi* to want, to need.

necio/cia *adj* ignorant; stupid, foolish; imprudent.

nefasto/ta *adj* unlucky.

negado/da *adj* incapable, unfit.

negar *vt* to deny; to refuse: —~**se** *vr*~ **a hacer** to refuse to do.

negocio *m* business, affair; transaction; firm; place of business.

negro/gra *adj* black: —*m* black: —*m/f* Black.
nené *m*, **nena** *f* baby.
neto/ta *adj* neat, pure; net.
neumático/ca *adj* pneumatic: —*m* tire.
neutro/tra *adj* neutral; neuter.
nevar *vi* to snow.
nevera *f* icebox.
ni *conj* neither, nor.
nido *m* nest; hiding place.
niebla *f* fog; mist.
nieta *f* granddaughter.
nieto *m* grandson.
nieve *f* snow.
niña *f* little girl; pupil, (of eye).
ningún, ninguno/na *adj* no: —*pn:* nobody; none; not one; neither.
niño/ña *adj* childish: —*m/f* child; infant: —**desde ~** from infancy, from a child: —*m* boy.
nitidez *f* clarity; brightness; sharpness.
nivel *m* level; standard; height: —**a ~** perfectly level.
no *adv* no; not: —*excl* no!
no obstante *adv* nevertheless, not-withstanding.
noche *f* night; evening; darkness: —**~ buena** Christmas Eve: —**~ vieja** New Year's Eve: —**¡buenas ~s!** good night!
noción *f* notion, idea.
nocivo/va *adj* harmful.
nogal *m* walnut tree.
nombrar *vt* to name; to nominate; to appoint.
nombre *m* name; title; reputation.
nómina *f* list; (com) payroll.
non *adj* odd, uneven: —*m* odd number.
nor(d)este *adj* northeast, north-eastern: —*m* north-east.
nórdico/ca *adj* northern; Nordic.
noria *f* water wheel; big wheel.
noroeste *adj* northwest, northwestern: —*m* north-west.
norte *adj* north, northern: —*m* north; (fig) rule, guide.
nos *pn* us; to us; for us; from us; to ourselves.
nosotros/tras *pn* we; us.
nostalgia *f* homesickness.
notar *vt* to note; to mark; to remark: —**~se** *vr* to be obvious.
noticia *f* information; note: —**~s** *fpl* news.
noticiario *m* newsreel; news bulletin.
notificar *vt* to notify, inform.
novato/ta *adj* inexperienced: —*m/f* beginner.
novecientos/tas *adj* nine hundred.
novedad *f* novelty; modernness; newness; piece of news; change.
noveno/na *adj* ninth.
noventa *adj* , *m* ninety.
novia *f* bride; girlfriend; fiancée.
noviembre *m* November.
novio *m* bridegroom; boyfriend; fiancé.
nube *f* cloud.
nublado/da *adj* cloudy: —*m* storm cloud.
nuca *f* nape (of the neck); scruff of the neck.
nudillo *m* knuckle.
nudo *m* knot.
nuera *f* daughter-in-law.
nuestro/tra *adj* our: —*pn* ours.
nueve *m*, *adj* nine.
nuevo/va *adj* new; modern; fresh: —*f* piece of news: —**¿que hay de ~?** is there any news?, what's new?
nuez *f* nut; walnut; Adam's apple: —**~ moscada** nutmeg.
número *m* number; cipher.
nunca *adv* never.
nutria *f* otter.
nutrir *vt* to nourish; to feed.

Ñ

ñato/ta *adj* snub-nosed.
ñoño/ña *adj* insipid; spineless; silly.

ñoñeria *f* insipidness.

O

o *conj* or; either.
obedecer *vt* to obey.
obeso/sa *adj* obese, fat.
objetar *vi* to object.
objeto *m* object; aim.
obligar *vt* to force: —**~se** *vr* to bind oneself.
obra *f* work; building, construction; play: —**por ~ de** thanks to.
obrero/ra *adj* working; labor *compd:* —*m/f* worker; laborer.
obsequiar *vt* to lavish attention on: —**~con** to present with.
observar *vt* to observe; to notice.
obstáculo *m* obstacle, impediment.
obstinarse *vr* to be obstinate: —**~ en** to persist in.
obstruir *vt* to obstruct: —**~se** *vr* to be blocked up,
be obstructed.
obtener *vt* to obtain; to gain.
ocasión *f* occasion, opportunity.
ocasionar *vt* to cause, occasion.
occidente *m* occident, west.
océano *m* ocean.
ochenta *m*, *adj* eighty.
ocho *m*, *adj* eight.
ochocientos *m*, *adj* eight hundred.
ocio *m* leisure; pastime.
octavilla *f* pamphlet.
octavo/va *adj* eighth.
octubre *m* October.
ocultar *vt* to hide, conceal.
ocupar *vt* to occupy; to hold (office): —**~se** *vr* **~ de, ~ en** to concern oneself with; to look after.

ocurrencia *f* event; bright idea.
ocurrir *vi* to occur, happen.
odiar *vt* to hate: ——**se** *vr* to hate one another.
oeste *adj* west, western: —*m* west.
ofender *vt* to offend; to injure: ——**se** *vr* to be vexed; to take offence.
oficina *f* office.
oficio *m* employment, occupation; ministry; function; trade, business.
ofrecer *vt* to offer; to present; to exhibit: ——**se** *vr* to offer oneself; to occur, present itself.
oído *m* hearing; ear.
oír *vt* , *vi* to hear; to listen (to).
ojal *m* buttonhole.
ojalá *conj* if only!, would that! **ojear** *vt* to eye, view; to glance.
ojera *f* bag under the eyes.
ojo *m* eye; sight; eye of a needle; arch of a bridge.
ola *f* wave.
oler *vt* to smell, scent: —*vi* to smell: ——** a** to smack of.
olfato *m* sense of smell.
olivo *m* olive tree.
olla *f* pan; stew: ——** exprés, ~ a presion** pressure cooker.
olmo *m* elm tree.
olor *m* smell, odor; scent.
olvidar *vt* to forget.
ombligo *m* navel.
once *m, adj* eleven.
onda *f* wave.
opaco/ca *adj* opaque; dark.
opinar *vt* to think: —*vi* to give one's opinion.
oponer *vt* to oppose: ——**se** *vr* to be opposed: ——** a** to oppose.
oposición *f* opposition: ——**ones** *fpl* public examinations *pl.*
oprimir *vt* to oppress; to crush; to press; to squeeze.
optar *vt* to choose, elect.
optativo/va *adj* optional.
óptimo/ma *adj* best.

opuesto/ta *adj* opposite; contrary; adverse.
orar *vi* to pray.
ordenado/da *adj* methodical; tidy.
ordenador *m* computer.
ordenanza *f* order; statute, ordi-nance; ordination.
ordenar *vt* to arrange; to order; to ordain: ——**se** *vr* to take holy orders.
ordeñar *vt* to milk.
oreja *f* ear.
orgullo *m* pride, haughtiness.
oriental *adj* oriental, eastern.
orientar *vt* to orient; to point; to direct; to guide: ——**se** *vr* to get one's bearings; to decide on a course of action.
orificio *m* orifice; mouth; aperture.
orilla *f* limit, border, margin; edge (of cloth); shore.
orín *m* rust.
orina *f* urine.
orinal *m* chamber pot.
oro *m* gold; ~**s** *mpl* diamonds *pl* (cards).
ortiga *f (bot)* nettle.
oruga *f (bot)* caterpillar.
orzuelo *m (med)* stye.
os *pn* you; to you.
osa *f* she-bear: —**O~ Mayor/Menor** Great/Little Bear.
osar *vi* to dare, venture.
oscuro/ra *adj* obscure; dark.
oso *m* bear: ——** blanco** polar bear.
ostentar *vt* to show: —*vi* to boast, brag.
ostra *f* oyster.
otoño *m* fall, autumn.
otorgar *vt* to concede; to grant.
otorrino/na, otorrinolaringólogo/ga *m/f* ear, nose and throat specialist.
otro/tra *adj* another; other.
oveja *f* sheep.
ovillo *m* ball of wool.
óvulo *m* ovum.
oxidar *vt* to rust: ——**se** *vr* to go rusty.
oyente *m/f* listener, hearer.

P

pacificar *vt* to pacify, appease.
pacotilla *f*: —**de ~** third-rate; cheap.
pactar *vt* to covenant; to contract; to stipulate.
padecer *vt* to suffer; to sustain (an injury); to put up with.
padrastro *m* stepfather.
padre *m* father: ——**s** *mpl* parents *pl.*
pagar *vt* to pay; to pay for; *(fig)* to repay: —*vi* to pay.
página *f* page.
pago *m* payment; reward.
país *m* country; region.
paisaje *m* landscape.
paisano/na *adj* of the same country: —*m/f* fellow countryman/woman.
paja *f* straw; *(fig)* trash.
pájaro *m* bird; sly, acute fellow.
pajita *f* (drinking) straw.
pala *f* spade, shovel.
palabra *f* word: —**de ~** by word of mouth.

paladar *m* palate; taste, relish.
palanca *f* lever.
palangana *f* basin.
palco *m* box (in a theater).
paleto/ta *m/f* rustic.
pálido/da *adj* pallid, pale.
palillo *m* small stick; toothpick: ——**s** *mpl* chopsticks *pl.*
paliza *f* beating, thrashing.
palma *f* palm tree; palm of the hand; palm leaf.
palmada *f* slap, clap: ——**s** *fpl* clapping of hands, applause.
palmera *f* palm tree.
palo *m* stick; cudgel; blow given with a stick; post; mast; bat; suit (at cards): ——**s** *mpl* masting.
paloma *f* pigeon, dove: ——** torcaz** ring dove: ——** zorita** wood pigeon.
palomilla *f* moth; wing nut; angle iron.
palpar *vt* to feel, touch.
palta *f* avocado (pear).

pámpano *m* vine branch.
pan *m* bread; loaf; food in general.
pana *f* corduroy.
pañal *m* diaper, nappy.
pandereta *f* tambourine.
pandilla *f* group; gang; clique.
paño *m* cloth; piece of cloth; duster, rag.
pantalla *f* screen; lampshade.
pantalón *m*, **pantalones** *mpl* trou-sers, pants *pl*.
pantano *m* marsh; reservoir; obstacle, difficulty.
pantorrilla *f* calf (of the leg).
pañuelo *m* handkerchief.
panza *f* belly, paunch.
papá *m* (*fam*) dad, pop.
papada *f* double chin.
papel *m* paper; writing; part, role (in a play): —~ **de estraza** brown paper: —~ **sellado** stamped paper.
papeleo *m* red tape.
paperas *fpl* mumps.
paquete *m* packet; parcel; package tour.
par *adj* equal; alike; even: —*m* pair; couple; peer: —**sin** ~ matchless.
para *prep* for; to , in order to; to wards.
parabrisas *m invar* windshield.
paracaídas *m invar* parachute.
parada *f* halt; suspension; pause; stop; shutdown; stopping place: —~ **deautobús** bus stop.
parado/da *adj* motionless; at a standstill; stopped; standing (up); unemployed.
paraguas *m invar* umbrella.
parar *vi* to stop, halt: —*vt* to stop, detain: —**sin** ~ instantly, without delay: —~**se** *vr* to stop, halt; to standup.
parecer *m* opinion, advice, counsel; countenance, air, mien: —*vi* to appear; to seem: —~**se** *vr* ~ **a** to resemble.
parecido/da *adj* resembling, like.
pared *f* wall: —~ **medianera** party wall.
pareja *f* pair, couple, brace.
pariente/ta *m/f* relative, relation.
parir *vt* to give birth to: —*vi* to give birth.
paro *m* strike; unemployment.
párpado *m* eyelid.
parra *f* vine raised on stakes or nailed to a wall.
párrafo *m* paragraph.
parrilla *f* grill; grille.
parte *m* message; report: —*f* part; side; party: —**de ocho dias a esta** ~ within these last eight days: — **de** ~ **a** ~ from side to side, through and through.
partera *f* midwife.
particular *adj* particular, special: —*m* private indi-vidual; particular matter or subject treated upon.
partida *f* departure; party; item in an account; parcel; game.
partido *m* party; match; team.
partir *vt* to part; to divide, separate; to cut; to break: —*vi* to depart: —~**se** *vr* to break (in two, etc).
parvulario *m* nursery school.
pasa *f* raisin.
pasadizo *m* narrow passage; narrow, covered way.
pasado/da *adj* past; bad; overdone; out of date: —~ **mañana** the day after tomorrow: —**la semana pasada** last week: —*m* past.
pasaje *m* passage; fare; passengers *pl*.
pasajero/ra *adj* transient; transitory; fugitive: —*m/f* traveler; passenger.

pasamanos *m invar* (hand)rail; bannister.
pasar *vt* to pass; to surpass; to suf-fer; to strain; to dissemble: —*vi* to pass; to happen: —~**se** *vr* to go over (to another party); to go bad or off.
pasarela *f* footbridge; gangway.
pasatiempo *m* pastime, amusement.
Pascua *f* Passover; Easter.
pasear *vt* to walk: —*vi* ~**se** *vr* to walk; to walk about.
pasmar *vt* to amaze; to numb; to chill: —~**se** *vr* to be astonished.
paso *m* pace, step; passage; manner of walking; flight of steps; accident: —(*ferro*) ~ **a nivel** grade cross-ing: —**al**~ on the way, in passing.
pasta *f* paste; dough; pastry; (*fam*)dough: —~**s** *fpl* pastries *pl*; pasta: —~ **de dientes** toothpaste.
pastel *m* cake; pie; crayon (for drawing).
pastilla *f* bar (of soap); tablet, pill.
pastor *m* shepherd; pastor.
pata *f* leg (of animal or furniture); foot: —**meter la** ~ to put one's foot in it.
patata *f* potato.
patear *vt* to kick; to stamp on.
patillas *fpl* sideburns *pl*.
patín *m* skate; runner.
patinar *vi* to skate; to skid; (*fam*) to blunder.
patio *m* courtyard; playground.
pato *m* duck.
patoso/sa *adj* (*fam*) clumsy.
patraña *f* lie.
patrocinar *vt* to sponsor; to back, support.
patrón/ona *m/f* boss, master/mistress; landlord/lady; patron saint: —*m* pattern.
patronal *adj* : —**la clase** ~ management.
patrulla *f* patrol.
paulatino/na *adj* gradual, slow.
pausar *vi* to pause.
pauta *f* guideline.
pavo *m* turkey: —~ **real** peacock.
pavor *m* dread, terror.
payaso/sa *m/f* clown.
payo/ya *m/f* non-Gipsy (for a Gipsy).
paz *f* peace; tranquillity, ease.
peaje *m* toll.
peana *f* pedestal; footstool.
peatón *m* pedestrian.
peca *f* freckle; spot.
pecado *m* sin.
pecho *m* chest; breast(s) (*pl*); teat; (*fig*) courage, valor: —**dar el** ~ **a** to suckle: —**tomar a** ~ to take to heart.
pechuga *f* breast of a fowl; (*fam*) bosom.
pedazo *m* piece, bit.
pedernal *m* flint.
pediatra *m/f* pediatrician.
pedicuro/ra *m/f* chiropodist.
pedir *vt* to ask for; to petition; to beg; to order; to need; to solicit: —*vi* to ask.
pedo *m* (*fam*) fart (*sl*): —**tirarse un** ~ to fart (*sl*).
pegamento *m* glue.
pegar *vt* to cement; to join, unite; to beat: —~ **fuego a** to set fire to: —*vi* to stick; to match: —~**se** *vr* to intrude; to steal in.
pegatina *f* sticker.
peinar *vt* to comb; to style.
peine *m* comb.
pelar *vt* to cut (hair); to strip off (feath-ers); to peel: —~**se** *vr* to peel off; to have one's hair cut.

peldaño *m* step (of a flight of stairs).
pelear *vt* to fight, combat: —**se** *vr* to scuffle.
pelele *m* dummy; man of straw.
película *f* film, thin covering; movie.
peligro *m* danger, peril; risk.
pelirrojo/ja *m/f* redhead: —*adj* red-haired.
pellejo *m* skin; hide, pelt; peel; wine skin; oilskin; drunkard.
pellizcar *vt* to pinch.
pelo *m* hair; pile; flaw (in precious stones).
pelota *f* ball.
peluca *f* wig.
peluquería *f* hairdresser's/barber's premises.
pelusa *f* bloom (on fruit); fluff.
pena *f* punishment, pain: —**a duras~s** with great difficulty or trouble.
pendiente *f* slope, declivity: —*m* earring: —*adj* pending; unsettled.
pene *m* penis.
penetrante *adj* deep; sharp; piercing; searching; biting.
penique *m* penny.
penoso/sa *adj* painful.
pensar *vi* to think.
pensativo/va *adj* pensive, thoughtful.
pensión *f* guest-house; pension.
penúltimo/ma *adj* penultimate, last but one.
penumbra *f* half-light.
penuria *f* penury, poverty, neediness, extreme want.
peña *f* rock, large stone.
peón *m* (day) laborer; foot soldier; pawn (at chess).
peor *adj*, *adv* worse: —**~ que ~** worse and worse.
pepino *m* cucumber.
pepita *f* kernel; pip.
pequeño/ña *adj* little, small; young.
pera *f* pear.
percatarse *vr*: —**~ de** to notice.
percha *f* coat hook; coat hanger; perch.
percibir *vt* to receive; to perceive, comprehend.
perder *vt* to lose; to waste; to miss: —**se** *vr* to go astray; to be lost; to be spoiled.
perdiz *f* partridge.
perdón *m* pardon; mercy: —**¡~!** sorry!
perdonar *vt* to pardon, forgive; to excuse.
perdurar *vi* to last; to still exist.
perecedero/ra *adj* perishable.
peregrino/na *adj* (fig) strange: —*m* pilgrim.
perejil *m* parsley.
pereza *f* laziness, idleness.
perfil *m* profile.
perforar *vt* to perforate; to drill; to punch a hole in: —*vi* to drill.
perfume *m* perfume.
pergamino *m* parchment.
periódico/ca *adj* periodical: —*m* newspaper.
periodista *m/f* journalist.
peripecia *f* vicissitude; sudden change.
periquito *m* budgie.
perito/ta *adj* skillful, experienced: — *m/f* expert; skilled worker; techn-ician.
perjudicar *vt* to prejudice, damage; to injure, hurt.
perjurar *vi* to perjure, swear falsely; to swear.
perla *f* pearl: —**de ~s** fine.
permanecer *vi* to stay; to continue to be.
permiso *m* permission, leave, license.
permitir *vt* to permit, allow.
permutar *vt* to exchange, permute.

pernera *f* trouser leg.
perno *m* bolt.
pernoctar *vi* to spend the night.
pero *m* kind of apple: —*conj* but, yet.
perogrullada *f* truism, platitude.
perol *m* large metal pan.
perro *m* dog.
perseguir *vt* to pursue; to persecute; to chase after.
perseverar *vi* to persevere, persist.
persiana *f* (Venetian) blind.
persistir *vi* to persist.
persona *f* person: —**de ~ a ~** from person to person.
personaje *m* celebrity; character.
persuadir *vt* to persuade: —**se** *vr* to be persuaded.
pertenecer *vi:* —**~ a** to belong to; to appertain, concern.
pértiga *f* long pole or rod.
pertinaz *adj* pertinacious; obstinate.
pertinente *adj* relevant; appropriate.
perturbar *vt* to perturb, disturb.
pervertir *vt* to pervert; to corrupt.
pesa *f* weight.
pesadez *f* heaviness, weight; gravity; slowness; peevishness, fretfulness; trouble; fatigue.
pesadilla *f* nightmare.
pesado/da *adj* peevish; troublesome; cumbersome; tedious; heavy, weighty.
pesar *m* sorrow, grief; repentance: —**a ~ de** in spite of, not withstanding: —*vi* to weigh; to repent: —*vt* to weigh.
pescado *m* fish (in general).
pescar *vt* to fish for, catch (fish): —*vi* to fish.
pescuezo *m* neck.
pésimo/ma *adj* very bad.
peso *m* weight, heaviness; balance scales *pl*.
pesquisa *f* inquiry, examination.
pestaña *f* eyelash.
pestañear *vi* to blink.
pestillo *m* bolt.
petróleo *m* crude oil, petroleum.
pez *m* fish: —*f* pitch.
pezón *m* nipple.
pezuña *f* hoof.
piadoso/sa *adj* pious; mild; merciful; moderate.
piar *vi* to squeak; to chirp.
pibe/ba *m/f* boy/girl.
picado/da *adj* pricked; minced, chopped; bad (tooth); cross.
picante *adj* hot, spicy; racy.
picaporte *m* door handle; latch.
picar *vt* to prick; to sting; to mince; to nibble: —*vi* to prick; to sting; to itch: —**se** *vr* to be piqued; to take offence; to be moth-eaten; to begin to rot.
pícaro/ra *adj* roguish; mischievous, malicious; sly: —*m/f* rogue, knave.
pico *m* beak; bill, nib; peak; pick-ax.
pie *m* foot; leg; basis; trunk (of trees); foundation; occasion: —**a ~** on foot.
piedad *f* piety; mercy, pity.
piedra *f* stone.
piel *f* skin; hide; peel.
pienso *m* fodder.
pierna *f* leg (human).
pieza *f* piece; room.
pila *f* battery; trough; font; sink; pile, heap: —**nombre de ~** first name.

píldora *f* pill.
pileta *f* basin; swimming pool.
pimentón *m* paprika.
pimienta *f* pepper.
pimiento *m* pepper, pimiento.
piña *f* pineapple; fir cone; group.
pincel *m* paintbrush.
pinchar *vt* to prick; to puncture.
pincho *m* thorn; snack.
ping-pong *m* table tennis.
pino *m (bot)* pine.
piñón *m* pine nut; pinion.
pintar *vt* to paint; to picture; to describe; to exagger-ate: —*vi* to paint; *(fam)* to count, to be important: —~**se** *vr* to put on make-up.
pintura *f* painting.
pinza *f* claw; clothes pin; pincers *pl*: —~**s** *fpl* twee-zers *pl.*
piojo *m* louse; troublesome hanger-on.
pipa *f* pipe; sunflower seed.
pipí *m (fam)*: —**hacer ~** to have to go (wee-wee).
piquete *m* prick, jab; hole; *(mil)*squad.
piragua *f* canoe.
piropo *m* compliment; flattery.
pisar *vt* to tread, trample; to stamp on (the ground); to hammer down: —*vi* to tread, walk.
piscina *f* swimming pool.
piso *m* apartment; tread, trampling; floor, sidewalk; floor, story.
pisotear *vt* to trample, tread underfoot.
pista *f* trace, footprint; clue.
pita *f (bot)* agave.
pitar *vt* to blow; to whistle at: —*vi* to whistle; to toot one's horn; to smoke.
pito *m* whistle; horn.
pizarra *f* slate.
pizca *f* mite; pinch.
placa *f* plate; badge.
placer *m* pleasure; delight: —*vt* to please.
plan *m* plan; design; plot; scheme.
plancha *f* plate; iron; gangway.
planear *vt* to plan: —*vi* to glide.
planicie *f* plain.
planificación *f* planning: —~ **familiar** family planning.
plano/na *adj* plain, level, flat: —*m* plan; ground plot, map: —~ **inclinado** *(ferro)* dead level.
plantación *f* plantation.
plantar *vt* to plant; to fix upright; to strike or hit (a blow); to found; to establish: —~**se** *vr* to stand upright.
plantilla *f* personnel; insole of a shoe.
plata *f* silver; plate (wrought silver); cash: —**en ~** briefly.
plátano *m* banana; plane tree.
plateado/da *adj* silvered; plated.
platicar *vi* to converse.
platillo *m* saucer: —~**s** *mpl* cymbals *pl*: —~ **volador/~ volante** flying saucer.
platino *m* platinum: —~**s** *mpl* contact points *pl.*
plato *m* dish; plate.
playa *f* beach.
playera *f* T-shirt: —~**s** *fpl* sneakers *pl.*
plaza *f* square; place; office, employ-ment; room; seat.
plazo *m* term; installment; expiry date.
plegar *vt* to fold; to crease.

pleito *m* contract, bargain; dispute, controversy, debate; lawsuit.
plenilunio *m* full moon.
pleno/na *adj* full; complete: —*m* ple-num.
pliego *m* sheet of paper.
pliegue *m* fold; pleat.
plisado/da *adj* pleated: —*m* pleating.
plomero *m* plumber.
plomo *m* lead: —**a ~** perpendicu-larly.
pluma *f* feather, plume.
población *f* population; town.
pobre *adj* poor.
poco/ca *adj* little, scanty; *(pl)* few: — *adv* little: —~ **a ~** gently; little by little: —*m* small part; little.
podar *vt* to prune.
poder *m* power, authority; command; force: —*vi* to be able to; to possess the power of doing or performing.
podrido/da *adj* rotten, bad; *(fig)*rotten.
poesía *f* poetry.
polea *f* pulley; *(mar)* tackle-block.
polideportivo *m* sports center.
polilla *f* moth.
pollera *f* skirt.
pollo *m* chicken.
polo *m* pole; ice lolly; polo; polo neck.
polvo *m* powder, dust.
pólvora *f* gunpowder.
pomada *f* cream, ointment.
pomelo *m* grapefruit.
pómez *f*: —**piedra ~** pumice stone.
pompa *f* pomp; bubble.
pómulo *m* cheekbone.
poner *vt* to put, place; to put on; to impose; to lay (eggs): —~**se** *vr* to oppose; to set (of stars); to become.
poniente *m* west; west wind.
ponzoña *f* poison.
popa *f (mar)* poop, stern.
por *prep* for; by; about; by means of; through; on account of.
porción *f* part, portion; lot.
porfiar *vt* to dispute obstinately; to persist in a pursuit.
pormenor *f* detail.
poro *m* pore.
porque *conj* because; since; so that.
porquería *f* nastiness, foulness; brut-ishness, rude-ness; trifle; dirty action.
porrón *m* spouted wine jar.
portada *f* portal, porch; frontis-piece.
portaequipajes *m invar* trunk (in car); baggage rack.
portarse *vr* to behave.
portátil *adj* portable.
portavoz *m/f* spokesman/woman.
porte *m* transportation (charges *pl*); deportment, demeanor, conduct.
portero *m* porter, gatekeeper.
porvenir *m* future.
posar *vi* to sit, pose: —*vt* to lay down (a burden): —~**se** *vr* to settle; to perch; to land.
posdata *f* postscript.
poseer *vt* to hold, possess.
posesivo/va *adj* possessive.
posibilitar *vt* to make possible; to make feasible.
poso *m* sediment, dregs *pl.*

posponer *vt* to postpone.

postal *adj* postal: —*f* postcard.

poste *m* post, pillar.

postergar *vt* to leave behind; to post-pone.

posterioridad *f*: —con ~ subse-quently, later.

postigo *m* wicket; postern; shutter.

postizo/za *adj* artificial (not natural): —*m* wig.

postrar *vt* to humble, humiliate: — ~se *vr* to pros-trate oneself.

postre *m* dessert.

postura *f* posture, position; attitude; bet, wager; agreement, conven-tion.

potable *adj* drinkable.

potaje *m* pottage; drink made up of several ingredi-ents; medley of various useless things.

potro/ra *m/f* colt; foal.

pozo *m* well.

practicar *vt* to practice.

práctico/ca *adj* practical; skillful, experienced.

prado *m* lawn; meadow.

precaver *vt* to prevent; to guard against.

preceder *vt* to precede, go before.

preciado/da *adj* esteemed, valued.

precinto *m* seal.

precio *m* price; value.

precioso/sa *adj* precious; (*fam*) beautiful.

precisamente *adv* precisely; exactly.

precisar *vt* to compel, oblige; to need.

preciso/sa *adj* necessary, requisite; precise, accurate; abstracted.

precoz *adj* precocious.

precursor/ra *m/f* harbinger, forerunner.

predecir *vt* to foretell.

predicar *vt* to preach.

predilecto/ta *adj* darling, favorite.

predisponer *vt* to predispose; to prejudice.

predominar *vi* to predominate, prevail.

preferir *vt* to prefer.

pregón *m* proclamation; hue and cry.

preguntar *vt* to ask; to question; to demand; to inquire.

prejuicio *m* prejudgement; preconception; preju-dice.

premiar *vt* to reward, remunerate.

premura *f* pressure, haste, hurry.

preñada *adj* pregnant.

prenda *f* pledge; garment; sweet-heart; person or thing dearly loved: —~s *fpl* accomplishments, talents *pl*.

prender *vt* to seize, catch, lay hold of; to imprison: —~se *vr* to catch fire: — *vi* to take root.

prensar *vt* to press.

preocupar(se) *vt (vr)* to worry.

preparar *vt* to prepare: —~se *vr* to be prepared.

prepucio *m* foreskin.

presa *f* capture, seizure; dike, dam.

presagio *m* omen.

prescindir *vi*: —~ de to do without; to dispense with.

presenciar *vt* to attend; to be present at; to witness.

presentar *vt* to present; to introduce; to offer; to show: —~se *vr* to present oneself; to appear; to run (as candidate); to apply.

presentir *vt* to have a premonition of.

preservativo *m* condom, sheath.

presidiario *m* convict.

presilla *f* clip; loop (in clothes).

presión *f* pressure, pressing.

presionar *vt* to press; (*fig*) to put pressure on.

preso/sa *m/f* prisoner.

prestar *vt* to lend.

presto/ta *adj* quick; prompt; ready: — *adv* soon; quickly.

presumir *vt* to presume, conjecture: —*vi* to be conceited.

presunto/ta *adj* supposed; so-called.

presupuesto *m* presumed cost; bud-get.

pretender *vt* to claim; to try, attempt.

pretendiente *m* pretender; suitor.

pretexto *m* pretext; pretence, excuse.

prevalecer *vi* to prevail; to triumph; to take root.

prevenir *vt* to prepare; to foresee, know in advance; to prevent; to warn: —~se *vr* to be prepared; to be predisposed.

prever *vt* to foresee, forecast.

previo/via *adj* previous.

previsión *f* foresight, prevision; forecast.

prima *f* bonus; (female) cousin.

primario/ria *adj* primary.

primavera *f* spring (the season).

primer(o)/ra *adj* first; prior; former: —*adv* first; rather, sooner.

primicias *f* first fruits *pl*.

primo/ma *m* cousin.

primogénito/ta *adj* , *m/f* first-born.

príncipe *m* prince.

principiante *m* beginner, learner.

principio *m* beginning, commencement; principle.

pringoso/sa *adj* greasy; sticky.

prisa *f* speed; hurry; urgency; promptness.

prismáticos *mpl* binoculars *pl*.

privación *f* deprivation, want.

privado/da *adj* private; particular.

proa *f (mar)* prow.

probador *m* fitting room.

probar *vt* to try; to prove; to taste: —*vi* to try.

probeta *f* test tube.

procedente *adj* reasonable; proper: —~ de com-ing from.

procesador *m*: —~ de textos word processor.

procesar *vt* to put on trial.

procurar *vt* to try; to obtain; to produce.

prodigar *vt* to waste, lavish.

producir *vt* to produce; (*jur*) to pro-duce as evidence: —~se *vr* to come about; to arise; to be made; to break out.

proeza *f* prowess, valor, bravery.

profanar *vt* to profane, desecrate.

profesor/ra *m/f* teacher.

prófugo *m* fugitive.

profundo/da *adj* profound.

programa *m* program(me).

prohibir *vt* to prohibit, forbid; to hinder.

prójimo *m* fellow creature; neigh-bor.

prole *f* offspring, progeny; race.

prolijidad *f* prolixity; minute attention to detail.

prólogo *m* prolog.

promedio *m* average; middle.

prometer *vt* to promise; to assure: —~se *vr* to be-come engaged.

promiscuo/cua *adj* promiscuous; confusedly mingled.

promover *vt* to promote, advance; to stir up.

promulgar *vt* to promulgate, pub-lish.

pronosticar *vt* to predict, foretell; to conjecture.
pronto/ta *adj* prompt; ready: —*adv* promptly.
pronunciamiento *m (jur)* publication; insurrection, sedition.
pronunciar *vt* to pronounce; to deliver: —~se *vr* to rebel.
propaganda *f* propaganda; advertising.
propagar *vt* to propagate.
propasar *vt* to go beyond, exceed.
propenso/sa *adj* prone, inclined.
propiamente *adv* properly; really.
propiciar *vt* to favor; to cause.
propiedad *f* property, possessions *pl;* right of property; propriety.
propina *f* tip.
propio/pia *adj* proper; own; typical; very.
proponer *vt* to propose.
proporcionar *vt* to provide.
propósito *m* aim, purpose: —**a ~** on purpose.
propuesta *f* proposal, offer; representation.
propulsar *vt* to propel; *(fig)* to promote.
prórroga *f* prolongation; extension; extra time.
prorrumpir *vi* to break forth, burst forth.
prosa *f* prose.
proscrito/ta *adj* banned.
proseguir *vt* to continue: —*vi* to continue, go on.
prospección *f* exploration; prospecting.
prosperar *vi* to prosper, thrive.
proteger *vt* protector.
protestar *vt* to protest; to make public declaration (of faith): —*vi* to protest.
provecho *m* profit; advantage.
proveedor/ra *m/f* purveyor, supplier.
provenir *vi* to arise, originate; to issue.
provocar *vt* to provoke; to lead to; to excite.
próximamente *adv* soon.
próximo/ma *adj* next; neighboring; close, nearby.
proyectar *vt* to throw; to cast; to screen; to plan.
prueba *f* proof; reason; argument; to ken; experiment; essay; attempt; relish, taste.
púa *f* sharp point, prickle; shoot; pick.
pubertad *f* puberty.
publicar *vt* to publish; to make public.
publicidad *f* publicity; advertising.
público/ca *adj* public: —*m* public; audi-ence; crowd.
puchero *m* pot; stew.
púdico/ca *adj* chaste, pure.
pudiente *adj* rich, opulent.
pudor *m* bashfulness.
pudrir *vt* to rot, putrefy: —~se *vr* to decay, rot.

pueblo *m* people *pl;* town, village; population; populace.
puente *m* bridge.
puerco/ca *adj* nasty; filthy, dirty; rude, coarse: —*m* pig, hog: —~ **espín** porcupine.
pueril *adj* childish; puerile.
puerro *m* leek.
puerta *f* door; doorway; gateway: — ~ **trasera** back door.
puerto *m* port, harbor; haven; pass.
pues *adv* then; therefore; well: —¡~! well, then.
puesto *m* place; particular spot; post, employment; barracks *pl;* stand.
púgil *m* boxer.
pujante *adj* powerful, strong; robust; stout, strapping.
Pulga *f* flea: —tener malas ~s to be easily piqued; to be ill-tempered.
pulgada *f* inch.
pulgar *m* thumb.
pulir *vt* to polish; to put the last touches to.
pulmón *m* lung.
pulpa *f* pulp; soft part (of fruit).
pulpería *f* small grocery store.
pulpo *m* octopus.
pulsar *vt* to touch; to play; to press.
pulsera *f* bracelet.
pulso *m* pulse; wrist; firmness or steadiness of the hand.
pulular *vi* to swarm.
pulverizador *m* spray gun.
puna *f (med)* mountain sickness.
puñado *m* handful.
puñal *m* dagger.
puño *m* fist; handful; wrist-band; cuff; handle.
punta *f* point; end; trace.
puntada *f* stitch.
puntal *m* prop, stay; buttress.
puntapié *m* kick.
puntería *f* aiming.
puntiagudo/da *adj* sharp-pointed.
puntilla *f* narrow lace edging: —**de ~son** tiptoe.
punto *m* point; end; spot; stitch; full stop.
puntual *adj* punctual; exact; reliable.
punzada *f* prick; sting; pain; compunction.
punzante *adj* sharp.
pupila *f* pupil (of eye).
puro/ra *adj* pure; mere; clear; genuine.
púrpura *f* purple.
purulento/ta *adj* purulent.
puta *f* whore.

Q

que *pn* that; who; which; what: —*conj* that; than.
¿qué? *adj* what?; which?: —*pn* what?; which?.
quebrantar *vt* to break; to crack; to burst; to pound, grind; to violate; to fatigue; to weaken.
quedar *vi* to stay: —~se *vr* to remain.
quedo/da *adj* quiet, still: —*adv* softly, gently.
quejarse *vr* to complain of.
quemar *vt* to burn; to kindle: —~se *vr* to be parched with heat; to burn oneself: —*vi* to be too hot.
querella *f* charge; dispute; complaint.

querer *vt* to want; to desire; to will; to love: —*m* will, desire.
querido/da *adj* dear, beloved: —*m/f* darling; lover: —~ mio, ~da mia my dear, my love, my darling.
queso *m* cheese.
quicio *m* hook, hinge (of a door).
quien *pn* who; whom.
¿quién? *pn* who?; whom?.
quienquiera *adj* whoever.
quieto/ta *adj* still, peaceable.

quilla *f* keel.
química *f* chemistry.
quina *f* Peruvian bark, quinine.
quince *adj*, *m* fifteen; fifteenth.
quincena *f* fortnight.
quinientos/tas *adj* five hundred.
quinta *f* country house; levy, drafting of soldiers.
quinto *adj* fifth: —*m* fifth; drafted soldier.
quiosco *m* bandstand; news stand.

quirúrgico/ca *adj* surgical.
quiste *m* cyst.
quitamanchas *m invar* stain remover.
quitanieves *m invar* snowplough.
quitar *vt* to take away, remove; to take off; to relieve; to annul: —~**se** *vr* to take off (clothes, etc); to withdraw.
quitasol *m* parasol.
quizá/quizás *adv* perhaps.

R

rábano *m* radish.
rabia *f* rage, fury.
rabo *m* tail.
racha *f* gust of wind: —**buena/mala** ~spell of good/bad luck.
racimo *m* bunch of grapes.
radiografía *f* x-ray.
ráfaga *f* gust; flash; burst.
raído/da *adj* scraped; worn-out; impudent.
raíz *f* root; base, basis; origin: — **bienes raices** *mpl* landed prop-erty.
raja *f* splinter, chip (of wood); chink, fissure.
rajatabla *f*: —**a** ~ *adv* strictly.
rallar *vt* to grate.
rama *f* branch (of tree, of family).
ramo *m* branch (of tree).
rampa *f* ramp.
rana *f* frog.
rancho *m* grub; ranch; small farm.
rancio/cia *adj* rank; rancid.
ranura *f* groove; slot.
rapar *vt* to shave; to plunder.
rapaz/za *adj* rapacious: —*m/f* young boy/girl.
rápido/da *adj* quick, rapid, swift.
rapiña *f* robbery.
raptar *vt* to kidnap.
raquítico/ca *adj* stunted; (*fig*) inade-quate.
raro/ra *adj* rare, scarce; extraordi-nary.
ras *m*: —**a** ~ **de** level with: —**a** ~ **de tierra** at ground level.
rascacielos *m invar* skyscraper.
rascar *vt* to scratch, scrape.
rasgar *vt* to tear, rip.
rasgo *m* dash, stroke; grand or mag-nanimous action: —~**s** *mpl* features *pl*.
rasguño *m* scratch.
raso *m* satin; glade: —~/**sa** *adj* plain; flat: —**al** ~ in the open air.
raspa *f* beard (of an ear of corn); backbone (of fish); stalk (of grapes); rasp.
raspar *vt* to scrape, rasp.
rastrear *vt* to trace; to inquire into: — *vi* to skim along close to the ground (of birds).
rastrillo *m* rake.
rastro *m* track; rake; trace.
rata *f* rat.
ratificar *vt* to ratify, confirm.
rato *m* moment: —**a** ~**s perdidos** in leisure time.
ratón *m* mouse.
raya *f* stroke; line; part; frontier; ray (fish); roach (fish).
rayar *vt* to draw lines on; to cross out; to underline; to cross; to rifle.

rayo *m* ray, beam (of light).
raza *f* race, lineage; quality; crack, fissure.
razonar *vi* to reason; to discourse, talk.
reaccionar *vi* to react.
real *adj* real, actual; royal: —*m (mil)* camp.
realidad *f* reality; sincerity.
realizador/ra *m/f* producer (in TV, etc).
realzar *vt* to raise, elevate; to emboss; to heighten.
reanimar *vt* to cheer, encourage; to reanimate.
reanudar *vt* to resume.
rebaja *f* abatement; deduction: —~**s** *fpl* sale.
rebanada *f* slice.
rebaño *m* flock (of sheep), herd (of cattle).
rebasar *vt* to exceed.
rebatir *vt* to resist; to parry, ward off; to refute; to repress.
rebeca *f* cardigan.
rebelarse *vr* to revolt; to rebel; to resist.
rebosar *vi* to run over, overflow; to abound.
rebotar *vt* to bounce; to clinch; to repel: —*vi* to rebound.
rebozar *vt* to wrap up; to fry in batter or bread-crumbs.
rebuznar *vi* to bray.
recado *m* message; errand.
recaída *f* relapse.
recalcar *vt* to stress, emphasize.
recalentar *vt* to heat again; to over-heat.
recambio *m* spare; refill.
recapacitar *vt* to reflect.
recargar *vt* to overload; to recharge; to charge again.
recatado/da *adj* prudent; circum-spect; modest.
recaudar *vt* to gather; to obtain; to recover.
recelo *m* dread; suspicion, mistrust.
receta *f* recipe; prescription.
rechazar *vt* to refuse; to repulse; to contradict.
recibir *vt* to receive, accept; to let in; to go to meet: —~**se** *vr* ~ **de** to qualify as.
recibo *m* receipt.
recién *adv* recently, lately.
reciente *adj* recent; new, fresh; modern.
recio/cia *adj* stout; strong, robust; coarse, thick; rude; arduous, rigid: — *adv* strongly, stoutly: —**hablar** ~ to talk loud.
recipiente *m* container.
reclamación *f* claim; reclamation; protest.
recluir *vt* to shut up.
reclutar *vt* to recruit.
recobrar *vt* to recover: —~**se** *vr* to recover (from sickness).
recodo *m* corner or angle jutting out.
recoger *vt* to collect; to take back; to get; to gather;

to shelter; to compile: —~se *vr* to take shelter or refuge; to retire; to withdraw from the world.

recompensa *f* compensation; recompense, reward.

reconfortar *vt* to comfort.

reconocer *vt* to recognize; to examine closely; to acknowledge; to consider; *(mil)* to reconnoiter.

reconstituyente *m* tonic.

reconversión *f:* —~ **industrial** industrial rationalization.

recopilar *vt* to compile.

recordar *vt* to remember; to remind: —*vi* to remember.

recorrer *vt* to run over, peruse; to cover.

recortar *vt* to cut out.

recostar *vt* to lean, recline: —~se *vr* to lie down.

recoveco *m* cubby hole; bend.

recreo *m* recreation; playtime (school).

recta *f* straight line.

rectángulo/la *adj* rectangular: —*m* rectangle.

rectitud *f* straightness; rectitude; justness, honesty; exactitude.

recto/ta *adj* straight; right; just, honest: —*m* rectum.

rector/ra *m/f* superior of a community or establishment; rector (of a university); curate, rector: —*adj* governing.

recuadro *m* box; inset.

recuento *m* inventory.

recuerdo *m* souvenir; memory.

recuperar *vt* to recover: —~se *vr* to recover (from sickness).

recurrir *vi:* —~ **a** to resort to.

red *f* net; network; snare.

redactar *vt* to draft; to edit.

redada *f:* —~ **policial** police raid.

redimir *vt* to redeem; to ransom.

redoblar *vt* to redouble; to rivet.

redondo/da *adj* round; complete.

reducir *adj* to reduce; to limit: —~se *vr* to diminish.

redundancia *f* superfluity, redun-dancy, excess.

reembolso *m* reimbursement; refund: —**contra ~** C.O.D.

referir *vt* to refer, relate, report: —~se *vr* to refer or relate to.

refinado/da *adj* refined; subtle, artful.

reflejar *vt* to reflect.

reflejo *m* reflex; reflection.

reflujo *m* reflux, ebb: —**flujo y ~** the tides *pl.*

reformar *vt* to reform; to correct; to restore: —~se *vr* to mend; to have one's manners reformed or cor-rected.

reforzar *vt* to strengthen, fortify; to encourage.

refrán *m* proverb.

refrescar *vt* to refresh: —~se *vr* to get cooler; to go out for a breath of fresh air: —*vi* to cool down.

refriega *f* affray, skirmish, fray.

refrigerador *m,* **refrigeradora** *f* refrigerator, fridge.

refuerzo *m* reinforcement.

refugiar *vt* to shelter: —~se *vr* to take refuge.

refunfuñar *vi* to snarl; to growl; to grumble.

regadera *f* watering can.

regalar *vt* to give (as present); to give away; to pamper; to caress.

regaliz *m* licorice.

regalo *m* present, gift; pleasure; com-fort.

regañadientes: —**a ~** *adv* reluctantly.

regañar *vt* to scold: —*vi* to growl; to grumble; to quarrel.

regar *vt* to water, irrigate.

regata *f* irrigation ditch; regatta.

regatear *vt (com)* to bargain over; to be mean with: —*vi* to haggle; to dribble (in sport).

regazo *m* lap.

regentar *vt* to rule; to govern.

régimen *m* regime, management; diet; *(gr)* rules *pl* of verbs.

registrar *vt* to survey; to inspect, examine; to record, enter in a register: —~se *vr* to register; to happen.

regla *f* rule, ruler; period.

reglamentar *vt* to regulate.

regocijar *vt* to gladden: —~se *vr* to rejoice.

regordete *adj* chubby, plump.

regresar *vi* to return, go back.

reguero *m* small rivulet; trickle of spilt liquid; drain, gutter.

regular *vt* to regulate, adjust: —*adj* regular; ordinary.

rehén *m* hostage.

rehuir *vt* to avoid.

rehusar *vt* to refuse, decline.

reimpresión *f* reprint.

reina *f* queen.

reincidir *vi:* —~ **en** to relapse into, fallback into.

reino *m* kingdom, reign.

reintegrar *vt* to reintegrate, restore: —~se *vr* to be reinstated or restored.

reír(se) *vi (vr)* to laugh.

reiterar *vt* to reiterate, repeat.

reivindicar *vt* to claim.

reja *f* ploughshare; lattice, grating.

rejoneador *m* mounted bullfighter.

relación *f* relation; relationship; report; account.

relajar *vt* to relax, slacken: —~se *vr* to relax.

relamerse *vr* to lick one's lips; to relish.

relámpago *m* flash of lightning.

relatar *vt* to relate, tell.

relato *m* story; recital.

relegar *vt* to relegate; to banish, exile.

relente *m* evening dew.

relieve *m* relief; *(fig)* prominence.

relinchar *vi* to neigh.

reliquia *f* residue, remains *pl;* (saintly) relic.

rellano *m* landing (of stairs).

rellenar *vt* to fill up; to stuff.

reloj *m* clock; watch.

relucir *vi* to shine, glitter; to excel, be brilliant.

relumbrar *vi* to sparkle, shine.

remachar *vt* to rivet; *(fig)* to drive home.

remache *m* rivet; clinch; obstinacy.

remanente *m* remainder; *(com)* balance; surplus.

remanso *m* stagnant water; quiet place.

remar *vi* to row.

rematar *vt* to terminate, finish; to sell off cheaply: —*vi* to end.

remedar *vt* to copy, imitate; to mimic.

remediar *vt* to remedy; to assist, help; to free from danger; to avoid.

remesa *f* shipment; remittance.

remilgado/da *adj* prim; affected.

remitente *m* sender.

remojar *vt* to steep; to dunk.

remolacha *f* beet.

remolcar *vt* to tow.

remordimiento *m* remorse.

remoto/ta *adj* remote, distant; far.
remover *vt* to stir; to move around.
remozar *vt* to rejuvenate; to renovate.
renacer *vi* to be born again; to revive.
renacuajo *m* tadpole.
rendija *f* crevice, crack, cleft.
rendir *vt* to subject, subdue: ——**se** *vr* to yield; to surrender; to be tired out.
renegar *vt* to deny; to disown; to detest, abhor: —*vi* to apostatize; to blaspheme, curse.
renglón *m* line; item.
reñir *vt* , *vi* to wrangle, quarrel; to scold, chide.
renombre *m* renown.
renovar *vt* to renew; to renovate; to reform.
renta *f* income; rent; profit.
reo *m* offender, criminal.
reparar *vt* to repair; to consider, observe; to parry: —*vi* ~ **en** to notice; to pass (at cards).
repartir *vt* to distribute; to deliver.
repasar *vt* to revise; to check; to mend.
repente: —de ~ *adv* suddenly.
repercutir *vi* to reverberate; to rebound.
repetir *vt* , *vi* to repeat.
repiquetear *vi* to ring merrily.
repisa *f* pedestal, stand; shelf; windowsill.
repleto/ta *adj* replete, very full.
replicar *vi* to reply.
repoblar *vt* to repopulate; to reafforest.
repollo *m* cabbage.
reponer *vt* to replace; to restore: ——**se** *vr* to recover lost health or property.
reportaje *m* report, article.
reposar *vi* to rest, repose.
repostería *f* confectioner's (store).
reprender *vt* to reprimand.
represa *f* dam; lake.
representar *vt* to represent; to play on the stage; to look (age).
reprimir *vt* to repress; to check; to contain.
reprobable *adj* reprehensible.
reprochar *vt* to reproach.
repuesto *m* supply; spare part.
repugnancia *f* reluctance; repugnance; disgust.
requerir *vt* to intimate, notify; to request; to require, need; to summon.
requesón *m* cottage cheese.
requiebro *m* endearing expression.
res *f* head of cattle.
resabio *m* (unpleasant) aftertaste; vicious habit, bad custom.
resaca *f* surge, surf; (*fig*) backlash; (*fam*) hangover.
resaltar *vi* to rebound; to jut out; to be evident; to stand out.
resbaladizo/za *adj* slippery.
resbalar(se) *vi* (*vr*) to slip, slide.
rescindir *vt* to rescind, annul.
rescoldo *m* embers *pl,* cinders *pl.*
resecarse *vr* to dry up.
reseña *f* review; account.
resentirse *vr:* —— **de** to suffer: —— **con** to resent.
reservar *vt* to keep; to reserve: ——**se** *vr* to preserve oneself; to keep to oneself.
resfriado *m* cold.
resguardar *vt* to preserve, defend: — ~**se** *vr* to be on one's guard.
residir *vi* to reside, dwell.
residuo *m* residue, remainder.

resistir *vt* to resist, oppose; to put up with: —*vi* to resist; to hold out.
resol *m* glare (of the sun).
resollar *vi* to wheeze; to take breath.
resolver *vt* to resolve, decide; to anal-yse: ——**se** *vr* to resolve, determine.
resoplar *vi* to snore; to snort.
resorte *m* spring.
respaldo *m* backing; endorsement; back of a seat.
respetar *vt* to respect; to revere.
respingo *m* start; jump.
respiradero *m* vent, breathing hole; rest, repose.
respirar *vi* to breathe.
resplandecer *vi* to shine; to glisten.
resplandor *m* splendor, brilliance.
responder *vt* to answer: —*vi* to answer; to corre-spond: —— **de** to be responsible for.
responso *m* prayer for the dead.
respuesta *f* answer, reply.
resquemor *m* resentment.
restablecer *vt* to re-establish: ——**se** *vr* to recover.
restallar *vi* to crack; to click.
restar *vt* to subtract, take away: —*vi* to be left.
restaurar *vt* to restore.
restituir *vt* to restore; to return.
resto *m* remainder, rest.
restregar *vt* to scrub, rub.
restringir *vt* to restrict, limit; to restrain.
resuelto/ta *adj* resolute, determined; prompt.
resultar *vi* to be; to turn out; to amount to.
resumir *vt* to abridge; to summarize.
retahíla *f* range, series.
retal *m* remnant.
retar *vt* to challenge.
retener *vt* to retain, keep back.
retentiva *f* memory.
retirar *vt* to withdraw, retire; to remove: ——**se** *vr* to retire, retreat; to go to bed.
reto *m* challenge; threat, menace.
retocar *vt* to retouch; to mend; to finish off (work).
retoñar *vi* to sprout.
retorcer *vt* to twist; to wring.
retozar *vi* to frisk, skip.
retraído/da *adj* shy.
retransmitir *vt* to broadcast; to relay; to retransmit.
retraso *m* delay; slowness; back-wardness; lateness: —(*ferro*) **el tren ha tenido** ~ the train is overdue or late.
retrato *m* portrait, effigy.
retrete *m* lavatory.
retribuir *vt* to repay.
retroceder *vi* to go backwards, fly back; to back down.
retrovisor *m* rear-view mirror.
retumbar *vi* to resound, jingle.
reúma *f* rheumatism.
reunir *vt* to reunite; to unite: ——**se** *vr* to gather, meet.
revancha *f* revenge.
revelar *vt* to reveal; to develop (pho-tographs).
reventar *vi* to burst, crack; to explode; to toil, drudge.
reverdecer *vi* to grow green again; to revive.
revés *m* back; wrong side; disappoint-ment, setback.
revisar *vt* to revise, review.
revisor *m* inspector; ticket collector.
revista *f* review, revision; magazine.

revolcarse *vr* to wallow.

revolotear *vi* to flutter.

revoltijo *m* confusion, disorder.

revoltoso/sa *adj* rebellious, unruly.

revolver *vt* to move about; to turnaround; to mess up; to revolve; ~**se** *vr* to turn round; to change (of the weather).

revuelta *f* turn; disturbance, revolt.

rey *m* king; king (in cards or chess).

rezagar *vt* to leave behind; to defer: ——**se** *vr* to remain behind.

rezar *vi* to pray, say one's prayers.

rezumar *vt* to ooze, leak.

ría *f* estuary.

riada *f* flood.

ribera *f* shore, bank.

rico/ca *adj* rich; delicious; lovely; cute.

riego *m* irrigation.

rienda *f* rein of a bridle: —**dar** ~**suelta** to give free rein to.

riesgo *m* risk, danger.

rifa *f* raffle, lottery.

rígido/da *adj* rigid, inflexible; severe.

riguroso/sa *adj* rigorous.

rimar *vi* to rhyme.

rímel, rimmel *m* mascara.

riña *f* quarrel, dispute.

rincón *m* (inside) corner.

rinoceronte *m* rhinoceros.

riñón *m* kidney.

río *m* river, stream.

riqueza *f* riches *pl*, wealth.

risa *f* laugh, laughter.

risco *m* steep rock.

ritmo *m* rhythm.

rizo *m* curl; ripple (on water).

robar *vt* to rob; to steal; to break into.

roble *m* oak tree.

robusto/ta *adj* robust, strong.

roca *f* rock.

rociar *vt* to sprinkle; to spray.

rocío *m* dew.

rodaja *f* slice.

rodaje *m* filming: —**en** ~ (*auto*) running in.

rodear *vi* to make a detour: —*vt* to surround, enclose.

rodilla *f* knee: —**de** ~**s** on one's knees.

rodillo *m* roller; rolling pin.

roer *vt* to gnaw; to corrode.

rogar *vt* , *vi* to ask for; to beg, entreat; to pray.

rojizo/za *adj* reddish.

rojo/ja *adj* red; ruddy.

rol *m* list, roll, catalog; role.

rollo *m* roll; coil.

romería *f* pilgrimage.

romero *m* (*bot*) rosemary.

rompecabezas *m invar* riddle; jigsaw.

romper *vt* to break; to tear up; to wear out; to break up (land): —*vi* to break (of waves); to break through.

ron *m* rum.

roña *f* scab, mange; grime; rust.

roncar *vi* to snore; to roar.

ronco/ca *adj* hoarse; husky; raucous.

ronda *f* night patrol; round (of drinks, cards, etc).

ronronear *vi* to purr.

ropa *f* clothes *pl;* clothing; dress.

rosa *f* rose; birthmark.

rosado/da *adj* pink; rosy.

rosca *f* thread (of a screw); coil, spiral.

rosquilla *f* doughnut.

rostro *m* face.

roto/ta *adj* broken, destroyed; debauched.

rótula *f* kneecap; ball-and-socket joint.

rotulador *m* felt-tip pen.

rótulo *m* inscription; label, ticket; placard, poster.

rotundo/da *adj* round; emphatic.

rozar *vt* to rub; to chafe; to nibble (the grass); to scrape; to touch lightly.

rubio/bia *adj* fair-haired, blond(e): — *m/f* blond/ blonde.

rudimento *m* principle; beginning: ——**s** *mpl* rudiments *pl*.

rudo/da *adj* rough, coarse; plain, simple; stupid.

rueda *f* wheel; circle; slice, round.

ruedo *m* rotation; border, selvage; arena, bullring.

ruego *m* request, entreaty.

rufián *m* pimp, pander; lout.

rugir *vi* to roar, bellow.

rugoso/sa *adj* wrinkled.

ruido *m* noise, sound; din, row; fuss.

ruin *adj* mean, despicable; stingy.

ruina *f* ruin, collapse; downfall, destruction: ——**s** *fpl* ruins *pl*.

ruiseñor *m* nightingale.

rulo *m* curler.

rumbo *m* (*mar*) course, bearing; road, route, way; course of events, pomp, ostentation.

rumboso/sa *adj* generous, lavish.

rústico/ca *adj* rustic: —*m/f* peasant.

ruta *f* route, itinerary.

rutina *f* routine; habit.

S

sábado *m* Saturday; (*j*ewish) Sabbath.

sábana *f* sheet; altar cloth.

sabañón *m* chilblain.

sabelotodo *m/f invar* know-all.

saber *vt* to know; to be able to; to find out, learn; to experience: —*vi*- **a** to taste of: —*m* learning, knowledge.

sabiduría *f* learning, knowledge; wis-dom.

sabio/bia *adj* sage, wise: —*m/f* sage, wise person.

sablazo *m* sword wound; (*fam*) sponging, scrounging.

sabor *m* taste, savor, flavor.

sabroso/sa *adj* tasty, delicious; pleas-ant; salted.

sabueso *m* bloodhound.

sacacorchos *m invar* corkscrew.

sacapuntas *m invar* pencil sharpener.

sacar *vt* to take out, extract; to get out; to bring out (a book etc); to takeoff (clothes); to receive, get; (*dep*) to serve.

sacerdote *m* priest.

saco *m* bag, sack; jacket.

sacudir *vt* to shake, jerk; to beat, hit.
sagaz *adj* shrewd, clever, sagacious.
sagrado/da *adj* sacred, holy.
sal *f* salt.
sala *f* large room; *(teat)* house, audito-rium; public hall; *(jur)* court; *(med)* ward.
salado/da *adj* salted; witty, amusing.
salario *m* salary.
salchicha *f* sausage.
salchichón *m* (salami-type) sausage.
saldo *m* settlement; balance; remain-der: —**s** *mpl* sale.
salida *f* exit, way out; leaving, depar-ture; production, output; *(com)* sale; sales outlet.
saliente *adj* projecting; rising; *(fig)* outstanding.
salir *vi* to go out, leave; to depart, set out; to appear; to turn out, prove: — **~se** *vr* to escape, leak.
salmo *m* psalm.
salmonete *m* red mullet.
salmuera *f* brine.
salón *m* living room, lounge; public hall.
salpicadero *m* dashboard.
salpicar *vt* to sprinkle, splash, spatter.
salsa *f* sauce.
saltamontes *m invar* grasshopper.
saltar *vt* to jump, leap; to skip, miss out: —*vi* to leap, jump; to bounce; *(fig)* to explode, blow up.
saltimbanqui *m/f* acrobat.
salubre *adj* healthy.
salud *f* health.
saludar *vt* to greet; *(mil)* to salute.
salvado *m* bran.
salvaguardar *vt* to safeguard.
salvaje *adj* savage.
salvar *vt* to save; to rescue; to overcome; to cross, jump across; to cover, travel; to exclude: —**~se** *vr* to escape from danger.
salvavidas *adj invar*: —**bote/chaleco/cinturón ~** lifeboat/life preserver/life belt.
salvia *f (bot)* sage.
salvo/va *adj* safe: —*adv* save, except (for).
San *adj* Saint (as title).
saña *f* anger, passion.
sanar *vt* , *vi* to heal.
sandalia *f* sandal.
sandez *f* folly, stupidity.
sandía *f* watermelon.
sangre *f* blood: —**a ~ fria** in cold blood: —**a ~ y fuego** without mercy.
sangriento/ta *adj* bloody, bloodstained, gory; cruel.
sano/na *adj* healthy, fit; intact, sound.
sapo *m* toad.
saquear *vt* to ransack, plunder.
sarampión *m* measles.
sarna *f* itch; mange; *(med)* scabies.
sarpullido *m (med)* rash.
sarro *m (med)* tartar.
sarta *f* string of beads, etc; string, row.
sartén *f* frying pan.
sastre *m* tailor.
satisfacer *vt* to satisfy; to pay (a debt): —**~se** *vr* to satisfy oneself; to take revenge.
sauce *m (bot)* willow.
saúco *m (bot)* elder.
savia *f* sap.
sazonar *vt* to ripen; to season.
se *pn reflexivo* himself; herself; itself; yourself; themselves; yourselves; each other; one another; oneself.
se(p)tiembre *m* September.
sebo *m* fat, grease.
secano *m* dry, arable land which is not irrigated.
secar *vt* to dry: —**~se** *vr* to dry up; to dry oneself.
seco/ca *adj* dry; dried up; skinny; cold (of character); brusque, sharp; bare.
secuestrar *vt* to kidnap; to confis-cate.
sed *f* thirst: —**tener ~** to be thirsty.
seda *f* silk.
sedal *m* fishing line.
sede *f* see; seat; headquarters.
sediento/ta *adj* thirsty; eager.
seducir *vt* to seduce; to bribe; to charm, attract.
segar *vt* to reap, harvest; to mow.
seguido/da *adj* continuous; successive; long-lasting: —*adv* straight (on); after; often.
seguir *vt* to follow, pursue; to continue: —*vi* to follow; to carry on: —**~se** *vr* to follow, ensue.
según *prep* according to.
segundo/da *adj* second: —*m* second (of time).
seguro/ra *adj* safe, secure; sure, certain; firm, constant: —*adv* for sure: — *m* safety device; insurance; safety, certainty.
seis *adj* , *m* six; sixth.
seiscientos/tas *adj* six hundred.
seísmo *m* earthquake.
sello *m* seal; stamp.
seleccionar *vt* to select, chose, pick.
selectivo *adj* selective.
selva *f* forest.
semáforo *m* traffic lights *pl;* signal.
semana *f* week.
sembrar *vt* to sow; to sprinkle, scatter.
semejante *adj* similar, like: —*m* fellowman.
semestral *adj* half-yearly.
semilla *f* seed.
sémola *f* semolina.
sempiterno/na *adj* everlasting.
seña *f* sign, mark, token; signal; *(mil)* password: —**s** *fpl* address.
señal *f* sign, token; symptom; signal; landmark; *(com)* deposit.
señalar *vt* to stamp, mark; to signpost; to point out; to fix, settle: —**~se** *vr* to distinguish oneself, excel.
sencillo/lla *adj* simple; natural; unaffected; single.
senda *f,* **sendero** *m* path, trail.
seno *m* bosom; lap; womb; hole, cavity; sinus: —**s** *mpl* breasts *pl.*
señor *m* man; gentleman; master; Mr; sir.
señora *f* lady; Mrs; madam; wife.
señorita *f* Miss; young lady.
señorito *m* young gentleman; rich kid.
sensación *f* sensation, feeling; sense.
sensato/ta *adj* sensible.
sensible *adj* sensitive; perceptible, appreciable; regrettable.
sentado/da *adj* sitting, seated; sedate; settled.
sentar *vt* to seat; *(fig)* to establish: —*vi* to suit: —**~se** *vr* to sit down.
sentido *m* sense; feeling; meaning: — **~/da** *adj* regrettable; sensitive.
sentir *vt* to feel; to hear; to perceive; to sense; to suffer from; to regret, be sorry for: —**~se** *vr* to feel; to feel pain; to crack (of walls, etc): —*m* opinion, judgement.

separar *vt* to separate: —**~se** *vr* to separate; to come away, come apart; to withdraw.
septentrional *adj* north, northern.
séptimo/ma *adj* seventh.
sepultar *vt* to bury, inter.
sequía *f* dryness; thirst; drought.
séquito *m* retinue, suite; group of sup-porters; aftermath.
ser *vi* to be; to exist: —**~ de** to come from; to be made of; to belong to: — *m* being.
serenata *f (mus)* serenade.
sereno *m* night watchman: —**~/na** *adj* serene, calm, quiet.
serie *f* series; sequence.
serio/ria *adj* serious; grave; reliable.
serpentear *vi* to wriggle; to wind, snake.
serpiente *f* snake.
serranía *f* range of mountains; moun-tainous country.
serrar *vt* to saw.
serrín *m* sawdust.
servicial *adj* helpful, obliging.
servilleta *f* napkin, serviette.
servir *vt* to serve; to wait on: —*vi* to serve; to be of use; to be in service: —**~se** *vr* to serve oneself, help oneself; to deign, please; to make use of.
sesenta *m, adj* sixty; sixtieth.
seso *m* brain.
sestear *vi* to take a nap.
seta *f* mushroom.
setecientos/tas *adj* seven hundred.
setenta *adj, m* seventy.
setiembre *m* September.
seto *m* fence; enclosure; hedge.
severo/ra *adj* severe, strict; grave, serious.
sexto/ta *adj, m* sixth.
si *conj* whether; if.
sí *adv* yes; certainly; indeed: —*pn* oneself; himself; herself; itself; yourself; themselves; yourselves; each other; one another.
siderúrgico/ca *adj* iron and steel *compd:* —*f* **la side-rúrgica** the iron and steel industry.
sidra *f* cider.
siempre *adv* always; all the time; ever; still: —**jamás** for ever and ever.
sien *f* temple (of the head).
sierra *f* saw; range of mountains.
siete *adj, m* seven.
sigilo *m* secrecy.
sigla *f* acronym; abbreviation.
siglo *m* century.
significado *m* significance, meaning.
significativo/va *adj* significant.
signo *m* sign, mark.
siguiente *adj* following, successive, next.
silbar *vt, vi* to hiss; to whistle.
silencio *m* silence: —¡~! silence! quiet!
silla *f* chair; saddle; seat: —**~ de ruedas** wheelchair.
silo *m* silo; underground wheat store.
silueta *f* silhouette; outline; figure.
silvestre *adj* wild, uncultivated; rustic.
símbolo *m* symbol.
simio *m* ape.
simpático/ca *adj* pleasant; kind.
simpatizar *vi:* —**~ con** to get on well with.
simular *vt* to simulate.
sin *prep* without.

sindicato *m* trade(s) union; syndicate.
sinfín *m:* —**un ~ de** a great many.
singular *adj* singular; exceptional; peculiar, odd.
siniestro/tra *adj* left; *(fig)* sinister: —*m* accident.
sino *conj* but; except; save; only: —*m* fate.
sinsabor *m* unpleasantness; disgust.
sinuoso/sa *adj* sinuous; wavy; winding.
sinvergüenza *m/f* rogue.
siquiera *conj* even if, even though: —*adv* at least.
sitio *m* place; spot; site, location; room, space; job, post; *(mil)* siege, blockade.
situar *vt* to place, situate; to invest: — **~se** *vr* to be established in place or business.
smoking *m* tuxedo.
sobaco *m* armpit, armhole.
sobar *vt* to handle, soften; to knead; to massage, rub hard; to rumple (clothes); to fondle.
soberbia *f* pride, haughtiness; magni-ficence.
sobornar *vt* to suborn, bribe.
sobrante *adj* remaining: —*m* surplus, remainder.
sobrar *vt* to exceed, surpass: —*vi* to be more than enough; to remain, be left.
sobre *prep* on; on top of; above, over; more than; besides: —*m* envelope.
sobrecargar *vt* to overload; *(com)* to surcharge.
sobredosis *f* overdose.
sobreentender *vt* to deduce: —**~se** *vr* **se sobreen-tiende que .**

it is implied that.
sobrellevar *vt* to carry; to tolerate.
sobremesa *f:* —**de ~** immediately after dinner.
sobrenombre *m* nickname.
sobrepasar *vt* to surpass.
sobresalto *m* start, scare; sudden shock.
sobrevenir *vi* to happen, come unexpectedly; to supervene.
sobrevivir *vi* to survive.
sobrevolar *vt* to fly over.
sobrino/na *m/f* nephew/niece.
sobrio/ria *adj* sober, frugal.
socarrón/ona *adj* sarcastic; ironic(al).
socavar *vt* to undermine.
socio/cia *m/f* associate, member.
socorrista *m/f* first aider; lifeguard.
socorro *m* help, aid, assistance, relief.
soez *adj* dirty, obscene.
sofá *m* sofa.
soga *f* rope.
soja *f* soya.
sol *m* sun; sunshine, sunlight.
solamente *adv* only, solely.
solapa *f* lapel.
solar *m* building site; piece of land; ancestral home of a family: —*adj* solar.
soldado *m/f* soldier: —**~ raso** private.
soldar *vt* to solder; to weld; to unite.
soledad *f* solitude; loneliness.
soler *vi* to be accustomed to, be in the habit of.
solicitar *vt* to ask for, seek; to apply for (a job); to canvass for; to chase after, pursue.
solidario/ria *adj* joint; mutually bind-ing.
soliloquio *m* soliloquy, monologue.
solista *m/f* soloist.
solitario/ria *adj* solitary: —*m* soli-taire: —*m/f* hermit.

sollozar *vi* to sob.

solo *m (mus)* solo: —**~la** *adj* alone, single: —**a solas** alone, unaided.

sólo *adv* only.

solomillo *m* sirloin.

soltar *vt* to untie, loosen; to set free, let out: —**~se** *vr* to get loose; to come undone.

soltero/ra *m/f* bachelor/singlewoman: —*adj* single, unmarried.

soltura *f* looseness, slackness; agility, activity; fluency.

solucionar *vt* to solve; to resolve.

sombra *f* shade; shadow.

sombrero *m* hat.

sombrilla *f* parasol.

sombrío/bría *adj* shady, gloomy; sad.

somero/ra *adj* superficial.

someter *vt* to conquer (a country); to subject to one's will; to submit; to subdue: —**~se** *vr* to give in, submit.

somnífero *m* sleeping pill.

sonar *vt* to ring: —*vi* to sound; to make a noise; to be pronounced; to be talked of; to sound familiar: —**~se** *vr* to blow one's nose.

soñar *vt , vi* to dream.

sondeo *m* sounding; boring; *(fig)*poll.

soneto *m* sonnet.

sonido *m* sound.

sonreír(se) *vi (vr)* to smile.

sonrisa *f* smile.

sonrojarse *vr* to blush.

sonsacar *vt* to wheedle; to cajole; to obtain by cunning.

sopa *f* soup; sop.

sopetón *m*: —**de ~** suddenly.

soplar *vt* to blow away, blow off; to blow up, inflate: —*vi* to blow, puff.

soplón/ona *m/f* telltale.

soportal *m* portico.

soportar *vt* to suffer, tolerate; to support.

sorber *vt* to sip; to inhale; to swallow; to absorb.

sorbete *m* sherbet; iced fruit drink.

sordo/da *adj* deaf; silent, quiet: —*m/f* deaf person.

sorprender *vt* to surprise.

sorteo *m* draw; raffle.

sortija *f* ring; ringlet, curl.

sortilegio *m* sorcery.

sosegar *vt* to appease, calm: —*vi* to rest.

soso/sa *adj* insipid, tasteless; dull.

sospechar *vt* to suspect.

sostén *m* support; bra; sustenance.

sostener *vt* to sustain, maintain: —**~se** *vr* to support or maintain oneself; to contrive, remain.

sota *f* knave (at cards).

sótano *m* basement, cellar.

su *pn* his, her, its, one's; their; your.

suave *adj* smooth, soft; delicate; gentle; mild, meek.

subalterno/na *adj* secondary; auxiliary.

subasta *f* auction.

subcampeón/ona *m/f* runner-up.

subestimar *vt* to underestimate.

subir *vt , vi* to raise, lift up; to go up; to climb, ascend, mount; to increase, swell; to get in, get on, board; to rise (in price).

súbito/ta *adj* sudden, hasty; unfore-seen.

sublevar *vt* to excite (a rebellion); to incite (a revolt): —**~se** *vr* to revolt.

submarino/na *adj* underwater: —*m* submarine.

subrayar *vt* to underline.

subsanar *vt* to excuse; to mend, repair; to overcome.

subsidio *m* subsidy, aid; benefit, allow-ance.

su(b)stancia *f* substance.

su(b)straer *vt* to remove; *(mat)* to subtract: —**~se** *vr* to avoid; to withdraw.

subterráneo/nea *adj* subterraneán; underground: —*m* underground passage; *(ferro)* underground (rail-way).

suburbio *m* slum quarter; suburbs *pl*.

subvencionar *vt* to subsidize.

sucedáneo/nea *adj* substitute: —*m* substitute (food).

suceder *vt* to succeed, inherit: —*vi* to happen.

suceso *m* event; incident.

sucesor/ra *m/f* successor; heir.

sucio/cia *adj* dirty, filthy; obscene; dishonest.

sucursal *f* branch (office).

sudar *vt , vi* to sweat.

sudeste *adj* southeast, southeastern: —*m* southeast.

sudoeste *adj* southwest, southwest-ern: —*m* southwest.

suegra *f* mother-in-law.

suegro *m* father-in-law.

suela *f* sole of the shoe.

sueldo *m* wages *pl*, salary.

suelo *m* ground; floor; soil, surface.

suelto/ta *adj* loose; free; detached; swift: —*m* loose change.

sueño *m* sleep; dream.

suero *m (med)* serum; whey.

suerte *f* fate, destiny, chance, lot, fortune, good luck; kind, sort.

sufrir *vt* to suffer; to bear, put up with; to support.

sugerir *vt* to suggest.

sujetador *m* fastener; bra.

sujetar *vt* to fasten, hold down; to subdue; to subject: —**~se** *vr* to subject oneself.

sujeto/ta *adj* fastened, secure; subject, liable: —*m* subject; individual.

sumamente *adv* extremely.

sumar *vt* to add, add up; to collect, gather: —*vi* to add up.

sumergir *vt* to submerge, sink; to immerse.

sumidero *m* sewer, drain.

suministrar *vt* to supply, furnish.

sumiso/sa *adj* submissive, docile.

sumo/ma *adj* great, extreme; highest, greatest: —**a lo ~** at most.

súper *f* four-star (gas).

superar *vt* to surpass; to overcome; to exceed, go beyond.

superficial *adj* superficial; shallow.

superficie *f* surface; area.

superintendente *m/f* superintendent, supervisor; floorwalker.

superior *adj* superior; upper; higher; better: —*m/f* superior.

supermercado *m* supermarket.

superviviente *m/f* survivor: —*adj* surviving.

suplente *m/f* substitute.

suplicar *vt* to beg (for), plead (for); to beg; to plead with.

suplicio *m* torture.

suplir *vt* to supply; to make good, make up for; to replace.

suponer *vt* to suppose: —*vi* to have authority.
suprimir *vt* to suppress; to abolish; to remove; to delete.
supuesto *m* assumption: —~/ta *adj* supposed: —~que *conj* since, granted that.
sur *adj* south, southern: —*m* south; south wind.
surco *m* furrow; groove.
surgir *vi* to emerge; to crop up.
surtido *m* assortment, supply.
surtir *vt* to supply, furnish, provide: — *vi* to spout, spurt.
suscitar *vt* to excite, stir up.
susodicho/cha *adj* above-men-tioned.
suspender *vt* to suspend, hang up; to stop; to fail (an exam etc).
suspicaz *adj* suspicious, mistrustful.
suspirar *vi* to sigh.
sustentar *vt* to sustain; to support, nourish.
susto *m* fright, scare.
sustraer *vt* to take away; to sub-tract.
susurrar *vi* to whisper; to murmur; to rustle: —~se *vr* to be whispered about.
sutil *adj* subtle; thin; delicate; very soft; keen, observant.
suyo/ya *adj* his; hers; theirs; one's; his; her; its own; one's own; their own: —**de** ~ per se: —**los** ~**s** *mpl* his own, near friends, relations, family, supporters.

T

tabaco *m* tobacco; (*fam*) cigarettes *pl*.
tabique *m* thin wall; partition wall.
tabla *f* board; shelf; plank; slab; index of a book; bed of earth in a garden.
tablero *m* plank, board; chessboard; dashboard; bulletin board; gambling den.
taburete *m* stool.
tacaño/ña *adj* mean, stingy; crafty.
tachar *vt* to find fault with; to erase.
tachuela *f* tack, nail.
tácito/ta *adj* tacit, silent; implied.
taco *m* stopper, plug; heel (of a shoe); wad; book of coupons; billiard cue.
tacón *m* heel.
tacto *m* touch, feeling; tact.
tahona *f* bakery.
taimado/da *adj* sly, cunning, crafty.
tajo *m* cut, incision; cleft, sheer drop; working area; chopping block.
tal *adj* such: —**con ~ que** provided that: —**no hay** ~ no such thing.
taladro *m* drill; borer, gimlet.
talante *m* mood; appearance; aspect; will.
talar *vt* to fell (trees); to desolate.
talega *f*, **talego** *m* bag; bagful.
talla *f* raised work; sculpture; stature, size; measure (of anything); hand, draw, turn (at cards).
tallar *vt* to cut, chop; to carve in wood; to engrave; to measure.
taller *m* workshop, laboratory.
tallo *m* shoot, sprout.
talón *m* heel; receipt; cheque.
tamaño *m* size, shape, bulk.
tambalearse *vr* to stagger, waver.
también *adv* also, as well; likewise; besides.
tambor *m* drum; drummer; ear-drum.
tamiz *m* fine sieve.
tampoco *adv* neither, nor.
tan *adv* so.
tanto *m* certain sum or quantity; point; goal: —~/ta *adj* so much, as much; very great: —*adv* so much, as much; so long, as long.
tapar *vt* to stop up, cover; to conceal, hide.
tapia *f* wall.
tapicería *f* tapestry; upholstery; upholsterer's (store).
tapiz *m* tapestry; carpet.

tapón *m* cork, plug, bung.
taquigrafía *f* shorthand.
taquilla *f* booking office; takings *pl*.
tardar *vi* to delay; to take a long time; to be late.
tarde *f* afternoon; evening: —*adv* late.
tarea *f* task.
tarima *f* platform; step.
tarjeta *f* card; visiting card: — ~ **postal** postcard.
tarro *m* pot.
tarta *f* cake.
tartamudear *vi* to stutter, stammer.
tarugo *m* wooden peg or pin.
tasar *vt* to appraise, value.
tatarabuelo/la *m/f* great-great-grandfather/mother.
tataranieto/ta *m/f* great-great-grandson/daughter.
tatuaje *m* tattoo; tattooing.
taurino/na *adj* bullfighting *compd*.
taza *f* cup; basin of a fountain.
te *pn* you.
té *m* (*bot*) tea.
teatro *m* theater, playhouse.
tebeo *m* comic.
techo *m* roof; ceiling.
tecla *f* key (of an organ, piano, etc).
técnico/ca *adj* technical.
tedio *m* boredom; dislike, abhorrence.
tejado *m* roof covered with tiles.
tejer *vt* to weave.
tejo *m* quoit; yew tree.
tejón *m* badger.
tela *f* cloth; material.
telaraña *f* cobweb.
telefax *m invar* fax; fax (machine).
televisor *m* television set.
telón *m* curtain, drape.
tema *m* theme.
temblar *vi* to tremble.
temer *vt* to fear, doubt: —*vi* to be afraid.
temerario/ria *adj* rash.
temible *adj* dreadful, terrible.
témpano *m* ice-floe.
templado/da *adj* temperate, tempered.
templar *vt* to temper, moderate, cool; to tune: —~se *vr* to be moderate.
temple *m* temperature; tempera; temperament; tuning: —**al** ~ painted in distemper.
temporada *f* time, season; epoch, period.

temprano/na *adj* early, anticipated: —*adv* early; very early, prematurely.
tenaz *adj* tenacious; stubborn.
tenaza(s) *f (pl)* tongs *pl*, pincers *pl*.
tender *vt* to stretch out; to expand; to extend; to hang out; to lay: —~se *vr* to stretch oneself out.
tendero/ra *m/f* shop-keeper.
tendón *m* tendon, sinew.
tenebroso/sa *adj* dark, obscure.
tenedor *m* holder, keeper, tenant; fork.
tener *vt* to have; to take; to hold; to possess: —~se *vr* to stand upright; to stop, halt; to resist; to adhere.
tenia *f* tapeworm.
teñir *vt* to tinge, dye.
tensar *vt* to tauten; to draw.
tentar *vt* to touch; to try; to tempt; to attempt.
tentempié *m (fam)* snack.
tenue *adj* thin; tenuous, slender.
terapia *f* therapy.
tercer(o)/ra *adj* third: —*m (jur)* third party.
tercio/cia *adj* third: —*m* third part.
terciopelo *m* velvet.
terco/ca *adj* obstinate.
tergiversar *vt* to distort.
terminante *adj* decisive; categorical.
terminar *vt* to finish; to end; to terminate: —*vi* to end; to stop.
termo *m* flask.
ternero/ra *m/f* calf; veal; heifer.
ternilla *f* gristle.
ternura *f* tenderness.
terrado *m* terrace.
terrateniente *m/f* landowner.
terraza *f* balcony; (flat) roof; terrace (in fields).
terremoto *m* earthquake.
terreno/na *adj* earthly, terrestrial: — *m* land, ground, field.
terrón *m* clod of earth; lump: —~ones *mpl* landed property.
terror *m* terror, dread.
terso/sa *adj* smooth, glossy.
tertulia *f* club, assembly, circle.
tesorero/ra *m* treasurer.
tesoro *m* treasure; exchequer.
testamento *m* will, testament.
testar *vt , vi* to make one's will.
testarudo/da *adj* obstinate.
testificar *vt* to attest, witness.
testigo *m* witness, deponent.
teta *f* breast.
tetera *f* teapot.
tetilla *f* nipple; teat (of a bottle).
tétrico/ca *adj* gloomy, sullen, surly.
tez *f* complexion, hue.
ti *pn* you; yourself.
tía *f* aunt; (fam) bird.
tibio/bia *adj* lukewarm.
tiburón *m* shark.
tiempo *m* time; term; weather; (gr)tense; occasion, opportunity; season.
tienda *f* tent; awning; tilt; shop.
tierno/na *adj* tender.
tierra *f* earth; land, ground; native country.
tieso/sa *adj* stiff, hard, firm; robust; valiant; stubborn.
tiesto *m* earthen pot.
tigre *m* tiger.

tijeras *fpl* scissors *pl*.
tilde *f* tilde (ñ).
tilo *m* lime tree.
timar *vt* to con; to swindle.
timbre *m* stamp; bell; timbre; stamp duty.
tímido/da *adj* timid; cowardly.
timón *m* helm, rudder.
tímpano *m* ear-drum; small drum.
tina *f* tub; bath (tub).
tinieblas *fpl* darkness; shadows *pl*.
tino *m* skill; judgement, prudence.
tinta *f* ink; tint, dye; color.
tinte *m* tint, dye; dry cleaner's.
tinto/ta *adj* dyed: —*m* red wine.
tío *m* uncle; (fam) guy.
tiovivo *m* merry-go-round.
típico/ca *adj* typical; characteristic; picturesque; traditional; regional.
tipo *m* type; norm; pattern; guy.
tiquismiquis *m invar* fussy person.
tira *f* abundance; strip.
tirachinas *m invar* slingshot.
tirado/da *adj* dirt-cheap; (fam) very easy: —*f* cast; distance; series; edition.
tirano/na *m/f* tyrant.
tirante *m* joist; stay; strap; brace: —*adj* taut, extended, drawn.
tirar *vt* to throw; to pull; to draw; to drop; to tend, aim at: —*vi* to shoot; to pull; to go; to tend to.
tirita *f* (sticking) plaster.
tiritar *vi* to shiver.
títere *m* puppet; ridiculous little fel-low.
titubear *vi* to stammer; to stagger; to hesitate.
titular *adj* titular: —*m/f* occupant: —*m* headline: —*vt* to title: —~se *vr* to obtain a title.
tiza *f* chalk.
tiznar *vt* to stain; to tarnish.
tizón *m* half-burnt wood.
toalla *f* towel.
tobillo *m* ankle.
tobogán *m* toboggan; roller-coaster; slide.
tocadiscos *m invar* record player.
tocado *m* headdress, headgear.
tocar *vt* to touch; to strike; (mus) to play; to ring (a bell): —*vi* to belong; to concern; to knock; to call; to be a duty or obligation.
tocino *m* bacon.
todavía *adv* even; yet; still.
todo/da *adj* all, entire; every: —*pn* everything, all: —*m* whole.
todopoderoso/sa *adj* almighty.
toldo *m* awning; parasol.
tomar *vt* to take; to seize, grasp; to understand; to interpret, perceive; to drink; to acquire: —*vi* to drink; to take.
tomavistas *m invar* cine-camera.
tomillo *m* thyme.
tomo *m* bulk; to me; volume.
tonada *f* tune, melody.
tonel *m* cask, barrel.
tonelada *f* ton; (mar) tonnage duty.
tónico/ca *adj* tonic, strengthening: — *m* tonic: —*f* tonic (water); (mus)tonic; (fig) keynote.
tontería *f* foolery, nonsense.
tonto/ta *adj* stupid, foolish.
topar *vt* to run into; to find.
topo *m* mole; stumbler.

toquilla *f* head-scarf; shawl.
tórax *m* thorax.
torbellino *m* whirlwind.
torcer *vt* to twist, curve; to turn; to sprain: —~**se** *vr* to bend; to go wrong: —*vi* to turn off.
torcido/da *adj* oblique; crooked.
tordo *m* thrush: —~/da *adj* speckled black and white.
torear *vt* to avoid; to tease: —*vi* to fight bulls.
tormenta *f* storm, tempest.
tornar *vt* to return; to restore: —~**se** *vr* to become: —*vi* to return: —~ **ahacer** to do again.
tornasolado *adj* iridescent; shimmer-ing.
torneo *m* tournament.
tornillo *m* screw.
torno *m* winch; revolution.
toro *m* bull.
toronja *f* grapefruit.
torpe *adj* dull, heavy; stupid.
torre *f* tower; turret; steeple.
torrefacto/ta *adj* roasted.
torta *f* cake; *(fam)* slap.
tortilla *f* omelet; pancake.
tortuga *f* tortoise; turtle.
tos *f* cough.
tosco/ca *adj* coarse, ill-bred, clumsy.
toser *vi* to cough.
tostado/da *adj* parched; sunburnt; light-yellow; light-brown.
tostar *vt* to toast, roast.
total *m* whole, totality: —*adj* total, entire: —*adv* in short.
tóxico/ca *adj* toxic: —*m* poison.
trabajar *vt* to work, labor; to persuade; to push: —*vi* to strive.
trabalenguas *m invar* tongue twister.
trabar *vt* to join, unite; to take hold of; to fetter, shackle.
tracción *f* traction: —~ **delantera/ trasera** front-wheel/rear-wheel drive.
traducir *vt* to translate.
traer *vt* to bring, carry; to attract; to persuade; to wear; to cause.
traficar *vi* to trade, do business, deal.
tragaluz *m* skylight.
tragaperras *m* o *f invar* slot machine.
tragar *vt* to swallow; to swallow up.
trago *m* drink; gulp; adversity, misfortune.
traicionar *vt* to betray.
traje *m* suit; dress; costume.
trajinar *vt* to carry: —*vi* to bustle about; to travel around.
trama *f* plot; weft, woof.
tramitar *vt* to transact; to negotiate; to handle.
tramo *m* section; piece of ground; flight of stairs.
tramoya *f* scene, theatrical decoration; trick.
trampa *f* trap, snare; trapdoor; fraud.
trampolín *m* trampoline; diving board.
tramposo/sa *adj* deceitful, swindling.
tranca *f* bar, crossbeam.
trance *m* danger; last stage of life; trance.
tranquilizar *vt* to calm; to reassure.
tranquilo/la *adj* tranquil, calm, quiet.
transbordador *m* ferry.
transbordo *m* transfer: —**hacer** ~ to change (trains).
transcurrir *vi* to pass; to turn out.

transeúnte *adj* transitory: —*m* passerby.
transigir *vi* to compromise.
tránsito *m* passage; transition; road, way; change; removal; death of holy or virtuous persons.
transmitir *vt* to transmit; to broadcast.
transparente *adj* transparent; see-through.
transpirar *vt* to perspire; to tran-spire.
tranvía *m* tram.
trapo *m* rag, tatter.
tráquea *f* windpipe.
tras *prep* after, behind.
trascender *vi* to smell; to come out: —~ **de** to go beyond.
trasegar *vt* to move about; to decant.
trasero/ra *adj* back: —*m* bottom.
trasfondo *m* background.
trasgredir *vt* to contravene.
trashumante *adj* migrating.
trasladar *vt* to transport; to transfer; to postpone; to transcribe, copy: —~**se** *vr* to move.
trasnochar *vi* to watch, sit up the whole night.
traspasar *vt* to remove, transport; to transfix, pierce; to return; to exceed (the proper bounds); to transfer.
traste *m* fret (of a guitar): —**dar al** ~**con algo** to ruin something.
trastero *m* lumber room.
trastienda *f* back room behind a shop.
trasto *m* piece of junk; useless person.
trastornar *vt* to overthrow, overturn; to confuse: —~**se** *vr* to go crazy.
trastrocar *vt* to invert (the order of).
tratar *vt* to traffic, trade; to use; to treat; to handle; to address; —~**se** *vr* to treat each other.
trato *m* treatment; manner, address; trade, traffic; conversation; *(com)* agreement.
través *m* *(fig)* reverse: —**de** *o* **al** ~ across, crossways: —**a** ~ **de** *prep* across; over; through.
travesía *f* crossing; cross-street; trajectory; *(mar)* side wind.
travieso/sa *adj* restless, uneasy, fidgety; lively; naughty.
trayecto *m* road; journey, stretch; course.
trazar *vt* to plan out; to project; to trace.
trébedes *fpl* trivet, tripod.
trébol *m* trefoil, clover.
trece *adj* , *m* thirteen; thirteenth.
trecho *m* space, distance of time or place: —**a** ~**s** at intervals.
tregua *f* truce, cessation of hostilities.
treinta *adj* , *m* thirty.
tremendo/da *adj* terrible, formidable; awful, grand.
tren *m* train, retinue; show, ostentation; *(ferro)* train: —~ **de granvelocidad** fast *or* express train: —~**de mercancias** freight train.
trenza *f* braid (in hair), plaited silk.
trepar *vi* to climb; to crawl.
tres *adj* , *m* three.
tresillo *m* three-piece suite; *(mus)* triplet.
tricotar *vi* to knit.
trigésimo/ma *adj* , *m* thirtieth.
trigo *m* wheat.
trillado/da *adj* beaten; trite, hackneyed: —**camino** ~ common routine.
trinar *vi* to trill, quaver; to be angry.
trinchar *vt* to carve, divide (meat).
trineo *m* sled.

trino *m* trill.

tripa *f* gut, intestine: ——**s** *fpl* guts; tripe.

tripulación *f* crew.

tripular *vt* to man; to drive.

tris *m invar*: ——**estar en un ~ de** to be on the point of.

triste *adj* sad, mournful, melancholy.

triturar *vt* to reduce to powder; to grind, pound.

triza *f*: ——**hacer ~s** to smash to bits; to tear to shreds.

trocar *vt* to exchange.

trompa *f* trumpet; proboscis; large top.

trompazo *m* heavy blow; accident.

trompeta *f* trumpet; ——*m* trum-peter.

tronar *vi* to thunder; to rage.

tronco *m* trunk; log of wood; stock.

tropel *m* confused noise; hurry; bustle, confusion; heap; crowd: ——**en ~** in a tumultuous and confused way.

tropezar *vi* to stumble: ——*vt* to meet accidentally.

trotamundos *m invar* globetrotter.

trotar *vi* to trot.

trozo *m* piece.

trucha *f* trout.

truco *m* knack; trick.

trueno *m* thunderclap.

trueque *m* exchange.

truncar *vt* to truncate, maim.

tu *adj* your.

tú *pn* you.

tubería *f* pipe; pipeline.

tubo *m* tube.

tuerca *f* nut.

tumba *f* tomb.

tumbar *vt* to knock down: ——*vi* to fall down: ——**se** *vr* to lie down to sleep.

tumbona *f* easy chair; beach chair.

tunda *f* beating.

tupido/da *adj* dense.

turbar *vt* to disturb, trouble: ——**se** *vr* to be disturbed.

turbio/bia *adj* muddy; troubled.

turno *m* turn; shift; opportunity.

turrón *m* nougat (almond cake).

tutear *vt* to address as 'tu'.

tutor *m* guardian, tutor.

tuyo/ya *adj* yours: ——**s** *pl* friends and relations of the party addressed.

U

u *conj* or (instead of *o* before an *o* or *ho*).

ubicar *vt* to place: ——**se** to be located.

ufanarse *vr* to boast.

últimamente *adv* lately.

ultimar *vt* to finalize; to finish.

último/ma *adj* last; latest; bottom; to p.

ultrajar *vt* to outrage; to despise; to abuse.

ultramar *adj* , *m* overseas.

ultramarinos *mpl* groceries.

umbral *m* threshold.

un/una *art* a, an: ——*adj* , *m* one (for **uno**).

uña *f* nail; hoof; claw, talon.

ungir *vt* to anoint.

ungüento *m* ointment.

únicamente *adv* only, simply.

único/ca *adj* only; singular, unique.

unidad *f* unity; unit; conformity; union.

unificar *vt* to unite.

unir *vt* to join, unite; to mingle; to bind, tie: ——**se** *vr* to associate.

uno *m* one: ——**~/una** *adj* one; sole, only: ——**~ a otro** one another: ——**~ a ~** one by one: ——**a una** jointly together.

untar *vt* to anoint; to grease; (*fam*) to bribe.

urbanidad *f* urbanity, politeness.

urbanismo *m* town planning.

urbanización *f* housing estate.

urdir *vt* to warp; to contrive.

urgencia *f* urgency; emergency; need, necessity.

urinario/ria *adj* urinary: ——*m* urinal.

urna *f* urn; ballot box.

urraca *f* magpie.

usado/da *adj* used; experienced; worn.

usar *vt* to use, make use of; to wear: ——**se** *vr* to be used.

usted *pn* you.

usuario *m* user.

útero *m* uterus, womb.

útil *adj* useful, profitable: ——*m* utility.

utilizar *vt* to use; to make useful.

uva *f* grape.

V

vaca *f* cow; beef.

vacaciones *fpl* vacation; holidays *pl*.

vacante *adj* vacant: ——*f* vacancy.

vaciar *vt* to empty, clear; to mold: ——*vi* to fall, decrease (of waters): ——**se** *vr* to empty.

vacilar *vi* to hesitate; to falter; to fail.

vacío/cía *adj* void, empty; unoccupied; concave; vain; presumptuous: ——*m* vacuum; emptiness.

vacuna *f* vaccine.

vacuno/na *adj* bovine, cow *compd*.

vagar *vi* to rove or loiter about; to wander.

vago/ga *adj* vagrant; restless; vague.

vagón *m* (*ferro*) wagon; carriage: ——**de mercancias** goods wagon.

vaho *m* steam, vapor.

vaina *f* pod, husk.

vaivén *m* fluctuation, instability; giddiness.

vajilla *f* crockery.

vale *m* OK; promissory note, IOU.

valer *vi* to be valuable; to be deserving; to cost; to

be valid; to be worth; to produce; to be current: —*vt* to protect, favor; to be worth; to be equivalent to: —**~se** *vr* to employ, make use of; to have recourse to.

valiente *adj* robust, vigorous; valiant, brave; boasting.

valija *f* suitcase.

valioso/sa *adj* valuable.

valla *f* fence; hurdle; barricade.

valle *m* valley.

valor *m* value; price; validity; force; power; courage, valor.

valorar *vt* to value; to evaluate.

vals *m invar* waltz.

valsar *vi* to waltz.

válvula *f* valve.

vanidoso/sa *adj* vain, showy; haughty; conceited.

vano/na *adj* vain; useless, frivolous; arrogant; futile: —**en ~** in vain.

vapor *m* vapor, steam; breath.

vaquero *m* cow-herd: —**~/ra** *adj* belonging to a cowman: —**~s** *mpl* jeans *pl*.

vara *f* rod; pole, staff; stick.

variar *vt* to vary; to modify; to change: —*vi* to vary.

varices *fpl* varicose veins *pl*.

varilla *f* small rod; curtain rod; spindle, pivot.

vario/ria *adj* varied, different; vague; variegated: —**~s** *pl* some; several.

varón *m* man, male.

vasco/ca *adj* , *m/f* Basque.

vasija *f* vessel.

vaso *m* glass; vessel; vase.

vástago *m* bud, shoot; offspring.

vasto/ta *adj* vast, huge.

vaticinar *vt* to divine, foretell.

vatio *m* watt.

vecindad *f* inhabitants of a place; neighborhood.

vecino/na *adj* neighboring; near: —*m* neighbor, inhabitant.

veinte *adj* , *m* twenty.

veintena *f* twentieth part; score.

vejar *vt* to vex; to humiliate.

vejez *f* old age.

vejiga *f* bladder.

vela *f* watch; watchfulness; night-guard; candle; sail: —**hacerse a la ~** to set sail.

velar *vi* to stay awake; to be attentive: —*vt* to guard, watch.

velero/ra *adj* swift-sailing.

veleta *f* weather cock.

vello *m* down; gossamer; short downy hair.

velo *m* veil; pretext.

velocidad *f* speed; velocity.

vena *f* vein.

venado *m* deer; venison.

vencer *vt* to defeat; to conquer, vanquish: —*vi* to win; to expire.

vendaje *m* bandage, dressing for wounds.

vendaval *m* gale.

vender *vt* to sell.

vendimia *f* grape harvest; vintage.

vendimiar *vt* to harvest, gather; to profit from (something).

veneno *m* poison, venom.

venerar *vt* to venerate, worship.

vengar *vt* to revenge, avenge: —**~se** *vr* to take revenge.

venida *f* arrival; return; overflow of a river.

venidero/ra *adj* future: —**~s** *mpl* posterity.

venir *vi* to come, arrive; to follow, succeed; to happen; to spring from: —**~se** *vr* to ferment.

venta *f* sale.

ventaja *f* advantage.

ventana *f* window; window shutter; nostril.

ventilar *vt* to ventilate; to fan; to discuss.

ventisca *f*, **ventisco** *m* snowstorm.

ventosidad *f* flatulence.

ventura *f* happiness; luck, chance, fortune: —**por ~** by chance.

ver *vt* to see, look at; to observe; to visit: —*vi* to understand; to see: —**~se** *vr* to be seen; to be conspicuous; to find oneself: —**~se con uno** to have a bone to pick with some-one: —*m* sense of sight; appear-ance.

veraneo *m* summer vacation.

verano *m* summer.

veras *fpl* truth, sincerity: —**de ~** in truth, really.

veraz *adj* truthful.

verbena *f* fair; dance.

verdad *f* truth, veracity; reality; reli-ability.

verdadero/ra *adj* true; real; sincere.

verde *m, adj* green.

verdura *f* verdure; vegetables *pl*, greens *pl*.

vereda *f* path, trail; sidewalk.

vergüenza *f* shame; bashfulness; con-fusion.

verificar *vt* to check, verify: —**~se** *vr* to happen.

verruga *f* wart.

vertedero *m* sewer, drain; tip.

verter *vt* to pour; to spill; to empty: — *vi* to flow.

vértice *m* vertex, zenith; crown (head).

vertiente *f* slope; waterfall, cas-cade.

vertiginoso/sa *adj* giddy.

vespertino/na *adj* evening *compd.*

vestíbulo *m* vestibule, lobby.

vestido *m* dress; clothes *pl*.

vestir *vt* to put on; to wear; to dress; to adorn; to cloak, disguise: —*vi* to dress: —**~se** to get dressed.

vestuario *m* clothes *pl;* uniform; ves-try; changing room.

veta *f* vein (in mines, wood, etc); streak; grain.

veteado/da *adj* veined; striped: —*m* veining; streaks.

veterano/na *adj* experienced, practiced: —*m* veteran, old soldier.

veterinaría *f* veterinary medicine.

veterinario/ria *m/f* veterinary surgeon.

vez *f* time; turn; return: —**cada ~** each time: —**una ~** once: —**a veces** sometimes, by turns.

veza *f* (*bot*) vetch.

vía *f* way; road, route; mode, manner, method; (*ferro*) railway line.

viajante *m* sales representative.

viajar *vi* to travel.

víbora *f* viper.

vibrar *vt* , *vi* to vibrate.

vicio *m* vice.

vid *f* (*bot*) vine.

vida *f* life.

vídeo *m* video.

vidriera *f* stained-glass window; shop window.

vidrio *m* glass.

vieira *f* scallop.

viejo/ja *adj* old; ancient, antiquated.

viento *m* wind; air.

vientre *m* belly.

viernes *m invar* Friday: **—V ~ Santo** Good Friday.

viga *f* beam; girder.

vigente *adj* in force.

vigésimo/ma *adj , m* twentieth.

vigía *f (mar)* lookout: *—m* watchman.

vigilar *vt* to watch over: *—vi* to keep watch.

vil *adj* mean, sordid, low; worthless; infamous; ungrateful.

vilipendiar *vt* to despise, revile.

villancico *m* Christmas carol.

vilo: —en ~ *adv* in the air; in suspense.

vinagre *m* vinegar.

vincular *vt* to link.

viñedo *m* vineyard.

vino *m* wine: **—~ tinto** red wine.

violar *vt* to rape; to violate; to pro-fane.

violentar *vt* to force.

violento/ta *adj* violent; forced; absurd; embarrassing.

violeta *f* violet.

violón *m* double bass.

virar *vi* to swerve.

viril *adj* virile, manly.

virtud *f* virtue.

viruela *f* smallpox.

visa *f,* **visado** *m* visa.

viscoso/sa *adj* viscous, glutinous.

visillos *mpl* net curtains *pl.*

visión *f* sight, vision; fantasy.

visitar *vt* to visit.

vislumbrar *vt* to catch a glimpse of; to perceive indistinctly.

visón *m* mink.

víspera *f* eve; evening before: **—~s** *pl* vespers.

vista *f* sight, view; vision; eyesight; appearance; looks *pl; prospect; intention; (jur)* trial: *—m* customs officer.

vistazo *m* glance.

vistoso/sa *adj* colorful, attractive, lively.

vitalicio/cia *adj* for life.

vitorear *vt* to shout, applaud.

vitrina *f* showcase.

viudo/a *f* widower, widow.

vivaz *adj* lively.

víveres *mpl* provisions.

vivero *m* nursery (for plants); fish farm.

vivienda *f* housing; flat, apartment.

viviente *adj* living.

vivir *vt* to live through; to go through: *—vi* to live; to last.

vivo/va *adj* alive; lively: **—al ~** to the life; very realistically.

vocablo *m* word, term.

vocal *f* vowel: *—m/f* member (of a committee): *—adj* vocal, oral.

vociferar *vt* to shout; to proclaim in aloud voice: *—vi* to yell.

volante *adj* flying: *—m (auto)* steering wheel; note; pamphlet; shuttlecock.

volar *vi* to fly; to pass swiftly (of time); to rush, hurry: *—vt* to blow up, explode.

volcán *m* volcano.

volcar *vt* to upset, overturn; to make giddy; to empty out; to exasperate: **—~se** *vr* to tip over.

volquete *m* tipcart; dump truck.

voltear *vt* to turn over; to overturn: **—** *vi* to roll over, tumble.

voltereta *f* tumble; somersault.

voluble *adj* unpredictable; fickle.

volumen *m* volume; size.

voluntad *f* will, willpower; wish, desire.

volver *vt* to turn (over); to turn upside down; to turn inside out: *vi* to return, go back: **—~se** *vr* to turnaround.

vórtice *m* whirlpool.

vos *pn* you.

vosotros/tras *pn pl* you.

votar *vi* to vow; to vote.

voz *f* voice; shout; rumor; word, term.

vuelo *m* flight; wing; projection of a building; ruffle, frill: **—cazar al ~** to catch in flight: **—~ chárter** charter flight.

vuelta *f* turn; circuit; return; row of stitches; cuff; change; bend, curve; reverse, other side; return journey.

vuestro/tra *adj* your: *—pn* yours.

WXYZ

xenofobia *f* xenophobia.

xilófono *m* xylophone.

y *conj* and.

ya *adv* already; now; immediately; atone; soon: *—conj* **~ que** since, seeing that: **—¡~!** of course!, sure!

yacimiento *m* deposit.

yate *m* yacht, sailing boat.

yedra *f* ivy.

yegua *f* mare.

yema *f* bud; leaf; yolk: **—~ del dedo** tip of the finger.

yerno *m* son-in-law.

yeso *m* gypsum; plaster: **—~ mate** plaster of Paris.

yo *pn* I: **—~ mismo** I myself.

yodo *m* iodine.

yogur *m* yogurt.

yunque *m* anvil.

yute *m* jute.

zafiro *m* sapphire.

zaguán *m* porch, hall.

zalamero/ra *adj* flattering: *—m/f* wheedler.

zamarra *f* sheepskin (jacket).

zambullirse *vr* to plunge into water, dive.

zampar *vt* to gobble down; to put away hurriedly: **—~se** *vr* to thrust oneself suddenly into any place; to crash, hurtle.

zanahoria *f* carrot.

zancada *f* stride.

zancudo/da *adj* long legged: *—m* mosquito.

zángano *m* drone; idler, slacker.

zanja *f* ditch, trench.

zapata *f* boot: **—~ de freno** *(auto)* brake shoe.

zapatilla *f* slipper; pump (shoe); *(dep)* trainer, training shoe.

zapato *m* shoe.
zarandear *vt* to shake vigorously.
zarcillo *m* earring; tendril.
zarpar *vi* to weigh anchor.
zarza *f* bramble.
zarzuela *f* Spanish light opera.
zócalo *m* plinth, base; baseboard.
zona *f* zone; area, belt.
zopenco/ca *adj* dull, very stupid.
zoquete *m* block; crust of bread; (*fam*) blockhead.
zorro/a *m* fox; cunning person.

zozobrar *vi (mar)* to founder; to capsize; (*fig*) to fail; to be anxious.
zueco *m* wooden shoe; clog.
zumbar *vt* to hit: —**se** *vr* to hit each other: —*vi* to buzz.
zumo *m* juice.
zurcir *vt* to darn; (*fig*) to join, unite; to hatch (lies).
zurdo/da *adj* left; left-handed.
zurrar *vt (fam)* to flog, lay into; (*fig*) to criticize harshly.

English–Spanish Dictionary

A

a *art* un, uno, una: —*prep* a, al, en.
abandon *vt* abandonar, dejar.
abash *vt* avergonzar, causar confusión.
abbey *n* abadía *f.*
abbot *n* abad *m.*
abbreviate *vt* abreviar, acortar.
abbreviation *n* abreviatura *f.*
abdicate *vt* abdicar; renunciar.
abdication *n* abdicación *f;* renuncia *f.*
abdomen *n* abdomen, bajo vientre *m.*
abduct *vt* secuestrar.
aberration *n* error *m;* aberración *f.*
abet *vt* : —**to aid and** ~ ser cómplicede.
abide *vt* soportar, sufrir.
ability *n* habilidad, capacidad.
ablaze *adj* en llamas.
able *adj* capaz, hábil.
able-bodied *adj* robusto/ta, vigoroso/sa.
ably *adv* con habilidad.
abnormal *adj* anormal.
abnormality *n* anormalidad *f.*
aboard *adv* a bordo.
abode *n* domicilio *m.*
abolish *vt* abolir, anular.
abolition *n* abolición, anulación *f.*
abominable *adj* abominable.
abomination *n* abominación *f.*
aboriginal *adj* aborigen.
abort *vi* abortar.
abortion *n* aborto *m.*
abound *vi* abundar.
about *prep* acerca de, acerca.
above *prep* encima.
aboveboard *adj* legitimo/ma.
abrasion *n* abrasión *f.*
abrasive *adj* abrasivo/va.
abroad *adv* en el extranjero.
abrupt *adj* brusco/ca.
abscess *n* absceso *m.*
abscond *vi* esconderse; huirse.
absence *n* ausencia *f.*
absent *adj* ausente.
absentee *n* ausente *m.*
absent-minded *adj* distraído/da.
absolute *adj* absoluto/ta.
absorb *vt* absorber.
abstain *vi* abstenerse.
abstinence *n* abstinencia *f.*
abstinent *adj* abstinente.
abstract *adj* abstracto/ta: —*n* extracto *m.*
abstraction *n* abstracción *f.*
absurd *adj* absurdo/da.
abundance *n* abundancia *f.*
abundant *adj* abundante.
abuse *vt* abusar; maltratar.
abusive *adj* abusivo/va, ofensivo/va.
abysmal *adj* abismal.
abyss *n* abismo *m.*

acacia *n* acacia *f.*
academic *adj* académico/ca.
academy *n* academia *f.*
accede *vi* acceder.
accelerate *vt* acelerar.
accelerator *n* acelerador *m.*
accent *n* acento *m;* to no *m.*
accentuate *vt* acentuar.
accept *vt* aceptar; admitir.
acceptable *adj* aceptable.
acceptance *n* aceptación *f.*
access *n* acceso *m;* entrada *f.*
accessible *adj* accesible.
accession *n* aumento.
accessory *n* accesorio *m.*
accident *n* accidente *m;* casualidad *f.*
acclaim *vt* aclamar, aplaudir.
accommodate *vt* alojar; complacer.
accommodation *n* alojamiento *m.*
accompany *vt* acompañar.
accomplice *n* cómplice *m.*
accomplish *vt* efectuar, completar.
accord *n* acuerdo, convenio *m.*
accordance *n*: —**in** ~ **with** deacuerdo con.
according *prep* segun, conforme.
accordion *n (mus)* acordeón *m.*
account *n* cuenta *f.*
accountability *n* responsabilidad *f.*
accountancy *n* contabilidad *f.*
accountant *n* contable, contador *m.*
accrue *vi* resultar, provenir.
accumulate *vt* acumular; amontonar.
accuracy *n* exactitud *f.*
accurate *adj* exacto/ta.
accursed *adj* maldito/ta.
accuse *vt* acusar; culpar.
accustom *vt* acostumbrar.
ache *n* dolor *m:* —*vi* doler.
achieve *vt* realizar; obtener.
achievement *n* realización *f.*
acid *adj* ácido/da; agrio/ria: —*n*ácido *m.*
acknowledge *vt* reconocer, confesar.
acne *n* acne *m.*
acorn *n* bellota *f.*
acoustics *n* acústica *f.*
acquaint *vt* informar, avisar.
acquaintance *n* conocimiento *m;* conocido *m.*
acquire *vt* adquirir.
acquisition *n* adquisición
acquit *vt* absolver.
acquittal *n* absolución *f.*
acre *n* acre *m.*
acrid *adj* acre.
acrimony *n* acrimonio *m.*
across *adv* de través.
action *n* acción *f.*
activate *vt* activar.
active *adj* activo/va.

activity *n* actividad *f.*
actor *n* actor *m.*
actress *n* actriz *f.*
actual *adj* real; efectivo/va.
actuary *n* actuario de seguros *m.*
acumen *n* agudeza *f.*
acute *adj* agudo/da; ingenioso/sa.
ad *n* aviso *m.*
adage *n* proverbio *m.*
adamant *adj* inflexible.
adapt *vt* adaptar.
adaptor *n* adaptador *m.*
add *vt* añadir, agregar: **—to ~ up** sumar.
adder *n* culebra *f;* víbora *f.*
addict *n* drogadicto *m.*
addiction *n* dependencia *f.*
addition *n* adición *f.*
additional *adj* adicional.
additive *n* aditivo *m.*
address *vt* dirigir: **—n** dirección *f.*
adenoids *npl* vegetaciones adenoideas *fpl.*
adept *adj* hábil.
adequacy *n* suficiencia *f.*
adequate *adj* adecuado/da; suficiente.
adhere *vi* adherir.
adhesion *n* adhesión *f.*
adhesive *adj* pegajoso/sa.
adhesiveness *n* adhesividad *f.*
adieu *adv* adiós: **—n** despedida *f.*
adjacent *adj* adyacente, contiguo/gua.
adjective *n* adjetivo *m.*
adjoining *adj* contiguo/gua.
adjournment *n* prorroga *f.*
adjudicate *vt* adjudicar.
adjust *vt* ajustar, acomodar.
adjustable *adj* ajustable.
adjustment *n* ajustamiento *m.*
ad lib *vt* improvisar.
administer *vt* administrar.
administration *n* administración *f.*
administrative *adj* administrativo/ va.
admirable *adj* admirable.
admiral *n* almirante *m.*
admire *vt* admirar.
admirer *n* admira/a *m/f* .
admission *adj* entrada *f.*
admit *vt* admitir.
admittance *n* entrada *f.*
admittedly *adj* de acuerdo que.
admonish *vt* amonestar.
ad nauseam *adv* hasta el cansancio.
adolescence *n* adolescencia *f.*
adopt *vt* adoptar.
adorable *adj* adorable.
adore *vt* adorar.
adorn *vt* adornar.
adrift *adv* a la deriva.
adult *adj* adulto/ta.
adulterate *vt* adulterar, corromper.
adulterer *n* adultero *m.*
adultery *n* adulterio *m.*
advance *vt* avanzar; promover.
advantage *n* ventaja *f.*
advantageous *adj* ventajoso/sa.
adventure *n* aventura *f.*
adventurous *adj* intrépido/da.
adverb *n* adverbio *m.*

adversary *n* adversario enemigo *m.*
adversity *n* calamidad *f;* infortunio *m.*
advertise *vt* anunciar.
advertisement *n* aviso *m.*
advice *n* consejo *m;* aviso *m.*
advisability *n* prudencia *f.*
advise *vt* aconsejar; avisar.
advocacy *n* defensa *f.*
advocate *n* abogado *m;* protector *m.*
aerial *n* antena *f.*
aerobics *npl* aerobic *m.*
aerometer *n* areómetro *m.*
aerosol *n* aerosol *m.*
afar *adv* lejos, distante.
affair *n* asunto *m;* negocio *m.*
affect *vt* conmover; afectar.
affection *n* cariño *m.*
affidavit *n* declaración jurada *f.*
affiliate *vt* afiliar.
affiliation *n* afiliación *f.*
affinity *n* afinidad *f.*
affirm *vt* afirmar, declarar.
affirmation *n* afirmación *f.*
affirmative *adj* afirmativo/va.
affix *vt* pegar: **—n (gr)** afijo *m.*
afflict *vt* afligir.
affliction *n* aflicción *f;* dolor *m.*
affluence *n* opulencia *f.*
affluent *adj* opulento/ta.
affray *n* asalto *m;* tumulto *m.*
aflame *adv* en llamas.
afloat *adv* flotante, a flote.
afore *prep* antes: **—adv** primero.
afraid *adj* espantado/da.
afresh *adv* de nuevo, otra vez.
after *prep* después.
afterbirth *n* secundinas *fpl.*
after-effects *npl* consecuencias *fpl.*
afterlife *n* vida venidera *f.*
aftermath *n* consecuencias *fpl.*
afternoon *n* tarde *f.*
aftershave *n* aftershave *m.*
aftertaste *n* resabio *m.*
afterwards *adv* después.
again *adv* otra vez.
against *prep* contra.
agate *n* ágata *f.*
age *n* edad *f;* vejez *f.*
agency *n* agencia *f.*
agenda *n* orden del día *m.*
agent *n* agente *m.*
aggrandizement *n* engrandecimiento *m.*
aggravate *vt* agravar, exagerar.
aggregate *n* agregado *m.*
aggregation *n* agregación *f.*
aggression *n* agresión *f.*
aggressor *n* agresor *m.*
aggrieved *adj* ofendido/da.
aghast *adj* horrorizado/da.
agile *adj* ágil; diestro/tra.
agitate *vt* agitar.
ago *adv* pasado.
agonizing *adj* atngustioso.
agony *n* agonía *f.*
agree *vt* convenir: **—vi** estar de acuerdo/da.
agreeable *adj* agradable; amable.
agreement *n* acuerdo *m.*

agriculture *n* agricultura *f.*
ah! *excl* ¡ah! ¡ay!
ahead *adv* más allá, delante de otro.
aid *vt* ayudar, socorrer.
AIDS *n* SIDA *m.*
ail *vt* afligir, molestar.
ailment *n* dolencia, indisposición *f.*
aim *vt* apuntar aspirar a; intentar.
air *n* aire *m:* —*vt* airear; ventilar.
air balloon *n* globo aerostático *m.*
airborne *adj* aerotransportado/da.
air-conditioning *n* climatización *f.*
aircraft *n* avión *m.*
air force *n* fuerzas aéreas *fpl.*
airline *n* línea aérea *f.*
airmail *n:* —**by** ~ por avión.
airplane *n* avión *m.*
airport *n* aeropuerto *m.*
airstrip *n* pista de aterrizaje *f.*
airy *adj* bien ventilado/da.
aisle *n* nave de una iglesia *f.*
akin *adj* parecido/da.
alabaster *n* alabastro *m.*
alarm *n* alarma *f:* —*vt* alarmar; inquietar.
alas *adv* desgraciadamente.
albeit *conj* aunque.
album *n* album *m.*
alchemy *n* alquimia *f.*
alcohol *n* alcohol *m.*
alcoholic *adj* alcohólico/ca: —*n* alcoholizado *m.*
alcove *n* nicho *m.*
alder *n* aliso *m.*
ale *n* cerveza *f.*
alert *adj* vigilante; alerto/ta.
algae *npl* alga *f.*
algebra *n* álgebra *f.*
alias *adj* alias.
alibi *n (law)* coartada *f.*
alien *adj* ajeno/na.
alienate *vt* enajenar.
alight *vi* apearse.
align *vt* alinear.
alike *adj* semejante, igual.
alive *adj* vivo/va, viviente; activo/va.
alkali *n* álcali *m.*
alkaline *adj* alcalino/na.
all *adj* todo/da.
allay *vt* aliviar.
allegation *n* alegación *f.*
allege *vt* alegar; declarar.
allegiance *n* lealtad, fidelidad *f.*
allegorical *adj* alegórico/ca.
allegory *n* alegoría *f.*
allergy *n* alergia *f.*
alley *n* callejuela *f.*
alliance *n* alianza *f.*
allied *adj* aliado/da.
alligator *n* caimán *m.*
allocate *vt* repartir.
allot *vt* asignar.
allow *vt* conceder; permitir; dar.
allowance *n* concesión *f.*
alloy *n* liga, mezcla *f.*
allspice *n* pimienta de Jamaica *f.*
allude *vt* aludir.
allure *n* fascinación *f.*
allusion *n* alusión *f.*

allusive *adj* alusivo/va.
alluvial *adj* aluvial.
ally *n* aliado *m:* —*vt* aliar.
almanac *n* almanaque *m.*
almighty *adj* omnipotente, todopoderoso/sa.
almond *n* almendra *f.*
almost *adv* casi; cerca de.
aloft *prep* arriba.
alone *adj* solo.
along *adv* a lo largo.
aloof *adv* lejos.
alphabet *n* alfabeto *m.*
alphabetical *adj* alfabético/ca.
alpine *adj* alpino/na.
already *adv* ya.
also *adv* también, además.
altar *n* altar *m.*
altarpiece *n* retablo *m.*
alter *vt* modificar.
alteration *n* alteración *f.*
alternate *adj* alterno/na: —*vt* alternar, variar.
alternator *n* alternador *m.*
alternative *n* alternativa *f.*
although *conj* aunque, no obstante.
altitude *n* altitud, altura *f.*
altogether *adv* del todo.
aluminum *n* aluminio *m.*
always *adv* siempre, constantemente.
a.m. *adv* de la mañana.
amalgam *n* amalgama *f.*
amalgamate *vt vi* amalgamar(se).
amaryllis *n (bot)* amarillas *f.*
amass *vt* acumular, amontonar.
amateur *n* aficionado *m.*
amateurish *adj* torpe.
amaze *vt* asombrar.
amazon *n* amazona *f.*
ambassador *n* embajador *m.*
amber *n* ámbar *m.*
ambidextrous *adj* ambidextro/tra.
ambiguity *n* ambigüedad, duda *f.*
ambiguous *adj* ambiguo: —~**ly** *adv* ambiguamente.
ambition *n* ambición *f.*
amble *vi* andar sin prisa.
ambulance *n* ambulancia *f.*
ambush *n* emboscada *f.*
amenable *adj* sensible.
amend *vt* enmendar.
amendment *n* enmienda *f.*
amends *npl* compensación *f.*
amenities *npl* comodidades *fpl.*
America *n* América *f.*
amethyst *n* amatista *f.*
amiable *adj* amable.
amiableness *n* amabilidad *f.*
amiably *adv* amablemente.
amicable *adj* amigable.
amid(st) *prep* entre, en medio de.
amiss *adv* : —**something's** ~ pasa algomalo.
ammonia *n* amoníaco *m.*
ammunition *n* municiones *fpl.*
amnesia *n* amnesia *f.*
amnesty *n* amnistía *f.*
amoral *adv* amoral.
amorous *adj* amoroso/sa.
amount *n* importe *m;* cantidad *f.*
amp(ere) *n* amperio *m.*

amphibian *n* anfibio *m*.
amphibious *adj* anfibio/bia.
amphitheater *n* anfiteatro *m*.
ample *adj* amplio/lia.
ampleness *n* amplitud, abundancia *f*.
amplifier *n* amplificador *m*.
amplify *vt* ampliar, extender.
amplitude *n* amplitud, extensión *f*.
amputate *vt* amputar.
amuse *vt* entretener, divertir.
amusement *n* diversión *f*.
amusing *adj* divertido/da.
an *art* un, uno, una.
anachronism *n* anacronismo *m*.
anemia *n* anemia *f*.
anesthetic *n* anestesia *f*.
analogy *n* analogía *f*.
analyse *vt* analizar.
anarchy *n* anarquía *f*.
anatomical *adj* anatómico/ca.
anatomy *n* anatomía *f* ancestor *n*: —~s *pl* antepasados *mpl* .
ancestral *adj* hereditario/ria.
ancestry *n* raza, alcurnia *f*.
anchor *n* ancla *f*: —*vi* anclar.
anchovy *n* anchoa *f*.
ancient *adj* antiguo.
and *conj* y, e.
anecdote *n* anécdota *f*
anemone *n (bot)* anémona *f*
angel *n* ángel *m*
anger *n* cólera *f*: —*vt* enojar, irritar.
angle *n* ángulo *m*: —*vt* pescar con cana.
anglicism *n* anglicismo *m*.
angry *adj* enojado/da.
anguish *n* ansia, angustia *f*
angular *adj* angular.
animal *n adj* animal *m*.
animation *n* animación *f*
aniseed *n* anís *m*
ankle *n* tobillo *m*.
annals *n* anales *mpl* .
annex *vt* anejar: —*n* anejo *m*.
annihilate *vt* aniquilar.
annihilation *n* aniquilación *f*.
anniversary *n* aniversario *m*.
annotate *vi* anotar.
announce *vt* anunciar, publicar.
announcement *n* anuncio *m*.
annoy *vt* molestar.
annual *adj* anual.
annunciation *n* anunciación *f*
anoint *vt* untar, ungir.
anomaly *n* anomalía, irregularidad *f*.
anon *adv* más tarde.
anonymity *n* anonimato *m*.
anonymous *adj* anónimo/ma.
anorexia *n* anorexia *f*.
another *adj* otro/tra.
answer *vt* responder.
answering machine *n* contestadorautomático *m*.
ant *n* hormiga *f*.
antagonize *vt* provocar.
antarctic *adj* antártico/ca.
antelope *n* antílope *m*.
antenna *npl* antena *f*.
anterior *adj* anterior, precedente.

anthem *n* himno *m*.
anthology *n* antología *f*
anthropology *n* antropología *f*
antibiotic *n* antibiótico *m*.
antibody *n* anticuerpo *m*.
Antichrist *n* Anticristo *m*.
anticipate *vt* anticipar, prevenir.
anticipation *n* anticipación *f*.
antidote *n* antídoto *m*.
antipodes *npl* antípodas *fpl*
antiquarian *n* anticuario *m*.
antiquated *adj* antiguo/gua.
antiquity *n* antigüedad *f*.
antiseptic *adj* antiséptico/ca.
antler *n* cuerna *f*.
anvil *n* yunque *m*.
anxiety *n* ansiedad, ansia *f*.
anxious *adj* ansioso/sa.
any *adj pn* cualquier, cualquiera; alguno, alguna
apart *adv* aparte, separadamente.
apartment *n* departamento *m*.
apathy *n* apatía *f*.
ape *n* mono *m*.
apologize *vt* disculpar.
apology *n* apología, defensa *f*.
apostrophe *n* apóstrofe *m*.
appall *vt* espantar, aterrar.
apparatus *n* aparato *m*.
apparent *adj* evidente, aparente.
apparition *n* aparición, visión *f*.
appeal *vi* apelar.
appear *vi* aparecer.
appease *vt* aplacar.
append *vt* anejar.
appendicitis *n* apendicitis *f*.
appendix *n* apéndice *m*.
appetite *n* apetito *m*.
applaud *vi* aplaudir.
apple *n* manzana *f*.
appliance *n* aparato *m*.
applicable *adj* aplicable.
applicant *n* aspirante, candidato *m*.
application *n* aplicación *f*; solicitud *f*.
applied *adj* aplicado/da.
apply *vt* aplicar.
appoint *vt* nombrar.
appointment *n* cita *f*; nombramiento *m*.
apportion *vt* repartir.
appraisal *n* estimación *f*.
appraise *vt* tasar; estimar.
appreciate *vt* apreciar; agradecer.
apprehend *vt* arrestar.
apprehension *n* aprensión *f*.
apprehensive *adj* aprensivo/va.
apprentice *n* aprendiz *m*.
approach *vt vi* aproximar(se).
appropriate *vt* apropiarse de: —*adj* apropiado/da.
approve (of) *vt* aprobar.
April *n* abril *m*.
apron *n* delantal *m*.
apse *n* ábside *m*.
apt *adj* apto/ta, idóneo/nea.
aptitude *n* aptitud *f*.
aquarium *n* acuario *m*.
Aquarius *n* Acuario *m*.
aqueduct *n* acueducto *m*.
arable *adj* labrantío/tía.

arbitrate *vt* arbitrar.
arcade *n* galería *f.*
arch *n* arco *m.*
archeology *n* arqueología *f.*
archaic *adj* arcaico/ca.
archbishop *n* arzobispo *m.*
archer *n* arquero *m.*
architect *n* arquitecto/ta *m/f.*
architecture *n* arquitectura *f.*
archives *npl* archivos *mpl* .
arctic *adj* ártico/ca.
area *n* área *f;* espacio *m.*
arena *n* arena *f.*
arguably *adv* posiblemente.
argue *vi* discutir.
argument *n* argumento *m,* controversia *f.*
arid *adj* árido/da, estéril.
aridity *n* sequedad *f.*
Aries *n* Aries *m.*
arise *vi* levantarse.
aristocracy *n* aristocracia *f.*
arithmetic *n* aritmética *f.*
ark *n* arca *f.*
arm *n* brazo *m;* arma *f.*
armament *n* armamento *m.*
armchair *n* sillón *m.*
armor *n* armadura *f.*
armpit *n* sobaco *m.*
army *n* ejercito *m.*
aroma *n* aroma *m.*
around *prep* alrededor de.
arouse *vt* despertar; excitar.
arraign *vt* acusar.
arraignment *n* acusación *f;* proceso criminal *m.*
arrange *vt* organizar.
arrangement *n* colocación *f;* arre-glo.
arrant *adj* consumado/da.
array *n* serie *f.*
arrears *npl* resto de una deuda *m;* atraso *m.*
arrest *n* arresto *m;* —*vt* detener, arrestar.
arrival *n* llegada *f.*
arrive *vi* llegar.
arrogance *n* arrogancia, presunción *f.*
arrogant *adj* arrogante, presuntuoso/sa: —~**ly** *adv* arrogantemente.
arrogate *vt* arrogarse.
arrogation *n* arrogación *f.*
arrow *n* flecha *f.*
arsenal *n (mil)* arsenal *m; (mar)* atara-zana, armería *f.*
arsenic *n* arsénico *m.*
art *n* arte *m.*
arterial *adj* arterial.
artery *n* arteria *f.*
artful *adj* ingenioso/sa.
art gallery *n* pinacoteca *f.*
arthritis *n* artritis *f.*
artichoke *n* alcachofa *f.*
article *n* articulo *m.*
articulate *vt* articular.
artifice *n* artificio *m.*
artillery *n* artillería *f.*
artisan *n* artesano/na *m/f* .
artist *n* artista *m.*
artistry *n* habilidad *f.*
artless *adj* sencillo, simple.
artlessness *n* sencillez *f.*
as *conj* como; mientras.

asbestos *n* asbesto *m.*
ascend *vi* ascender, subir.
ascribe *vt* atribuir.
ash *n (bot)* fresno *m;* ceniza *f*
ashamed *adj* avergonzado/da.
ashtray *n* cenicero *m.*
Ash Wednesday *n* miércoles deceniza *m.*
ask *vt* pedir, rogar, preguntar por.
askew *adv* de lado.
asleep *adj* dormido/da.
asparagus *n* espárrago *m.*
aspect *n* aspecto *m.*
aspen *n* álamo temblón *m.*
asphalt *n* asfalto *m.*
asphyxia *n (med)* asfixia *f.*
asphyxiate *vt* asfixiar.
asphyxiation *n* asfixia *f.*
aspiration *n* aspiración *f.*
aspire *vi* aspirar, desear.
aspirin *n* aspirina *f.*
ass *n* asno *m*: —**she** ~ burra *f.*
assassin *n* asesino *m.*
assassinate *vt* asesinar.
assault *n* asalto *m.*
assemble *vt* reunir, convocar.
assembly *n* asamblea *f.*
assert *vt* sostener, mantener.
assess *vt* valorar.
assessment *n* valoración *f.*
assets *npl* bienes *mpl* .
assign *vt* asignar.
assimilate *vt* asimilar.
assist *vt* asistir, ayudar.
assistance *n* asistencia *f.*
assistant *n* asistente, ayudante *m.*
associate *vt* asociar.
association *n* asociación, sociedad *f.*
assortment *n* surtido *m.*
assume *vt* asumir; suponer.
assurance *n* seguro *m.*
assure *vt* asegurar.
asterisk *n* asterisco *m.*
asthma *n* asma *f.*
asthmatic *adj* asmático/ca.
astonish *vt* pasmar, sorprender.
astringent *adj* astringente.
astrologer *n* astrólogo/ga *m/f* .
astrology *n* astrología *f.*
astronaut *n* astronauta *m/f* .
astronomer *n* astrónomo *m.*
astronomy *n* astronomía *f.*
astute *adj* astuto/ta.
asylum *n* asilo, refugio *m.*
at *prep* a; en.
atheism *n* ateísmo *m.*
atheist *n* ateo *m,* atea *f.*
athlete *n* atleta *m/f* .
atlas *n* atlas *m.*
atmosphere *n* atmósfera *f.*
atom *n* átomo *m.*
atomic *adj* atómico/ca.
atrocious *adj* atroz.
atrocity *n* atrocidad, enormidad *f.*
attach *vt* adjuntar.
attaché *n* agregado *m.*
attack *vt* atacar; acometer.
attempt *vi* intentar; probar, experimentar.

attend *vt* servir; asistir.
attendant *n* sirviente *m*.
attention *n* atención *f;* cuidado *m*.
attentive *adj* atento/ta; cuidadoso/sa.
attest *vt* atestiguar.
attic *n* desván *m;* guardilla *f*.
attorney *n* abogado *m*.
attract *vt* atraer.
attraction *n* atracción *f;* atractivo *m*.
auburn *adj* moreno/na, castaño/ña.
auction *n* subasta *f*.
auctioneer *n* subastador/a.
audacious *adj* audaz.
audible *adj* perceptible al oído.
audience *n* audiencia *f*.
audit *n* auditoría *f*.
augment *vt* aumentar, acrecentar.
August *n* agosto *m*.
august *adj* augusto/a.
aunt *n* tia *f*.
au pair *n* au pair *f*.
aura *n* aura *f*.
auspicious *adj* propicio/cia.
austere *adj* austero/ra, severo/ra;
authentic *adj* auténtico/ca.
authenticate *vt* autenticar.
authenticity *n* autenticidad *f*.
author *n* autor *m;* escritor *m*.
authorization *n* autorización *f*.
authorize *vt* autorizar.

authority *n* autoridad *f*.
auto *n* carro, coche *m*.
autograph *n* autógrafo *m*.
automatic *adj* automático/ca.
autonomy *n* autonomía *f*.
autopsy *n* autopsia *f*.
auxiliary *adj* auxiliar, asistente.
available *adj* disponible.
avalanche *n* alud *m*.
avarice *n* avaricia *f*.
avenue *n* avenida *f*.
avert *vt* desviar, apartar.
aviary *n* pajarera *f*.
avoid *vt* evitar, escapar.
await *vt* aguardar.
awake *vt* despertar.
award *vt* otorgar: —*n* premio *m*.
aware *adj* consciente; vigilante.
away *adv* ausente, fuera.
awe *n* miedo, temor *m*.
awful *adj* tremendo/da; horroroso/sa.
awhile *adv* un rato, algún tiempo.
awkward *adj* torpe, rudo/da.
awning *n (mar)* toldo *m*.
awry *adv* oblicuamente, torcidamente.
axe *n* hacha *f*.
axiom *n* axioma *m*.
axis *n* eje *m*.
axle *n* eje *m*.

B

baboon *n* cinocéfalo *m*.
baby *n* niño pequeño *m*.
bachelor *n* soltero *m;* bachiller *m*.
back *n* dorso *m*.
backbone *n* hueso dorsal, espinazo *m*.
backer *n* partidario/ria *m*.
backgammon *n* juego de chaquete otablas *m*.
background *n* fondo *m*.
backlash *n* reacción *f*.
backpack *n* mochila *f*.
backside *n* trasero *m*.
backward *adj* tardo/da, lento/ta.
bacon *n* tocino *m*.
bad *adj* mal, malo.
badge *n* señal *f;* símbolo *m*.
badger *n* tejón *m*.
badminton *n* bádminton *m*.
baffle *vt* confundir.
bag *n* saco *m;* bolsa *f*.
baggage *n* bagaje, equipaje *m*.
bail *n* fianza, caución (juratoria) *f*.
bailiff *n* alguacil *m*.
bake *vt* cocer en horno.
bakery *n* panadería *f*.
baking powder *n* levadura *f*.
balance *n* balanza *f;* equilibrio *m*.
balcony *n* balcón *m*.
bald *adj* calvo/va.
ball *n* bola *f;* pelota *f;* baile *m*.
ballad *n* balada *f*.
ballerina *n* bailarina *f*.

ballet *n* ballet *m*.
balloon *n* globo *m*.
ballpoint (pen) *n* bolígrafo *m*.
balm, balsam *n* bálsamo *m*.
balustrade *n* balaustrada *f*.
bamboo *n* bambú *m*.
ban *n* prohibición *f*.
banal *adj* vulgar.
banana *n* plátano *m*.
band *n* faja *f;* cuadrilla *f*.
bandage *n* venda *f*.
bandit *n* bandido/da *m/f*.
bang *n* golpe *m*.
bangle *n* brazalete *m*.
banister(s) *n(pl)* pasamanos *m*.
banjo *n* banjo *m*.
bank *n* orilla (de rió) *f;* montón detierra *m;* banco *m*.
bank account *n* cuenta de banco *f*.
bankrupt *adj* insolvente.
banner *n* bandera *f*.
banquet *n* banquete *m*.
baptize *vt* bautizar.
bar *n* bar *m;* barra *f*.
barbecue *n* barbacoa *f*.
barber *n* peluquero *m*.
bare *adj* desnudo/da, descubierto/ta.
barely *adv* apenas.
bargain *n* ganga *f*.
barge *n* barcaza *f*.
bark *n* corteza *f*.
barley *n* cebada *f*.

barn *n* granero.
barometer *n* barómetro *m*.
baron *n* barón *m*.
barracks *npl* cuartel *m*.
barrel *n* barril *m*.
barren *adj* estéril, infructuoso/sa.
barrier *n* barrera *f*; obstáculo *m*.
barter *vi* baratar.
base *n* fondo *m*; base *f*; basa *f*.
baseball *n* béisbol *m*.
basement *n* sótano *m*.
basic *adj* básico/ca.
basin *n* jofaina, bacía *f*.
basis *n* base *f*; fundamento *m*.
basket *n* cesta, canasta *f*.
basketball *n* baloncesto *m*.
bastard *n, adj* bastardo/da *m/f*.
bat *n* murciélago *m*.
batch *n* serie *f*.
bath *n* baño *m*.
bathe *vt (vi)* bañar(se).
bathing suit *n* traje de baño *m*.
bathroom *n* (cuarto de) baño *m*.
baths *npl* piscina *f*.
battery *n* batería *f*.
battle *n* combate *m*.
bawdy *adj* indecente.
bay *n* bahía *f*; laurel.
bazaar *n* bazar *m*.
be *vi* ser; estar.
beach *n* playa, orilla *f*.
beacon *n* almenara *f*.
beagle *n* sabueso *m*.
beak *n* pico *m*.
beam *n* rayo de luz *m*; travesaño *m*.
bean *n* haba *f*.
beansprouts *npl* brotes de soja *mpl*.
bear *vt* llevar alguna cosa como carga; sostener; soportar.
bear *n* oso *m*.
beard *n* barba *f*.
bearer *n* portador/a *m/f*.
beast *n* bestia *f*.
beat *vt* golpear; to car (un tambor).
beatify *vt* beatificar, santificar.
beautiful *adj* hermoso/sa, bello.
beauty *n* hermosura, belleza *f*.
because *conj* porque, a causa de.
bed *n* cama *f*.
bedroom *n* dormitorio *m*.
bee *n* abeja *f*.
beech *n* haya *f*.
beef *n* carne de vaca *f*.
beefburger *n* hamburguesa *f*.
beefsteak *n* bistec *m*.
beeline *n* línea recta *f*.
beer *n* cerveza *f*.
beetle *n* escarabajo *m*.
befall *vi* suceder, acontecer.
before *adv , prep* antes de; delante.
beg *vt* mendigar.
beggar *n* mendigo/ga *m/f*.
begin *vt vi* comenzar, empezar.
beginning *n* principio *m*.
begrudge *vt* envidiar.
behave *vi* comportarse.
behind *prep* detrás; atrás.

beige *adj* color beige.
belch *vi* eructar.
belief *n* fe, creencia *f*.
believe *vt* creer.
believer *n* creyente, fiel.
bell *n* campana *f*.
bellows *npl* fuelle *m*.
belly *n* vientre *m*; panza *f*.
belong *vi* pertenecer.
beloved *adj* querido/da, amado/da.
below *adv , prep* debajo, inferior; abajo.
belt *n* cinturón, cinto *m*.
bench *n* banco *m*.
bend *vt* encorvar, inclinar, plegar.
beneath *adv , prep* debajo, abajo.
benefit *n* beneficio *m*; utilidad *f*; provecho *m*.
benevolence *n* benevolencia *f*.
benevolent *adj* benévolo.
benign *adj* benigno/na.
bent *n* inclinación *f*.
bereave *vt* privar.
bereavement *n* perdida *f*.
beret *n* boina *f*.
berry *n* baya *f*.
beset *vt* acosar.
beside(s) *prep* al lado de; excepto.
best *adj* mejor.
bestial *adj* bestial, brutal.
bestow *vt* dar, conferir.
bestseller *n* bestseller *m*.
bet *n* apuesta *f*.
betray *vt* traicionar.
betroth *vt* contraer esponsales.
betting *n* juego *m*.
between *prep* entre, en medio de.
beverage *n* bebida *f*.
beware *vi* guardarse.
bewitch *vt* encantar, hechizar.
beyond *prep* más allá.
bias *n* propensión.
bib *n* babador *m*.
Bible *n* Biblia *f*.
bibliography *n* bibliografía *f*.
bicycle *n* bicicleta *f*.
bid *vt* mandar, ordenar; ofrecer.
biennial *adj* bienal.
bifocals *npl* anteojos bifocales *mpl*.
big *adj* grande, lleno/na.
bigamist *n* bígamo/ma *m/f*.
bigamy *n* bigamia *f*.
bigot *n* fanático/ca *m/f*.
bike *n* bici *f*.
bikini *n* bikini *m*.
bile *n* bilis *f*.
bilingual *adj* bilingüe.
bill *n* pico de ave *m*; billete.
billboard *n* cartelera *f*.
billet *n* alojamiento *m*.
billfold *n* cartera.
billiards *npl* billar *m*.
billion *n* billón *f*.
bin *n* cubo de la basura *m*.
binder *n* encuadernador/a *m/f*.
bingo *n* bingo *m*.
binoculars *npl* prismáticos *mpl*.
biographer *n* biógrafo/fa *m/f*.
biography *n* biografía *f*.

biological *adj* biológico/ca.
biology *n* biología *f.*
birch *n* abedul *m.*
bird *n* ave *f.*; pájaro *m.*
birth *n* nacimiento *m.*
birthday *n* cumpleaños *m invar.*
biscuit *n* bizcocho *m.*
bishop *n* obispo *m.*
bit *n* bocado *m;* pedacito *m.*
bitch *n* perra *f.*
bite *vt* morder; picar.
bitter *adj* amargo/ga.
bitumen *n* betún *m.*
bizarre *adj* raro/ra.
blab *vi* chismear.
black *adj* negro/gra, oscuro/ra.
blackberry *n* zarzamora *f.*
blackbird *n* mirlo *m.*
blackboard *n* pizarra *f.*
blackmail *n* chantaje *m;* —*vt* chantajear.
blacksmith *n* herrero *m.*
bladder *n* vejiga *f.*
blade *n* hoja *f;* filo *m.*
blame *vt* culpar.
blameless *adj* inocente.
blank *adj* blanco/ca.
blanket *n* manta *f.*
blaspheme *vt* blasfemar, jurar.
blasphemy *n* blasfemia *f.*
blatant *adj* obvio.
blaze *n* llama *f.*
bleed *vi, vt* sangrar.
blemish *vt* manchar.
bless *vt* bendecir.
blessing *n* bendición *f.*
blight *vt* arruinar.
blind *adj* ciego/ga.
blink *vi* parpadear.
bliss *n* felicidad (eterna) *f.*
blister *n* ampolla *f.*
blitz *n* bombardeo aéreo *m.*
blizzard *n* huracán *m.*
bloated *adj* hinchado/da.
blob *n* gota *f.*
bloc *n* bloque *m.*
block *n* bloque *m;* obstáculo *m.*
blockade *n* bloqueo *m;* —*vt* bloquear.
blond *adj* rubio/bia.
blood *n* sangre *f.*
blood group *n* grupo sanguíneo *m.*
blood poisoning *n* envenenamiento de la sangre.*m.*
blood pressure *n* presión de sangre *f.*
blood sausage *n* morcilla *f.*
blood test *n* análisis de sangre *m.*
blood transfusion *n* transfusion desangre *f.*
bloom *n* flor *f; (also fig):* —*vi* florecer.
blossom *n* flor *f.*
blot *vt* manchar.
blotchy *adj* muy manchado/da.
blouse *n* blusa *f.*
blow *vi* soplar; sonar.
blubber *n* grasa de ballena *f.*
blue *adj* azul.
bluebell *n* campanilla *f.*
blueprint *n (fig)* anteproyecto *m.*
blunder *n* desatino *m.*
blunt *adj* obtuso/sa; grosero/ra.

blush *n* rubor *m;* sonrojo *m.*
boar *n* verraco *m:* —**wild** ~ jabalí *m.*
board *n* tabla *f;* mesa *f.*
boarder *n* pensionista *m.*
boarding card *n* tarjeta de embar-que *f.*
boast *vi* jactarse.
boat *n* barco *m.*
bobsleigh *n* bob *m.*
bodice *n* corsé *m.*
body *n* cuerpo *m;* individuo *m;* gre-mio *m.*
body-building *n* culturismo *m.*
bodyguard *n* guardaespaldas *m.*
boil *vi* hervir; bullir.
bold *adj* ardiente, valiente; audaz.
bolt *n* cerrojo *m.*
bomb *n* bomba *f.*
bond *n* ligadura *f;* vinculo *m.*
bondage *n* esclavitud, servidumbre *f.*
bone *n* hueso *m.*
bonfire *n* hoguera *f.*
bonny *adj* bonito/ta.
bonus *n* cuota, prima *f.*
book *n* libro *m.*
bookcase *n* armario para libros *m.*
bookmarker *n* registro *m.*
bookstore *n* librería *f.*
boom *n* trueno *m.*
boon *n* presente, regalo *m.*
booth *n* barraca, cabaña *f.*
booty *n* botín *m;* presa *f;* saqueo *m.*
border *n* orilla *f;* borde *m.*
borderline *n* frontera *f.*
bore *vt* taladrar; barrenar; fastidiar.
boredom *n* aburrimiento *m.*
borrow *vt* pedir prestado/da.
bosom *n* seno, pecho *m.*
boss *n* jefe *m;* patrón/ona *m/f.*
botany *n* botánica *f.*
botch *vt* chapuzar.
both *adj* ambos.
bother *vt* preocupar; fastidiar.
bottle *n* botella *f.*
bottom *n* fondo *m.*
bough *n* brazo del árbol *m;* ramo *m.*
boulder *n* canto rodado *m.*
bounce *vi* rebotar.
bound *n* limite *m;* salto *m.*
boundary *n* limite *m;* frontera *f.*
bouquet *n* ramillete de flores *m.*
bourgeois *adj* burgués.
bout *n* ataque *m.*
bow *vt* encorvar, doblar.
bow *n* arco *m.*
bowels *npl* intestinos *mpl .*
bowl *n* taza; bola *f.*
bow tie *n* pajarita *f.*
box *n* caja, cajita *f.*
boxer *n* boxeador *m.*
boxing *n* boxeo *m.*
box office *n* taquilla *f.*
boy *n* muchacho *m;* niño *m.*
boycott *vt* boicotear: —*n* boicot *m.*
boyfriend *n* novio *m.*
bra *n* sujetador *m.*
bracelet *n* brazalete *m.*
bracket *n* puntal *m;* paréntesis *m.*
brag *n* jactancia *f;* —*vi* jactarse.

braid *n* pliegue *m*, trenza *f:* —*vt* trenzar.
brain *n* cerebro *m*.
brake *n* freno *m:* —*vt vi* frenar.
bran *n* salvado *m*.
branch *n* ramo *m;* rama *f*.
brand *n* marca *f*.
brandy *n* coñac *m*.
brass *n* latón *m*.
brassiere *n* sujetador *m*.
brave *adj* bravo/va, valiente.
bravery *n* valor *m*.
brawl *n* pelea *f*.
brazier *n* brasero *m*.
breach *n* rotura *f*.
bread *n* pan *m*.
breadth *n* anchura *f*.
break *vt* romper; quebrantar.
breakage *n* rotura *f*.
breakfast *n* desayuno *m:* —*vi* desa-yunar.
breast *n* pecho, seno *m*.
breastbone *n* esternón *m*.
breath *n* aliento *m*, respiración *f;* soplode aire *m*.
breathe *vt vi* respirar; exhalar.
breathtaking *adj* pasmoso/sa.
breed *n* casta, raza *f*.
breeze *n* brisa *f*.
brevity *n* brevedad, concisión *f*.
brew *vt* hacer; tramar, mezclar.
bribe *n* cohecho, soborno *m*.
bribery *n* cohecho, soborno *m*.
bric-a-brac *n* baratijas *fpl*.
brick *n* ladrillo *m*.
bricklayer *n* albañil *m*.
bride *n* novia *f*.
bridegroom *n* novio *m*.
bridesmaid *n* madrina de boda *f*.
bridge *n* puente *m/f*.
brief *adj* breve, conciso/sa, sucinto/ta.
briefcase *n* cartera *f*.
brigade *n (mil)* brigada *f*.
bright *adj* claro/ra, luciente, brillante.
brighten *vt* pulir, dar lustre.
brilliant *adj* brillante.
bring *vt* llevar, traer.
brisk *adj* vivo/va, alegre, jovial; fresco/ca.
brisket *n* pecho (de un animal) *m*.
briskly *adj* vigorosamente.
bristle *n* cerda, seta *f:* —*vi* erizarse.
bristly *adj* cerdoso/sa, lleno/na decerdas.
brittle *adj* quebradizo, frágil.
broach *vt* comenzar a hablar de.
broad *adj* ancho.
broadcast *n* emisión *f*.
broadcasting *n* radiodifusión *f*.
broaden *vt vi* ensanchar(se).
broadly *adv* anchamente.
broad-minded *adj* tolerante.
brocade *n* brocado *m*.
broccoli *n* brécol *m*.
brochure *n* folleto *m*.
broil *vt* asar a la parrilla.
broken *adj* roto/ta.
broker *n* corredor/a *m/f*.
bronchial *adj* bronquial.
bronchitis *n* bronquitis *f*.
bronze *n* bronce *m*.
brooch *n* broche *m*.

brook *n* arroyo *m*.
broom *n* hiniesta *f;* escoba *f*.
broth *n* caldo *m*.
brothel *n* burdel *m*.
brother *n* hermano *m*.
brother-in-law *n* cuñado *m*.
brow *n* caja *f;* frente *f;* cima *f*.
browbeat *vt* intimidar.
brown *adj* moreno/na; castaño/ña.
browse *vt* ramonear.
bruise *vt* magullar.
brunette *n* morena *f*.
brunt *n* choque *m*.
brush *n* cepillo *m;* escobilla *f*.
brusque *adj* brusco/ca.
Brussels sprout *n* col de Bruselas *f*.
brutal *adj* brutal.
brutality *n* brutalidad *f*.
brute *n* bruto *m*.
bubble *n* burbuja *f*.
bubblegum *n* chicle *m*.
bucket *n* cubo, pozal *m*.
buckle *n* hebilla *f*.
bucolic *adj* bucólico/ca.
bud *n* pimpollo, botón *m:* —*vi* brotar.
Buddhism *n* Budismo *m*.
buddy *n* compañero *m*.
budge *vi* moverse.
budgerigar *n* periquito *m*.
budget *n* presupuesto *m*.
buff *n* entusiasta *m*.
buffalo *n* búfalo *m*.
buffet *n* buffet *m*.
buffoon *n* bufón, chocarrero *m*.
bug *n* chinche *m*.
bugle(horn) *n* trompa de caza *f*.
build *vt* edificar; construir.
building *n* edificio *m;* construcción *f*.
bulb *n* bulbo *m;* cebolla *f*.
bulge *vi* combarse: —*n* bombeo *m*.
bulk *n* masa *f;* volumen *m*.
bulky *adj* grueso/sa, grande.
bull *n* toro *m*.
bulldog *n* dogo *m*.
bulldozer *n* aplanadora *f*.
bullet *n* bala *f*.
bullfight *n* corrida de toros *f*.
bullfighter *n* toreo *m*.
bullfighting *n* los toros *mpl*.
bullion *n* oro o plata en barras *m* o *f*.
bullock *n* novillo capado *m*.
bullring *n* plaza de toros *f*.
bully *n* valentón *m:* —*vt* tiranizar.
bumblebee *n* abejorro *m*.
bump *n* hinchazón *f*.
bun *n* bollo *m;* mono *m*.
bunch *n* ramo *m*.
bundle *n* fardo *m*, haz *m*.
bung *n* tapón *m*.
bungalow *n* bungalow *m*.
bunk *n* litera *f*.
bunker *n* refugio *m;* bunker *m*.
burden *n* carga *f:* —*vt* cargar.
bureau *n* armario *m;* escritorio *m*.
bureaucracy *n* burocracia *f*.
burglar *n* ladrón *m*.
burial *n* enterramiento *m;* exequias *fpl*.

burial place n cementerio m.
burly adj corpulento/ta, fornido/da.
burn vt quemar, abrasar, incendiar: — vi arder: —n quema dura f.
burner n quemador m; mechero m.
burning adj ardiente.
burrow n conejera f.
bursar n tesorero m.
burse n bolsa, lonja f.
burst vi reventar; abrirse.
bury vt enterrar, sepultar; esconder.
bus n autobús m.
bush n arbusto, espinal m.
busily adv diligentemente, apresuradamente.
business n asunto m; negocios mpl .
businessman n hombre de negocios m.
bust n busto m.
bus-stop n parada de autobuses f.
bustle vi hacer ruido.
busy adj ocupado/da; entrometido/da.
busybody n entrometido m.
but conj pero; mas.

butcher n carnicero m.
butcher's (shop) n carnicería f.
butler n mayordomo m.
butter n mantequilla f.
buttercup n (bot) ranúnculo m.
butterfly n mariposa f.
buttocks npl posaderas fpl.
button n botón m.
buttonhole n ojal m.
buttress n estribo m; apoyo m.
buxom adj frescachona.
buy vt comprar.
buzz n susurro, zumbido m: —vi zumbar.
buzzard n ratonero común m.
buzzer n timbre m.
by prep por; a, en; de; cerca, al lado de.
bypass n carretera de circunvalación f.
by-product n derivado m.
bystander n mirador m.
byte n (comput) byte m.
byword n proverbio, refrán m.

C

cab n taxi m.
cabbage n berza, col f.
cabin n cabaña.
cabinet n consejo á ministros m; gabinete m.
cable n (mar) cable m.
cable car n teleférico m.
cactus n cacto m.
cadaver n cadáver m.
cadet n cadete m.
cadge vt mangar.
cafeteria n cantina f.
cage n jaula f.
cake n bollo m; to rtita f.
calculate vt calcular.
calculator n calculadora f.
calendar n calendario m.
calf n ternero m.
call vt llamar, nombrar.
calligraphy n caligrafía f.
callous adj calloso/sa.
calm n calma, tranquilidad.
calorie n caloría f.
Calvinist n calvinista m.
camel n camello m.
cameo n camafeo m.
camera n máquina fotográfica f.
camomile n manzanilla f.
camouflage n camuflaje m.
camp n campo m.
campaign n campana f.
camping n camping m.
campsite n camping m.
can vi poder: —n lata f.
canal n estanque m; canal m.
cancel vt cancelar; anular.
cancer n cáncer m.
Cancer n Cáncer m (signo del zodiaco).
caress n caricia f.
caretaker n portero m.

cargo n cargamento de navío m.
caricature n caricatura f.
carnal adj carnal; sensual.
carnation n clavel m.
carnival n carnaval m.
carpenter n carpintero m.
carpentry n carpintería f.
carpet n alfombra f.
carrier n portador m.
carrot n zanahoria f.
carry vt llevar, conducir.
cart n carro m; carreta f.
cartilage n cartílago m.
carton n caja f.
cartoon n dibujo animado m.
carve vt cincelar.
carving n escultura f.
case n caja f; maleta f.
cash n dinero contante m.
cashmere n cachemira f.
cask n barril, tonel m.
casserole n cazuela f.
cassette n cassette m.
cassock n sotana f.
castanets npl castañetas fpl.
castaway n réprobo m.
caste n casta f.
castigate vt castigar.
castle n castillo m.
castrate vt castrar.
castration n capadura f.
casual adj casual.
cat n gato m; gata f.
catalog(ue) n catalogo m.
cataract n cascada f; catarata f.
catarrh n catarro m; reuma f.
catastrophe n catástrofe f.
catch vt coger.
catchphrase n lema m.

catechism *n* catecismo *m*.
candid *adj* cándido/da, sencillo/lla.
candle *n* candela *f*; vela *f*.
candlestick *n* candelero *m*.
candy *n* caramelo *m*.
cane *n* cana *f*; bastón *m*.
cannabis *n* canabis *f*.
cannibal *n* caníbal *m*.
cannibalism *n* canibalismo *m*.
cannon *n* cañón *m*.
canoe *n* canoa *f*.
canon *n* canon *m*; regla *f*.
can opener *n* abrelatas *m invar*.
canopy *n* dosel, pabellón *m*.
canter *n* medio galope *m*.
canvas *n* cañamazo *m*.
canyon *n* cañón *m*.
cap *n* gorra *f*.
capability *n* capacidad *f*.
capable *adj* capaz.
cape *n* cabo, promontorio *m*.
capital *adj* capital; principal.
capitalism *n* capitalismo *m*.
Capitol *n* Capitolio *m*.
capitulate *vi* capitular.
Capricorn *n* Capricornio *m* (signo delzodiaco).
capsule *n* cápsula *f*.
captain *n* capitán *m*.
captivate *vt* cautivar.
capture *n* captura *f*; presa *f*.
car *n* coche, carro *m*; vagón *m*.
carafe *n* garrafa *f*.
caramel *n* caramelo *m*.
carat *n* quilate *m*.
carbohydrates *npl* hidratos de car-bono *mpl* .
carcass *n* cadáver *m*.
card *n* naipe *m*; carta *f*.
cardboard *n* cartón *m*.
cardinal *adj* cardinal, principal.
care *n* cuidado *m*; solicitud *f*.
career *n* carrera *f*.
categorize *vt* clasificar.
category *n* categoría *f*.
caterpillar *n* oruga *f*.
cathedral *n* catedral *f*.
catholic *adj* , *n* católico *m*.
Catholicism *n* catolicismo *m*.
cattle *n* ganado *m*.
cauliflower *n* coliflor *f*.
cause *n* causa *f*; razón *f*; motivo *m*.
causeway *n* arrecife *m*.
caustic *adj* , *n* cáustico *m*.
cauterize *vt* cauterizar.
caution *n* prudencia.
cavalry *n* caballería *f*.
cave *n* caverna *f*.
caviar *n* caviar *m*.
cease *vt* parar, suspender.
cedar *n* cedro *m*.
cede *vt* ceder.
ceiling *n* techo *m*.
celebrate *vt* celebrar.
celery *n* apio *m*.
celibacy *n* celibato *m*.
cell *n* celdilla *f*; célula *f*; cueva *f*.
cellar *n* sótano *m*.
cellophane *n* celofán *m*.

cement *n* cemento.
cemetery *n* cementerio *m*.
cenotaph *n* cenotafio *m*.
censor *n* censor *m*.
census *n* censo *m*.
cent *n* centavo *m*.
center *n* centro *m*.
centigrade *n* centígrado *m*.
centiliter *n* centilitro *m*.
centimeter *n* centímetro *m*.
centipede *n* escolopendra *f*.
central *adj* central.
centralize *vt* centralizar.
century *n* siglo *m*.
ceramic *adj* cerámico/ca.
ceremony *n* ceremonia *f*.
certain *adj* cierto/ta, evidente.
certificate *n* certificado, testimonio *m*.
certify *vt* certificar, afirmar.
cervical *adj* cervical.
chaffinch *n* pinzón *m*.
chain *n* cadena *f*.
chair *n* silla *f*.
chamber *n* cámara *f*.
chameleon *n* camaleón *m*.
champagne *n* champaña *m*.
championship *n* campeonato *m*.
chance *n* ventura, suerte *f*; oportunidad *f*.
chancellor *n* canciller *m*.
change *vt* cambiar.
channel *n* canal *m*.
chant *n* canto (llano) *m*.
chaos *n* caos *m*.
chapel *n* capilla *f*.
chaplain *n* capellán *m*.
chapter *n* capitulo *m*.
character *n* carácter *m*.
charcoal *n* carbón de leña *m*.
charge *vt* cargar; acusar, imputar.
charity *n* caridad.
charlatan *n* charlatán/tana *m/f* .
charm *n* encanto *m*.
charter flight *n* vuelo charter *m*.
chauffeur *n* chófer *m*.
chauvinist *n* machista *m*.
cheap *adj* barato/ta.
cheat *vi* engañar, defraudar.
check *n* cheque *m*.
checkmate *n* mate *m*.
checkout *n* caja *f*.
cheek *n* mejilla *f*.
cheese *n* queso *m*.
chef *n* jefe de cocina *m*.
chemical *adj* químico/ca.
chemist *n* químico *m*.
cheroot *n* puro *m*.
f; cherry *n* cereza *f*.
cherub *n* querubín *m*.
chess *n* ajedrez *m*.
chest *n* pecho *m*.
chestnut *n* castaña *f*.
chew *vt* mascar, masticar.
chewing gum *n* chicle *m*.
chicken *n* pollo *m*.
chickenpox *n* varicela *f*.
chickpea *n* garbanzo *m*.
chief *adj* principal.

chilblain n sabañón m.
child n niño m; niña f.
childhood n infancia, niñez f.
children npl de **child** niños mpl .
chimney n chimenea f.
chimpanzee n chimpancé m.
chin n barbilla f.
chiropodist n pedicuro m.
chirp vi chirriar.
chlorine n cloro m.
chloroform n cloroformo m.
chocolate n chocolate m.
choice n elección, preferencia f.
choir n coro m.
choke vt sofocar.
cholera n cólera m.
choose vt escoger, elegir.
chop vt tajar, cortar: —n chuleta f.
chore n faena f.
Christ n Cristo m.
christen vt bautizar.
Christianity n cristianismo m; cristiandad f.
Christmas n Navidad f.
chrome n cromo m.
chronicle n crónica f.
chronological adj cronológico/ca.
chubby adj gordo/da.
chunk n trozo m.
church n iglesia f.
churchyard n cementerio m.
cider n sidra f.
cigar n cigarro m.
cigarette n cigarrillo m.
cinder n carbonilla f.
cinema n cine m.
cinnamon n canela f.
circle n círculo m.
circumcize vt circuncidar.
circumcision n circuncisión f.
circumference n circunferenciacircuito m.
circumflex n acento circunflejo m.
circumstance n circunstancia.
circus n circo m.
cistern n cisterna f.
cite vt citar.
citizen n ciudadano m.
city n ciudad f.
civic adj cívico/ca.
civil adj civil, cortés.
civilization n civilización f.
clairvoyant n clarividente m/f.
clam n almeja f.
clammy adj viscoso/sa.
clamor n clamor m.
clan n familia, tribu, raza f.
clandestine adj clandestino/na.
clap vt aplaudir.
claret n clarete m.
clarify vt clarificar, aclarar.
clarinet n clarinete m.
clarity n claridad f.
class n clase f; orden f.
classic(al) adj clásico/ca: —n autorclásico m.
classify vt clasificar.
classmate n compañero de clase m.
classroom n aula f.
clause n cláusula f.

claw n garra f.
clay n arcilla f.
clean adj limpio/pia; casto/ta: —vt limpiar.
cleanse vt limpiar, purificar; purgar.
clear adj claro/ra.
clemency n clemencia f.
clement adj clemente, benigno/na.
clergy n clero m.
clerical adj clerical, eclesiástico/ca.
clerk n dependiente m; oficinista m.
clever adj listo/ta; hábil.
client n cliente m/f.
cliff n acantilado m.
climate n clima m.
climax n clímax m.
climb vt escalar, trepar.
cling vi colgar, adherirse.
clinic n clínica f.
clip vt cortar.
clique n camarilla f.
cloak n capa f.
cloakroom n guardarropa m.
clock n reloj m.
clog n zueco m.
cloister n claustro, monasterio m.
close vt cerrar; concluir, terminar.
closet n armario m.
close-up n primer plano m.
clot n grumo m; embolia f.
cloth n paño m.
clothe vt vestir.
clothes npl ropa f.
clothes pin n pinza f.
cloud n nube f.
clout n tortazo m.
clove n clavo m.
clover n trébol m.
clown n payaso m.
coach n autocar, autobús m.
coagulate vt coagular, cuajar.
coal n carbón m.
coalition n coalición, confederación f.
coarse adj basto/ta; grosero/ra.
coast n costa f.
coastguard n guardacostas m invar.
coat n chaqueta f; abrigo m.
coat hanger n percha f.
cobbler n zapatero m.
cobweb n telaraña f.
cocaine n cocaína f.
cock n gallo m; macho m.
cockle n caracol de mar m.
cockpit n cabina f.
cockroach n cucaracha f.
cocktail n cóctel m.
cocoa n coco m; cacao m.
coconut n coco m.
cod n bacalao m.
code n código m.
cod-liver oil n aceite de hígado debacalao m.
coffee n café m.
coffer n cofre m; caja f.
coffin n ataúd m.
cog n diente (de rueda) m.
cognac n coñac m.
cogwheel n rueda dentada f.
cohabit vi cohabitar.

coherence n coherencia f.
cohesion n coherencia f.
cohesive adj cohesivo.
coil n rollo m.
coin n moneda f.
coincide vi coincidir.
coke n coque m.
colander n colador, pasador m.
cold adj frío/ría.
cold sore n herpes labial m.
coleslaw n ensalada de col f.
colic n cólico m.
collaborate vt cooperar.
collapse vi hundirse.
collapsible adj plegable.
collar n cuello m.
collarbone n clavícula f.
collate vt comparar.
collateral adj colateral.
colleague n colega m.
collect vt recoger; coleccionar.
collection n colección f; compilación f.
college n colegio m.
collide vi chocar.
colloquial adj familiar.
collusion n colusión f.
colon n dos puntos mpl ; (med) colon m.
colonel n (mil) coronel m.
colonial adj colonial.
colonize vt colonizar.
colony n colonia f.
color n color m.
colossal adj colosal.
colt n potro m.
column n columna f.
columnist n columnista m.
coma n coma f.
comatose adj comatoso/sa.
comb n peine m: —vt peinar.
combat n combate m.
combination n combinación f.
combine vt combinar.
combustion n combustión f.
come vi venir.
comedy n comedia f.
comet n cometa f.
comfort n confort m.
comfortable adj cómodo/da.
comma n (gr) coma f.
command vt comandar.
commemorate vt conmemorar; celebrar.
commence vt , vi comenzar.
commencement n principio m.
commend vt encomendar.
commensurate adj proporcionado/da.
comment n comentario m.
commentator n comentador m.
commerce n comercio m.
commercial adj comercial.
commiserate vt compadecer.
commission n comisión f.
commit vt cometer.
committee n comité m.
commodity n comodidad f.
common adj común.
commotion n tumulto m.
communicate vt comunicar.

communion n comunión f.
communism n comunismo m.
community n comunidad f.
commute vt conmutar.
compact adj compacto/ta.
compact disc n disco compacto m.
companion n compañero/ra.
company n compañía, sociedad f.
compare vt comparar.
compartment n compartimiento m.
compass n brújula f.
compassion n compasión f.
compatriot n compatriota m.
compensate vt compensar.
compensation n compensación f.
compère n presentador m.
compete vi concurrir.
competent adj competente.
competition n competencia f.
competitor n competidor, rival m.
compilation n compilación f.
complain vi quejarse, lamentarse.
complement n complemento m.
complex adj complejo/ja.
complexion n tez f; aspecto m.
complicate vt complicar.
component adj componente.
compose vt componer.
composer n autor m.
composite adj compuesto/ta.
composition n composición f.
comprehend vt comprender, contener; entender.
compress vt comprimir.
comprise vt comprender.
compromise n compromiso m.
compulsive adj compulsivo/va.
computer n ordenador m.
comrade n camarada.
con vt estafar: —n estafa f.
concave adj cóncavo/va.
conceal vt ocultar, esconder.
concede vt conceder.
conceit n concepto m, capricho m.
conceive vt concebir, comprender.
concentrate vt concentrar.
concept n concepto m.
conception n concepción f.
concern vt concernir, importar.
concert n concierto m.
concession n concesión f; privilegio m.
concise adj conciso/sa.
conclude vt concluir.
conclusion n conclusión.
concord n concordia, armonía f.
concrete n concreto m.
concussion n concusión f.
condemn vt condenar.
condensation n condensación f.
condiment n condimento m; salsa f.
condition vt condicionar.
conditional adj condicional.
condom n condón m.
conduct n conducta f.
conductor n conductor m.
conduit n conducto m.
cone n cono m.
confection n confitura f.

confectioner's (shop) n pastelería f.
conference n conferencia f.
confess vt, vi confesar(se).
confession n confesión f.
confessional n confesionario m.
confetti n confeti m.
confidant n confidente.
confide vt, vi confiar; fiarse.
confidence n confianza, seguridad f.
confident adj cierto/ta, seguro/ra; confiado/da.
confine vt limitar; aprisionar.
confirm vt confirmar; ratificar.
confiscate vt confiscar.
conflagration n conflagración f.
conflict n conflicto m; combate m; pelea f.
conflicting adj contradictorio/ria.
confluence n confluencia f.
conform vt, vi conformar(se).
conformity n conformidad.
confound vt turbar, confundir.
confront vt afrontar; confrontar.
confrontation n enfrentamiento m.
confuse vt confundir.
congeal vt, vi helar, congelar(se).
congenial adj congenial.
congenital adj congénito/ta.
congested adj atestado/da.
congestion n congestión f; acumulación f.
congratulate vt congratular, felicitar.
congratulations npl felicidades fpl.
congratulatory adj congratulatorio/ria.
congregate vt congregar.
congress n congreso m; conferencia f.
congruity n congruencia f.
coniferous adj (bot) conífero/ra.
conjecture n conjetura.
conjugal adj conyugal.
conjugate vt (gr) conjugar.
conjunction n conjunción f.
conjuncture n coyuntura f.
conjure vi conjurar.
con man n timador m.
connect vt juntar, unir.
connection n conexión f.
connivance n connivencia f.
connive vi tolerar.
connoisseur n conocedor/a m/f.
conquer vt conquistar; vencer.
conqueror n vencedor/a, conquistador/a m/f.
conquest n conquista f.
conscience n conciencia f.
consciousness n conciencia f.
conscript n conscripto m.
conscription n reclutamiento m.
consecrate vt consagrar.
consecration n consagración f.
consecutive adj consecutivo/va.
consensus n consenso m.
consent n consentimiento m; aprobación f.
consequence n consecuencia f.
consequent adj consecutivo/va.
conservation n conservación f.
conservative adj conservativo/va.
conservatory n conservatorio m.
conserve vt conservar.
consider vt considerar.
considerable adj considerable.

considerate adj considerado/da.
consideration n consideración f.
consign vt consignar.
consignment n consignación f.
consist vi consistir.
consistency n consistencia f.
consistent adj consistente.
consolation n consolación f; consuelo m.
console vt consolar.
consolidate vt, vi consolidar(se).
consolidation n consolidación f.
consonant adj consonante.
consort n consorte, socio m.
conspicuous adj conspicuo/cua.
conspiracy n conspiración f.
conspirator n conspirador/a m/f.
conspire vi conspirar.
constancy n constancia.
constant adj constante.
constellation n constelación f.
constipated adj estreñido/da.
constituency n junta electoral f.
constituent n constitutivo m.
constitute vt constituir.
constitution n constitución f.
constitutional adj constitucional.
constrict vt constreñir, estrechar.
construct vt construir, edificar.
construction n construcción f.
consul n cónsul m.
consulate, consulship n consulado m.
consult vt, vi consultar(se).
consultation n consulta f.
consume vt consumir.
consumer n consumidor/a m/f.
consumption n consumo m.
contact n contacto m.
contact lenses npl lentes de contacto mpl.
contagious adj contagioso/sa.
contain vt contener.
container n recipiente m.
contaminate vt contaminar.
contamination n contaminación f.
contemplate vt contemplar.
contemplation n contemplación f.
contempt n desprecio, desdén m.
contend vi contender.
content adj contento/ta, satisfecho/cha.
contention n contención, altercación f.
contest vt contestar, disputar, litigar.
contestant n concursante/ta m/f.
context n contexto m.
continent adj continente.
contingency n contingencia f.
contingent n contingente m; cuota f.
continue vt continuar.
contort vt torcer.
contortion n contorsión f.
contour n contorno m.
contraband n contrabando m.
contraception n contracepción f.
contraceptive n anticonceptivo m.
contract vt contraer; abreviar; contratar.
contraction n contracción f; abrevia-tura f.
contradict vt contradecir.
contradiction n contradicción, oposi-ción f.
contraption n artilugio m.

contrary *adj* contrario/ria, opuesto/ta.
contrast *n* contraste *m.*
contrasting *adj* opuesto/ta.
contributary *adj* contributario/ria.
contribute *vt* contribuir, ayudar.
contrive *vt* inventar, trazar.
control *n* control *m;* inspección *f:* —*vt* controlar; manejar; restringir; gobernar.
controversial *adj* polémico/ca.
controversy *n* controversia *f.*
conurbation *n* urbanización *f.*
convalesce *vi* convalecer.
convalescence *n* convalecencia *f.*
convene *vt* convocar; juntar, unir.
convenient *adj* conveniente.
convent *n* convento *m.*
convention *n* convención *f.*
converge *vi* converger.
conversation *n* conversación *f.*
converse *vi* conversar; platicar.
conversely *adv* mutuamente, recíprocamente.
convert *vt , vi* convertir(se).
convertible *adj* convertible.
convex *adj* convexo/xa.
convey *vt* transportar; transmitir, transferir.
conveyance *n* transporte *m.*
conveyancer *n* notario *m.*
conviction *n* convicción *f.*
convince *vt* convencer.
convivial *adj* sociable; hospitalario/ria.
convoke *vt* convocar, reunir.
convoy *n* convoy *m.*
convulse *vt* conmover, convulsionar.
convulsion *n* convulsión *f.*
convulsive *adj* convulsivo/va.
cook *n* cocinero *m;* cocinera *f:* —*vt* cocinar.
cool *adj* fresco/ca; indiferente.
cooperate *vi* cooperar.
cooperation *n* cooperación *f.*
coordinate *vt* coordinar.
coordination *n* coordinación *f.*
cop *n (fam)* poli *m.*
copier *n* copiadora *f.*
copious *adj* copioso/sa, abundante.
copper *n* cobre *m.*
copulate *vi* copularse.
copy *n* copia *f.*
copying machine *n* copiadora *f.*
coral *n* coral *m.*
cord *n* cuerda *f;* cable *m.*
cordial *adj* cordial.
corduroy *n* pana *f.*
core *n* cuesco *m;* interior *m.*
cork *n* alcornoque *m;* corcho *m.*
corkscrew *n* tirabuzón *m.*
corn *n* maíz *m;* grano *m;* callo *m.*
corncob *n* mazorca *f.*
cornea *n* córnea *f.*
corner *n* rincón *m;* esquina *f.*
cornet *n* corneta *f.*
cornflakes *npl* copos de maíz *mpl .*
cornice *n* cornisa *f.*
coronary *n* infarto *m.*
coronation *n* coronación *f.*
coroner *n* oficial que hace la inspección jurídica de los cadáveres *m.*
corporation *n* corporación *f.*

corps *n* cuerpo (de ejercito) *m.*
correct *vt* corregir; enmendar.
correctness *n* exactitud *f.*
correspond *vi* corresponder.
correspondence *n* correspondencia *f.*
corridor *n* pasillo *m.*
corrode *vt* corroer.
corrosive *adj , n* corrosivo *m.*
corrupt *vt* corromper; sobornar.
corruption *n* corrupción *f;* depravación *f.*
corset *n* corsé *m.*
cosily *adv* cómodamente.
cosmetic *adj* cosmético/ca.
cosmic *adj* cósmico/ca.
cosmonaut *n* cosmonauta *m.*
cosmopolitan *adj* cosmopolita.
cosset *vt* mimar.
cost *n* coste, precio *m:* —*vi* costar.
costume *n* traje *m.*
cosy *adj* cómodo/da.
cottage *n* casita, casucha *f.*
cotton *n* algodón *m.*
cotton wool *n* algodón hidrófilo *m.*
couch *n* sofá *m.*
couchette *n* litera *f.*
cough *n* tos *f:* —*vi* toser.
council *n* concilio, consejo *m.*
counsel *n* consejo, aviso *m.*
count *vt* contar, numerar; calcular.
counter *n* mostrador *m;* ficha *f.*
counterfeit *vt* contrahacer, imitar, falsear.
counterpart *n* parte correspond-iente *f.*
countersign *vt* refrendar.
countess *n* condesa *f.*
countless *adj* innumerable.
countrified *adj* rústico/ca.
country *n* país *m;* campo *m;* región *f;* patria *f.*
county *n* condado *m.*
coup *n* golpe *m.*
couple *n* par *m.*
couplet *n* copla *f;* par *m.*
coupon *n* cupón *m.*
courage *n* coraje, valor *f.*
courageous *adj* corajudo/da, valeroso/sa: —**~ly** *adv* valerosamente.
courier *n* correo, mensajero/ra *m/f ,* expreso *m.*
course *n* curso *m;* carrera *f;* camino *m;* ruta *f.*
court *n* corte *f.*
courteous *adj* cortés.
courtesy *n* cortesía *f.*
courthouse *n* palacio de justicia *m.*
courtyard *n* patio *m.*
cousin *n* primo *m;* prima *f.*
cove *n (mar)* ensenada, caleta *f.*
covenant *n* contrato *m.*
cover *n* cubierta *f;* abrigo *m.*
cover letter *n* carta de explicación *f.*
covert *adj* cubierto/ta; oculto/ta, secreto/ta.
cover-up *n* encubrimiento *m.*
covet *vt* codiciar.
cow *n* vaca *f.*
coward *n* cobarde *m/f .*
cowardice *n* cobardía, timidez *f.*
cowboy *n* vaquero *m.*
cower *vi* agacharse.
cowherd *n* vaquero *m.*
crab *n* cangrejo *m.*

crab apple *n* manzana silvestre *f.*
crack *n* crujido *m;* hendedura, quebraja *f.*
cracker *n* buscapiés *m invar;* galleta *f.*
crackle *vi* crujir, chillar.
cradle *n* cuna *f.*
craft *n* arte.
craftsman *n* artífice, artesano *m.*
craftmanship *n* artesanía *f.*
crafty *adj* astuto/ta, artificioso/sa.
cramp *n* calambre *m.*
cranberry *n* arandilla *f.*
crane *n* grulla *f;* grua *f.*
crash *vi* estallar.
crash helmet *n* casco *m.*
crass *adj* craso/sa.
crater *n* cráter *m;* boca de volcán *f.*
cravat *n* pañuelo *m.*
crave *vt* rogar, suplicar.
craving *adj* insaciable.
crawl *vi* arrastrar.
crayfish *n* cangrejo de río *m.*
crayon *n* lápiz *m.*
craze *n* manía *f.*
craziness *n* locura *f.*
crazy *adj* loco/ca.
cream *n* crema *f.*
creamy *adj* cremoso.
crease *n* pliegue *m.*
create *vt* crear; causar.
creation *n* creación *f;* elección *f.*
creator *n* creador/a *m/f.*
creature *n* criatura *f.*
credence *n* creencia, fe *f.*
credibility *n* credibilidad *f.*
credible *adj* creíble.
credit *n* crédito *m.*
creditable *adj* estimable.
credit card *n* tarjeta de crédito *f.*
creed *n* credo *m.*
creek *n* arroyo, rio *m.*
creep *vi* arrastrar, serpear.
creeper *n (bot)* enredadera *f.*
cremate *vt* incinerar cadáveres.
cremation *n* cremación *f.*
crematorium *n* crematorio *m.*
crescent *adj* creciente.
cress *n* berro *m.*
crest *n* cresta *f.*
crevasse *n* grieta (de glaciar) *f.*
crevice *n* raja, hendedura *f.*
crew *n* banda, tropa *f.*
crib *n* cuna *f;* pesebre *m.*
cricket *n* grillo *m;* criquet *m.*
crime *n* crimen *m.*
criminal *adj* criminal.
crimson *adj , n* carmesí *m.*
cripple *n, adj* cojo/ja *m/f.*
crisis *n* crisis *f.*
crisp *adj* crujiente.
crispness *n* encrespadura *f.*
criss-cross *adj* entrelazado/da.
criterion *n* criterio *m.*
critic *n* crítico *m;* crítica *f.*
criticize *vt* criticar, censurar.
crochet *n* ganchillo *m.*
crockery *n* loza *fl.*
crocodile *n* cocodrilo *m.*

crook *n (fam)* ladrón *m.*
crooked *adj* torcido/da; perverso/sa.
cross *n* cruz *f.*
crossbar *n* travesaño *m.*
crossbreed *n* raza cruzada *f.*
cross-country *n* carrera a campotraviesa *f.*
crossing *n* cruce *m;* paso a nivel *m.*
cross-reference *n* contrarreferencia *f.*
crotch *n* entrepierna *f.*
crouch *vi* agacharse, bajarse.
crow *n* cuervo *m.*
crowd *n* publico *m.*
crown *n* corona *f.*
crown prince *n* príncipe real *m.*
crucial *adj* crucial.
crucible *n* crisol *m.*
crucifix *n* crucifijo *m.*
crucifixion *n* crucifixión *f.*
crude *adj* crudo/da, imperfecto/ta.
cruel *adj* cruel.
cruelty *n* crueldad *f.*
cruet *n* vinagrera *f.*
cruiser *n* crucero *m.*
crumb *n* miga *f.*
crumble *vt* desmigajar.
crumple *vt* arrugar.
crunchy *adj* crujiente.
crusade *n* cruzada *f.*
crush *vt* apretar, oprimir.
crust *n* costra *f;* corteza *f.*
crutch *n* muleta *f.*
crux *n* lo esencial.
cry *vt , vi* gritar; exclamar; llorar.
crypt *n* cripta (bóveda subterránea) *f.*
cryptic *adj* enigmático/ca.
crystal *n* cristal *m.*
cub *n* cachorro *m.*
cube *n* cubo *m.*
cuckoo *n* cuclillo, cuco *m.*
cucumber *n* pepino *m.*
cuddle *vt* abrazar.
cudgel *n* garrote, palo *m.*
cue *n* taco (de billar) *m.*
cuff *n* puñada *f;* vuelta *f.*
cull *vt* escoger, elegir.
culminate *vi* culminar.
culpable *adj* culpable.
cult *n* culto *f.*
cultivate *vi* cultivar.
cultivation *n* cultivación *f.*
cultural *adj* cultural.
culture *n* cultura *f.*
cumulative *adj* cumulativo/va.
cunning *adj* astuto/ta; intrigante.
cup *n* taza, jícara *f; (bot)* cáliz *m.*
cupboard *n* armario *m.*
curable *adj* curable.
curb *n* freno *m;* bordillo *m.*
curd *n* cuajada *f.*
cure *n* cura *f;* remedio *m.*
curiosity *n* curiosidad *f;* rareza *f.*
curious *adj* curioso/sa: **—~ly** *adv* curiosamente.
curl *n* rizo de pelo *m.*
curly *adj* rizado/da.
currant *n* pasa *f.*
currency *n* moneda *f.*
current *adj* corriente.

current affairs npl actualidades fpl.
currently adv corrientemente; actualmente.
curry n curry m.
curse vt maldecir.
cursor n cursor m.
curt adj sucinto/ta.
curtail vt acortar.
curtain n cortina f; telón (en los teatros) m.
curvature n curvatura f.
curve vt encorvar: —n curva f.
cushion n cojín m; almohada f.
custard n natillas fpl.
custodian n custodio m.
custody n custodia f; prisión f.
custom n costumbre f, uso m.
customary adj usual, acostumbrado/da, ordinario/ria.
customer n cliente m/f.
customs npl aduana f.
customs duty n derechos de aduana mpl.
customs officer n aduanero/ra m/f.
cut vt cortar; separar.
cutback n reducción f.

cute adj lindo/da.
cutlery n cuchillería f.
cutlet n chuleta f.
cut-rate adj a precio reducido.
cut-throat n asesino m: —adj encarnizado/da.
cutting n cortadura f: —adj cortante; mordaz.
cyanide n cianuro m.
cycle n ciclo m; bicicleta f: —vi ir en bicicleta.
cycling n ciclismo m.
cyclist n ciclista m/f.
cyclone n ciclón m.
cygnet n pollo del cisne m.
cylinder n cilindro m; rollo m.
cylindric(al) adj cilíndrico/ca.
cymbals n címbalo m.
cynic(al) adj cínico/ca; obsceno/na: — n cínico m (filósofo).
cynicism n cinismo m.
cypress n ciprés m.
cyst n quiste m.
czar n zar m.

D

dad(dy) n papa m.
daddy-long-legs n típula m.
daffodil n narciso m.
dagger n puñal m.
daily adj diario/ria.
dainty adj delicado/da.
dairy n lechería f.
dairy produce n productos lácteos mpl.
daisy n margarita f.
damage n daño m; perjuicio m.
damask n damasco m.
damn vt condenar.
damnation n perdición f.
damp adj húmedo/da.
dampen vt mojar.
dampness n humedad f.
dance n danza f; baile m.
dandelion n diente de león m.
dandruff n caspa f.
danger n peligro m.
dare vi atreverse.
daredevil n atrevido m.
dark adj oscuro/ra.
darling n, adj querido m.
darn vt zurcir.
dart n dardo m.
dartboard n diana f.
dash vi irse de prisa.
dashboard n tablero de instrumentos m.
data n datos mpl.
database n base de datos f.
date n fecha f; cita f.
daughter n hija f: —— in-law nuera f.
dawn n alba f: —vi amanecer.
day n día m.
dazzle vt deslumbrar.
deacon n diácono m.
dead adj muerto/ta.
deadline n fecha tope f.

deadlock n punto muerto m.
deaf adj sordo/da.
deal n convenio m; transacción f.
dean n deán m.
dear adj querido/da. caro/ra.
dearness n carestía f.
death n muerte f.
debacle n desastre m.
debar vt excluir.
debase vt degradar.
debate n debate m; polémica f.
debilitate vt debilitar.
debt n deuda f.
decade n década f.
decadence n decadencia f.
decaffeinated adj descafeinado/da.
decay vi decaer; pudrirse.
deceit n engaño m.
deceive vt engañar.
December n diciembre m.
decent adj decente.
decide vt , vi decidir; resolver.
deciduous adj (bot) de hoja caduca.
decimal adj decimal.
decipher vt descifrar.
decision n decisión.
declare vt declarar.
decline vt (gr) declinar; evitar.
decompose vt descomponer.
decorate vt decorar, adornar.
decoration n decoración f.
decorum n decoro m.
decrease vt disminuir.
decree n decreto m.
dedicate vt dedicar; consagrar.
dedication n dedicación f.
deduce vt deducir.
deep adj profundo/da.
deep-freeze n congeladora f.

deer n ciervo m.
defamation n difamación f.
defeat n derrota f: —vt derrotar.
defect n defecto m.
defend vt defender.
defense n defensa f.
defensive adj defensivo/va.
defer vt aplazar.
deficient adj insuficiente.
deficit n déficit m.
define vt definir.
definition n definición f.
deflate vt desinflar.
deflect vt desviar.
deform vt desfigurar.
defraud vt estafar.
defuse vt desactivar.
degenerate vi degenerar.
degrade vt degradar.
degree n grado m; titulo m.
dehydrated adj deshidratado/da.
deity n deidad, divinidad f.
dejection n desaliento m.
delay vt demorar: —n retraso m.
delegate vt delegar: —n delegado m.
delete vt tachar; borrar.
delicacy n delicadeza f.
delicate adj delicado/da.
delicious adj delicioso/sa.
delight n delicia f.
delinquent n delincuente m.
delirium n delirio m.
deliver vt entregar.
delivery n entrega f; parto m.
delivery truck n camioneta f.
delude vt engañar.
deluge n diluvio m.
demagog(ue) n demagogo m.
demand n demanda f.
demean vi rebajarse.
demented adj demente.
demise n desaparición f.
democracy n democracia f.
democrat n demócrata m/f.
demolish vt demoler.
demon n demonio, diablo m.
demonstrate vt demostrar.
demoralize vt desmoralizar.
demote vt degradar.
demure adj modesto/ta.
den n guarida f.
denial n negación f.
denims npl vaqueros mpl.
denomination n valor m.
denote vt denotar.
denounce vt denunciar.
dense adj denso/sa.
density n densidad f.
dental adj dental.
dentist n dentista m/f.
denture npl dentadura postiza f.
denunciation n denuncia f.
deny vt negar.
deodorant n desodorante m.
depart vi partir(se).
department n departamento m.
department store n gran almacén m.

departure lounge n sala de embarque f.
depend vi depender.
depict vt pintar, retratar; describir.
deplore vt deplorar, lamentar.
deport vt deportar.
deposit vt depositar.
depositor n depositante m.
depot n depósito m.
deprave vt depravar.
depravity n depravación f.
deprecate vt lamentar.
depreciate vi depreciarse.
depreciation n depreciación f.
depress vt deprimir.
depressed adj deprimido/da.
depression n depresión f.
deprivation n privación f.
deprive vt privar.
depth n profundidad f.
deputation n diputación f.
deputize vi suplir a.
deputy n diputado m.
derelict adj abandonado/da.
deride vt burlar.
derision n mofa f.
derivative n derivado m.
derive vt, vi derivar(se).
derogatory adj despectivo/va.
descend vi descender.
descendant n descendiente m.
descent n descenso m.
describe vt describir.
description n descripción f.
descriptive adj descriptivo/va.
desecrate vt profanar.
desert n desierto m.
deserve vt merecer.
design vt diseñar.
designate vt nombrar.
designedly adv de propósito.
designer n diseñador m.
desirable adj deseable.
desire n deseo m.
desk n escritorio m.
desolate adj desierto/ta.
despair n desesperación f.
desperado n bandido m.
desperate adj desesperado/da.
despise vt despreciar.
despite prep a pesar de.
despoil vt despojar.
despondency n abatimiento m.
despot n déspota m/f.
dessert n postre m.
destination n destino m.
destine vt destinar.
destiny n destino m; suerte f.
destitute adj indigente.
destroy vt destruir.
destruction n destrucción.
detach vt separar.
detail n detalle m.
detain vt retener; detener.
detect vt detectar.
detection n descubrimiento m.
detective n detective m/f.
deter vt disuadir.

detergent *n* detergente *m*.
deteriorate *vt* deteriorar.
determination *n* resolución *f*.
determine *vt* determinar.
deterrent *n* fuerza de disuasión *f*.
detest *vt* detestar.
detonate *vi* detonar.
detonation *n* detonación *f*.
detour *n* desviación *f*.
detriment *n* perjuicio *m*.
devaluation *n* devaluación *f*.
devastate *vt* devastar.
develop *vt* desarrollar.
development *n* desarrollo *m*.
deviate *vi* desviarse.
deviation *n* desviación *f*.
device *n* mecanismo *m*.
devil *n* diablo, demonio *m*.
devious *adj* taimado/da.
devise *vt* inventar.
devote *vt* dedicar.
devour *vt* devorar.
devout *adj* devoto/ta.
dew *n* rocío *m*.
dexterity *n* destreza *f*.
diabetes *n* diabetes *f*.
diabetic *n* diabético *m*.
diadem *n* diadema *f*.
diagnosis *n (med)* diagnosis *f*.
diagonal *adj* , *n* diagonal (*f*).
diagram *n* diagrama *m*.
dial *n* cuadrante *m*.
dialect *n* dialecto *m*.
dialog(ue) *n* dialogo *m*.
diameter *n* diámetro *m*.
diamond *n* diamante *m*.
diaper *n* pañal *m*.
diaphragm *n* diafragma *m*.
diarrhea *n* diarrea *f*.
diary *n* diario *m*.
dice *npl* dados *mpl* .
dictate *vt* dictar.
dictation *n* dictado *m*.
dictatorship *n* dictadura *f*.
diction *n* dicción *f*
dictionary *n* diccionario *m*.
didactic *adj* didáctico/ca.
die[1] *vi* morir.
die[2] *n* dado *m*.
diesel *n* diesel *m*.
diet *n* dieta *f*; régimen *m*.
differ *vi* diferenciarse.
difference *n* diferencia *f*.
different *adj* diferente.
difficult *adj* dificil.
dig *vt* cavar.
digest *vt* digerir.
digestion *n* digestión *f*.
digger *n* excavadora *f*.
digit *n* dígito *m*.
digital *adj* digital.
dignity *n* dignidad *f*.
dike *n* dique *m*.
dilate *vt* , *vi* dilatar(se).
dilemma *n* dilema *m*.
dilute *vt* diluir.
dim *adj* turbio/bia.

dimension *n* dimensión, extensión *f*.
diminish *vt* , *vi* disminuir(se).
dimple *n* hoyuelo *m*.
din *n* alboroto *m*.
dine *vi* cenar.
diner *n* café *m*, restaurante (económico) *m*.
dinghy *n* lancha neumática *f*.
dingy *adj* sombrío/ria.
dinner *n* cena *f*.
dinosaur *n* dinosaurio *m*.
diocese *n* diócesis *f*.
dip *vt* mojar.
diphtheria *n* difteria *f*.
diploma *n* diploma *m*.
diplomacy *n* diplomacia *f*.
diplomat *n* diplomático/ca *m/f* .
dire *adj* calamitoso/sa.
direct *adj* directo/ta: —*vt* dirigir.
direction *n* dirección *f*.
directly *adj* directamente.
director *n* director/a *m/f* .
directory *n* guía *f*.
dirt *n* suciedad *f*.
disability *n* incapacidad *f*.
disabled *adj* minusválido/da.
disadvantage *n* desventaja *f*: —*vt* perjudicar.
disagree *vi* no estar de acuerdo.
disappear *vi* desaparecer.
disappoint *vt* decepcionar.
disapprove *vt* desaprobar.
disaster *n* desastre *m*.
disbelieve *vt* desconfiar.
discard *vt* descartar.
discern *vt* discernir, percibir.
discharge *vt* descargar; pagar (una deuda).
disciple *n* discípulo *m*.
discipline *n* disciplina *f*: —*vt* disciplinar.
disclose *vi* revelar.
disco *n* discoteca *f*.
discomfort *n* incomodidad *f*.
discontent *n* descontento *m*: —*adj* malcontento/ta.
discontinue *vi* interrumpir.
discord *n* discordia *f*.
discount *n* descuento *m*; rebaja *f*.
discover *vt* descubrir.
discreet *adj* discreto/ta.
discriminate *vt* distinguir.
discuss *vt* discutir.
discussion *n* discusión *f*.
disease *n* enfermedad *f*.
disembark *vt* , *vi* desembarcar.
disentangle *vt* desenredar.
disfigure *vt* desfigurar.
disgrace *n* ignominia *f*.
disgruntled *adj* descontento/ta.
disguise *vt* disfrazar.
disgust *n* aversión *f*: —*vt* repugnar.
dish *n* fuente *f*; plato *m*.
disheveled *adj* desarreglado/da.
dishonest *adj* deshonesto/ta.
dishonesty *n* falta de honradez *f*.
dishonor *n* deshonra, ignominia *f*.
dishtowel *n* trapo de fregar *m*.
dishwasher *n* lavaplatos *m*.
disillusion *vt* desilusionar.
disillusioned *adj* desilusionado/da.
disincentive *n* freno *m*.

disinclination *n* aversión *f.*
disinclined *adj* reacio/cia.
disinfect *vt* desinfectar.
disinfectant *n* desinfectante *m.*
disinherit *vt* desheredar.
disintegrate *vi* disgregarse.
disinterested *adj* desinteresado/da.
disjointed *adj* inconexo/xa.
disk *n* disco, disquete *m.*
diskette *n* disco, disquete *m.*
dislike *n* aversión *f.*
dislocate *vt* dislocar.
dislocation *n* dislocación *f.*
dislodge *vt , vi* desalojar.
disloyal *adj* desleal.
disloyalty *n* deslealtad *f.*
dismal *adj* triste.
dismantle *vt* desmontar.
dismay *n* consternación *f.*
dismember *vt* despedazar.
dismiss *vt* despedir.
dismissal *n* despedida *f.*
disobedience *n* desobediencia *f.*
disobedient *adj* desobediente.
disobey *vt* desobedecer.
disorderly *adj* desarreglado/da.
disorganized *adj* desorganizado/da.
disorientated *adj* desorientado/da.
disown *vt* desconocer.
disparage *vt* despreciar.
disparaging *adj* despreciativo/va.
disparity *n* disparidad *f.*
dispassionate *adj* desapasionado/da.
dispatch *vt* enviar.
dispel *vt* disipar.
dispensary *n* dispensario *m.*
dispense *vt* dispensar; distribuir.
disperse *vt* disipersar.
dispirited *adj* desalentado/da.
displace *vt* desplazar.
display *vt* exponer.
displeased *adj* disgustado/da.
displeasure *n* disgusto *m.*
disposable *adj* desechable.
disposal *n* disposición *f.*
dispose *vt* disponer; arreglar.
disposition *n* disposición *f.*
dispossess *vt* desposeer.
disproportionate *adj* desproporcionado/da.
disprove *vt* refutar.
dispute *n* disputa, controversia *f.*
disqualify *vt* incapacitar.
disregard *vt* desatender: —*n* desdén *m.*
disreputable *adj* de mala fama.
disrespectful *adj* irreverente.
disrobe *vt* desnudar.
disrupt *vt* interrumpir.
disruption *n* interrupción *f.*
dissatisfaction *n* descontento/ta.
dissatisfied *adj* insatisfecho/cha.
dissect *vt* disecar.
dissection *n* disección *f.*
dissent *vi* disentir.
dissertation *n* disertación *f.*
dissident *n* disidente *m.*
dissimilar *adj* distinto.
dissolution *n* disolución *f.*

dissolve *vt* disolver.
dissuade *vt* disuadir.
distance *n* distancia *f:* —**at a ~** delejos: —*vt* apartar.
distant *adj* distante.
distillery *n* destilería *f.*
distinct *adj* distinto/ta.
distinction *n* distinción *f.*
distinctive *adj* distintivo/va.
distinguish *vt* distinguir.
distort *vt* retorcer.
distorted *adj* distorsionado/da.
distortion *n* distorción *f.*
distract *vt* distraer.
distracted *adj* distraído/da.
distraction *n* distracción *f;* confusión *f.*
distraught *adj* enloquecido/da.
distress *n* angustia *f.*
distribute *vt* distribuir, repartir.
distribution *n* distribución *f.*
district *n* distrito *m.*
disturb *vt* molestar.
disturbance *n* disturbio *m.*
disturbing *adj* inquietante.
disused *adj* abandonado/da.
ditch *n* zanja *f.*
ditto *adv* idem.
diuretic *adj (med)* diurético/ca.
diver *n* buzo *m.*
diverge *vi* divergir.
diverse *adj* diverso/sa, diferente.
diversion *n* diversión *f.*
diversity *n* diversidad *f.*
divert *vt* desviar; divertir.
divide *vt* dividir: —*vi* dividirse.
divine *adj* divino/na.
divinity *n* divinidad *f.*
divorce *n* divorcio *m.*
DJ *n* pinchadiscos *m.*
do *vt* hacer, obrar.
docile *adj* dócil, apacible.
dockyard *n (mar)* astillero *m.*
doctor *n* médico/ca *m/f .*
doctrine *n* doctrina *f.*
document *n* documento *m.*
documentary *adj* documental.
doe *n* gama *f:* —— **rabbit** coneja *f.*
dog(ue) *n* perro *m.*
do-it-yourself *n* bricolaje *m.*
doll *n* muñeca *f.*
dollar *n* dólar *m.*
dolphin *n* delfín *m.*
dome *n* cúpula *f.*
domestic *adj* doméstico/ca.
domesticity *n* domesticidad *f.*
domicile *n* domicilio *m.*
dominant *adj* dominante.
dominate *vi* dominar.
domineer *vi* dominar.
dominion *n* dominio *m.*
dominoes *npl* domino *m.*
donate *vt* donar.
donation *n* donación *f.*
donkey *n* asno, borrico *m.*
donor *n* donante *m.*
door *n* puerta *f.*
doorbell *n* timbre *m.*
doorman *n* portero *m.*

doormat *n* felpudo *m.*
dormouse *n* lirón *m.*
dose *n* dosis *f.*
dossier *n* expediente *m.*
dot *n* punto *m.*
dote *vi* adorar.
double *adj* doble.
doubly *adj* doblemente.
doubt *n* duda, sospecha *f.*
doubtful *adj* dudoso/sa.
doubtless *adv* sin duda.
dough *n* masa *f.*
douse *vt* apagar.
dove *n* paloma *f.*
dovecot *n* palomar *m.*
dowdy *adj* mal vestido/da.
down *n* plumón *m;* flojel *m:* —*prep* abajo.
downfall *n* ruina *f.*
downhearted *adj* desanimado/da.
downpour *n* aguacero *m.*
downtown *adv* al centro (de la ciudad).
dowry *n* dote *f.*
doze *vi* dormitar.
dozen *n* docena *f.*
dozy *adj* soñoliento/ta.
drab *adj* gris.
draft *n* borrador *m;* quinta *f;* corrientede aire *f.*
dragon *n* dragón *m.*
dragonfly *n* libélula *f.*
drain *vt* desaguar.
drake *n* ánade macho *m.*
drama *n* drama *m.*
dramatic *adj* dramático/ca.
dramatize *vt* dramatizar.
dramatist *n* dramaturgo/ga *m/f* .
drape *vt* cubrir.
drapes *npl* cortinas *fpl.*
drastic *adj* drástico/ca.
draw *vt* tirar; dibujar.
drawback *n* desventaja *f.*
drawer *n* cajón *m.*
drawing *n* dibujo *m.*
drawing room *n* salón *m.*
dread *n* terror, espanto *m:* —*vt* temer.
dreadful *adj* espantoso/sa.
dream *n* sueno *m:* —*vi* sonar.
drench *vt* empapar.
dress *vt* vestir: —*n* vestido *m.*
dresser *n* aparador *m.*
dressing gown *n* bata *f.*
dressing table *n* tocador *m.*
dressmaker *n* modista *f.*
dried *adj* seco/ca.
drill *n* taladro *m.*
drink *vt , vi* beber.
drinkable *adj* potable.
drip *vi* gotear.
drive *vt* manejar.
driver *n* conductor *m.*
driveway *n* entrada *f.*
drizzle *vi* lloviznar.
droop *vi* decaer.
drop *n* gota *f.*
drought *n* seguía *f.*

drown *vt* anegar.
drowsiness *n* somnolencia *f.*
drowsy *adj* soñoliento/ta.
drudgery *n* trabajo monótono *m.*
drug *n* droga *f:* —*vt* drogar.
drug addict *n* drogadicto *m.*
drug store *n* farmacia *f.*
drum *n* tambor *m:* —*vi* tocar el tambor.
drummer *n* batería *m.*
drumstick *n* palillo de tambor *m.*
drunk *adj* borracho/cha.
drunkard *n* borracho *m.*
drunkenness *n* borrachera *f.*
dry *adj* seco/ca.* *vt* secar.
dry goods store *n* mercería, camiseria *f.*
dry rot *n* podredumbre *f.*
dual *adj* doble.
dubbed *adj* doblado/da.
dubious *adj* dudoso/sa.
duck *n* pato *m.*
duckling *n* patito *m.*
dud *adj* estropeado/da.
due *adj* debido/da.
duel *n* duelo *m.*
duet *n (mus)* duo *m.*
dull *adj* lerdo/da.
insípido/da.
duly *adv* debidamente; puntualmente.
dumb *adj* mudo/da.
dumbbell *n* pesa *f.*
dumbfounded *adj* pasmado/da.
dummy *n* maniquí *m;* imbécil *m.*
dumpling *n* bola de masa *f.*
dumpy *adj* gordito/ta.
dunce *n* zopenco *m.*
dune *n* duna *f.*
dung *n* estiércol *m.*
dungarees *npl* mono *m.*
dungeon *n* calabozo *m.*
dupe *n* bobo *m.*
duplicity *n* duplicidad *f.*
durability *n* durabilidad *f.*
durable *adj* duradero/ra.
duration *n* duración *f.*
during *prep* mientras, durante eltiempo que.
dusk *n* crepúsculo *m.*
dust *n* polvo *m.*
duster *n* plumero *m.*
dutch courage *n* valor fingido *m.*
duteous *adj* fiel, leal.
dutiful *adj* obediente.
duty *n* deber *m;* obligación *f.*
dwarf *n* enano *m;* enana *f.*
dwell *vi* habitar, morar.
dwelling *n* habitación *f;* domicilio *m.*
dwindle *vi* mermar, disminuirse.
dye *vt* teñir: —*n* tinte *m.*
dynamic *adj* dinámico/ca.
dynamite *n* dinamita *f.*
dynamo *n* dinamo *f.*
dynasty *n* dinastía *f.*
dysentery *n* disenteria *f.*
dyspepsia *n (med)* dispepsia *f.*

E

each *pn* cada uno, cada una.
eager *adj* entusiasmado/da.
eagle *n* águila *f.*
eaglet *n* aguilucho *m.*
ear *n* oreja *f.*
earache *n* dolor de oídos *m.*
eardrum *n* tímpano (del oído) *m.*
early *adj* temprano/na.
earn *vt* ganar; conseguir.
earnest *adj* serio/ria.
earth *n* tierra *f.*
earthenware *n* loza de barro *f.*
earthquake *n* terremoto *m.*
earthworm *n* lombriz *f.*
earthy *adj* sensual.
earwig *n* tijereta *f.*
ease *n* comodidad *f;* facilidad *f.*
easel *n* caballete *m.*
easily *adv* fácilmente.
east *n* este *m;* oriente *m.*
Easter *n* Pascua de Resurrección *f.*
easterly *adj* del este.
eastern *adj* del este, oriental.
easy *adj* fácil; cómodo/da.
easy chair *n* sillón *m*
eat *vt* comer.
ebb *n* reflujo *m.*
ebony *n* ébano *m.*
eccentric *adj* excéntrico/ca.
echo *n* eco *m.*
eclectic *adj* ecléctico/ca.
eclipse *n* eclipse *m.*
ecology *n* ecología *f.*
economics *npl* economía *f.*
economy *n* economía *f.*
ecstasy *n* éxtasis *m.*
eczema *n* eczema *m.*
eddy *n* reflujo de agua *m.*
edge *n* filo *m.*
edict *n* edicto, mandato *m.*
edit *vt* dirigir; redactar.
edition *n* edición *f.*
editor *n* director *m.*
educate *vt* educar.
education *n* educación *f.*
eel *n* anguila *f.*
effect *n* efecto *m.*
effective *adj* eficaz..
effeminate *adj* afeminado/da.
effervescence *n* efervescencia *f.*
efficacy *n* eficacia *f.*
efficient *adj* eficaz.
effigy *n* efigie, imagen *f.*
effort *n* esfuerzo *m.*
egg *n* huevo *m.*
eggplant *n* berenjena *f.*
ego(t)ist *n* egoísta *m/f.*
eight *num* ocho.
eighteen *num* dieciocho.
eighth *adj* octavo.
eighty *num* ochenta.

either *pn* cualquiera.
eject *vt* expeler, desechar.
elastic *adj* elástico/ca.
elation *n* regocijo *m.*
elbow *n* codo *m.*
elder *n* saúco *m* (árbol): —*adj* mayor.
elect *vt* elegir.
election *n* elección *f.*
electrician *n* electricista *m/f.*
electricity *n* electricidad *f.*
elegance *n* elegancia *f.*
elegant *adj* elegante, delicado/da.
elegy *n* elegía *f.*
element *n* elemento *m.*
elephant *n* elefante *m.*
elevate *vt* elevar, alzar.
elevator *n* ascensor *m.*
eleven *num* once.
eleventh *adj* onceno, undécimo.
elf *n* duende *m.*
elicit *vt* sacar de.
eligible *adj* elegible.
eliminate *vt* eliminar, descartar.
elk *n* alce *m.*
elm *n* olmo *m.*
elocution *n* elocución *f.*
elongate *vt* alargar.
elope *vi* escapar, huir.
elopement *n* fuga *f.*
eloquence *n* elocuencia *f.*
else *pn* otro/ra.
elsewhere *adv* en otra parte.
elude *vt* eludir, evitar.
embargo *n* prohibición *f.*
embark *vt* embarcar.
embarrass *vt* avergonzar.
embarrassment *n* desconcierto *m.*
embassy *n* embajada *f.*
embed *vt* empotrar; clavar.
embellish *vt* hermosear.
embers *npl* rescoldo *m.*
embezzle *vt* desfalcar.
embitter *vt* amargar.
emblem *n* emblema *m.*
embrace *vt* abrazar.
embroider *vt* bordar.
embroil *vt* embrollar; confundir.
embryo *n* embrión *m.*
emerald *n* esmeralda *f.*
emerge *vi* salir, proceder.
emergency *n* emergencia *f.*
emery *n* esmeril *m.*
emigrant *n* emigrante *m.*
emigrate *vi* emigrar.
eminent *adj* eminente.
emission *n* emisión *f.*
emit *vt* emitir.
emotion *n* emoción *f.*
emperor *n* emperador *m.*
emphasis *n* énfasis *m.*
emphasize *vt* hablar con énfasis.

empire *n* imperio *m.*
employ *vt* emplear, ocupar.
employee *n* empleado *m.*
employer *n* patrón *m;* empresario *m.*
empress *n* emperatriz *f.*
empty *adj* vacío/cia.
emulate *vt* emular.
emulsion *n* emulsión *f.*
enable *vt* capacitar.
enact *vt* promulgar.
enamel *n* esmalte *m.*
enchant *vt* encantar.
enchanting *adj* encantador.
encircle *vt* cercar, circundar.
enclose *vt* cercar, circunvalar.
encore *adv* otra vez, de nuevo.
encounter *n* encuentro *m.*
encourage *vt* animar.
encouragement *n* estimulo, patrocinio *m.*
encroach *vt* usurpar.
encumber *vt* embarazar, cargar.
encyclopedia *n* enciclopedia *f.*
end *n* fin *m.*
endanger *vt* peligrar.
endear *vt* encarecer.
endeavor *vi* esforzarse; intentar.
endemic *adj* endémico/ca.
ending *n* conclusión.
endive *n (bot)* endibia *f.*
endless *adj* infinito/ta.
endorse *vt* endosar; aprobar.
endow *vt* dotar.
endure *vt* sufrir, soportar.
enemy *n* enemigo/ga.
energetic *adj* enérgico/ca.
energy *n* energía, fuerza *f.*
enforce *vt* hacer cumplir.
engine *n* motor *m;* locomotora *f.*
engineer *n* ingeniero *m.*
engrave *vt* grabar.
enhance *vt* aumentar.
enigma *n* enigma *m.*
enjoy *vt* gozar.
enjoyment *n* disfrute *m;* placer *m.*
enlarge *vt* engrandecer.
enlist *vt* alistar.
enliven *vt* animar.
enmity *n* enemistad *f;* odio *m.*
enormous *adj* enorme.
enough *adv* bastante; basta.
enrage *vt* enfurecer.
enrapture *vt* arrebatar.
enrich *vt* enriquecer.
enrol *vt* registrar.
enrolment *n* inscripción *f.*
ensign *n (mil)* bandera *f.*
enslave *vt* esclavizar.
ensue *vi* seguirse.
ensure *vt* asegurar.
entangle *vt* enmarañar.
enter *vt* entrar; admitir.
enterprise *n* empresa *f.*
entertain *vt* divertir; hospedar.
entertainer *n* artista *m/f.*
entertainment *n* entretenimiento, pasatiempo *m.*
enthralling *adj* cautivador.
enthusiasm *n* entusiasmo *m.*

entice *vt* tentar; seducir.
entire *adj* entero/ra, completo/ta.
entitle *vt* intitular; conferir algúnderecho.
entity *n* entidad *f.*
entrance *n* entrada *f.*
entreat *vt* rogar, suplicar.
entrepreneur *n* empresario *m.*
entrust *vt* confiar.
entry *n* entrada *f.*
entwine *vt* entrelazar.
envelop *n* envolver.
envelope *vt* sobre *m.*
enviable *adj* envidiable.
environment *n* medio ambiente *m.*
environs *npl* vecindad *f.*
envisage *vt* prever; concebir.
envoy *n* enviado *m.*
envy *n* envidia.
ephemeral *adj* efímero/ra.
epic *adj* épico/ca.
epidemic *adj* epidémico/ca.
epilogue *n* epílogo *m.*
Epiphany *n* Epifanía *f.*
episcopacy *n* episcopado *m.*
episcopal *adj* episcopal.
episcopalian *n* anglicano *m.*
episode *n* episodio *m.*
epistle *n* epístola *f.*
epithet *n* epíteto *m.*
epoch *n* época *f.*
equal *adj* igual.
equalize *vt* igualar.
equality *n* igualdad, uniformidad *f.*
equally *adv* igualmente.
equate *vt* equiparar (con).
equation *n* ecuación *f.*
equator *n* ecuador *m.*
equatorial *adj* ecuatorial.
equestrian *adj* ecuestre.
equilibrium *n* equilibrio *m.*
equinox *n* equinoccio *m.*
equip *vt* equipar.
equipment *n* equipaje *m.*
equitable *adj* equitativo/va.
equity *n* equidad *f.*
equivalent *adj , n* equivalente *m.*
era *n* era *f.*
eradicate *vt* desarraigar.
eradication *n* extirpación *f.*
erase *vt* borrar.
eraser *n* goma de borrar *f.*
erect *vt* erigir; establecer.
ermine *n* armiño *m.*
erode *vt* erosionar.
erotic *adj* erótico/ca.
err *vi* vagar, errar.
errand *n* recado.
erratic *adj* errático/ca.
erroneous *adj* erróneo/nea.
error *n* error *m.*
erudite *adj* erudito/ta.
erupt *vi* entrar en erupción; hacererupción.
eruption *n* erupción *f.*
escalate *vi* extenderse.
escalator *n* escalera móvil *f.*
escapade *n* travesura *f.*
escape *vt* evitar; escapar.

escapism *n* escapismo *m*.
escort *n* escolta *f*: —*vt* escoltar.
esoteric *adj* esotérico/ca.
especial *adj* especial.
essay *n* ensayo *m*.
essence *n* esencia *f*.
essential *n* esencia *f*: —*adj* esencial.
establish *vt* establecer.
establishment *n* establecimiento *m*.
estate *n* estado *m*.
esteem *vt* estimar, apreciar.
estimate *vt* estimar, apreciar.
estuary *n* estuario.
etch *vt* grabar al aguafuerte.
eternal *adj* eterno/na.
eternity *n* eternidad *f*.
ether *n* éter *m*.
ethical *adj* ético/ca.
ethics *npl* ética *f*.
ethnic *adj* étnico/ca.
ethos *n* genio *m*.
etiquette *n* etiqueta *f*.
etymology *n* etimología *f*.
Eucharist *n* Eucaristía *f*.
eulogy *n* elogio *m*.
eunuch *n* eunuco *m*.
euphemism *n* eufemismo *m*.
evacuate *vt* evacuar.
evacuation *n* evacuación *f*.
evade *vt* evadir.
evaluate *vt* evaluar.
evangelical *adj* evangélico/ca.
evaporate *vt* evaporar.
evasion *n* evasión *f*.
evasive *adj* evasivo/va.
eve *n* víspera *f*.
even *adj* llano/na, igual; par, semejante: —*adv* aun; aun cuando, supuesto que; no obstante.
evening *n* tarde *f*.
event *n* acontecimiento, evento *m*.
eventuality *n* eventualidad *f*.
ever *adv* siempre.
every *adj* cada uno o cada una.
evict *vt* desahuciar.
eviction *n* desahucio *m*.
evidence *n* evidencia *f*.
evil *adj* malo/la, depravado/da.
evocative *adj* sugestivo/va.
evoke *vt* evocar.
evolution *n* evolución *f*.
evolve *vt*, *vi* evolucionar.
ewe *n* oveja *f*.
exacerbate *vt* exacerbar.
exact *adj* exacto/ta.
exacting *adj* exigente.
exaggerate *vt* exagerar.
exaggeration *n* exageración *f*.
exalt *vt* exaltar.
exaltation *n* exaltación.
examination *n* examen *m*.
examine *vt* examinar.
examiner *n* inspector/a *m/f*.
example *n* ejemplar *m;* ejemplo *m*.
excavate *vt* excavar.
excavation *n* excavación *f*.
exceed *vt* exceder.
exceedingly *adv* extremamente, ensumo grado.

excel *vt* sobresalir.
excellence *n* excelencia *f*.
excellent *adj* excelente.
except *vt* exceptuar, excluir: —~ **(ing)** *prep* excepto, a excepción de.
exception *n* excepción, exclusión *f*.
exceptional *adj* excepcional.
excerpt *n* extracto *m*.
excess *n* exceso *m*.
excessive *adj* excesivo/va.
exchange *vt* cambiar; trocar.
exchange rate *n* tipo de cambio *m*.
excitability *n* excitabilidad *f*.
excitable *adj* excitable.
excite *vt* excitar; estimular.
excited *adj* emocionado/da.
excitement *n* estímulo *m*, excitación *f*.
exclaim *vi* exclamar.
exclamation *n* exclamación *f*.
exclamation mark *n* punto de admiración *m*.
exclamatory *adj* exclamatorio/ria.
exclude *vt* excluir; exceptuar.
exclusion *n* exclusión, *f*.
exclusive *adj* exclusivo/va.
excommunicate *vt* excomulgar.
excommunication *n* excomunión *f*.
excrement *n* excremento *m*.
excruciating *adj* atroz.
excursion *n* excursión *f*.
excusable *adj* excusable.
excuse *vt* disculpar.
execute *vt* ejecutar.
execution *n* ejecución *f*.
executioner *n* ejecutor/a.
executive *adj* ejecutivo/va.
executor *n* testamentario/ria, albacea *m/f*.
exemplary *adj* ejemplar.
exemplify *vt* ejemplificar.
exempt *adj* exento/ta.
exemption *n* exención *f*.
exercise *n* ejercicio *m*.
exercise book *n* cuaderno *m*.
exertion *n* esfuerzo *m*.
exhale *vt* exhalar.
exhaust *n* escape *m*.
exhausted *adj* agotado/da.
exhaustion *n* agotamiento *m*.
exhaustive *adj* comprensivo/va.
exhibit *vt* exhibir; mostrar.
exhibition *n* exposición *f*.
exhilarating *adj* estimulante.
exhort *vt* exhortar, excitar.
exhume *vt* exhumar.
exile *n* destierro *m*.
exist *vi* existir.
existence *n* existencia *f*.
exit *n* salida *f*: —*vi* hacer mutis.
exit ramp *n* vía de acceso *f*.
exodus *n* éxodo *m*.
exonerate *vt* exonerar.
exhorbitant *adj* exorbitante.
exorcize *vt* exorcizar, conjurar.
exorcism *n* exorcismo *m*.
exotic *adj* exótico/ca.
expand *vt* extender, dilatar.
expatriate *vt* expatriar.
expect *vt* esperar.

expectant mother *n* mujer encinta *f.*
expediency *n* conveniencia *f.*
expedition *n* expedición *f.*
expel *vt* expeler, desterrar.
expend *vt* expender.
expendable *adj* prescindible.
expenditure *n* gasto, desembolso *m.*
expense *n* gasto *m;* coste *m.*
experience *n* experiencia *f;* practica *f.*
experienced *adj* experimentado/da.
experiment *n* experimento *m.*
expert *adj* experto/ta.
expertise *n* pericia *f.*
expiration *n* expiración *f.*
expire *vi* expirar.
explain *vt* explanar, explicar.
explanation *n* explanación, explicación *f.*
expletive *adj* expletivo/va.
explicit *adj* explícito/ta.
explode *vt , vi* estallar, explotar.
exploit *vt* explotar.
exploitation *n* explotación *f.*
exploration *n* exploración *f.*
exploratory *adj* exploratorio/ria.
explore *vt* explorar.
explorer *n* explorador *m.*
explosion *n* explosión *f.*
explosive *adj , n* explosivo *m.*
exponent *n (math)* exponente *m.*
export *vt* exportar.
expose *vt* exponer; mostrar.
exposed *adj* expuesto/ta.
exposition *n* exposición *f.*
expostulate *vi* debatir, contender.
exposure *n* exposición *f.*
expound *vt* exponer.
express *vt* exprimir; representar.
expression *n* expresión *f.*
expressionless *adj* sin expresión(cara).
expressway *n* autopista *f.*
expulsion *n* explosión *f.*
expurgate *vt* expurgar.
exquisite *adj* exquisito/ta.

extend *vt* extender.
extension *n* extensión *f.*
extensive *adj* extenso/sa.
extent *n* extensión *f.*
extenuate *vt* extenuar.
exterior *adj , n* exterior *m.*
exterminate *vt* exterminar.
extermination *n* exterminación *f.*
external *adj* externo/na.
extinct *adj* extinto/ta.
extinction *n* extinción *f.*
extinguish *vt* extinguir.
extinguisher *n* extintor *m.*
extol *vt* alabar, magnificar.
extort *vt* sacar por fuerza.
extortion *n* extorsión *f.*
extortionate *adj* excesivo/va.
extra *adv* extra.
extract *vt* extraer.
extracurricular *adj* extraescolar.
extradition *n (law)* extradición *f.*
extramarital *adj* extramatrimonial.
extraneous *adj* extraño/ña.
extraordinary *adj* extraordinario/ria.
extravagance *n* extravagancia *f.*
extravagant *adj* extravagante.
extreme *adj* extremo/ma.
extremist *adj , n* extremista *m/f .*
extremity *n* extremidad *f.*
extrovert *adj , n* extrovertido *m.*
exuberance *n* exuberancia *f.*
exuberant *adj* exuberante.
exult *vt* exultar.
exultation *n* exultación *f;* regocijo *m.*
eye *n* ojo *m: —vt* ojear, contemplar, observar.
eyeball *n* globo del ojo *m.*
eyebrow *n* ceja *f.*
eyelash *n* pestaña *f.*
eyelid *n* párpado *m.*
eyesight *n* vista *f.*
eyewitness *n* testigo ocular *m.*
eyrie *n* aguilera *f.*

F

fabric *n* tejido *m.*
fabricate *vt* fabricar.
fabulous *adj* fabuloso/sa.
facade *n* fachada *f.*
face *n* cara, faz *f;* superficie *f.*
facet *n* faceta *f.*
facetious *adj* chistoso/sa.
facile *adj* fácil.
facilitate *vt* facilitar.
facility *n* facilidad *f.*
facsimile *n* facsímile *m;* telefax *m.*
fact *n* hecho *m.*
faction *n* facción *f.*
factor *n* factor *m.*
factory *n* fabrica *f.*
faculty *n* facultad *f.*
fad *n* moda , manía *f.*
fade *vi* decaer.
fail *vt* suspender, reprobar; fallar a.

failure *n* falta *f;* culpa *f.*
faint *vi* desmayarse, debilitarse.
faint-hearted *adj* cobarde.
fair *adj* hermoso/sa, bello/la; blanco/ca; rubio/bia;
claro/ra, sereno/na; favorable; recto/ta, justo/ta;
franco/ca: *—adv* limpio: *—n* feria *f.*
fairly *adv* justamente.
fairy *n* hada *f.*
faith *n* fe *f;* dogma de fe *m.*
faithfulness *n* fidelidad *f.*
fake *n* falsificación *f.*
falcon *n* halcón *m.*
fall[1] *n* otoño *m.*
fall[2] *vi* caer(se).
fallacy *n* falacia.
fallible *adj* falible.
false *adj* falso/sa.
falsify *vt* falsificar.
fame *n* fama *f.*

famed *adj* celebrado/da, famoso/sa.
familiar *adj* familiar.
family *n* familia *f.*
famine *n* hambre *f;* carestía *f.*
famous *adj* famoso/sa.
fan *n* abanico *m;* aficionado *m.*
fanatic *adj , n* fanático *m.*
fanciful *adj* imaginativo/va.
fancy *n* fantasía, imaginación *f.*
fanfare *n (mus)* fanfarria *f.*
fang *n* colmillo *m.*
fantastic *adj* fantástico/ca.
fantasy *n* fantasía *f.*
far *adv* lejos.
faraway *adj* remoto/ta.
farce *n* farsa *f.*
fare *n* precio *m;* tarifa *f.*
farm *n* finca *f,* granja *f.*
farmer *n* estanciero *m;* granjero *m.*
fascinate *vt* fascinar, encantar.
fascism *n* fascismo.
fashion *n* moda *f;* forma.
fashionable *adj* a la moda.
fashion show *n* desfile de modelos *m.*
fast *vi* ayunar; *adv* rápidamente.
fasten *vt* abrochar.
fastidious *adj* fastidioso/sa.
fat *adj* gordo/da.
fatal *adj* fatal.
fate *n* hado, destino *m.*
fateful *adj* fatídico/ca.
father *n* padre *m.*
father-in-law *n* suegro *m.*
fatherland *n* patria *f.*
fathom *n* braza (medida) *f.*
fatigue *n* fatiga *f.*
fatty *adj* graso/sa.
faucet *n* espita *f.*
fault *n* falta, culpa *f.*
fauna *n* fauna *f.*
faux pas *n* plancha *f.*
favor *n* favor.
favorite *n* favorito *m.*
fawn *n* cervato *m.*
fax *n* facsímil(e) *m;* telefax *m.*
fear *vi* temer; —*n* miedo *m.*
fearful *adj* medroso/sa, temeroso/sa.
feasible *adj* factible.
feast *n* banquete.
feat *n* hecho *m.*
feather *n* pluma *f.*
feature *n* característica *f;* rasgo *m.*
February *n* febrero *m.*
federal *adj* federal.
federalist *n* federalista *m/f .*
federation *n* federación *f.*
fed-up *adj* harto/ta.
fee *n* honorarios *mpl .*
feeble *adj* flaco/ca, débil.
feed *vt* nutrir; alimentar.
feedback *n* reacción *f.*
feel *vt* sentir; to car.
feign *vt* inventar, fingir.
feline *adj* gatuno/na.
fellowship *n* compañerismo *m.*
felon *n* criminal *m/f .*
felony *n* crimen *m.*

felt *n* fieltro *m.*
female *n* hembra *f:* —*adj* femenino/na.
feminine *adj* femenino/na.
feminist *n* feminista *m/f .*
fence *n* cerca *f;* defensa *f.*
fennel *n (bot)* hinojo *m.*
fern *n (bot)* helecho *m.*
ferocious *adj* feroz.
ferret *n* hurón *m.*
ferry *n* barca de pasaje *f.*
fertile *adj* fértil, fecundo/da.
fester *vi* enconarse.
festival *n* fiesta *f;* festival *m.*
fetch *vt* ir a buscar.
fete *n* fiesta *f.*
fetus *n* feto *m.*
feud *n* riña, contienda *f.*
feudal *adj* feudal.
fever *n* fiebre *f.*
feverish *adj* febril.
few *adj* poco/ca.
fewer *adj* menor.
fewest *adj* los menos.
fiancé *n* novio *m.*
fiancée *n* novia *f.*
fib *n* mentira *f.*
fibre *n* fibra, hebra *f.*
fickle *adj* voluble.
fiction *n* ficción *f.*
fiddle *n* violín *m;* trampa *f.*
fidelity *n* fidelidad *f.*
field *n* campo *m.*
fieldmouse *n* ratón de campo *m.*
fierce *adj* fiero/ra, feroz.
fierceness *n* fiereza, ferocidad *f.*
fiery *adj* ardiente; apasionado/da.
fifteen *adj , n* quince.
fifteenth *adj , n* decimoquinto/ta.
fifth *adj , n* quinto/ta.
fiftieth *adj , n* quincuagésimo/ma.
fifty *adj , n* cincuenta.
fig *n* higo *m.*
fight *vt , vi* reñir; batallar; combatir.
fig-leaf *n* hoja de higuera *f.*
figurative *adj* figurativo/va.
figure *n* figura.
filament *n* filamento *m.*
fill *vt* llenar; hartar.
fillet *n* filete *m.*
filling station *n* estación de servicio *f.*
fillip *n (fig)* estímulo *m.*
filly *n* potra *f.*
film *n* película *f;* film *m.*
filter *n* filtro *m.*
filth(iness) *n* inmundicia, porquería *f.*
fin *n* aleta *f.*
final *adj* final, último/ma.
finalize *vt* concluir.
finance *n* fondos *mpl .*
financier *n* financiero *m.*
find *vt* hallar, descubrir.
finesse *n* sutileza *f.*
finger *n* dedo *m.*
fingernail *n* uña *f.*
finish *vt* acabar, terminar, concluir.
finite *adj* finito/ta.
fir *n* abeto *m.*

fire *n* fuego *m;* incendio *m.*
firearm *n* arma de fuego *f.*
firefly *n* luciérnaga *f.*
firewood *n* leña *f.*
fireworks *npl* fuegos artificiales *mpl* .
firm *adj* firme, estable.
firmament *n* firmamento *m.*
firmness *n* firmeza *f.*
first *adj* primero/ra.
fiscal *adj* fiscal.
fish *n* pez *m.*
fishbone *n* espina *f.*
fisherman *n* pescador *m.*
fishy *adj (fig)* sospechoso/sa.
fist *n* puño *m.*
fitness *n* salud *f.*
five *adj* , *n* cinco.
fix *vt* fijar.
fixation *n* obsesión *f.*
fizzy *adj* gaseoso/sa.
flabbergasted *adj* pasmado/da.
flabby *adj* blando/da.
flaccid *adj* flojo/ja.
flag *n* bandera *f.*
flagpole *n* asta de bandera *f.*
flagrant *adj* flagrante; notorio/ria.
flagship *n* navío almirante *m.*
flair *n* aptitud especial *f.*
flake *n* copo *m.*
flamboyant *adj* vistoso/sa.
flame *n* llama *f.*
flamingo *n* flamenco *m.*
flammable *adj* inflamable.
flank *n* ijada *f.*
flannel *n* franela *f.*
flare *vi* lucir, brillar.
flash *n* flash *m.*
flashlight *n* antorcha *f.*
flask *n* frasco *m.*
flat *adj* llano/na, plano/na.
flatness *n* llanura *f.*
flatten *vt* allanar.
flatter *vt* adular.
flattery *n* adulación *f.*
flatulence *n (med)* flatulencia *f.*
flaunt *vt* ostentar.
flavor *n* sabor *m.*
flavorless *adj* soso/sa.
flaw *n* falta *m.*
flawless *adj* sin defecto.
flax *n* lino *m.*
flea *n* pulga *f.*
fleck *n* mota *f.*
flee *vt* huir de.
fleece *n* vellón *m.*
fleet *n* flota *f.*
flesh *n* carne *f.*
flex *n* cordón *m.*
flexibility *n* flexibilidad *f.*
flexible *adj* flexible.
flight *n* vuelo *m.*
flight attendant *n* tripulante auxiliar *m.*
flimsy *adj* débil; fútil.
flinch *vi* encogerse.
fling *vt* lanzar.
flint *n* pedernal *m.*
flip *vt* arrojar.

flippant *adj* petulante.
flipper *n* aleta *f.*
flirt *vi* coquetear: —*n* coqueta *f.*
flirtation *n* coquetería *f.*
flock *n* manada *f.*
flog *vt* azotar.
flogging *n* tunda, zurra *f.*
flood *n* diluvio *m;* inundación *f.*
flooding *n* inundación *f.*
floodlight *n* foco *m.*
floor *n* suelo, piso *m.*
floorboard *n* tabla *f.*
flop *n* fracaso *m.*
floppy *adj* flojo/ja.
flora *n* flora *f.*
floral *adj* floral.
florescence *n* florescencia *f.*
florid *adj* florido/da.
florist *n* florista *m/f* .
florist's (shop) *n* florería *f.*
flotilla *n (mar)* flotilla *f.*
flounder *n* platija (pez de mar) *f.*
flour *n* harina *f.*
flourish *vi* florecer.
flout *vt* burlarse de.
flow *vi* fluir.
flower *n* flor *f.*
flowerbed *n* cuadro (en un jardín) *m.*
flowerpot *n* tiesto de flores *m.*
flowery *adj* florido/da.
fluctuate *vi* fluctuar.
fluctuation *n* fluctuación *f.*
fluency *n* fluidez *f.*
fluent *adj* fluido/da.
fluff *n* pelusa *f.*
fluid *adj* , *n* fluido/da *m.*
fluidity *n* fluidez *f.*
fluke *n (sl)* chiripa *f.*
fluoride *n* fluoruro *m.*
flurry *n* ráfaga *f;* agitación *f.*
flute *n* flauta *f.*
flutter *vi* revolotear; estar en agitación.
flux *n* flujo *m.*
fly *vt* pilotar; transportar: —*vi* volar.
flying saucer *n* platillo volante *m.*
foal *n* potro *m.*
foam *n* espuma *f.*
foamy *adj* espumoso/sa.
focus *n* foco.
fodder *n* forraje *m.*
foe *n adv* ersario/ria *m/f* , enemigo *m.*
fog *n* niebla *f.*
foggy *adj* nebuloso/sa.
fold *n* redil *m;* pliegue *m.*
folder *n* carpeta *f.*
folding *adj* plegable.
foliage *n* follaje *m.*
folio *n* folio *m.*
folk *n* gente *f.*
folklore *n* folklore *m.*
folk song *n* canción folklórica *f.*
follow *vt* seguir; acompañar.
follower *n* seguidor/a *m/f* .
following *adj* siguiente.
folly *n* extravagancia *f.*
foment *vt* fomentar.
fond *adj* cariñoso/sa.

fondle *vt* acariciar.
fondness *n* gusto *m;* cariño *m.*
font *n* pila bautismal *f.*
food *n* comida *f.*
food mixer *n* batidora *f.*
food poisoning *n* botulismo *m.*
fool *n* loco/ca, tonto/ta *m/f.*
foolish *adj* bobo/ba, tonto/ta.
foolscap *n* papel tamaño folio *m.*
foot *n* pie *m;* pata *f.*
footage *n* imágenes *fpl.*
footnote *n* nota de pie *f.*
footpath *n* senda *f.*
footprint *n* huella *f.*
for *prep* por, a causa de; para.
forbid *vt* prohibir.
force *n* fuerza *f;* poder, vigor *m.*
forced *adj* forzado/da.
forceful *adj* enérgico/ca.
forceps *n* fórceps *m.*
ford *n* vado *m.*
fore *n:* —**to the ~** en evidencia.
forearm *n* antebrazo *m.*
foreboding *n* presentimiento *m.*
forecast *vt* pronosticar.
forecourt *n* patio *m.*
forefather *n* abuelo, antecesor *m.*
forefinger *n* índice *m.*
forefront *n:* —**in the ~ of** en la vanguardia de.
forego *vt* ceder.
foreground *n* delantera *f.*
forehead *n* frente *f.*
foreign *adj* extranjero/ra; extraño/ña.
foreigner *n* extranjero/ra, forastero/ra *m/f.*
foreign exchange *n* divisas *fpl.*
foreleg *n* pata delantera *f.*
foreman *n* capataz *m.*
foremost *adj* principal.
forensic *adj* forense.
forerunner *n* precursor/a *m/f.*
foresee *vt* prever.
foresight *n* previsión *f.*
forest *n* bosque *m;* selva *f.*
forester *n* guardabosque *m.*
forestry *n* silvicultura *f.*
foretaste *n* muestra *f.*
foretell *vt* predecir, profetizar.
forethought *n* providencia *f.*
forever *adv* para siempre.
foreword *n* prefacio *m.*
forfeit *n* confiscación *f.*
forge *n* fragua *f;* fabrica de metales *f.*
forger *n* falsificador/a *m/f.*
forgery *n* falsificación *f.*
forget *vt* olvidar.
forgetful *adj* olvidadizo/za.
forget-me-not *n (bot)* nomeolvides *m.*
forgive *vt* perdonar.
forgiveness *n* perdón *m.*
fork *n* tenedor *m.*
form *n* forma *f;* modelo *m;* modo *m.*
formal *adj* formal.
formality *n* formalidad *f.*
format *n* formato *m.*
formation *n* formación *f.*
formative *adj* formativo/va.
former *adj* precedente; anterior.

formidable *adj* formidable.
formula *n* fórmula *f.*
formulate *vt* formular.
forsake *vt* dejar.
fort *n* castillo *m.*
forthright *adj* franco/ca.
forthwith *adj* inmediatamente.
fortieth *adj* , *n* cuadragésimo *m.*
fortification *n* fortificación *f.*
fortify *vt* fortificar.
fortitude *n* fortaleza *f.*
fortnight *n* quince días *mpl* .
fortress *n (mil)* fortaleza *f.*
fortuitous *adj* impensado/da.
fortunate *adj* afortunado/da.
fortune *n* fortuna, suerte *f.*
fortune-teller *n* sortílego/ga.
forty *adj* , *n* cuarenta.
forum *n* foro *m.*
forward *adj* avanzado/da; delantero/ra.
forwardness *n* precocidad *f;* audacia *f.*
fossil *adj* , *n* fósil *m.*
foster *vt* criar.
foul *adj* sucio/cia, puerco/ca; impuro/ra.
found *vt* fundar, establecer.
foundation *n* fundación *f.*
founder *n* fundador/a *m/f.*
foundling *n* niño expósito *m,* niñaexpósita *f.*
foundry *n* fundería *f.*
fount, fountain *n* fuente *f.*
fountainhead *n* origen de fuente *m.*
four *adj* , *n* cuatro.
fourfold *adj* cuádruple.
fourteen *adj* , *n* catorce.
fourteenth *adj* , *n* decimocuarto/ta.
fourth *adj* , *n* cuarto/ta: —*n* cuarto *m:* —**ly** *adv* en cuarto lugar.
fowl *n* ave *f.*
fox *n* zorra *f.*
fracas *n* riña *f.*
fraction *n* fracción *f.*
fracture *n* fractura *f.*
fragile *adj* frágil; débil.
fragility *n* fragilidad *f.*
fragment *n* fragmento *m.*
fragrance *n* fragancia *f.*
fragrant *adj* fragante, oloroso/sa.
frail *adj* frágil, débil.
frailty *n* fragilidad *f;* debilidad *f.*
frame *n* armazón *m;* marco, cerco *m.*
franchise *n* sufragio *m.*
frank *adj* franco/ca, liberal.
frankly *adv* francamente.
frantic *adj* frenético/ca.
fraternize *vi* hermanarse.
fraternity *n* fraternidad *f.*
fraud *n* fraude *m.*
fraudulent *adj* fraudulento/ta.
fraught *adj* cargado/da, lleno/na.
freak *n* monstruo *m;* fenómeno *m.*
freckle *n* peca *f.*
freckled *adj* pecoso/sa.
free *adj* libre; liberal; suelto/ta.
freedom *n* libertad *f.*
freehold *n* propiedad vitalicia *f.*
free-for-all *n* riña general *f.*
freelance *adj* , *adv* por cuenta propia.

freemason n francmasón m.
freemasonry n francmasonería f.
freeway n autopista f.
freewheel vi ir en punto muerto.
freeze vi helar(se).
freezer n congeladora f.
freight n carga f; flete m.
freighter n fletador m.
frenzy n frenesí m; locura f.
frequency n frecuencia f.
fresco n fresco m.
fresh adj fresco/ca; nuevo/va.
freshly adv nuevamente.
freshman n novicio m.
freshwater adj de agua dulce.
fret vi agitarse.
friar n fraile m.
friction n fricción f.
Friday n viernes m: —**Good** ~ ViernesSanto m.
friend n amigo m; amiga f.
friendship n amistad f.
frieze n friso m.
frigate n (mar) fragata f.
fright n espanto, terror m.
frighten vt espantar.
frigid adj frío/ría, frígido/da.
fringe n franja f.
frisk vt cachear.
frivolity n frivolidad f.
frock n vestido m.
frog n rana f.
frolic vi juguetear.
from prep de; después; desde.
front n parte delantera f; fachada f; paseo marítimo m; frente m.
frontal adj de frente.
frontier n frontera f.
frost n helada f; hielo m.
froth n espuma (de algún líquido) f.
frown vt mirar con ceño.
frozen adj helado/da.
fruit n fruta f; fruto m.
fruiterer n frutero m.
fruiterer's (shop) n frutería f.
fruit juice n jugo de fruta m.
fruitless adj estéril; inútil.

fruit salad n ensalada de frutas f.
fruit tree n frutal m.
frustrate vt frustrar; anular.
fry vt freír.
frying pan n sartén f.
fuchsia n (bot) fucsia f.
fuel n combustible m.
fuel tank n deposito m.
fugitive adj , n fugitivo m.
fulcrum n fulcro m.
fulfill vt cumplir; realizar.
fulfillment n cumplimiento m.
full adj lleno/na.
full moon n plenilunio m; luna llena f.
fulsome adj exagerado/da.
fumble vi manejar torpemente.
fume vi humear; encolerizarse.
fun n diversión f; alegría f.
function n función f.
functional adj funcional.
fund n fondo m.
fundamental adj fundamental.
funeral n funerales mpl .
fungus n hongo m; seta f.
funnel n embudo m.
funny adj divertido/da; curioso/sa.
fur n piel f.
furious adj furioso/sa.
furnace n horno m; hornaza f.
furnish vt amueblar.
furnishings npl muebles mpl .
furniture n muebles mpl .
furrow n surco m.
furry adj peludo/da.
furthermore adv además.
fury n furor m; furia f; ira f.
fuse vt , vi fundir; derretirse.
fuse box n caja de fusibles f.
fusion n fusión f.
fuss n lío m; alboroto m.
fussy adj jactancioso/sa.
futile adj fútil, frívolo/la.
futility n futilidad f.
future adj futuro/ra.
fuzzy adj borroso/sa; muy rizado/da.

G

gable n aguilón m.
gag n mordaza f; chiste m.
gage n calibre m.
gaiety n alegría f.
gain n ganancia f.
gala n fiesta f.
galaxy n galaxia f.
gale n vendaval m.
gallant adj galante.
gallery n galería f.
gallon n galón m (medida).
gallop n galope m.
gallows n horca f.
galore adv en abundancia.
gambit n estrategia f.

gamble vi jugar; especular f.
gambler n jugador m.
game n juego m; pasatiempo m.
gamekeeper n guardabosques m.
gaming n juego m.
gammon n jamón m.
gander n ganso m.
gang n pandilla, banda f.
gangrene n gangrena f.
gangster n gangster m.
gangway n pasarela f.
gap n hueco m; claro m; intervalo m.
garage n garaje m.
garbage n basura f.
garbage can n cubo de la basura m.

garden *n* jardín *m*.
gargoyle *n* gárgola *f*.
genius *n* genio *m*.
genteel *adj* refinado, elegante.
gentile *n* gentil.
gentle *adj* suave.
gentleman *n* caballero *m*.
gentry *n* alta burguesía *f*.
gents *n* aseos *mpl* .
genuine *adj* genuino/na.
genus *n* genero *m*.
geographer *n* geógrafo/fa *m/f* .
geography *n* geografía *f*.
geology *n* geología *f*.
geometry *n* geometría *f*.
geranium *n* (bot) geranio *m*.
germ *n* (bot) germen *m*.
germinate *vi* brotar.
gesticulate *vi* gesticular.
gesture *n* gesto*m*.
get *vt* ganar; conseguir, obtener.
geyser *n* géiser *m m*.
ghastly *adj* espantoso/sa.
gherkin *n* pepinillo *m*.
ghost *n* fantasma *m*.
ghostly *adj* fantasmal.
giant *n* gigante *m*.
giddy *adj* vertiginoso/sa.
gift *n* regalo*m*.
giggle *vi* reírse tontamente.
gin *n* ginebra *f*.
ginger *n* jengibre *m*.
ginger-haired *adj* pelirrojo/ja.
giraffe *n* jirafa *f*.
girl *n* muchacha, chica *f*.
girlfriend *n* amiga *f*; novia *f*.
giro *n* giro postal *m*.
girth *n* cincha *f*; circunferencia *f*.
give *vt* , *vi* dar.
glacier *n* glaciar *m*.
glad *adj* alegre, contento/ta.
gladiator *n* gladiator *m*.
glamor *n* encanto*m*.
gland *n* glándula *f*.
garish *adj* ostentoso/sa.
garland *n* guirnalda *f*.
garlic *n* ajo *m*.
garment *n* prenda *f*.
garnish *vt* guarnecer *m*.
garter *n* liga *f*.
gas *n* gas *m*.
gasoline, gas *n* gasolina *f*.
gash *n* cuchillada *f*.
gasp *vi* jadear.
gastric *adj* gástrico/ca.
gastronomic *adj* gastronómico/ca.
gate *n* puerta *m*.
gateway *n* puerta *f*.
gather *vt* recoger.
gathering *n* reunión *f*.
gaudy *adj* chillón/ona.
gauze *n* gasa *f*.
gay *adj* alegre; vivo/va; gay.
gazelle *n* gacela *f*.
gazette *n* gaceta *f*.
gazetteer *n* gacetero *m*.
gear *n* atavío *m*; vestido *m*.

gearbox *n* caja de cambios *f*.
gel *n* gel *m*.
gelatin(e) *n* jaletina, jalea *f*.
gelignite *n* gelignita *f*.
gem *n* joya *f*.
Gemini *n* Géminis *m* (signo del zodiaco).
gender *n* género *m*.
gene *n* gen *m*.
genealogy *n* genealogía *f*.
general *adj* general, común.
generalize *vt* generalizar.
generation *n* generación *f*.
generic *adj* genérico/ca.
generosity *n* generosidad.
generous *adj* generoso/sa.
genetics *npl* genética *f*.
genial *adj* genial.
genitals *npl* genitales *mpl* .
glare *n* deslumbramiento *m*.
glass *n* vidrio.
glean *vt* espigar; recoger.
glee *n* alegría *f*; gozo *m*.
glib *adj* con poca sinceridad, elocuente pero falso.
glide *vi* resbalar.
glimmer *n* vislumbre *f*.
glimpse *n* vislumbre *f*.
glint *vi* centellear.
glisten, glitter *vi* relucir, brillar.
gloat *vi* ojear con admiración.
global *adj* mundial.
globe *n* globo *m*; esfera *f*.
gloom, gloominess *n* oscuridad *f*; melancolía.
glorify *vt* glorificar, celebrar.
glory *n* gloria, fama, celebridad *f*.
gloss *n* glosa *f*; lustre *m*.
glossary *n* glosario *m*.
glove *n* guante *m*.
glow *vi* arder; inflamarse; relucir.
glower *vi* mirar con ceño.
glue *n* cola *f*.
glum *adj* abatido/da, triste.
glut *n* hartura, abundancia *f*.
gluttony *n* glotonería *f*.
glycerine *n* glicerina *f*.
gnarled *adj* nudoso/sa.
gnash *vt* , *vi* rechinar; crujir los dien-tes.
gnat *n* mosquito *m*.
gnaw *vt* roer.
gnome *n* gnomo *m*.
go *vi* ir, irse.
goal *n* meta *f*; fin *m*.
goaltender *n* portero *m*.
gobble *vt* engullir, tragar.
go-between *n* mediador/a *m/f* .
goblet *n* copa *f*.
goblin *n* espíritu ambulante, duende *m*.
God *n* Dios *m*.
godchild *n* ahijado, hijo de pila *m*.
goddaughter *n* ahijada, hija depila *f*.
goddess *n* diosa *f*.
godfather *n* padrino *m*.
godmother *n* madrina *f*.
godsend *n* don del cielo *m*.
godson *n* ahijado *m*.
goggle-eyed *adj* bizco/ca.
goggles *npl* anteojos *mpl* .
gold *n* oro *m*.

goldfish *n* pez de colores *m*.
gold-plated *adj* chapado/da enoro.
golf *n* golf *m*.
golf course *n* campo de golf *m*.
golfer *n* golfista *m/f*.
gondolier *n* gondolero/ra *m/f*.
gone *adj* ido/da; perdido/da; pasado/da; gastado/da; muerto/ta.
gong *n* atabal chino *m*.
good *adj* bueno/na.
goodbye ! *excl* ¡adiós!
Good Friday *n* Viernes Santo *m*.
good-looking *adj* guapo/pa.
goodness *n* bondad *f*.
goodwill *n* benevolencia, bondad *f*.
goose *n* ganso *m; oca f*.
gooseberry *n* grosella espinosa *f*.
gorge *n* barranco *m*.
gorgeous *adj* maravilloso/sa.
gorilla *n* gorila *m*.
gorse *n* aulaga *f*.
gory *adj* sangriento/ta.
goshawk *n* azor *m*.
gospel *n* evangelio *m*.
gossamer *n* vello *m*.
gossip *n* charla *f*.
gothic *adj* gótico/ca.
gout *n* gota *f* (enfermedad).
govern *vt* gobernar, dirigir.
governess *n* gobernadora *f*.
government *n* gobierno *m*.
governor *n* gobernador *m*.
gown *n* toga *f*.
grab *vt* agarrar.
grace *n* gracia.
graceful *adj* gracioso/sa.
gracious *adj* gracioso/sa.
gradation *n* gradación *f*.
grade *n* grado *m*.
grade crossing *n* paso a nivel *m*.
gradient *n (rail)* pendiente.
gradual *adj* gradual.
graduate *vi* graduarse.
graduation *n* graduación *f*.
graffiti *n* pintadas *fpl*.
graft *n* injerto *m*.
grain *n* grano *m*.
gram *n* gramo *m* (peso).
grammar *n* gramática *f*.
granary *n* granero *m*.
grand *adj* grande, ilustre.
grandchild *n* nieto *m; nieta f*.
grandad *n* abuelo *m*.
granddaughter *n* nieta *f*.
grandeur *n* grandeza *f*.
grandfather *n* abuelo *m*.
grandiose *adj* grandioso/sa.
grandma *n* abuelita *f*.
grandmother *n* abuela *f*.
grandparents *npl* abuelos *mpl*.
grand piano *n* piano de cola *m*.
grandson *n* nieto *m*.
grandstand *n* tribuna *f*.
granite *n* granito *m*.
granny *n* abuelita *f*.
grant *vt* conceder.
granule *n* gránulo *m*.

grape *n* uva *f*: —bunch of ~s racimode uvas *m*.
grapefruit *n* toronja *f*.
graph *n* gráfica *f*.
graphics *n* artes gráficas *fpl*; gráficos *mpl*.
grasp *vt* empuñar.
grass *n* hierba *f*.
grasshopper *n* saltamontes *m*.
grassland *n* pampa , pradera *f*.
grass snake *n* culebra *f*.
gratify *vt* contentar; gratificar.
gratifying *adj* grato/ta.
grating *n* rejado *m*.
gratis *adv* gratis.
gratitude *n* gratitud *f*.
grave *n* sepultura *f*.
gravel *n* cascajo *m*.
gravestone *n* piedra sepulcra *f*.
graveyard *n* cementerio *m*.
gravity *n* gravedad *f*.
gravy *n* jugo de la carne *f; salsa f*.
gray *adj* gris.
graze *vt* pastorear.
grease *n* grasa *f*: —vt untar.
greasy *adj* grasiento/ta.
great *adj* gran, grande.
greatcoat *n* sobretodo *m*.
greatness *n* grandeza *f*.
greedily *adv* vorazmente.
greediness, greed *n* gula *f*: codicia *f*.
Greek *n* griego (idioma) *m*.
green *adj* verde.
greengrocer *n* verdulero *m*.
greenhouse *n* invernadero *m*.
greet *vt* saludar, congratular.
greeting *n* saludo *m*.
greeting(s) card *n* tarjeta de felicitaciones *f*.
grenade *n (mil)* granada *f*.
grenadier *n* granadero *m*.
greyhound *n* galgo *m*.
greyish *adj* pardusco/ca.
grid *n* reja *f; red f*.
grief *n* dolor *m*.
grieve *vt* agraviar.
grievous *adj* doloroso/sa.
griffin *n* grifo *m*.
grill *n* parrilla *f*.
grim *adj* feo, fea.
grimace *n* visaje *m*.
grime *n* porquería *f*.
grin *n* mueca *f*.
grind *vt* moler.
grinder *n* molinero *m*.
grip *n* asimiento *m*.
grisly *adj* horroroso/sa.
gristle *n* tendón, nervio *m*.
grit *n* gravilla *f; valor m*.
groan *vi* gemir, suspirar.
grocer *n* tendero/ra, abarrotero/ram/f*.
groceries *npl* comestibles *mpl*.
groin *n* ingle *f*.
groom *n* establero *m*.
groove *n* ranura *f*.
gross *adj* grueso/sa.
grotesque *adj* grotesco/ca.
grotto *n* gruta *f*.
ground *n* tierra *f*.
ground floor *n* planta baja *f*.

group *n* grupo *m.*.
grouse *n* urogallo *m:* —*vi* quejarse.
grove *n* arboleda *f.*
grovel *vi* arrastrarse.
grow *vt* cultivar: —*vi* crecer, aumentarse.
growl *vi* regañar, gruñir.
grown-up *n* adulto *m.*
grub *n* gusano *m.*
grubby *adj* sucio/cia.
grudge *n* rencor, odio *m;* envidia *f:* —*vt* , *vi*envidiar.
gruesome *adj* horrible.
gruff *adj* brusco/ca.
grumble *vi* gruñir; murmurar.
grunt *vi* gruñir.
G-string *n* taparrabo *m.*
guarantee *n* garantía *f.*
guard *n* guardia *f.*
guardianship *n* tutela *f.*
guerrilla *n* guerrillero *m.*
guess *vt* , *vi* conjeturar; adivinar; suponer.
guest *n* huésped/a.
guffaw *n* carcajada *f.*
guide *vt* guiar, dirigir: —*n* guía *m.*
guidebook *n* guía *f.*
guild *n* gremio *m.*
guile *n* astucia *f.*
guilt *n* culpabilidad *f.*
guilty *adj* reo, rea, culpable.

guinea pig *n* cobayo *m.*
guise *n* manera *f.*
guitar *n* guitarra *f.*
gulf *n* golfo *m.*
gull *n* gaviota *f.*
gullet *n* esófago *m.*
gullible *adj* crédulo/la.
gully *n* barranco *m.*
gulp *n* trago *m.*
gum *n* goma *f.*
gum tree *n* árbol gomero *m.*
gun *n* pistola *f;* escopeta *f.*
gunboat *n* cañonera *f.*
gunpowder *n* pólvora *f.*
gunshot *n* escopetazo *m.*
gurgle *vi* gorgotear.
guru *n* gurú *m.*
gush *vi* brotar.
gusset *n* escudete *m.*
gut *n* intestino *m.*
gutter *n* canalón *m;* arroyo *m.*
guy *n* tío *m;* tipo *m.*
gym(nasium) *n* gimnasio *m.*
gymnast *n* gimnasta *m/f :*
gynecologist *n* ginecólogo/ga *m/f .*
Gypsy *n* gitano/na *m/f .*
gyrate *vi* girar.

H

haberdasher *n* camisero/ra, mercero/ ra *m/f .*
habit *n* costumbre *f.*
habitable *adj* habitable.
habitat *n* hábitat *m.*
habitual *adj* habitual.
haddock *n* merlango *m.*
hag *n* bruja *f.*
hail *n* granizo *m.*
hair *n* pelo; cabello *m.*
hairbrush *n* cepillo *m.*
haircut *n* corte de pelo *m.*
hairdresser *n* peluquero *m.*
hairdryer *n* secador de pelo *m.*
hairspray *n* laca *f.*
hairstyle *n* peinado *m.*
half *n* mitad *f.*
half-caste *adj* mestizo/za.
hall *n* vestíbulo *m.*
hallow *vi* consagrar, santificar.
hallucination *n* alucinación *f.*
halo *n* halo *m.*
halt *vi* parar.
halve *vt* partir por mitad.
ham *n* jamón *m.*
hamburger *n* hamburguesa *f.*
hamlet *n* aldea *f.*
hammer *n* martillo *m.*
hammock *n* hamaca *f.*
hamper *n* cesto *f.*
hamstring *vt* desjarretar.
hand *n* mano *f.*
handbag *n* cartera *f.*
handful *n* puñado *m.*

handicap *n* desventaja *f.*
handicraft *n* artesanía *f.*
handkerchief *n* pañuelo *m.*
handle *n* mango, puño *m;* asa; manija *f.*
handshake *n* apretón de manos *m.*
handsome *adj* guapo/pa.
handwriting *n* letra *f.*
handy *adj* practico/ca.
hang *vt* colgar.
hanger *n* percha *f.*
hangover *n* resaca *f.*
happen *vi* pasar; acontecer.
happiness *n* felicidad *f.*
happy *adj* feliz.
harass *vt* cansar, fatigar.
harbinger *n* precursor *m.*
harbor *n* puerto *m.*
hard *adj* duro/ra, firme.
harden *vt* , *vi* endurecer(se).
hardiness *n* robustez *f.*
hardly *adv* apenas.
hardship *n* penas *fpl.*
hard-up *adj* sin plata.
hardware store *n* ferretería *f.*
hardy *adj* fuerte.
hare *n* liebre *f.*
hare-lipped *adj* labihendido/da.
haricot *n* alubia *f.*
harlequin *n* arlequín *m.*
harm *n* mal, daño *m.*
harmful *adj* perjudicial.
harmless *adj* inocuo/cua.
harmonic *adj* armónico/ca.

harmonious *adj* armonioso/sa.
harmonize *vt* armonizar.
harmony *n* armonía *f.*
harp *n* arpa *f.*
harpoon *n* arpón *m.*
harsh *adj* duro/ra; austero/ra.
harvest *n* cosecha *f.*
hearing aid *n* audífono *m.*
hearse *n* coche fúnebre *m.*
heart *n* corazón *m.*
heart attack *n* infarto *m.*
heartburn *n* acedia *f.*
hearth *n* hogar *m.*
heartily *adv* sinceramente.
heartless *adj* cruel.
hearty *adj* cordial.
heat *n* calor *m.*
heater *n* calentador *m.*
heathen *n* pagano *m.*
heating *n* calefacción *f.*
heatwave *n* ola de calor *f.*
heaven *n* cielo *m.*
heavily *adv* pesadamente.
heavy *adj* pesado/da.
Hebrew *n* hebreo *m.*
heckle *vt* interrumpir.
hectic *adj* agitado/da.
hedge *n* seto *m.*
hedgehog *n* erizo *m.*
heed *vt* hacer caso de.
heedless *adj* descuidado/da.
heel *n* talón *m.*
hefty *adj* grande.
heifer *n* ternera *f.*
height *n* altura *f;* altitud *f.*
heinous *adj* atroz.
heir *n* heredero/ra *m/f.*
heirloom *n* reliquia de familia *f.*
helicopter *n* helicóptero *m.*
hell *n* infierno *m.*
helm *n (mar)* timón *m.*
helmet *n* casco *m.*
help *vt , vi* ayudar, socorrer.
helper *n* ayudante *m.*
helpful *adj* útil.
helping *n* ración *f.*
helpless *adj* indefenso/sa.
hem *n* ribete *m.*
he-man *n* macho *m.*
harvester *n* cosechadora *f.*
hash *n* hachís *m.*
hassock *n* cojín de paja *m.*
haste *n* apuro *m.*
hasten *vt* acelerar.
hasty *adj* apresurado/da.
hat *n* sombrero *m.*
hatch *vt* incubar; tramar *f.*
hatchet *n* hacha *f.*
hatchway *n (mar)* escotilla *f.*
hate *n* odio.
hateful *adj* odioso/sa.
hatred *n* odio, aborrecimiento *m.*
haughty *adj* altanero/ra, orgulloso/sa.
haul *vt* tirar: —*n* botín *m.*
hauler *n* transportista *m/f.*
haunch *n* anca *f.*
haunt *vt* frecuentar, rondar.

have *vt* haber; tener, poseer.
haven *n* asilo *m.*
havoc *n* estrago *m.*
hawk *n* halcón *m.*
hawthorn *n* espino blanco *m.*
hay *n* heno *m.*
hazard *n* riesgo *m.*
haze *n* niebla *f.*
hazel *n* avellano *m.*
hazelnut *n* avellana *f.*
hazy *adj* oscuro/ra.
he *pn* el.
head *n* cabeza *f.*
head *n* cakeza *f.*
headache *n* dolor de cabeza *m.*
headlamp *n* faro *m.*
headline *n* titular *m.*
headmaster *n* director *m.*
headphones *npl* auriculares *mpl .*
heal *vt , vi* curar.
health *n* salud */healthy adj* sano/na.
heap *n* montón *m.*
hear *vt* oír; escuchar.
hearing *n* oído *m.*
hemisphere *n* hemisferio *m.*
hemorrhage *n* hemorragia *f.*
hemorrhoids *npl* hemorroides *mpl .*
hemp *n* cáñamo *m.*
hen *n* gallina *f.*
henchman *n* secuaz *m.*
henceforth, henceforward *adv* de aquí en adelante.
hepatitis *n* hepatitis *f.*
her *pn* su; ella; de ella; a ella.
herald *n* heraldo *m.*
heraldry *n* heráldica *f.*
herb *n* hierba *fl.*
herbaceous *adj* herbáceo/cea.
herbalist *n* herbolario *m.*
herbivorous *adj* herbívoro/ra.
herd *n* rebaño *m.*
here *adv* aquí, acá.
hereabout(s) *adv* aquí alrededor.
hereafter *adv* en el futuro.
hereby *adv* por esto.
hereditary *adj* hereditario/ria.
heresy *n* herejía *f.*
heretic *n* hereje *m/f .*
heritage *n* patrimonio *m.*
hermetic *adj* hermético/ca.
hermit *n* ermitaño/ña *m/f .*
hermitage *n* ermita *f.*
hernia *n* hernia *f.*
hero *n* héroe *m.*
heroic *adj* heroico/ca.
heroine *n* heroína *f.*
heroism *n* heroísmo *m.*
heron *n* garza *f.*
herring *n* arenque *m.*
herself *pn* ella misma.
hesitant *adj* vacilante.
hesitate *vt* dudar; tardar.
heterosexual *adj , n* heterosexual *m.*
hew *vt* tajar; cortar.
heyday *n* apogeo *m.*
hi *excl* ¡hola!
hiatus *n (gr)* hiato *m.*
hibernate *vi* invernar.

hiccup *n* hipo *m.*
hickory *n* noguera americana *f.*
hide *vt* esconder*f.*
hideaway *n* escondite *m.*
hideous *adj* horrible.
hierarchy *n* jerarquía *f.*
hieroglyphic *adj* jeroglífico/ca.
hi-fi *n* estéreo, hi-fi *m.*
high *adj* alto/ta; elevado/da.
highlight *n* punto culminante *m.*
highway *n* carretera *f.*
hike *vi* ir de excursión.
hijack *vt* secuestrar.
hilarious *adj* alegre.
hill, hillock *n* colina *f.*
him *pn* le, lo, el.
himself *pn* el mismo, se, si mismo.
hinder *vt* impedir.
hindrance *n* impedimento, obstáculo *m.*
hinge *n* bisagra *f.*
hip *n* cadera *f.*
hippopotamus *n* hipopótamo *m.*
hire *vt* alquilar.
his *pn* su, suyo, de el.
Hispanic *adj* hispano/na; hispánico/ca.
hiss *vt , vi* silbar.
historian *n* historiador *m.*
history *n* historia *f.*
hit *vt* golpear.
hitch *vt* atar.
hitch-hike *vi* hacer autostop.
hive *n* colmena *f.*
hoax *n* trampa *f.*
hobble *vi* cojear.
hobby *n* pasatiempo *m.*
hockey *n* hockey *m.*
hodge-podge *n* mezcolanza *f.*
hoe *n* azadón *m.*
hog *n* cerdo, puerco *m.*
hoist *vt* alzar.
hold *vt* tener; detener; contener.
hole *n* agujero *m.*
holiday *n* día de fiesta *m*: —**s** *pl* vacaciones *fpl.*
hollow *adj* hueco/ca.
holly *n (bot)* acebo *m.*
hollyhock *n* malva hortense *f.*
holocaust *n* holocausto *m.*
holster *n* pistolera *f.*
holy *adj* santo/ta.
holy week *n* semana santa *f.*
homage *n* homenaje *m.*
home *n* casa *f.*
home address *n* domicilio *m.*
homely *adj* casero/ra.
homeopathist *n* homeopatista *m/f .*
homeopathy *n* homeopatía *f.*
homesick *adj* nostálgico/ca.
homework *n* deberes *mpl .*
homicide *n* homicidio *m;* homicida *m.*
homosexual *adj , n* homosexual *m.*
honest *adj* honrado/da.
honesty *n* honradez *f.*
honey *n* miel *f.*
honeycomb *n* panal *m.*
honeymoon *n* luna de miel *f.*
honeysuckle *n (bot)* madreselva *f.*
honor *n* honra *f;* honor *m:* —*vt* honrar.

honorary *adj* honorario/ria.
hood *n* capo *m;* capucha *f.*
hoof *n* pezuña *f.*
hook *n* gancho *m.*
hooligan *n* gamberro *m.*
hoop *n* aro *m.*
hooter *n* sirena *f.*
hop *n (bot)* lúpulo.
hope *n* esperanza *f.*
horde *n* horda *f.*
horizon *n* horizonte *m.*
horizontal *adj* horizontal.
hormone *n* hormona *f.*
horn *n* cuerno *m.*
hornet *n* avispón *m.*
horny *adj* calloso/sa.
horoscope *n* horóscopo *m.*
horrendous *adj* horrendo/da.
horrible *adj* horrible.
horrid *adj* horrible.
horrific *adj* horroroso/sa.
horrify *vt* horrorizar.
horror *n* horror, terror *m.*
hors d'oeuvre *n* entremeses *mpl .*
horse *n* caballo *m*
horse chestnut *n* castaño de Indias *m.*
horsefly *n* moscarda *f.*
horseradish *n* rábano silvestre *m.*
horticulture *n* horticultura, jardinería *f.*
horticulturist *n* jardinero/ra *m/f .*
hosepipe *n* manga *f.*
hosiery *n* calcetería *f.*
hospital *n* hospital *m.*
hospitality *n* hospitalidad *f.*
host *n* anfitrión *m;* hostia *f.*
hostage *n* rehén *m.*
hostess *n* anfitriona *f.*
hostile *adj* hostil.
hot *adj* caliente; cálido/da.
hotbed *n* semillero *m.*
hotel *n* hotel *m.*
hotelier *n* hotelero/ra *m/f .*
hour *n* hora *f.*
hour-glass *n* reloj de arena *m.*
house *n* casa *f.*
household *n* familia *f.*
houseless *adv* sin casa.
housewife *n* ama de casa *f.*
hovel *n* choza, cabaña *f.*
hover *vi* flotar.
how *adv* cómo.
howl *vi* aullar.
hub *n* centro *m.*
hue *n* color *m.*
hug *vt* abrazar: —*n* abrazo *m.*
huge *adj* vasto/ta, enorme.
hum *vi* canturrear.
human *adv* humano/na.
humane *adv* humano/na.
humanist *n* humanista *m/f .*
humanitarian *adj* humanitario/ria.
humanity *n* humanidad *f.*
humble *adj* humilde.
humid *adj* húmedo/da.
humidity *n* humedad *f.*
humiliate *vt* humillar.
humming-bird *n* colibrí *m.*

humor n sentido del humor m.
humorist n humorista m./ f
humorous adj gracioso/sa.
hundred adj ciento.
hundredth adj centésimo.
hundredweight n quintal m.
hunger n hambre f.
hunt vt cazar; perseguir.
hunter n cazador/a m/f.
hurdle n valla f.
hurricane n huracán m.
hurt vt hacer daño; ofender.
hurtful adj dañoso/sa: —~ly adv dañosamente.
husband n marido m.
hush! excl ¡chitón!, ¡silencio!.
husk n cáscara f.

hut n cabaña f.
hutch n conejera f.
hyacinth n jacinto m.
hydraulic adj hidráulico/ca.
hydrofoil n aerodeslizador m.
hydrogen n hidroala f.
hyena n hiena f.
hygiene n higiene f.
hymn n himno m.
hypermarket n hipermercado m.
hyphen n (gr) guión m.
hypocrisy n hipocresía f.
hypocrite n hipócrita m/f.
hysterical adj histérico/ca.
hysterics npl histeria f.

I

I pn yo.
ice n hielo m: —vt helar.
ice cream n helado m.
ice rink n pista de hielo f.
icicle n carámbano m.
idea n idea f.
ideal adj ideal.
identical adj idéntico/ca.
identification n identificación f.
identify vt identificar.
identity n identidad f.
ideology n ideología f.
idiom n idioma m.
idiosyncrasy n idiosincrasia f.
idiot n idiota, necio m.
idiotic adj tonto/ta, bobo/ba.
idle adj desocupado/da.
idol n ídolo m.
idolatry n idolatría f.
idyllic adj idílico/ca.
i.e.adv esto es.
if conj si, aunque.
ignite vt encender.
ignoble adj innoble.
ignorance n ignorancia f.
ignorant adj ignorante.
ignore vt no hacer caso de.
ill adj malo/la, enfermo/ma.
ill-advised adj imprudente.
illegal adj ~ly adv ilegal(mente).
illegible adj ilegible.
illegitimate adj ilegítimo/ma.
ill feeling n rencor m.
illiterate adj analfabeto/ta.
illness n enfermedad f.
illogical adj ilógico/ca.
illuminate vt iluminar.
illusion n ilusión f.
illustrate vt ilustrar.
illustration n ilustración f.
image n imagen f.
imagination n imaginación f.
imagine vt imaginarse.
imbalance n desequilibrio m.
imbecile adj imbécil.

imitate vt imitar, copiar.
imitation n imitación, copia f.
immaculate adj inmaculado/da.
immature adj inmaduro/ra.
immediate adj inmediato/ta.
immense adj inmenso/sa.
immigrant n inmigrante m.
immigration n inmigración f.
imminent adj inminente.
immodest adj inmodesto/ta.
immoral adj inmoral.
immortal adj inmortal.
immune adj inmune.
imp n diablillo, duende m.
impact n impacto m.
impair vt disminuir.
impartial adj ~ly adv imparcial(mente).
impatience n impaciencia f.
impede vt estorbar.
impel vt impeler.
impending adj inminente.
imperative adj imperativo/va.
imperfect adj imperfecto/ta.
imperial adj imperial.
impersonal adj, ~ly adv impersonal(mente).
impetus n ímpetu m.
impiety n irmpiedad f.
implant vt implantar.
implement n herramienta.
implore vt suplicar.
imply vt suponer.
impolite adj maleducado/da.
import vt importar.
importance n importancia f.
important adj importante.
impose vt imponer.
impostor n impostor m.
impotence n impotencia f.
impotent adj impotente.
impound vt embargar.
impoverish vt empobrecer.
impractical adj poco práctico/ca.
imprecise adj impreciso/sa.
impress vt impresionar.
impression n impresión f; edición f.

impressive *adj* impresionante.
imprint *n* sello *m:* —*vt* imprimir; estampar.
improbable *adj* improbable.
improper *adj* impropio/pia.
improve *vt*, *vi* mejorar.
improvise *vt* improvisar.
impulse *n* impulso *m*.
impure *adj* impuro/ra.
impurity *n* impureza *f*.
in *prep* en.
inability *n* incapacidad *f*.
inaccessible *adj* inaccesible.
inaccurate *adj* inexacto/ta.
inadequate *adj* inadecuado/da, defectuoso/sa.
inadmissible *adj* inadmisible.
inadvertently *adv* sin querer.
inappropriate *adj* impropio/pia.
inaudible *adj* inaudible.
inaugurate *vt* inaugurar.
in-between *adj* intermedio/dia.
inborn, inbred *adj* innato/ta.
incapable *adj* incapaz.
incarcerate *vt* encarcelar.
incarnation *n* encarnación *f*.
incendiary *n* bomba incendiaria *f*.
incense *n* incienso *m*.
incentive *n* incentivo *m*.
incessant *adj* incesante.
incest *n* incesto *m*.
inch *n* pulgada *f*.
incident *n* incidente *m*.
incinerator *n* incinerador *m*.
inclination *n* inclinación.
incline *vt*, *vi* inclinar(se).
include *vt* incluir.
inclusive *adj* inclusivo/va.
incognito *adv* de incógnito.
incoherent *adj* incoherente.
income *n* renta *f*
incompatible *adj* incompatible.
incompetence *n* incompetencia *f*.
incomplete *adj* incompleto/ta.
incomprehensible *adj* incomprensible.
inconceivable *adj* inconcebible.
incontinence *n* incontinencia *f*.
inconvenience *n* incomodidad *f*.
incorrect *adj* incorrecto/ta.
increase *vt* acrecentar, aumentar
incredible *adj* increíble.
incubate *vi* incubar.
incubator *n* incubadora *f*.
incurable *adj* incurable.
indecency *n* indecencia *f*.
indecent *adj* indecente: —~**ly** *adv* indecentemente.
indecisive *adj* indeciso/sa.
indeed *adv* verdaderamente, de veras.
independence *n* independencia *f*.
independent *adj* independiente.
indescribable *adj* indescriptible.
index *n* índice *m*.
indicate *vt* indicar.
indifference *n* indiferencia *f*.
indigenous *adj* indígena.
indigestion *n* indigestión *f*.
indignation *n* indignación *f*.
indigo *n* añil *m*.
indirect *adj* indirecto/ta.

indiscreet *adj* indiscreto/ta.
indispensable *adj* indispensable.
indistinguishable *adj* indistinguible.
individual *adj* individual *m*.
indoors *adv* dentro.
indulge *vt*, *vi* conceder; ser indulgente.
industrialist *n* industrial *m*.
industry *n* industria *f*.
inedible *adj* no comestible.
ineffective, ineffectual *adj* ineficaz.
inefficiency *n* ineficacia *f*.
ineligible *adj* ineligible.
inept *adj* incompetente.
inequality *n* desigualdad *f*.
inevitable *adj* inevitable.
inexpensive *adj* económico/ca.
inexperience *n* inexperiencia *f*.
inexpert *adj* inexperto/ta.
inexplicable *adj* inexplicable.
infallible *adj* infalible.
infamy *n* infamia *f*.
infancy *n* infancia *f*.
infant *n* niño/ña *m/f*.
infantile *adj* infantil.
infantry *n* infantería *f*.
infatuation *n* infatuación *f*.
infect *vt* infectar.
infection *n* infección *f*.
inferior *adj* inferior.
infernal *adj* infernal.
inferno *n* infierno *m*.
infest *vt* infestar.
infidelity *n* infidelidad *f*.
infinite *adj* infinito/ta.
infinitive *n* infinitivo *m*.
infinity *n* infinito *m;* infinidad *f*.
infirm *adj* enfermo/ma.
infirmary *n* enfermería *f*.
infirmity *n* fragilidad, enfermedad *f*.
inflammation *n* inflamación *f*.
inflatable *adj* inflable.
inflate *vt* inflar, hinchar.
inflation *n* inflación *f*.
inflict *vt* imponer.
influence *n* influencia *f*.
influenza *n* gripe *f*.
inform *vt* informar.
informal *adj* informal.
information *n* información *f*.
infrastructure *n* infraestructura *f*.
infuriate *vt* enfurecer.
infusion *n* infusión *f*.
ingenious *adj* ingenioso/sa.
ingenuity *n* ingeniosidad *f*.
ingot *n* barra de metal *f*.
ingrained *adj* inveterado/da.
ingratitude *n* ingratitud *f*.
ingredient *n* ingrediente *m*.
inhabit *vt*, *vi* habitar.
inhabitant *n* habitante *m*.
inhale *vt* inhalar.
inherent *adj* inherente.
inherit *vt* heredar.
inheritance *n* herencia *f*.
inhibit *vt* inhibir.
inhospitable *adj* inhospitalario/ria.
inhuman *adj* inhumano/na.

inhumanity *n* inhumanidad, crueldad *f.*
initial *adj* inicial.
initiate *vt* iniciar.
initiative *n* iniciativa *f.*
inject *vt* inyectar.
injection *n* inyección *f.*
injure *vt* herir.
injury *n* daño *m.*
injustice *n* injusticia *f.*
ink *n* tinta *f.*
inkling *n* sospecha *f.*
inlaid *adj* taraceado/da.
in-laws *npl* suegros *mpl* .
inlay *vt* taracear.
inlet *n* entsenada *f.*
inmate *n* preso *m.*
inn *n* posada *f.*; mesón *m.*
innkeeper *n* posadero/ra, mesonero/ra *m/f.*
innocence *n* inocencia *f.*
innocent *adj* inocente.
innovate *vt* innovar.
innovation *n* innovación *f.*
innuendo *n* indirecta, insinuación *f.*
inoffensive *adj* inofensivo/va.
inorganic *adj* inorgánico/ca.
inpatient *n* paciente interno *m.*
input *n* entrada *f.*
inquest *n* encuesta judicial *f.*
inquire *vt , vi* preguntar.
inquiry *n* pesquisa *f.*
inquisition *n* inquisición *f.*
inquisitive *adj* curioso/sa.
insane *adj* loco/ca, demente.
insanity *n* locura *f.*
inscription *n* inscripción *f.*
inscrutable *adj* inescrutable.
insect *n* insecto *m.*
insecticide *n* insecticida *m.*
insecure *adj* inseguro/ra.
insensitive *adj* insensible.
inseparable *adj* inseparable.
insert *vt* introducir.
insertion *n* inserción *f.*
inside *n* interior *m: —adv* dentro.
inside out *adv* al revés; a fondo.
insignia *npl* insignias *fpl.*
insignificant *adj* insignificante.
insincere *adj* poco sincero/ra.
insipid *adj* insípido/da.
insist *vi* insistir.
insole *n* plantilla *f.*
insolence *n* insolencia *f.*
insoluble *adj* insoluble.
insomnia *n* insomnio *m.*
insomuch *conj* puesto que.
inspect *vt* examinar, inspeccionar.
inspection *n* inspección *f.*
inspire *vt* inspirar.
instability *n* inestabilidad *f.*
instance *n* ejemplo *m.*
instant *adj* inmediato/ta.
instead (of) *pr* por, en lugar de, en vezde.
instill *vt* inculcar.
instinct *n* instinto *m.*
instinctive *adj* instintivo/va.
institute *vt* establecer: *—n* instituto *m.*
institution *n* institución *f.*

instruct *vt* instruir, enseñar.
instruction *n* instrucción *f.*
instrument *n* instrumento *m.*
instrumental *adj* instrumental.
insufferable *adj* insoportable.
insufficient *adj* insuficiente.
insulate *vt* aislar.
insulin *n* insulina *f.*
insult *vt* insultar: *—n* insulto *m.*
insurance *n* (com) seguro *m.*
insure *vt* asegurar.
intact *adj* intacto/ta.
integral *adj* íntegro/gra.
integrate *vt* integrar.
integrity *n* integridad *f.*
intellect *n* intelecto *m.*
intelligence *n* inteligencia *f.*
intend *vi* tener intención.
intense *adj* intenso/sa.
intensity *n* intensidad *f.*
intention *n* intención *f.*
inter *vt* enterrar.
interaction *n* interacción *f.*
intercourse *n* relaciones sexuales *fpl.*
interest *vt* interesar.
interesting *adj* interesante.
interest rate *n* tipo de interés *m.*
interfere *vi* entrometerse.
interference *n* interferencia *f.*
interior *adj* interior.
interlude *n* intermedio *m.*
intermediate *adj* intermedio/dia.
interment *n* entierro *m;* sepultura *f.*
intermission *n* descanso *m.*
intermittent *adj* intermitente.
internal *adj* interno/na.
international *adj* internacional.
interpret *vt* interpretar.
interpretation *n* interpretación *f.*
interpreter *n* intérprete *m/f.*
interregnum *n* interregno *m.*
interrelated *adj* interrelacionado/da.
interrogate *vt* interrogar.
interrogation *n* interrogatorio *m.*
interrogative *adj* interrogativo/va.
interrupt *vt* interrumpir.
interruption *n* interrupción *f.*
intersect *vi* cruzarse.
intersection *n* cruce *m.*
intersperse *vt* esparcir.
intertwine *vt* entretejer.
interval *n* intervalo *m.*
intervene *vi* intervenir.
intervention *n* intervención *f.*
interview *n* entrevista *f.*
interviewer *n* entrevistador/a *m/f.*
intestine *n* intestino *m.*
intimacy *n* intimidad *f.*
intimate *n* amigo/ga íntimo/ma.
intimidate *vt* intimidar.
into *prep* en, dentro, adentro.
intolerable *adj* intolerable.
intolerance *n* intolerancia *f.*
intoxicate *vt* embriagar.
intravenous *adj* intravenoso/sa.
intrepid *adj* intrépido/da.
intricate *adj* intricado/da.

intrigue *n* intriga *f.* —*vi* intrigar.
intriguing *adj* fascinante.
intrinsic *adj* intrínseco/ca.
introduce *vt* introducir.
introduction *n* introducción *f.*
introvert *n* introvertido *m.*
intrude *vi* entrometerse.
intruder *n* intruso/sa *m/f.*
intuition *n* intuición *f.*
intuitive *adj* intuitivo/va.
inundate *vt* inundar.
inundation *n* inundación *f.*
invade *vt* invadir.
invalid *adj* inválido/da.
invalidate *vt* invalidar, anular.
invaluable *adj* inapreciable.
invariable *adj* invariable.
invariably *adv* invariablemente.
invasion *n* invasión *f.*
invent *vt* inventar.
invention *n* invento *m.*
inventor *n* inventor *m.*
inventory *n* inventario *m.*
inversion *n* inversión *f.*
invert *vt* invertir.
invest *vt* invertir.
investigate *vt* investigar.
investment *n* inversión *f.*
invigilate *vt* vigilar.
invigorating *adj* vigorizante.
invincible *adj* invencible.
invisible *adj* invisible.
invitation *n* invitación *f.*
invite *vt* invitar.
invoice *n (com)* factura *f.*
involuntarily *adv* involuntariamente.
involve *vt* implicar.

involvement *n* compromiso *m.*
iodine *n (chem)* yodo *m.*
IOU (I owe you) *n* vale *m.*
irate, ireful *adj* enojado/da.
iris *n* iris *m.*
irksome *adj* fastidioso/sa.
iron *n* hierro *m:* —*adj* férreo/rea: —*vt* planchar.
ironic *adj* irónico/ca: —~ly *adv* conironía.
ironwork *n* herraje *m:* —~s *pl* herrería *f.*
irony *n* ironía *f.*
irradiate *vt* irradiar.
irrational *adj* irracional.
irreconcilable *adj* irreconciliable.
irregular *adj* ~ly *adv* irregular(mente).
irrelevant *adj* impertinente.
irreparable *adj* irreparable.
irresistible *adj* irresistible.
irresponsible *adj* irresponsable.
irrigate *vt* regar.
irrigation *n* riego *m.*
irritable *adj* irritable.
irritant *n (med)* irritante *m.*
irritate *vt* irritar.
island *n* isla *f.*
isle *n* isla *f.*
isolate *vt* aislar.
issue *n* asunto *m.*
it *pn* el, ella, ello, lo, la, le.
italic *n* cursiva *f.*
itch *n* picazón *f:* —*vi* picar.
item *n* artículo *m.*
itemize *vt* detallar.
itinerary *n* itinerario *m.*
its *pn* su, suyo.
itself *pn* el mismo, la misma, lo mismo.
ivory *n* marfil *m.*
ivy *n* hiedra *f.*

J

jab *vt* clavar.
jabber *vi* farfullar.
jack *n* gato *m;* sota *f.*
jackal *n* chacal *m.*
jackboots *npl* botas militares *fpl.*
jackdaw *n* grajo *m.*
jacket *n* chaqueta *f.*
jack-knife *vi* colear.
jackpot *n* premio gordo *m.*
jade *n* jade *m.*
jagged *adj* dentado/da.
jaguar *n* jaguar *m.*
jail *n* cárcel *f.*
jailer *n* carcelero/ra *m/f.*
jam *n* conserva *f;* mermelada de frutas *f.*
jangle *vi* sonar.
January *n* enero *m.*
jargon *n* jerigonza *f.*
jasmine *n* jazmín *m.*
jaundice *n* ictericia *f.*
jaunt *n* excursión *f.*
jaunty *adj* alegre.
javelin *n* jabalina *f.*
jaw *n* mandíbula *f.*

jay *n* arrendajo *m.*
jazz *n* jazz *m.*
jealous *adj* celoso/sa.
jealousy *n* celos *mpl* ; envidia *f.*
jeans *npl* vaqueros *mpl* .
jeep *n* jeep *m.*
jeer *vi* befar.
jelly *n* jalea, gelatina *f.*
jellyfish *n* aguamar *m;* medusa *f.*
jeopardize *vt* arriesgar.
jersey *n* jersey *m.*
jest *n* broma *f.*
jester *n* bufón/ona *m/f* .
Jesuit *n* jesuita *m.*
Jesus *n* Jesús *m.*
jet *n* avión a reacción *m*
jettison *vt* desechar.
jetty *n* muelle *m.*
Jew *n* judío/día *m/f* .
jewel *n* joya *f.*
jewelry *n* joyería *f.*
Jewish *adj* judío/día.
jib *n (mar)* foque *m.*
jibe *n* mofa *f.*

jig *n* giga *f.*
jigsaw *n* rompecabezas *m.*
jilt *vt* dejar.
job *n* trabajo *m.*
jockey *n* jinete *m/f.*
jocular *adj* jocoso/sa, alegre.
jog *vi* hacer footing.
jogging *n* footing *m.*
join *vt* juntar, unir.
joiner *n* carpintero/ra *m/f.*
joinery *n* carpintería *f.*
joint *n* articulación *f.*
jointly *adv* conjuntamente.
joke *n* broma *f:* —*vi* bromear.
joker *n* comodín *m.*
jollity *n* alegría *f.*
jolly *adj* alegre.
jolt *vt* sacudir: —*n* sacudida *f.*
jostle *vt* codear.
journal *n* revista *f.*
journalism *n* periodismo *m.*
journalist *n* periodista *m/f.*
journey *n* viaje *m:* —*vt* viajar.
jovial *adj* jovial.
joy *n* alegría *f;* jubilo *m.*
jubilant *adj* jubiloso/sa.
jubilation *n* jubilo/la, regocijo *m.*
jubilee *n* jubileo *m.*
Judaism *n* judaísmo *m.*
judge *n* juez/a *m/f:* —*vt* juzgar.
judgment *n* juicio *m.*
judicial *adj* ~**ly** *adv* judicial(mente).
judiciary *n* judicatura *m.*

judicious *adj* prudente.
judo *n* judo *m.*
juggle *vi* hacer juegos malabares.
juggler *n* malabarista *m/f.*
juice *n* jugo *m;* suco *m.*
juicy *adj* jugoso/sa.
jukebox *n* gramola *f.*
July *n* julio *m.*
jumble *vt* mezclar
jump *vi* saltar
jumper *n* suéter *m.*
jumpy *adj* nervioso/sa.
juncture *n* coyuntura *f.*
June *n* junio *m.*
jungle *n* selva *f.*
junior *adj* más joven.
juniper *n* (*bot*) enebro *m.*
junk *n* basura *f;* baratijas *fpl.*
junta *n* junta *f.*
jurisdiction *n* jurisdicción *f.*
jurisprudence *n* jurisprudencia *f.*
jurist *n* jurista *m/f.*
jury *n* jurado *m.*
just *adj* justo/ta.
justice *n* justicia *f.*
justification *n* justificación *f.*
justify *vt* justificar.
justly *adv* justamente.
justness *n* justicia *f.*
jut *vi:* —**to ~ out** sobresalir.
jute *n* yute *m.*
juvenile *adj* juvenil.
juxtaposition *n* yuxtaposición *f.*

K

kaleidoscope *n* calidoscopio *m.*
kangaroo *n* canguro *m.*
karate *n* karate *m.*
kebab *n* pincho *m.*
keel *n* (*mar*) quilla *f.*
keen *adj* agudo/da; vivo/va.
keep *vt* mantener; guardar; conservar.
keeper *n* guardián/ana *m/f.*
keepsake *n* recuerdo *m.*
keg *n* barril *m.*
kennel *n* perrera *f.*
kernel *n* fruta *f;* meollo *m.*
kerosene *n* kerosene *m.*
ketchup *n* catsup *m.*
kettle *n* hervidor *m.*
key *n* llave *f; (mus)* clave *f;* tecla *f.*
keyboard *n* teclado *m.*
keyhole *n* ojo de la cerradura *m.*
key ring *n* llavero *m.*
khaki *n* caqui *m.*
kick *vt , vi* patear.
kid *n* chico *m.*
kidnap *vt* secuestrar.
kidnapper *n* secuestrador/a *m/f.*
kidney *n* riñón *m.*
killer *n* asesino/na *m/f.*
killing *n* asesinato *m.*
kiln *n* horno *m.*

kilo *n* kilo *m.*
kilobyte *n* kiloocteto *m.*
kilogram *n* kilo *m.*
kilometer *n* kilómetro *m.*
kilt *n* falda escocesa *f.*
kin *n* parientes *mpl.*
kind *adj* cariñoso/sa: —*n* genero *m.*
kind-hearted *adj* bondadoso/sa.
kindle *vt , vi* encender.
kindly *adj* bondadoso/sa.
kindness *n* bondad *f.*
kindred *adj* emparentado/da.
kinetic *adj* cinético/ca.
king *n* rey *m.*
kingdom *n* reino *m.*
kingfisher *n* martín pescador *m.*
kiosk *n* quiosco *m.*
kiss *n* beso *m:* —*vt* besar.
kit *n* equipo *m.*
kitchen *n* cocina *f.*
kite *n* cometa *f.*
kitten *n* gatillo *m.*
knack *n* don *m.*
knapsack *n* mochila *f.*
knave *n* bribón.
knead *vt* amasar.
knee *n* rodilla *f.*
kneel *vi* arrodillarse.

knell *n* toque de difuntos *m*.
knife *n* cuchillo *m*.
knight *n* caballero *m*.
knit *vt* , *vi* tejer.
knitting needle *n* aguja de tejer *f*.
knitwear *n* prendas de punto *fpl*.
knob *n* bulto *m*.
knock *vt* , *vi* golpear.
knocker *n* aldaba *f*.
knock-kneed *adj* patizambo/ba.
knock-out *n* K.O. *m*.

knoll *n* cima de una colina *f*.
knot *n* nudo *m*; lazo *m*: —*vt* anudar.
knotty *adj* escabroso/sa.
know *vt* , *vi* conocer; saber.
know-all *n* sabelotodo *m/f* .
know-how *n* conocimientos *mpl* .
knowing *adj* entendido/da: —**ly** *adv* a sabiendas.
knowledge *n* conocimiento *m*.
knowledgeable *adj* bien informado/da.
knuckle *n* nudillo *m*.

L

label *n* etiqueta *f*.
laboratory *n* laboratorio *m*.
laborious *adj* laborioso/sa.
labor *n* trabajo *m*.
laborer *n* peón *m*.
labyrinth *n* laberinto *m*.
lace *n* cordón.
lacerate *vt* lacerar.
lack *vt* , *vi* faltar.
lacquer *n* laca *f*.
lad *n* muchacho *m*.
ladder *n* escalera *f*.
ladle *n* cucharón *m*.
lady *n* señora *f*.
lag *vi* quedarse atrás.
lager *n* cerveza (rubia) *f*.
lagoon *n* laguna *f*.
lake *n* lago *m*.
lamb *n* cordero *m*: —*vi* parir.
lame *adj* cojo/ja.
lament *vt* , *vi* lamentar(se).
lamp *n* lámpara *f*.
lampoon *n* sátira *f*.
lampshade *n* pantalla *f*.
lance *n* lanza *f*.
lancet *n* lanceta *f*.
land *n* país *m*; tierra *f*.
landing *n* desembarco *m*.
landmark *n* lugar conocido *m*.
landscape *n* paisaje *m*.
lane *n* callejuela *f*.
language *n* lengua *f*; lenguaje *m*.
lank *adj* lacio/cia.
lanky *adj* larguirucho.
lantern *n* linterna *f*; farol *m*.
lap *n* regazo *m*.
lapel *n* solapa *f*.
lapse *n* lapso *m*.
larceny *n* latrocinio *m*.
larch *n* alerce *m*.
lard *n* manteca de cerdo *f*.
larder *n* despensa *f*.
large *adj* grande.
lark *n* alondra *f*.
larva *n* larva, oruga *f*.
laryngitis *n* laringitis *f*.
larynx *n* laringe *f*.
lascivious *adj* lascivo/va.
laser *n* láser *m*.
lash *n* latigazo *m*.

lasso *n* lazo *m*.
latitude *n* latitud *f*.
latter *adj* último/ma.
lattice *n* celosía *f*.
laugh *vi* reir.
laughter *n* risa *f*.
launch *vt* , *vi* lanzar(se): —*n (mar)* lancha *f*.
launching *n* lanzamiento *m*.
launder *vt* lavar.
laundry *n* lavandería *f*.
laurel *n* laurel *m*.
lava *n* lava *f*.
lavatory *n* water *m*.
lavender *n (bot)* espliego *m*, lavándula *f*.
lavish *adj* pródigo/ga: —**ly** *adv* pródigamente:
 —*vt* disipar.
law *n* ley *f*; derecho *m*.
law court *n* tribunal *m*.
lawn *n* pasto *m*.
lawnmower *n* cortacésped *m*.
law suit *n* proceso *m*.
lawyer *n* abogado/da *m/f* .
laxative *n* laxante *m*.
lay *vt* poner.
layabout *n* vago/ga *m/f* .
layer *n* capa *f*.
layout *n* composición *f*.
laze *vi* holgazanear.
laziness *n* pereza *f*.
lazy *adj* perezoso/sa.
lead *n* plomo *m*.
leader *n* jefe/fa *m/f* .
leaf *n* hoja *f*.
leaflet *n* folleto *m*.
last *adj* último/ma.
league *n* liga, alianza *f*.
lasting *adj* duradero/ra, permanente.
leak *n* escape *m*.
latch *n* picaporte *m*.
lean *vt* , *vi* apoyar(se).
late *adj* tarde; difunto/ta.
leap *vi* saltar
latent *adj* latente.
leap year *n* año bisiesto *m*.
lathe *n* torno *m*.
learn *vt* , *vi* aprender.
lather *n* espuma *f*.
lease *n* arriendo *m*: —*vt* arrendar.
leash *n* correa *f*.
least *adj* mínimo/ma.

leather n cuero m.
leave n licencia f; permiso m.
lecherous adj lascivo/va.
lecture n conferencia f.
ledge n reborde m.
ledger n (com) libro mayor m.
leech n sanguijuela f.
leek n (bot) puerro m.
left adj izquierdo/da.
left-handed adj zurdo/da.
leftovers npl sobras fpl.
leg n pierna f
legacy n herencia f.
legal adj legal.
legalize vt legalizar.
legend n leyenda f.
legendary adj legendario/ria.
legible adj legible.
legion n legión f.
legislate vt legislar.
legislation n legislación f.
leisure n ocio m: ––ly adj sin prisa: –at ~ desocupado/da.
lemon n limón m.
lemonade n limonada f.
lend vt prestar.
length n largo m; duración f.
lenient adj indulgente.
lens n lente f.
Lent n Cuaresma f.
lentil n lenteja f.
leopard n leopardo m.
leotard n leotardo m.
leper n leproso/sa m/f.
leprosy n lepra f.
lesbian n lesbiana f.
less adj menor.
lesson n lección f.
let vt dejar, permitir.
lethal adj mortal.
lethargy n letargo m.
letter n letra f; carta f.
lettuce n lechuga f.
leukemia n leucemia f.
level adj llano/na, igual.
lever n palanca f.
leverage n influencia f.
levy n leva (de tropas) f.
lexicon n léxico m.
liability n responsabilidad f.
liable adj sujeto/ta; responsable.
liaise vi enlazar.
liaison n enlace m.
liar n embustero m.
libel n difamación f; –vt difamar.
liberal adj liberal.
liberate vt libertar.
liberation n liberación f.
liberty n libertad f.
Libra n Libra f.
librarian n bibliotecario m.
library n biblioteca f.
license n licencia f.
lick vt lamer.
lid n tapa f.
lie n mentira f.
life n vida f.

lifelike adj natural.
life preserver n chaleco salvavidas m.
lift vt levantar.
ligament n ligamento m.
light n luz f.
light bulb n foco m; bombilla f.
lighter n encendedor m.
lighthouse n (mar) faro m.
lightning n relámpago m.
like adj semejante; igual.
likeness n semejanza f.
lilac n lila f.
lily n lirio m.
lima beans npl haba gruesa f.
limb n miembro m.
lime n cal f; lima f.
limestone n piedra caliza f.
limit n limitem.
line n línea f.
linen n lino m.
liner n transatlántico m.
linger vi persistir.
lingerie n ropa interior f.
linguist n lingüista m.
lining n forro m.
link n eslabón m.
linoleum n linóleo m.
lintel n dintel m.
lion n león m.
lip n labio m.
liqueur n licor m.
liquid adj líquido/da
liquor n licor m.
liquorice n orozuz m; regalicia f.
lisp vi cecear.
list n lista f.
listen vi escuchar.
literature n literatura f.
lithe adj ágil.
lithograph n litografía f.
litigation n litigio m.
liter n litro m.
litter n litera f.
little adj pequeño/ña, poco/ca
live vi vivir; habitar.
liver n hígado m.
livestock n ganado m.
living n vida f: –adj vivo/va.
living room n sala de estar f.
lizard n lagarto m.
load vt cargar**loaf** n pan m.
loam n marga f.
loan n préstamo m.
loathe vt aborrecer.
loathing n aversión f.
lobby n vestíbulo m.
lobe n lóbulo m.
lobster n langosta f.
local adj local.
locality n localidad f.
locate vt localizar.
location n situación f.
loch n lago m.
lock n cerradura f.
locker n vestuario m.
locket n medallón m.
locomotive n locomotora f.

locust *n* langosta *f.*
loft *n* desván *m.*
lofty *adj* alto/ta.
log *n* leño *m.*
logic *n* lógica *f.*
logo *n* logotipo *m.*
loiter *vi* merodear.
lollipop *n* pirulí *m.*
loneliness *n* soledad *f.*
long *adj* largo/ga.
longitude *n* longitud *f.*
look *vi* mirar *f.*
looking glass *n* espejo *m.*
loop *n* lazo *m.*
loose *adj* suelto/ta.
loot *vt* saquear: —*n* botín *m.*
lop *vt* desmochar.
lord *n* señor *m.*
lose *vt* perder.
loss *n* perdida *f.*
lotion *n* loción *f.*
lottery *n* lotería *f.*
loud *adj* fuerte: —**~ly** *adv* fuerte.
loudspeaker *n* altavoz *m.*
lounge *n* salón *m.*
louse *n* piojo *(pl* lice) *m.*
lout *n* gamberro *m.*
love *n* amor, cariño *m.*
lovely *adj* hermoso/sa.
lover *n* amante *m.*
low *adj* bajo/ja.

loyal *adj* leal; fiel.
lozenge *n* pastilla *f.*
lubricant *n* lubricante *m.*
lubricate *vt* lubricar.
luck *n* suerte *f;* fortuna *f.*
lucrative *adj* lucrativo/va.
ludricrous *adj* absurdo/da.
lug *vt* arrastrar.
luggage *n* equipaje *m.*
lull *vt* acunar: —*n* tregua *f.*
lullaby *n* nana *f.*
lumbago *n* lumbago *m.*
lumber *n* madera de construccion *f*
luminous *adj* luminoso/sa.
lump *n* terrón *m.*
lunacy *n* locura *f.*
lunar *adj* lunar.
lunatic *adj* loco/ca.
lunch, luncheon *n* merienda *f.*
lungs *npl* pulmones *mpl* .
luscious *adj* delicioso/sa.
lush *adj* exuberante.
lust *n* lujuria, sensualidad *f.*
luster *n* lustre *m.*
luxurious *adj* lujoso/sa.
luxury *n* lujo *m.*
lymph *n* linfa *f.*
lynx *n* lince *m.*
lyrical *adj* lírico/ca.
lyrics *npl* letra *f.*

M

macaroni *n* macarrones *mpl* .
macaroon *n* almendrado *m.*
mace *n* maza *f;* macis *f.*
machine *n* maquina *f.*
machinery *n* maquinaria, mecanica *f.*
mackerel *n* escombro *m.*
mad *adj* loco, furioso, rabioso.
madam *n* madama, senora *f.*
madhouse *n* casa de locos *f.*
madness *n* locura *f.*
magazine *n* revista *f.*
maggot *n* gusano *m.*
magic *n* magia *f.*
magician *n* mago *m*
magistrate *n* magistrado *m.*
magnet *n* iman *m.*
magnetic *adj* magnetico.
magnificent *adj* magnifico.
magnify *vt* aumentar.
magnifying glass *n* lupa *f.*
magnitude *n* magnitud *f.*
magpie *n* urraca *f.*
mahogany *n* caoba *f.*
mail *n* correo *m.*
mailman *n* cartero *m.*
maim *vt* mutilar.
main *adj* principal.
maintain *vt* mantener.
maintenance *n* mantenimiento *m.*
maize *n* maiz *m.*

majesty *n* majestad *f.*
major *adj* principal
make *vt* hacer, crear.
make-up *n* maquillaje *m.*
malaria *n* malaria *f.*
male *adj* masculino: —*n* macho *m.*
malice *n* malicia *f.*
malicious *adj* malicioso.
mall *n* centro comercial *m.*
malleable *adj* maleable.
mallet *n* mazo *m.*
mallows *n (bot)* malva *f.*
malnutrition *n* desnutricion *f.*
malpractice *n* negligencia *f.*
malt *n* malta *f.*
maltreat *vt* maltratar.
mammal *n* mamifero *m.*
mammoth *adj* gigantesco.
man *n* hombre *m.*
manage *vt* , *vi* manejar, dirigir.
management *n* direccion *f.*
manager *n* director *m.*
mandate *n* mandato *m.*
mane *n* crines del caballo *fpl.*
maneuvre *n* maniobra *f.*
mangle *n* rodillo *m.*
mangy *adj* sarnoso.
manhood *n* edad viril *f.*
mania *n* mania *f.*
maniac *n* maniaco *m.*

manipulate *vt* manejar.
mankind *n* genero humano *m*.
man-made *n* artificial.
manner *n* manera *f;* modo *m*
mansion *n* palacio *m*.
mantelpiece *n* repisa de chimenea *f.*
manual *adj , n* manual *m*.
manufacture *n* fabricacion *f.*
manufacturer *n* fabricante *m*.
manuscript *n* manuscrito *m*.
many *adj* muchos, muchas.
map *n* mapa *m*.
maple *n* arce *m*.
mar *vt* estropear.
marathon *n* maraton *m*.
marble *n* marmol *m*.
March *n* marzo *m*.
mare *n* yegua *f.*
margarine *n* margarina *f.*
margin *n* margen *m; borde m*.
marigold *n (bot)* calendula *f.*
marijuana *n* marijuana *f.*
marine *adj* marinom.
marital *adj* marital.
mark *n* marca *f.*
market *n* mercado *m*.
marmalade *n* mermelada de naranja *f.*
maroon *adj* marron.
marquee *n* entoldado *m*.
marriage *n* matrimonio *m*
marrow *n* medula *f.*
marry *vi* casar(se).
marsh *n* pantano *m*.
marshy *adj* pantanoso.
martyr *n* martir *m*.
marvel *n* maravilla *f.*
marvelous *adj* maravilloso.
marzipan *n* mazapan *m*.
mascara *n* rimel *m*.
masculine *adj* masculino.
mask *n* mascara *f.*
masochist *n* masoquista *m*.
mason *n* albanil *m*.
mass *n* masa *f;* misa *f;*
massacre *n* carniceria, matanza *f.*
massage *n* masaje *m*.
massive *adj* enorme.
mast *n* mastil *m*.
masterpiece *n* obra maestra *f.*
masticate *vt* masticar.
mat *n* estera *f.*
match *n* fosforo *m*, cerilla *f.*
mate *n* companero *m: —vt* acoplar.
mathematics *npl* matematicas *fpl.*
matinee *n* funcion de la tarde *f.*
mating *n* aparejamiento *m*.
matriculate *vt* matricular.
matriculation *n* matriculacion *f.*
matt *adj* mate.
matter *n* materia, substancia *f.*
mattress *n* colchon *m*.
mature *adj* maduro.
mauve *adj* de color malva.
maximum *n* maximo *m*.
May *n* mayo *m*.
mayonnaise *n* mayonesa *f.*
mayor *n* alcalde *m*.

maze *n* laberinto *m*.
me *pn* me; mi.
meal *n* comida *f;* harina *f.*
mean *adj* tacano.
meander *vi* serpentear.
meaning *n* sentido, significado *m*.
meantime, meanwhile *adv* mientrastanto.
measles *npl* sarampion *m*.
measurement *n* medida *f.*
meat *n* carne *f.*
mechanic *n* mecanico *m*.
mechanism *n* mecanismo *m*.
medal *n* medalla *f.*
media *npl* medios de comunicacion *mpl .*
medical *adj* medico.
medicate *vt* medicinar.
medicine *n* medicina *f.*
medieval *adj* medieval.
mediocre *adj* mediocre.
meditate *vi* meditar.
meditation *n* meditacion *f.*
Mediterranean *adj* mediterraneo.
medium *n* medio *m*.
meet *vt* encontrar.
meeting *n* reunion *f.*
megaphone *n* megafono *m*.
melancholy *n* melancolia *f.*
mellow *adj* maduro.
mellowness *n* madurez *f.*
melody *n* melodia *f.*
melon *n* melon *m*.
melt *vt* derretir.
member *n* miembro *m*.
membrane *n* membrana *f.*
memento *n* memento *m*.
memoir *n* memoria *f.*
memorandum *n* memorandum *m*.
memorial *n* monumento conmemorativo *m*.
memory *n* memoria *f;* recuerdo *m*.
menace *n* amenaza *f.*
menagerie *n* casa de fieras *f.*
mend *vt* reparar.
menial *adj* domestico.
meningitis *n* meningitis *f.*
menopause *n* menopausia *f.*
menstruation *n* menstruacion *f.*
mental *adj* mental.
mention *n* mencion *f.*
mentor *n* mentor *m*.
menu *n* menu *m;* carta *f.*
merchandise *n* mercancia *f.*
merchant *n* comerciante *m*.
mercury *n* mercurio *m*.
mercy *n* compasion *f.*
mere *adj* mero.
meridian *n* meridiano *m*.
merit *n* merito *m*.
mermaid *n* sirena *f.*
merry *adj* alegre.
merry-go-round *n* tiovivo *m*.
mesh *n* malla *f.*
mesmerize *vt* hipnotizar.
mess *n* lio *m*.
message *n* mensaje *m*.
metabolism *n* metabolismo *n*.
metal *n* metal *m*.
metallic *adj* metalico.

metamorphosis n metamorfosis f.
metaphor n metafora f.
meteor n meteoro m.
meteorological adj meteorológico.
meteorology n meteorologia f.
meter[1] n medidor m.
meter[2] n metro m.
method n metodo m.
methodical adj metodico.
Methodist n metodista m.
metric adj metrico.
metropolis n metropoli f.
metropolitan adj metropolitano.
mettle n valor m.
mew vi maullar.
mezzanine n entresuelo m.
microbe n microbio m.
microphone n microfono m.
microchip n microplaqueta f.
microscope n microscopio m.
microwave n horno microondas m.
mid adj medio.
midday n mediodia m.
middle adj mediom.
midge n mosca f.
midget n enano m.
midnight n medianoche f.
midst n medio, centro m.
midsummer n pleno verano m.
midwife n partera f.
might n poder m; fuerza f.
mighty adj fuerte.
migraine n jaqueca f.
migrate vi emigrar.
migration n emigracion f.
mike n microfono m.
mild adj apacible; suave.
mildew n moho m.
mileage n kilometraje m.
milieu n ambiente m.
militant adj militante.
military adj militar.
milk n leche f.
milkshake n batido m
milky adj lechoso: —**M~ Way** n Via Lactea f.
mill n molino m.
millennium n milenio m.
miller n molinero m.
milligram n miligramo m.
milliliter n mililitro m.
millimeter n milimetro m.
milliner n sombrerero.
million n millon m.
millionaire n millonario m.
millionth adj n millonésimo.
mime n mimo m.
mimic vt imitar.
mince vt picar.
mind n mente f.
mine pn mio, mia, mi: —n mina: —vi minar.
miner n minero m.
mineral adj , n mineral m.
mineral water n agua mineral f.
mingle vt mezclar.
miniature n miniatura f.
minimal adj minimo.
minimum n minimum m.

mining n explotacion minera f.
minister n ministro m.
mink n vison m.
minnow n pecicillo m (pez).
minor adj menor
mint n (bot) menta f.
minus adv menos.
minute adj diminuto.
minute n minuto m.
miracle n milagro m.
mirage n espejismo m.
mire n fango m.
mirror n espejo m.
mirth n alegria f.
misbehave vi portarse mal.
miscarry vi abortar.
miscellaneous adj varios, varias.
miser n avaro m.
miserable adj miserable.
miserly adj mezquino, tacano.
misery n miseria f.
mislay vt extraviar.
mislead vt enganar.
misogynist n misogino m.
Miss n senorita f.
miss vt perder; echar de menos.
missile n misil m.
mission n mision f.
missionary n misionero m.
mist n niebla f.
mistake vt entender mal
Mister n Senor m.
mistletoe n (bot) muerdago m.
mistress n amante f.
mistrust vt desconfiar.
mitigate vt mitigar.
mitigation n mitigacion f.
miter n mitra f.
mittens npl manoplas fpl.
mix vt mezclar.
mixer n licuadora f.
mixture n mezcla f.
moan n gemido m.
moat n foso m.
mob n multitud f.
mobile adj movil.
mode n modo m.
model n modelo m.
moderate adj moderado.
moderation n moderacion f.
modern adj moderno.
modernize vt modernizar.
modest adj modesto.
modesty n modestia f.
modify vt modificar.
module n modulo m.
mogul n magnate m.
mohair n mohair m.
moist adj humedo.
moisture n humedad f.
mold n molde m.
mole n topo m.
molecule n molecula f.
molest vt importunar.
mom n mama f.
moment n momento m.
momentum n impetu m.

mommy *n* mama *f.*
monarch *n* monarca *m.*
monarchy *n* monarquia *f.*
monastery *n* monasterio *m.*
Monday *n* lunes *m.*
monetary *adj* monetario.
money *n* moneda *f;* dinero *m.*
mongol *n* mongolico *m.*
mongrel *adj , n* mestizo *m.*
monk *n* monje *m.*
monkey *n* mono *m.*
monopoly *n* monopolio *m.*
monotonous *adj* monotono.
monsoon *n (mar)* monzon *m.*
monster *n* monstruo *m.*
month *n* mes *m.*
monthly *adj , adv* mensual (mente).
monument *n* monumento *m.*
mood *n* humor *m.*
moody *adj* malhumorado.
moon *n* luna *f.*
moor *n* paramo.
moorland *n* paramo *m.*
moose *n* alce *m.*
mop *n* fregona *f.*
mope *vi* estar triste.
moped *n* ciclomotor *m.*
morality *n* etica, moralidad *f.*
morbid *adj* morboso.
more *adj , adv* mas.
moreover *adv* ademas.
morgue *n* deposito de cadaveres *m.*
morning *n* manana *f:* —good ~ buenos dias *mpl .*
moron *n* imbecil *m.*
morphine *n* morfina *f.*
morse *n* morse *m.*
morsel *n* bocado *m.*
mortal *adj* mortal
mortality *n* mortalidad *f.*
mortar *n* mortero *m.*
mortgage *n* hipoteca *f.*
mortify *vt* mortificar.
mortuary *n* deposito de cadaveres *m.*
mosaic *n* mosaico *m.*
mosque *n* mezquita *f.*
mosquito *n* mosquito *m.*
moss *n (bot)* musgo *m.*
most *adj* la mayoria de.
motel *n* motel *m.*
moth *n* polilla *f.*
mother *n* madre *f.*
mother-in-law *n* suegra *f.*
mother-of-pearl *n* nacar *m.*
motif *n* tema *m.*
motion *n* movimiento *m.*
motive *n* motivo *m.*
motor *n* motor *m.*
motorbike *n* moto *f.*
motorcycle *n* motocicleta *f.*
motor vehicle *n* automovil *m.*
motto *n* lema *m.*
mount *n* monte *m.*
mountain *n* montana *f.*
mountaineering *n* montañismo *m.*
mourn *vt* lamentar.
mourner *n* doliente *m.*
mourning *n* luto *m.*

mouse *n (pl* mice *)* raton *m.*
mousse *n* mousse *f.*
mouth *n* boca *f;*
mouthful *n* bocado *m.*
mouthwash *n* enjuague *m.*
mouthwatering *adj* apetitoso.
move *vt* mover.
movement *n* movimiento *m.*
movies *n* pelicula *f;* el cine
moving *adj* conmovedor.
mow *vt* segar.
mower *n* cortacesped *m;* mocion *f.*
Mrs *n* senora *f.*
much *adj , adv* mucho.
muck *n* suciedad *f.*
mucous *adj* mocoso.
mud *n* barro *m.*
muddle *vt* confundir *m;* confusion *f.*
muffle *vt* embozar.
mug *n* jarra *f.*
mulberry *n* mora *f.*
mule *n* mulo *m,* mula *f.*
multiple *adj* multiplo *m.*
multiplication *n* multiplicacion *f.*
multiply *vt* multiplicar.
multitude *n* multitud *f.*
mumble *vt , vi* refunfunar.
mummy *n* momia *f.*
mumps *npl* paperas *fpl.*
munch *vt* mascar.
mundane *adj* trivial.
municipal *adj* municipal.
municipality *n* municipalidad *f.*
mural *n* mural *m.*
murder *n* asesinato *m;* homicidio *m.*
murky *adj* sombrio.
murmur *n* murmullo.
muscle *n* musculo *m.*
muse *vi* meditar.
museum *n* museo *m.*
mushroom *n (bot)* seta *f;* champinon *m.*
music *n* musica *f.*
musician *n* musico *m.*
musk *n* musco *m.*
muslin *n* muselina *f.*
mussel *n* marisco *m.*
must *v aux* estar obligado.
mustache *n* bigote *m.*
mustard *n* mostaza *f.*
mute *adj* mudo, silencioso.
mutilate *vt* mutilar.
mutter *vt , vi* murmurar.
mutton *n* carnero *m.*
mutual *adj* mutuo, mutual.
muzzle *n* bozal *m.*
my *pn* mi, mis; mio, mia; mios, mias.
myriad *n* miriada *f.*
myrrh *n* mirra *f.*
myrtle *n* mirto, arrayan *m.*
myself *pn* yo mismo.
mysterious *adj* misterioso.
mystery *n* misterio *m.*
mystic(al) *adj* mistico.
mystify *vt* dejar perplejo.
mystique *n* misterio *m.*
myth *n* mito *m.*
mythology *n* mitologia *f.*

N

nag *n* jaca *f;* —*vt* reganar.
nagging *adj* persistente.
nail *n* una *f;* garra *f;* clavo *m.*
naive *adj* ingenuo.
naked *adj* desnudo.
name *n* nombre *m.*
nameless *adj* anonimo.
namely *adv* a saber.
namesake *n* tocayo *m.*
nanny *n* ninera *f.*
nap *n* sueno ligero *m.*
nape *n* nuca *f.*
napkin *n* servilleta *f.*
narcissus *n (bot)* narciso *m.*
narcotic *adj* , *n* narcotico *m.*
narrate *vt* narrar.
narrative *adj* narrativo.
narrow *adj* angosto, estrecho.
nasal *adj* nasal.
nasty *adj* sucio, puerco.
natal *adj* nativo; natal.
nation *n* nacion *f.*
nationalize *vt* nacionalizar.
nationalism *n* nacionalismo *m.*
nationalist *adj* , *n* nacionalista *m.*
nationality *n* nacionalidad *f.*
native *adj* nativo *m.*
native language *n* lengua materna *f.*
Nativity *n* Navidad *f.*
natural *adj* natural.
naturalize *vt* naturalizar.
naturalist *n* naturalista *m.*
nature *n* naturaleza *f.*
naught *n* cero *m.*
naughty *adj* malo.
nausea *n* nausea.
nauseous *adj* fastidioso.
nautic(al), naval *adj* nautico, naval.
nave *n* nave (de la iglesia) *f.*
navel *n* ombligo *m.*
navigate *vi* navegar.
navigation *n* navegacion *f.*
navy *n* marina *f.*
Nazi *n* nazi *m.*
near *prep* cerca de.
nearby *adj* cercano.
nearly *adv* casi.
near-sighted *adj* miope.
nebulous *adj* nebuloso.
necessarily *adv* necesariamente.
necessary *adj* necesario.
necessity *n* necesidad *f.*
neck *n* cuello *m.*
necklace *n* collar *m.*
necktie *n* corbata *f.*
nectar *n* nectar *m.*
need *n* necesidad *f.*
needle *n* aguja *f.*
needless *adj* superfluo.
needlework *n* costura *f*
needy *adj* necesitado, pobre.

negation *n* negacion *f.*
negative *adj* negativo.
neglect *vt* descuidar.
negligee *n* salto de cama *m.*
negligence *n* negligencia *f*
negligible *adj* insignificante.
negotiate *vt* , *vi* negociar (con).
negotiation *n* negociacion *f;* negocio *m.*
Negress *n* negra *f.*
Negro *adj* , *n* negro *m.*
neighbor *n* vecino *m.*
neighborhood *n* vecindad *f;* vecindario *m.*
neither *conj* ni: —*pn* ninguno.
neon *n* neon *m.*
neon light *n* luz de neon *f.*
nephew *n* sobrino *m.*
nepotism *n* nepotismo *m.*
nerve *n* nervio *m;* valor *m.*
nerve-racking *adj* espantoso.
nervous *adj* nervioso; nervudo.
nervous breakdown *n* crisis nerviosa *f.*
nest *n* nido *m.*
nest egg *n (fig)* ahorros *mpl* .
nestle *vt* anidarse.
net *n* red *f.*
netball *n* basquet *m.*
nettle *n* ortiga *f.*
network *n* red *f.*
neurosis *n* neurosis *f* invar.
neurotic *adj* , *n* neurotico *m.*
neuter *adj (gr)* neutro.
neutral *adj* neutral.
neutrality *n* neutralidad *f.*
neutron *n* neutron *m.*
never *adv* nunca, jamas.
nevertheless *adv* no obstante.
new *adj* nuevo.
news *npl* novedad, noticias *fpl.*
newscaster *n* presentador *m.*
newspaper *n* periodico *m.*
next *adj* proximo.
nib *n* pico *m.*
nibble *vt* picar.
nice *adj* simpatico.
niche *n* nicho *m.*
nickel *n* niquel *m*
nickname *n* mote.
nicotine *n* nicotina *f.*
niece *n* sobrina *f.*
niggling *adj* insignificante.
night *n* noche *f.*
nightclub *n* cabaret *m.*
nightfall *n* anochecer *m.*
nightingale *n* ruisenor *m.*
nightmare *n* pesadilla *f.*
nihilist *n* nihilista *m.*
nimble *adj* ligero, activo, listo, agil.
nine *adj* , *n* nueve.
nineteen *adj* , *n* diecinueve.
nineteenth *adj* , *n* decimonono.
ninetieth *adj* , *n* nonagesimo.

ninety *adj* , *n* noventa.
ninth *adj* , *n* nono, noveno.
nip *vt* pellizcar; morder.
nipple *n* pezon *m;* tetilla *f.*
nit *n* liendre *f.*
nitrogen *n* nitrogeno *m.*
no *adv* no.
nobility *n* nobleza *f.*
noble *adj* noble.
nobleman *n* noble *m.*
nobody *n* nadie, ninguna persona *f.*
nocturnal *adj* nocturnal.
noise *n* ruido *m.*
noisy *adj* ruidoso, turbulento.
nominate *vt* nombrar.
nomination *n* nominacion *f.*
nominee *n* candidato *m.*
non-alcoholic *adj* no alcoholico.
nonchalant *adj* indiferente.
nondescript *adj* no descrito.
none *adj* nadie, ninguno.
nonentity *n* nulidad *f.*
nonetheless *adv* sin embargo.
nonsense *n* disparate *m.*
noodles *npl* fideos *mpl* .
noon *n* mediodia *m.*
noose *n* lazo corredizo *m.*
nor *conj* ni.
normal *adj* normal.
north *n* norte *m.*
North America *n* America del Norte *f.*
northeast *n* nor(d)este *m.*
northerly, northern *adj* norteno.
North Pole *n* polo artico *m.*
northwest *n* nor(d)oeste *m.*
nose *n* nariz *f*
nosebleed *n* hemorragia nasal *f.*
nostalgia *n* nostalgia *f.*
nostril *n* ventana de la nariz *f.*
not *adv* no.
notable *adj* notable.
notably *adv* especialmente.
notary *n* notario *m.*
notch *n* muesca *f.*
note *n* nota, marca *f.*
notebook *n* librito de apuntes *m.*
noted *adj* afamado, celebre.
nothing *n* nada *f.*

notice *n* noticia *f;* aviso *m.*
notification *n* notificacion *f.*
notify *vt* notificar.
notion *n* nocion *f.*
notoriety *n* notoriedad *f.*
notwithstanding *conj* no obstante, aunque.
nougat *n* turron *m.*
nought *n* cero *m.*
noun *n (gr)* sustantivo *m.*
nourish *vt* nutrir, alimentar.
novel *n* novela *f.*
novelist *n* novelista *m.*
novelty *n* novedad *f.*
November *n* noviembre *m.*
novice *n* novicio *m.*
now *adv* ahora.
nowadays *adv* hoy (en) dia.
nowhere *adv* en ninguna parte.
noxious *adj* nocivo, danoso.
nozzle *n* boquilla *f.*
nuance *n* matiz *m.*
nuclear *adj* nuclear.
nucleus *n* nucleo *m.*
nude *adj* desnudo.
nudge *vt* dar un codazo a.
nudist *n* nudista *m.*
nudity *n* desnudez *f.*
null *adj* nulo.
nullify *vt* anular.
numb *adj* entorpecido.
number *n* numero *m.*
numerous *adj* numeroso.
nun *n* monja *f.*
nunnery *n* convento de monjas *m.*
nuptial *adj* nupcial *fpl.*
nurse *n* enfermera *f.*
nursery *n* guarderia infantil *f*
nursery rhyme *n* cancion infantil *f.*
nursery school *n* parvulario *m.*
nursing home *n* clinica de reposo *f.*
nurture *vt* criar.
nut *n* nuez *f.*
nutcrackers *npl* cascanueces *m.*
nutmeg *n* nuez moscada *f.*
nutritious *adj* nutritivo.
nut shell *n* cascara de nuez *f.*
nylon *n* nilon *m.*

O

oak *n* roble *m.*
oar *n* remo *m.*
oasis *n* oasis *f.*
oat *n* avena *f.*
oath *n* juramento *m.*
obedience *n* obediencia *f.*
obese *adj* obeso, gordo.
obey *vt* obedecer.
obituary *n* necrologia *f.*
object *n* objeto *m: —vt* objetar.
objective *adj* , *n* objetivo *m.*
oblige *vt* obligar.
obliterate *vt* borrar.

oblivion *n* olvido *m.*
oblong *adj* oblongo.
obnoxious *adj* odioso.
oboe *n* oboe *m.*
obscene *adj* obsceno.
obscenity *n* obscenidad *f.*
obscure *adj* oscuro.
observatory *n* observatorio *m.*
observe *vt* observar, mirar.
obsess *vt* obsesionar.
obsolete *adj* en desuso.
obstacle *n* obstaculo *m.*
obstinate *adj* obstinado.

obstruct *vt* obstruir; impedir.
obtain *vt* obtener, adquirir.
obvious *adj* obvio, evidente.
occasion *n* ocasion *f.*
occupant, occupier *n* ocupador *m*
occupation *n* ocupacion *f;* empleo *m.*
occupy *vt* ocupar.
occur *vi* pasar.
ocean *n* oceano *m;* alta *mar f.*
ocher *n* ocre *m.*
octave *n* octava *f.*
October *n* octubre *m.*
octopus *n* pulpo *m.*
odd *adj* impar.
oddity *n* singularidad.
odious *adj* odioso.
odor *n* olor *m.*
of *prep* de.
off *adv* desconectado; apagado.
offence *n* ofensa *f.*
offend *vt* ofender.
offensive *adj* ofensivo.
offer *vt* ofrecer.
offering *n* sacrificio *m.*
office *n* oficina *f.*
officer *n* oficial, empleado *m.*
official *adj* oficial.
offspring *n* prole *f.*
ogle *vt* comerse con los ojos.
oil *n* aceite *m.*
oil painting *n* pintura al oleo *f.*
oil rig *n* torre de perforacion *f.*
oil tanker *n* petrolero *m.*
ointment *n* unguento *m.*
OK, okay *excl* vale.
old *adj* viejo; antiguo.
old age *n* vejez *f.*
olive *n* olivo *m.*
omelet *n* tortilla de huevos *f.*
omen *n* agüero.
ominous *adj* ominoso.
omission *n* omisión *f.*
omit *vt* omitir.
omnipotence *n* omnipotencia *f.*
on *prep* sobre, encima, en; de; a.
one *adj* un, uno.
oneself *pn* si mismo; si misma.
ongoing *adj* continuo.
onion *n* cebolla *f.*
onlooker *n* espectador *m.*
only *adj* unico, solo.
onus *n* responsabilidad *f.*
onwards *adv* adelante.
opaque *adj* opaco.
open *adj* abierto; *vi* abrirse.
open-minded *adj* imparcial.
opera *n* opera *f.*
operate *vi* obrar.
operation *n* operacion *f.*
operational *adj* operacional.
operative *adj* operativo.
operator *n* operario *m;* operador *m.*
ophthalmic *adj* oftálmico.
opinion *n* opinion *f.*
opinion poll *n* sondeo *m.*
opponent *n* antagonista *m.*
opportune *adj* oportuno.

opportunity *n* oportunidad *f.*
oppose *vt* oponerse.
opposite *adj* opuesto; contrario.
opposition *n* oposicion *f.*
oppress *vt* oprimir.
oppression *n* opresion *f.*
optic(al) *adj* optico *f.*
optician *n* optico *m.*
optimist *n* optimista *m.*
optimum *adj* optimum.
option *n* opcion *f;* deseo *m.*
opulent *adj* opulento.
or *conj* o; u.
oracle *n* oraculo *m.*
oral *adj* oral.
orange *n* naranja *f.*
orbit *n* orbita *f.*
orchard *n* huerto *m.*
orchestra *n* orquesta *f.*
orchid *n* orquidea *f.*
order *n* orden *mf;* regla *f;* mandar.
ordinary *adj* ordinario.
ore *n* mineral *m.*
organ *n* organo *m.*
organic *adj* organico.
organization *n* organizacion *f.*
organize *vt* organizar.
organism *n* organismo *m.*
organist *n* organista *m.*
orgasm *n* orgasmo *m.*
orgy *n* orgia *f.*
oriental *adj* oriental.
orifice *n* orificio *m.*
origin *n* origen *m.*
original *adj* original.
originate *vi* originar.
ornament *n* ornamento *m.*
ornate *adj* adornado.
orphan *adj* , *n* huerfano *m.*
orphanage *n* orfanato *m.*
orthodox *adj* ortodoxo.
orthopedic *adj* ortopedico.
oscillate *vi* oscilar.
osprey *n* aguila marina *f.*
ostensibly *adv* aparentemente.
ostentatious *adj* ostentoso.
osteopath *n* osteopata *m.*
ostrich *n* avestruz *m.*
other *pn* otro.
otter *n* nutria *f.*
ouch *excl* ¡ay!
ought *v aux* deber, ser menester.
ounce *n* onza *f.*
our, ours *pn* nuestro, nuestra, nuestros, nuestras.
ourselves *pn pl* nosotros mismos.
out *adv* fuera.
outbreak *n* erupcion *f.*
outcast *n* paria *m.*
outcome *n* resultado *m.*
outcry *n* clamor *m.*
outdo *vt* exceder a otro, sobrepujar.
outer *adj* exterior.
outermost *adj* extremo; lo mas exterior.
outfit *n* vestidos *mpl* ; ropa *f.*
outlet *n* enchufe *m.*
outline *n* contorno *m*
outlook *n* perspectiva *f.*

out-of-date *adj* caducado; pasado demoda.
outpatient *n* paciente externo *m*.
output *n* rendimiento *m*.
outrage *n* ultraje *m*.
outrageous *adj* ultrajoso.
outside *n* superficie *f*: exterior *m*.
outsider *n* forastero *m*.
outskirts *npl* alrededores *mpl* .
outstanding *adj* excepcional.
outwit *vt* enganar a uno a fuerza detretas.
oval *n* ovalo *m*: —*adj* oval.
ovary *n* ovario *m*.
oven *n* horno *m*.
ovenproof *adj* resistente al horno.
over *prep* sobre, encima.
overbearing *adj* despotico.
overcharge *vt* sobrecargar.
overcoat *n* abrigo *m*.
overdose *n* sobredosis *f*.
overdue *adj* retrasado.
overeat *vi* atracarse.
overflow *vt* , *vi* inundar.
overhaul *vt* revisar.

overkill *n* exceso de medios *m*.
overlap *vi* traslaparse.
overleaf *adv* al dorso.
overload *vt* sobrecargar.
overpower *vt* predominar, oprimir.
overseas *adv* en ultramar: —*adj* extranjero.
oversee *vt* inspeccionar.
overshadow *vt* eclipsar.
overstate *vi* exagerar.
overstep *vt* exceder, pasar de.
overtake *vt* sobrepasar.
overtime *n* horas extra *fpl*.
overtone *n* tono *m*.
owe *vt* deber.
owl *n* buho *m*.
own *adj* propio.
owner *n* dueno, propietario *m*.
ownership *n* posesion *f*.
ox *n* buey *m*.
oxidize *vt* oxidar.
oxygen *n* oxigeno *m*.
oyster *n* ostra *f*.
ozone *n* ozono *m*.

P

pa *n* papa *m*.
pace *n* paso *m*.
pacemaker *n* marcapasos *m*.
pacific(al) *adj* pacifico.
pacify *vt* pacificar.
package *n* paquete *m*.
packet *n* paquete *m*.
packing *n* embalaje *m*.
pact *n* pacto *m*.
pad *n* bloc *m*.
paddle *vi* remar
paddock *n* corral *m*.
paddy *n* arrozal *m*.
pagan *adj* , *n* pagano *m*.
page *n* pagina *f*.
pain *n* pena *f*; castigo *m*; dolor *m*.
parallel *adj* paralelo.
paralysis *n* paralisis *f*.
paralytic(al) *adj* paralitico.
paralyze *vt* paralizar.
paramedic *n* ambulanciero *m*.
paramount *adj* supremo.
paranoid *adj* paranoico.
parasite *n* parásito *m*.
parasol *n* parasol *m*.
parcel *n* paquete *m*.
parch *vt* resecar.
pardon *n* perdon *m*.
parent *n* padre *m*; madre *f*.
palpable *adj* palpable.
paltry *adj* irrisorio; mezquino.
pamphlet *n* folleto *m*.
pan *n* cazuela *f*.
pancake *n* bunuelo *m*.
pandemonium *n* jaleo *m*.
pane *n* cristal *m*.
panel *n* panel *m*
pang *n* angustia *f*.

panic *adj* , *n* panico *m*.
pansy *n* (*bot*) pensamiento *m*.
pant *vi* jadear.
panther *n* pantera *f*.
pantry *n* despensa *f*.
pants *npl* pantalones *mpl* .
papacy *n* papado *m*.
papal *adj* papal.
paper *n* papel *m*.
paperback *n* libro de bolsillo *m*.
paper clip *n* clip *m*.
paperweight *n* sujetapapeles *m*.
paprika *n* pimienta hungara *f*.
parachute *n* paracaidas *m*.
paradise *n* paraiso *m*.
paradox *n* paradoja *f*.
paragon *n* modelo perfecto *m*.
paragraph *n* parrafo *m*.
painkiller *n* analgesico *m*.
paint *vt* pintar.
paintbrush *n* pincel *m*.
painter *n* pintor *m*.
painting *n* pintura *f*.
pair *n* par *m*.
pajamas *npl* pijama *m*.
palatial *adj* palatino.
pale *adj* palido; claro.
pallet *n* pallet *m*.
palliative *adj* , *n* paliativo *m*.
pallid *adj* palido.
pallor *n* palidez *f*.
palm *n* (*bot*) palma *f*.
parentage *n* parentela *f*.
Palm Sunday *n* Domingo de Ramos *m*.
parental *adj* paternal.
parenthesis *n* parentesis *m*.
parish *n* parroquia *f*.
parity *n* paridad *f*.

park n parque m.
parliament n parlamento m.
parlor n sala de recibimiento f.
parody n parodia f.
parrot n papagayo m.
parsley n (bot) perejil m.
parsnip n (bot) chirivia f.
part n parte f.
participate vi participar (en).
particle n particula f.
particular adj particular.
parting n separacion f.
partition n particion.
partner n socio, companero m.
partridge n perdiz f.
party n partido m; fiesta f.
pass vt pasar.
passage n pasaje m
passbook n libreta de depositos f.
passenger n pasajero m.
passion n pasion f
passionate adj apasionado.
passive adj pasivo.
Passover n Pascua f.
passport n pasaporte m.
password n contrasena f.
past adj pasado.
pasta n pasta f.
paste n pasta f.
pastime n pasatiempo m f.
pastor n pastor m.
pastry n pasteleria f.
pasture n pasto m.
patch n remiendo m; parche m.
patent adj patente.
pathetic adj patetico.
patience n paciencia f.
patient adj paciente.
patio n patio m.
patriot n patriota m.
patriotism n patriotismo m.
patrol n patrulla f.
patron n patron m.
patronize vt patrocinar.
pattern n patron m; dibujo m.
pauper n pobre m.
pause n pausa f.
pave vt empedrar.
pavilion n pabellon m.
paw n pata f.
pay vt pagar.
pea n guisante m.
peace n paz f.
peach n melocoton m.
peacock n pavon, pavo real m.
peak n cima f.
peanut n cacahuete m.
pear n pera f.
pearl n perla f.
peasant n campesino m.
pebble n guija f.
peculiar adj peculiar.
pedal n pedal m.
pedestal n pedestal m.
pedestrian n peaton m.
pedigree n genealogia f.
f; **peel** vt pelar.

peg n clavija f.
pelican n pelicano m.
pen n boligrafo m; pluma f
penal adj penal.
pence n d pl of penny.
pencil n lapiz m.
pendulum n pendulo m.
penetrate vt penetrar.
penguin n pinguino m.
penicillin n penicilina f.
peninsula n peninsula f.
penis n pene m.
penitence n penitencia f.
penitentiary n encierro m.
penknife n navaja f.
penny n penique m.
pension n pension f.
pensive adj pensativo.
Pentecost n Pentecostes m.
penthouse n atico m.
people n pueblo m; naciongente f.
pepper n pimienta f.
peppermint n menta f.
perceive vt percibir.
percentage n porcentaje m.
perception n percepcion f.
percolator n cafetera de filtro f.
percussion n percusion f; golpe m.
perennial adj perenne; perpetuo.
perfect adj perfecto.
perform vt ejecutar.
performance n ejecucion f.
perfume n perfume m; fragancia f: —vt perfumar.
perhaps adv quiza, quizas.
peril n peligro m.
period n periodo m.
periodical n jornal, periodico m.
perk n extra m.
perm n permanente f.
permanent adj, ~ly adv permanente (mente).
permissible adj licito.
permission n permiso m.
permit vt permitir.
perplex vt confundir.
persecute vt perseguir.
persevere vi perseverar.
persist vi persistir.
person n persona f.
personality n personalidad f.
personnel n personal m.
perspective n perspectiva f.
perspiration n transpiracion f.
perspire vi transpirar.
persuade vt persuadir.
perturb vt perturbar.
peruse vt leer.
perverse adj perverso.
pessimist n pesimista m.
pester vt molestar.
pet n animal domestico m.
petal n (bot) petalo m.
petition n presentacion, peticion f.
petroleum n petroleo m.
petticoat n enaguas fpl.
petty adj mezquino.
pewter n peltre m.
phantom n fantasma m.

pharmacist *n* farmacéutico *m*.
pharmacy *n* farmacia *f*.
phase *n* fase *f*.
pheasant *n* faisan *m*.
phenomenon *n* fenomeno *m*.
phial *n* redomilla *f*.
philosopher *n* filosofo *m*.
philosophy *n* filosofia *f*.
phlegm *n* flema *f*.
phobia *n* fobia *f*.
phone *n* telefono *m*.
photocopier *n* fotocopiadora *f*.
photocopy *n* fotocopia *f*.
photograph *n* fotografia *f*: —*vt* fotografiar.
photographic *adj* fotografico.
photography *n* fotografia *f*.
phrase *n* frase *f*.
physical *adj* fisico.
physician *n* medico *m*.
physicist *n* fisico *m*.
physiotherapy *n* fisioterapia *f*.
physique *n* fisico *m*.
pianist *n* pianista *m*, *f*.
piano *n* piano *m*.
piccolo *n* flautin *m*.
pick *vt* escoger, elegir.
pickle *n* escabeche *m*.
picnic *n* comida, merienda *f*.
picture *n* pintura *f*.
picturesque *adj* pintoresco.
pie *n* pastel *m; tarta *f*.
piece *n* pedazo *m; pieza *f*.
pierce *vt* penetrar, agujerear.
pig *n* cerdo *m*.
pigeon *n* paloma *f*.
pigtail *n* trenza *f*.
pike *n* lucio *m; pica *f*.
pile *n* estaca *f; pila *f; monton *m*.
pilgrim *n* peregrino *m*.
pill *n* pildora *f*.
pillar *n* pilar *m*.
pillow *n* almohada *f*.
pilot *n* piloto *m*.
pimple *n* grano *m*.
pin *n* alfiler *m*.
pinball *n* fliper *m*.
pincers *n* pinzas *fpl*.
pinch *vt* pellizcar.
pine *n (bot)* pino *m*.
pineapple *n* pina *f, ananas *m*.
pink *n* rosa *f*.
pinnacle *n* cumbre *f*.
pint *n* pinta *f*.
pioneer *n* pionero *m*.
pious *adj* pio.
pip *n* pepita *f*.
pipe *n* tubo.
pirate *n* pirata *m*.
pirouette *n* pirueta.
Pisces *n* Piscis *m* (signo del zodiaco).
piss *n (sl)* meados *mpl* .
pistol *n* pistola *f*.
piston *n* embolo *m*.
pit *n* hoyo *m; mina *f*.
pitcher *n* cantaro, jarro *m*.
pitchfork *n* horca *f*.
pity *n* piedad, compasion *f*.

pivot *n* eje *m*.
pizza *n* pizza *f*.
placard *n* pancarta *f*.
placate *vt* apaciguar.
place *n* lugar, sitio *m*.
placid *adj* placido.
plagiarism *n* plagio *m*.
plague *n* peste, plaga *f*.
plaice *n* platija *f* (pez).
plaid *n* tartan *m*.
plain *adj* liso, llano.
plaintiff *n (law)* demandador *m*.
plan *n* plano *m*.
plane *n* avion *m; plano *m*.
planet *n* planeta *m*.
plank *n* tabla *f*.
plant *n* planta *f*.
plantation *n* plantacion *f*.
plaque *n* placa *f*.
plaster *n* yeso *m*.
plastic *adj* plastico.
plate *n* plato *m*.
plateau *n* meseta *f*.
platform *n* plataforma *f*.
platinum *n* platino *m*.
platoon *n (mil)* peloton *m*.
play *n* juego *m*.
playboy *n* playboy *m*.
player *n* jugador *m*
plea *n* defensa *f*.
pleasant *adj* agradable.
please *vt* agradar.
pleasure *n* gusto, placer *m*.
pleat *n* pliegue *m*.
plentiful *adj* copioso.
plethora *n* pletora, replecion *f*.
pleurisy *n* pleuresia *f*.
pliers *npl* alicates *mpl* .
plinth *n* plinto *m*.
plough *n* arado *m*.
ploy *n* truco *m*.
plug *n* tapon *m*.
plum *n* ciruela *f*.
plumage *n* plumaje *m*.
plumb *n* plomada *f*.
plumber *n* plomero *m*.
plume *n* pluma *f*.
plump *adj* gordo.
plunder *vt* saquear.
plunge *vi* sumergir(se), precipitarse.
pluperfect *n (gr)* pluscuamperfecto *m*.
plural *adj* , *n* plural *m*.
plus *n* signo de mas *m*.
plush *adj* de felpa.
plutonium *n* plutonio *m*.
plywood *n* madera contrachapada *f*.
pneumatic *adj* neumatico.
pneumonia *n* pulmonia *f*.
poach *vt* escalfar.
pocket *n* bolsillo *m*.
pod *n* vaina *f*.
poem *n* poema *m*.
poet *n* poeta *m*.
poetry *n* poesia *f*.
poignant *adj* punzante.
point *n* punta *f; punto *m*.
point-blank *adv* directamente.

poise *n* peso *m;* equilibrio *m.*
poison *n* veneno *m.*
poker *n* atizador *m;* poker *m.*
polar *adj* polar.
pole *n* polo *m.*
police *n* policia *f.*
policy *n* politica *f.*
polio *n* polio *f.*
polish *vt* pulir, alisar.
polite *adj* pulido, cortes.
politician *n* politico *m.*
politics *npl* politica *f.*
polka *n* polca *f.*
pollen *n (bot)* polen *m.*
pollute *vt* ensuciar.
pollution *n* polucion, contaminacion *f.*
polo *n* polo *m.*
polyester *n* poliester *m.*
polytechnic *n* politecnico *m.*
pomegranate *n* granada *f.*
pomp *n* pompa *f;* esplendor *m.*
pompom *n* borla *f.*
pompous *adj* pomposo.
pond *n* estanque *m.*
ponder *vt* ponderar, considerar.
ponderous *adj* ponderoso, pesado.
pontoon *n* ponton *m.*
pony *n* jaca *f.*
pool *n* charca *f;* piscina.
poor *adj* pobre.
pop *n* papá *m.*
popcorn *n* palomitas *fpl.*
Pope *n* papa *m.*
poplar *n* alamo *m.*
poppy *n (bot)* amapola *f.*
popular *adj ,* ~ly *adv* popular(mente).
populate *vi* poblar.
population *n* poblacion *f.*
porcelain *n* porcelana *f.*
porch *n* portico *m.*
porcupine *n* puerco espin *m.*
pore *n* poro *m.*
pork *n* carne de puerco *f.*
pornography *n* pornografia *f.*
porous *adj* poroso.
porpoise *n* marsopa *f.*
porridge *n* gachas de avena *fpl.*
port *n* puerto *m m.*
portable *adj* portatil.
portal *n* portal *m f.*
porter *n* portero *m.*
portfolio *n* cartera *f.*
porthole *n* portilla *f.*
portico *n* portico *m.*
portion *n* porcion *f.*
portly *adj* rollizo.
portrait *n* retrato *m.*
portray *vt* retratar.
pose *n* postura *f;* pose *f.*
posh *adj* elegante.
position *n* posicion *f.*
positive *adj* positivo.
posse *n* peloton *m.*
possess *vt* poseer.
possession *n* posesion *f.*
possibility *n* posibilidad *f.*
possible *adj* posible.

post *n* correo *m;* puesto *m.*
postage stamp *n* sello *m.*
postcard *n* tarjeta postal *f.*
poster *n* cartel *m.*
posterior *n* trasero *m.*
posterity *n* posteridad *f.*
postgraduate *n* posgraduado *m.*
posthumous *adj* postumo.
post office *n* correos *m.*
postpone *vt* diferir.
posture *n* postura *f.*
posy *n* ramillete de flores *m.*
pot *n* marmita *f.*
potato *n* patata *f;* papa *f.*
potent *adj* potente.
potential *adj* potencial.
pothole *n* bache *m.*
potion *n* pocion *f.*
potter *n* alfarero *m.*
pottery *n* cerámica *f.*
pouch *n* bolsa *f.*
poultice *n* cataplasma *f.*
poultry *n* aves caseras *fpl.*
pound *n* libra *f;* libra esterlina *f.*
pour *vt* echar; servir.
pout *vi* ponerse cenudo.
poverty *n* pobreza *f.*
powder *n* polvo *m.*
power *n* poder *m.*
practicable *adj* practicable; hacedero.
practical *adj* práctico: —ly *adv* prácticamente.
practicality *n* factibilidad *f.*
practice *n* practica *f.*
pragmatic *adj* pragmático.
prairie *n* pampa *f.*
praise *n* renombre *m.*
prattle *vi* charlar: —*n* charla *f.*
prawn *n* gamba *f.*
pray *vi* rezar.
prayer *n* oracion *f.*
preach *vi* predicar.
preacher *n* pastor *m.*
precaution *n* precaucion *f.*
precede *vt* anteceder.
precious *adj* precioso.
precise *n* preciso.
precision *n* precision *f.*
preconception *n* preocupacion *f.*
predator *n* animal de rapina *m.*
predict *vt* predecir.
prediction *n* prediccion *f.*
predominant *adj* predominante.
predominate *vt* predominar.
preface *n* prefacio *m.*
prefer *vt* preferir.
preference *n* preferencia *f.*
prefix *vt* prefijar.
pregnancy *n* embarazo *m.*
pregnant *adj* embarazada.
prehistoric *adj* prehistorico.
prejudice *n* perjuicio *m.*
preliminary *adj* preliminar.
prelude *n* preludio *m.*
premature *adj* prematuro.
premier *n* primer ministro *m.*
premises *npl* establecimiento *m.*
premium *n* premio *m.*

premonition *n* presentimiento *m*.
prepare *vt* preparar(se).
preposition *n* preposicion *f*.
preposterous *adj* prepostero; absurdo.
prerequisite *n* requisito *m*.
prerogative *n* prerrogativa *f*.
prescribe *vi* prescribir; recetar.
prescription *n* prescripcion *f*.
present *n* regalo *m*.
presentation *n* presentacion *f*.
preservation *n* preservacion *f*.
preservative *n* preservativo *m*.
preserve *vt* preservar.
preside *vi* presidir.
presidency *n* presidencia *f*.
president *n* presidente *m*.
press *vt* empujar *n* prensa.
pressure *n* presion *f*.
prestige *n* prestigio *m*.
presume *vt* presumir, suponer.
pretence *n* pretexto *m*; pretension *f*.
pretend *vi* pretender.
preterite *n* preterito *m*.
pretext *n* pretexto *m*.
pretty *adj* lindo.
prevent *vt* prevenir.
preview *n* preestreno *m*.
previous *adj* previo.
prey *n* presa *f*.
price *n* precio *m*; premio *m*.
prick *vt* punzar, picar.
pride *n* orgullo *m*.
priest *n* sacerdote *m*.
priggish *adj* afectado.
prim *adj* peripuesto.
primary *adj* primario.
primate *n* primado *m*.
primeval *adj* primitivo.
primitive *adj* primitivo.
primrose *n (bot)* primula *f*.
prince *n* principe *m*.
princess *n* princesa *f*.
principle *n* principio *m*.
printer *n* impresor *m*.
prior *adj* anterior.
priority *n* prioridad *f*.
priory *n* priorato *m*.
prism *n* prisma *m*.
prison *n* prision, carcel *f*.
prisoner *n* prisionero *m*.
pristine *adj* pristino.
privacy *n* soledad *f*.
private *adj* secreto, privado; particular.
private eye *n* detective privado *m*.
privet *n* alhena *f*.
privilege *n* privilegio *m*.
prize *n* premio *m*.
probability *n* probabilidad *f*.
probable *adj* probable.
probation *n* prueba *f*.
problem *n* problema *m*.
procedure *n* procedimiento
proceed *vi* proceder.
process *n* proceso *m*.
procession *n* procesion *f*.
proclaim *vt* proclamar.
proclamation *n* proclamacion *f*.

procure *vt* procurar.
prod *vt* empujar.
prodigal *adj* prodigo.
prodigious *adj* prodigioso.
prodigy *n* prodigio *m*.
produce *vt* producir
product *n* producto *m*; obra *f*; efecto *m*.
production *n* produccion *f*.
profane *adj* profano.
profess *vt* profesar.
profession *n* profesion *f*.
professor *n* profesor, catedrático *m*.
proficient *adj* proficiente.
profile *n* perfil *m*.
profit *n* ganancia *f*.
profound *adj* profundo.
profuse *adj* profuso.
program *n* programa *m*.
progress *n* progreso *m*.
prohibit *vt* prohibir.
project *vt* proyectar
prominent *adj* prominente, saledizo.
promiscuous *adj* promiscuo.
promise *n* promesa *f*.
promontory *n* promontorio *m*.
promote *vt* promover.
promotion *n* promocion *f*.
prone *adj* inclinado.
prong *n* diente *m*.
pronoun *n* pronombre *m*.
pronounce *vt* pronunciar.
proof *n* prueba *f*.
propaganda *n* propaganda *f*.
propel *vt* impeler.
propeller *n* helice *f*.
propensity *n* propension *f*.
proper *adj* propio.
property *n* propiedad *f*.
prophecy *n* profecia *f*.
prophesy *vt* profetizar.
prophet *n* profeta *m*.
prophetic *adj* profetico.
proportion *n* proporcion *f*.
proportional *adj* proporcional.
proposal *n* propuesta *f*.
propose *vt* proponer.
proposition *n* proposicion *f*.
proprietor *n* propietario *m*.
propriety *n* propiedad *f*.
pro rata *adv* a prorrateo.
prosaic *adj* prosaico.
prose *n* prosa *f*.
prosecute *vt* proseguir.
provide *vt* proveer.
province *n* provincia *f*
provincial *adj* , *n* provincial
provided *conj*: —— **that** con tal que.
pulpit *n* pulpito *m*.
providence *n* providencia *f*.
pulsate *vi* pulsar. *m*.
provision *n* provision *f*.
proviso *n* estipulacion *f*.
provocation *n* provocacion *f*.
provocative *adj* provocativo.
provoke *vt* provocar.
prowess *n* proeza *f*.
prowl *vi* rondar.

proximity *n* proximidad *f.*
proxy *n* poder *m;* apoderado *m.*
prudence *n* prudencia *f.*
prudent *adj* prudente.
pulse *n* pulso *m;* legumbres *fpl.*
pumice *n* piedra pomez *f.*
pummel *vt* aporrear.
pump *n* bomba *f.*
pumpkin *n* calabaza *f.*
pun *n* equivoco, chiste *m.*
punch *n* punetazo *m.*
punctual *adj* puntual.
punctuate *vi* puntuar.
punctuation *n* puntuacion *f.*
pungent *adj* picante.
punish *vt* castigar.
punishment *n* castigo *m.*
prosecution *n* prosecucion *f.*
prosecutor *n* acusador *m.*
prospect *n* perspectiva *f.*
prospectus *n* prospecto *m.*
prosper *vi* prosperar.
prosperity *n* prosperidad *f.*
prostitute *n* prostituta *f.*
prostitution *n* prostitucion *f.*
prostrate *adj* postrado.
protagonist *n* protagonista *m.*
protect *vt* proteger.
protection *n* proteccion *f.*
protective *adj* protectorio.
protector *n* protector, patrono *m.*
protege *n* protegido *m.*
protein *n* proteina *f.*
protest *vi* protestar.
Protestant *n* protestante *m.*
protester *n* manifestante *m.*
protocol *n* protocolo *m.*
prototype *n* prototipo *m.*
protracted *adj* prolongado.
protrude *vi* sobresalir.
proud *adj* soberbio, orgulloso.
prove *vt* probar.
proverb *n* proverbio *m.*
prudish *adj* gazmono.
prussic acid *n* acido prúsico *m.*
pry *vi* espiar, acechar.
psalm *n* salmo *m.*
pseudonym *n* seudonimo *m.*
psyche *n* psique *f.*
psychiatrist *n* psiquiatra *m.*
psychiatry *n* psiquiatria *f.*

psychic *adj* psiquico.
psychoanalysis *n* psicoanalisis *m.*
psychoanalyst *n* psicoanalista *m.*
psychological *adj* psicologico.
psychologist *n* psicologo *m.*
psychology *n* psicologia *f.*
puberty *n* pubertad *f.*
public *adj* publico
publicize *vt* publicitar.
publicity *n* publicidad *f.*
publish *vt* publicar.
publisher *n* publicador *m.*
pucker *vt* arrugar, hacer pliegues.
puddle *n* charco *m.*
puff *n* soplo *m.*
pull *vt* tirar.
pulley *n* polea *f.*
pullover *n* jersey *m.*
pulp *n* pulpa *f.*
punk *n* punki *m.*
punt *n* barco llano *m.*
pup *n* cachorro *m.*
pupil *n* alumno *m.*
puppet *n* titere *m.*
puppy *n* perrito *m.*
purchase *vt* comprar.
pure *adj* puro.
puree *n* pure *m.*
purification *n* purificacion *f.*
purify *vt* purificar.
puritan *n* puritano *m.*
purity *n* pureza *f.*
purple *adj* purpureo.
purpose *n* intencion *f.*
purr *vi* ronronear.
purse *n* bolsa *f;* cartera *f.*
pursue *vi* perseguir.
pursuit *n* perseguimiento *m.*
purveyor *n* abastecedor *m.*
push *vt* empujar
pusher *n* traficante de drogas *m.*
push-up *n* plancha *f.*
put *vt* poner, colocar.
putrid *adj* podrido.
putty *n* masilla *f.*
puzzle *n* acertijo *m.*
puzzling *adj* extrano.
pylon *n* torre de conduccion electrica *f.*
pyramid *n* piramide *f.*
python *n* piton atigrado *m.*

Q

quarantine *n* cuarentena *f.*
quadrangle *n* cuadrangulo *m.*
quadrant *n* cuadrante *m.*
quadrilateral *adj* cuadrilatero.
quadruped *n* cuadrupedo *m.*
quadruple *adj* cuadruplo.
quadruplet *n* cuatrillizo *m.*
quagmire *n* tremedal *m.*
quail *n* codorniz *f.*
quaint *adj* pulido; exquisito.

quake *vi* temblar; tiritar.
qualification *n* calificacion *f.*
qualify *vt* calificar.
quality *n* calidad *f.*
qualm *n* escrupulo *m.*
quandary *n* incertidumbre *f.*
quantitative *adj* cuantitativo.
quantity *n* cantidad *f.*
quarrel *n* rina, contienda *f.*
quarrelsome *adj* pendenciero.

quarry *n* cantera *f.*
quarter *n* cuarto *m*r.
quarterly *adj* trimestral.
quartermaster *n (mil)* comisario *m.*
quartet *n (mus)* cuarteto *m.*
quartz *n (min)* cuarzo *m.*
quash *vt* fracasar; anular.
quay *n* muelle *m.*
queasy *adj* nauseabundo.
queen *n* reina *f.*
queer *adj* extraño.
quell *vt* calmar.
quench *vt* apagar.
query *n* cuestion.
quest *n* pesquisa *f.*
quack *vi* graznar.
question *n* pregunta *f;* cuestion *f.*
questionable *adj* cuestionable.
question mark *n* punto de interrogación *m.*
questionnaire *n* cuestionario *m.*
quibble *vi* buscar evasivas.
quick *adj* rapido.
quicken *vt* apresurar.

quicksand *n* arena movediza *f.*
quicksilver *n* azogue, mercurio *m.*
quick-witted *adj* agudo, perspicaz.
quiet *adj* callado.
quinine *n* quinina *f.*
quintet *n (mus)* quinteto *m.*
quintuple *adj* quintuplo.
quintuplet *n* quintillizo *m.*
quip *n* indirecta *f:* —*vt* echar pullas.
quirk *n* peculiaridad *f.*
quit *vt* dejar.
quite *adv* bastante.
quits *adv* ¡en paz!.
quiver *vi* temblar.
quixotic *adj* quijotesco.
quiz *n* concurso *m.*
quizzical *adj* burlon.
quota *n* cuota *f.*
quotation *n* citacion, cita *f.*
quotation marks *npl* comillas *fpl.*
quote *vt* citar.
quotient *n* cociente *m.*

R

rabbi *n* rabi *m.*
rabbit *n* conejo *m.*
rabble *n* gentuza *f.*
rabid *adj* rabioso.
rabies *n* rabia *f.*
race *n* raza.
rack *n* rejilla *f.*
racket *n* ruido *m;* raqueta *f.*
racy *adj* picante.
radiance *n* brillantez *f.*
radiant *adj* radiante.
radiate *vt , vi* radiar.
radiation *n* radiacion *f.*
radiator *n* radiador *m.*
radical *adj , ~ly adv* radical(mente).
radio *n* radio *f.*
radioactive *adj* radioactivo.
radish *n* rabano *m.*
radius *n* radio *f.*
raffle *n* rifa *f.*
raft *n* balsa *f.*
rafter *n* par *m;* viga *f.*
rag *n* trapo *m.*
rage *n* rabia *f.*
raid *n* incursion *f.*
rail *n* baranda, barandilla *f.*
railroad, railway *n* ferrocarril *m.*
rain *n* lluvia *f.*
rainbow *n* arco iris *m.*
raise *vt* levantar, alzar.
raisin *n* pasa *f.*
rake *n* rastro *m.*
ram *n* carnero *m.*
ramble *vi* divagar.
ramification *n* ramificacion *f.*
ramp *n* rampa *f.*
rampant *adj* exuberante.
ramshackle *adj* en ruina.

ranch *n* hacienda *f.*
rancid *adj* rancio.
rancor *n* rencor *m.*
random *adj* fortuito, sin orden.
range *vt* colocar, ordenar.
ransack *vt* saquear.
ransom *n* rescate *m.*
rape *n* violacion *f.*
rapid *adj* rapido.
rapist *n* violador *m.*
rapture *n* rapto *m.*
rare *adj* raro.
rascal *n* picaro *m.*
rash *adj* precipitado *m;* erupción(cutánea) *f.*
raspberry *n* frambuesa *f.*
rat *n* rata *f.*
rate *n* tasa *f,* precio, valor *m.*
rather *adv* mas bien; antes.
ratification *n* ratificacion *f.*
ratify *vt* ratificar.
ratio *n* razon *f.*
ration *n* racion *f.*
rational *adj* racional.
ravage *vt* saquear.
rave *vi* delirar.
raven *n* cuervo *m.*
ravine *n* barranco *m.*
ravish *vt* encantar.
ravishing *adj* encantador.
raw *adj* crudo.
ray *n* rayo de luz *m;* raya *f* (pez).
raze *vt* arrasar.
razor *n* navaja *f.*
reach *vt* alcanzar.
react *vi* reaccionar.
reaction *n* reaccion *f.*
read *vt* leer.
readable *adj* legible.

reader *n* lector *m*.
readjust *vt* reajustar.
ready *adj* listo, pronto.
real *adj* real.
realization *n* realizacion *f*.
realize *adv* darse cuenta de; realizar.
reality *n* realidad *f*.
realm *n* reino *m*.
ream *n* resma *f*.
reap *vt* segar.
reappear *vi* reaparecer.
rear *n* parte trasera *ft*.
rearmament *n* rearme *m*.
reason *n* razon *f*; causa *f*: —*vt*, *vi* razonar.
reassure *vt* tranquilizar, alentar; *(com)*asegurar.
rebel *n* rebelde *m/f*.
rebellion *n* rebelion *f*.
rebound *vi* rebotar.
rebuke *vt* reprender.
rebut *vi* repercutir.
recede *vi* retroceder.
receipt *n* recibo *m*.
receive *vt* recibir.
recent *adj* reciente.
reception *n* recepcion *f*.
recess *n* descanso *m*.
recession *n* retirada *f*; *(com)* recesion *f*.
recipe *n* receta *f*.
recipient *n* recipiente *m*.
recital *n* recital *m*.
recite *vt* recitar.
reckless *adj* temerario.
reckon *vt* contar.
recline *vt*, *vi* reclinar(se).
recluse *n* recluso/a *m/f*.
recognize *vt* reconocer.
recommend *vt* recomendar.
recommendation *n* recomendacion *f*.
recompense *n* recompensa *f*.
reconcile *vt* reconciliar.
reconsider *vt* considerar de nuevo.
record *vt* registrar; grabar.
recourse *n* recurso *m*.
recover *vt* recobrar; recuperar.
recovery *n* convalecencia *f*; recobro *m*.
recreation *n* recreacion *f*; recreo *m*.
recruit *vt* reclutar.
rectangle *n* rectangulo *m*.
rectify *vt* rectificar.
rectilinear *adj* rectilineo.
rector *n* rector *m*.
recur *vi* repetirse.
red *adj* rojo; tinto: —*n* rojo *m*.
redeem *vt* redimir.
redemption *n* redencion *f*.
redhot *adj* candente, ardiente.
redress *vt* corregir.
reduce *vt* reducir.
reduction *n* reduccion *f*.
reed *n* cana *f*.
reek *n* mal olor.
refectory *n* refectorio *m*.
refer *vt*, *vi* referir.
referee *n* arbitro *m*.
reference *n* referencia.
refine *vt* refinar.
refit *vt* reparar.

reflect *vt*, *vi* reflejar.
reflection *n* reflexion *f*.
reflex *adj* reflejo.
reform *vt*, *vi* reformar(se).
refresh *vt* refrescar.
refreshment *n* refresco.
refrigerator *n* nevera *f*.
refuge *n* refugio, asilo *m*.
refugee *n* refugiado *m/f*.
refund *vt* devolver.
refurbish *vt* restaurar.
refusal *n* negativa *f*.
refuse *vt* rehusar.
refute *vt* refutar.
regal *adj* real.
regard *vt* estimar.
regardless *adv* a pesar de todo.
regatta *n* regata *f*.
regime *n* regimen *m*.
region *n* region *f*.
register *n* registro *m*.
registrar *n* registrador *m*.
registration *n* registro *m*.
registry *n* registro *m*.
regular *adj* regular.
regulation *n* regulacion *f*.
reign *n* reinado, reino *m*.
reinforce *vt* reforzar.
reinstate *vt* reintegrar.
reject *vt* rechazar.
rejection *n* rechazo *m*.
rejoice *vt*, *vi* regocijar(se).
relapse *vi* recaer.
relate *vt*, *vi* relatar.
relation *n* relacion *f*.
relationship *n* parentesco *m*; relacion *f*.
relative *adj* relativo.
relax *vt*, *vi* relajar.
release *vt* soltar, libertar.
relic *n* reliquia *f*.
relief *n* relieve *m*.
relieve *vt* aliviar.
religion *n* religion *f*.
rely *vi* confiar en; contar con.
remain *vi* quedar.
remains *npl* restos *mpl*.
remark *n* observacion, nota *f*.
remedial *adv* curativo.
remedy *n* remedio *m*.
remember *vt* acordarse de; recordar.
remind *vt* recordar.
remit *vt*, *vi* remitir.
remorse *n* remordimiento *m*.
remote *adj* remoto.
remove *vt* quitar.
renew *vt* renovar.
renovate *vt* renovar.
rent *n* renta *f*.
rental *n* alquiler *m*.
repair *vt* reparar.
repeat *vt* repetir.
repel *vt* repeler.
repetition *n* repeticion *f*.
replace *vt* reemplazar.
reply *n* respuesta *f*.
repose *vt*, *vi* reposar.
represent *vt* representar.

reproduce *vt* reproducir.
reproduction *n* reproduccion *f.*
reptile *n* reptil *m.*
republic *n* republica *f.*
repugnance *n* repugnancia *f.*
repulse *vt* repulsar.
request *n* peticion.
require *vt* requerir.
rescue *vt* librar.
research *vt* investigar.
resemble *vt* asemejarse.
resent *vt* resentirse.
reserve *vt* reservar.
residence *n* residencia *f.*
resign *vt* , *vi* resignar.
resin *n* resina *f.*
resist *vt* resistir, oponerse.
resolve *vt* , *vr* resolver(se).
resort *vi* recurrir.
resource *n* recurso *m.*
respect *n* respecto *m.*
respite *n* suspension *f.*
respond *vt* responder.
rest *n* reposo *m.*
restless *adj* insomne.
restore *vt* restaurar.
restrict *vt* restringir.
result *vi* resultar.
resume *vt* resumir.
résumé *n* curriculum *m.*
resurrection *n* resurreccion *f.*
resuscitate *vt* resucitar.
retail *vt* revender *f.*
retain *vt* retener.
reticence *n* reticencia *f.*
retina *n* retina *f.*
retire *vt* , *vi* retirar(se).
retreat *n* retirada *f.*
return *vt* retribuir; restituir; devolver.
reveal *vt* revelar.
revenge *vt* vengar: —*n* venganza *f.*
revenue *n* renta *f* .
revere *vt* reverenciar.
reverse *vt* trastrocar.
review *vt* rever.
revise *vt* rever; repasar.
revival *n* restauracion *f.*
revolt *vi* rebelarse.
revolution *n* revolucion *f.*
revolve *vt* revolver.
revue *n* revista *f.*
reward *n* recompensa *f.*
rheumatism *n* reumatismo *m.*
rhinoceros *n* rinoceronte *m.*
rhombus *n* rombo *m.*
rhubarb *n* ruibarbo *m.*
rhyme *n* rima *f.*
rhythm *n* ritmo *m.*
rib *n* costilla *f.*
ribbon *n* liston *m.*
rice *n* arroz *m.*
rich *adj* rico.
riches *npl* riqueza *f.*
rickets *n* raquitis *f.*
rid *vt* librar.
riddle *n* enigma *m.*
ride *vi* cabalgar.

ridge *n* espinazo.
ridiculous *adj* ridiculoso.
rifle *n* rifle *m.*
right *adj* derecho, recto; justo.—*n* derecho *m;* título *m;* privilegio *m.*
rigid *adj* rigido.
rigor *n* rigor *m.*
rind *n* corteza *f.*
rinse *vt* lavar, limpiar.
rise *vi* levantarse.
risk *n* riesgo, peligro *m.*
rite *n* rito *m.*
ritual *adj* , *n* ritual *m.*
rival *adj* emulo.
river *n* rio *m.*
road *n* camino *m.*
roadsign *n* senal de trafico *f.*
roar *vi* rugir.
roast *vt* asar.
rob *vt* robar.
robber *n* robador, ladron *m.*
robbery *n* robo *m.*
robust *adj* robusto.
rock *n* roca *f.*
rocket *n* cohete *m.*
rodent *n* roedor *m.*
rogue *n* bribon *m.*
roll *vt* rodar.
Roman Catholic *adj* , *n* catolico/a *m/f* (romano/a).
romance *n* romance *m.*
roof *n* tejado *m.*
room *n* habitacion, sala *f.*
roomy *adj* espacioso.
root *n* raiz *f.*
rope *n* cuerda *f.*
rosary *n* rosario *m.*
rose *n* rosa *f.*
rosebed *n* campo de rosales *m.*
rosebud *n* capullo de rosa *m.*
rosemary *n* (bot) romero *m.*
rosette *n* roseta *f.*
rot *vi* pudrirse.
rotten *adj* podrido.
rouble *n* rublo *m.*
rouge *n* arrebol *m.*
rough *adj* aspero.
roulette *n* ruleta *f.*
round *adj* redondo.
rouse *vt* despertar.
route *n* ruta *f.*
routine *adj* rutinario.
row *n* camorra *f.*
row *n* (line) hilera, fila *f:* —*vt* (mar)remar, bogar.
royal *adj* real.
royalty *n* realeza, dignidad real *f.*
rub *vt* estregar, fregar, frotar.
rubber *n* caucho *m*, goma *f.*
rubber-band *n* goma, gomita *f.*
rubric *n* rubrica *f.*
ruby *n* rubi *m.*
rudder *n* timon *m.*
rude *adj* rudo, brutal.
rudiment *n* rudimentos *mpl* .
rue *vi* compadecerse.
rug *n* alfombra *f.*
rugby *n* rugby *m.*
ruin *n* ruina *f.*

ruinous *adj* ruinoso.
rule *n* mando *m;* regla *f.*
ruler *n* gobernador *m;* regla *f.*
rum *n* ron *m.*
rumor *n* rumor *m.*
run *vt* dirigir; organizar, *vi* correr.
runaway *n* fugitivo.
rung *n* escalon.
runway *n* pista de aterrizaje *f.*
rupture *n* rotura *f.*
rural *adj* rural.

ruse *n* astucia *f.*
rush *n* junco *m;* rafaga *f.*
rusk *n* galleta *f.*
russet *adj* bermejo.
rust *n* herrumbre *f.*
rustic *adj* rustico.
rustle *vi* crujir.
rut *n* celo *m.*
ruthless *adj* cruel.
rye *n (bot)* centeno *m.*

S

Sabbath *n* sabado *m.*
sabotage *n* sabotaje *m.*
saccharin *n* sacarina *f.*
sachet *n* sobrecito *m.*
sack *n* saco *m: —vt* despedir.
sacrament *n* sacramento *m.*
sacred *adj* sagrado.
sacredness *n* santidad *f.*
sacrifice *n* sacrificio *m.*
sacrilege *n* sacrilegio *m.*
sad *adj* triste.
saddle *n* silla *f.*
sadness *n* tristeza *f.*
safari *n* safari *m.*
safe *adj* seguro; *n* caja fuerte *f.*
safety *n* seguridad *f*
saffron *n* azafran *m.*
sage *n (bot)* salvia *f.*
Sagittarius *n* Sagitario *m* (signo delzodiaco).
sago *n (bot)* zagu *m.*
sail *n* vela *f.*
sailor *n* marinero *m.*
saint *n* santo *m;* santa *f.*
sake *n* causa, razon *f.*
salad *n* ensalada *f.*
salamander *n* salamandra *f.*
salary *n* sueldo *m.*
sale *n* venta *f.*
sales clerk *n* dependiente *m.*
salient *adj* saliente.
saline *adj* salino.
saliva *n* saliva *f.*
salmon *n* salmon *m.*
salmon trout *n* trucha salmonada *f.*
saloon *n* bar *m.*
salt *n* sal *f.*
salubrious *adj* salubre.
salutation *n* salutacion *f.*
salute *vt* saludar.
same *adj* mismo, idéntico/a
sample *n* muestra *f;* ejemplo *m.*
sanctify *vt* santificar.
sanctuary *n* santuario *m.*
sand *n* arena *f.*
sandal *n* sandalia *f.*
sandstone *n* piedra arenisca *f.*
sandwich *n* bocadillo *m.*
sane *adj* sapo.
sanitarium *n* sanatorio *m.*
sanity *n* juicio sano *m.*

sap *n* savia *f.*
sapling *n* arbolito *m.*
sapphire *n* zafir *m.*
sarcasm *n* sarcasmo *m.*
sarcophagus *n* sarcofago.
sardine *n* sardina *f.*
Satan *n* Satanas *m.*
satchel *n* mochila *f.*
satellite *n* satelite *m.*
satin *n* raso *m.*
satire *n* satira *f.*
satisfaction *n* satisfaccion *f.*
satisfy *vt* satisfacer.
Saturday *n* sabado *m.*
satyr *n* satiro *m.*
sauce *n* salsa *f.*
saucepan *n* cazo *m.*
saucer *n* platillo *m.*
sausage *n* salchicha *f.*
savage *adj* salvaje
savagery *n* crueldad *f.*
savannah *n* sabana *f.*
save *vt* salvar.
saveloy *n* chorizo *m.*
Savior *n* Salvador *m.*
savory *adj* sabroso.
saw *n* sierra *f.*
saxophone *n* saxofono *m.*
say *vt* decir.
saying *n* dicho *m.*
scab *n* rona *f.*
scald *vt* escaldar.
scale *n* balanza *f.*
scalp *n* cabellera *f.*
scamp *n* bribon.
scampi *npl* gambas *fpl.*
scan *vt* escudrinar.
scandal *n* escandalo *m.*
scandalize *vt* escandalizar.
scar *n* cicatriz *f.*
scarce *adj* raro.
scare *vt* espantar.
scarf *n* bufanda *f.*
scarlet *n* escarlata *f.*
scarp *n* escarpa *f.*
scene *n* escena *f.*
scenery *n* vista *f.*
schedule *n* horario *m.*
scheme *n* proyecto, plan *m.*
schism *n* cisma *m.*

scholar *n* estudiante *m*
school *n* escuela *f.*
schoolteacher *n* maestro, profesor, ra *m/f.*
science *n* ciencia *f.*
scientist *n* cientifico, ca *m/f.*
scissors *npl* tijeras *fpl.*
scooter *n* moto *f.*
scorch *vt* quemar.
scorn *vt , vi* despreciar.
Scorpio *n* Escorpion *m* (signo delzodiaco).
scorpion *n* escorpion *m.*
Scotch *n* whisky escoces *m.*
scoundrel *n* picaro *m.*
scramble *vi* arrapar.
scrap *n* migaja *f;* sobras *fpl.*
scrape *vt , vi* raer, raspar.
scraper *n* rascador *m.*
scratch *vt* rascar.
scrawl *vt , vi* garrapatear.
scream, screech *vi* chillar.
screen *n* pantalla *f.*
screenplay *n* guion *m.*
screw *n* tornillo *m.*
screwdriver *n* destornillador *m.*
scribble *vt* escarabajear.
scribe *n* escritor *m.*
script *n* guion *m;* letra *f.*
Scripture *n* Escritura sagrada *f.*
scruffy *adj* desalinado.
scruple *n* escrupulo *m.*
scullery *n* fregadero *m.*
sculptor *n* escultor, ra *m/f.*
sculpture *n* escultura *f.*
scum *n* espuma *f;* escoria *f.*
scurvy *n* escorbuto *m.*
scythe *n* guadana *f.*
sea *n* mar *m/f : —adj* de mar.
sea breeze *n* viento de mar *m.*
seafood *n* mariscos *mpl .*
sea front *n* paseo maritimo *m.*
seagull *n* gaviota *f.*
sea horse *n* hipocampo *m.*
tra *m/f ;* **seal** *n* sello *m;* foca *f.*
seam *n* costura *f.*
seaman *n* marinero *m.*
sea plane *n* hidroavion *m.*
sear *vt* cauterizar.
search *vt* examinar, buscar.
seashore *n* ribera *f,* litoral *m.*
seasick *adj* mareado.
season *n* estacion *f.*
seasoning *n* condimento *m.*
seat *n* asiento *m;* silla *f.*
seat belt *n* cinturon de seguridad *m.*
seaweed *n* alga marina *f.*
seclude *vt* apartar.
seclusion *n* separacion *f.*
second *adj* segundo.
secondary *adj* secundario.
secondhand *n* segunda mano *f.*
secret *adj , n* secreto *m.*
secretary *n* secretario, ria *m/f .*
sect *n* secta *f.*
section *n* seccion *f.*
sector *n* sector *m.*
secular *adj* secular.
secure *adj* seguro.

security *n* seguridad *f.*
sedate *adj* sosegado.
sedative *n* sedativo *m.*
sedge *n (bot)* junco *m.*
sediment *n* sedimento *m*
sedition *n* sedicion *f.*
seduce *vt* seducir.
seducer *n* seductor *m.*
seduction *n* seduccion *f.*
seductive *adj* seductivo.
see *vt , vi* ver**seed** *n* semilla.
seedy *adj* desaseado.
seek *vt , vi* buscar.
seem *vi* parecer.
seemliness *n* decensia *f.*
seesaw *n* vaiven *m.*
seethe *vi* hervir.
segment *n* segmento *m.*
seize *vt* asir.
seizure *n* captura *f.*
seldom *adv* raramente.
select *vt* elegir.
selection *n* seleccion *f.*
self *n* uno mismo.
selfish *adj* egoista.
self-portrait *n* autorretrato *m.*
selfsame *adj* identico.
sell *vt , vi* vender.
semen *n* semen *m.*
semester *n* semestre *m.*
semicircle *n* semicirculo *m.*
semicircular *adj* semicircular.
semicolon *n* punto y coma *m.*
seminary *n* seminario *m.*
senate *n* senado *m.*
senator *n* senador, ra *m/f .*
send *vt* enviar.
sender *n* remitente *m.*
senile *adj* senil.
senior *n* mayor *m.*
senna *n (bot)* sena *f.*
sensation *n* sensacion *f.*
sense *n* sentido *m.*
sensibility *n* sensibilidad *f.*
sensible *adj* sensato/a, juicioso/a..
sensitive *adj* sensitivo.
sensual, sensuous *adj* sensual.
sensuality *n* sensualidad *f.*
sentence *n* oracion *f;* sentencia *f.*
sentiment *n* sentimiento *m.*
sentinel, sentry *n* centinela *m.*
separate *vt (vi)* separar(se).
separation *n* separacion *f.*
September *n* se(p)tiembre *m.*
sepulcher *n* sepulcro *m.*
sequel *n* continuacion *f.*
sequence *n* serie *f.*
seraph *n* serafin *m.*
serenade *n* serenata *f.*
serene *adj* seneno.
serenity *n* serenidad *f.*
serf *n* siervo *m.*
sergeant *n* sargento *m.*
serial *adj* consecutivo.
series *n* serie *f.*
serious *adj* serio, grave.
sermon *n* sermon *f.*

serious *adj* seroso.
serpent *n* serpiente *f.*
serpentine *adj* serpentino.
serrated *adj* serrado.
serum *n* suero *m.*
servant *n* criado *m;* criada *f.*
serve *vt , vi* servir.
service *n* servicio *m.*
servile *adj* servil.
session *n* junta *f;* sesion *f.*
set *vt* poner, colocar, fijar.
setter *n* perro de muestra *m.*
seven *adj , n* siete.
seventeen *adj , n* diez y siete, diecisiete.
seventeenth *adj , n* decimoseptimo.
seventh *adj , n* septimo.
seventieth *adj , n* septuagesimo.
seventy *adj , n* setenta.
sever *vt , vi* separar.
several *adj , pn* varios.
severance *n* separacion *f.*
severe *adj* severo.
severity *n* severidad *f.*
sew *vt , vi* coser.
sewer *n* albanal *m.*
sex *n* sexo *m.*
sexist *adj n* sexista *m/f .*
sexual *adj* sexual.
sexy *adj* sexy.
shade *n* sombra.
shadow *n* sombra *f.*
shaft *n* flecha, saeta *f.*
shake *vt* sacudir; agitar.
shallow *adj* somero.
sham *vt* enganar.
shame *n* verguenza *f.*
shamefaced *adj* vergonzoso.
shampoo *n* champu *m.*
shamrock *n* trebol *m.*
shank *n* pierna *f.*
shanty *n* chabola *f.*
shantytown *n* barrio de chabolas *m.*
shape *vt , vi* formar; *n* forma *m.*
shapeless *adj* informe.
shapely *adj* bien hecho.
share *n* parte, porcion *f;* compartir.
shark *n* tiburon *m.*
sharp *adj* agudo.
shatter *vt* destrozar.
shave *vt* afeitar.
shaver *n* maquina de afeitar *f.*
shawl *n* chal *m.*
she *pn* ella.
sheaf *n* gavilla *f*
shear *vt* atusar.
sheath *n* vaina *f.*
shed *vt* verter; cabana *f.*
sheen *n* resplandor *m.*
sheep *n* oveja *f.*
sheer *adj* puro, claro.
sheet *n* sabana *f.*
sheet lightning *n* relampagueamiento *m.*
shelf *n* anaquel *m.*
shell *n* cascara *f;* concha *f.*
shelter *n* guardia *f;* amparo *m.*
shepherd *n* pastor *m.*
sherbet *n* sorbete *m.*

sheriff *n* sherif *m.*
sherry *n* jerez *m.*
shield *n* escudo *m.*
shift *vi* cambiarse.
shinbone *n* espinilla *f.*
shine *vi* lucir, brillar.
shiny *adj* brillante.
ship *n* nave *f;* barco *m.*
shipwreck *n* naufragio *m.*
shirt *n* camisa *f.*
shit *excl (sl)* ¡mierda!
shiver *vi* tiritar de frio.
shoal *n* banco *m.*
shock *n* choque *m.*
shock absorber *n* amortiguador *m.*
shoddy *adj* de pacotilla.
shoe *n* zapato *m.*
shoelace *n* correa de zapato *f.*
shoemaker *n* zapatero *m.*
shoot *vt* tirar.
shopper *n* comprador, ra *m/f .*
shopping *n* compras *fpl.*
shopping mall *n* centro comercial *m.*
shore *n* costa, ribera *f.*
short *adj* corto breve.
short-sighted *adj* corto de vista.
shot *n* tiro *m.*
shotgun *n* escopeta *f.*
shoulder *n* hombro *m.*
shout *vi* gritar, aclamar.
shove *vt , vi* empujar.
shovel *n* pala *f.*
show *vt* mostrar.
showy *adj* ostentoso.
shred *n* cacho, pedazo.
shrewd *adj* astuto.
shriek *vt , vi* chillar
shrimp *n* camaron *m.*
shrine *n* relicario *m.*
shrink *vi* encogerse.
shroud *n* cubierta *f.*
Shrove Tuesday *n* martes de carnaval *m.*
shrub *n* arbusto *m.*
shrug *vt* encogerse de hombros.
shun *vt* huir, evitar.
shut *vt* cerrar.
shutter *n* contraventana *f.*
shuttle *n* lanzadera *f.*
shuttlecock *n* volante *m.*
shy *adj* timido.
shyness *n* timidez *f.*
sick *adj* malo, enfermo.
sickle *n* hoz *f.*
sickness *n* enfermedad *f.*
side *n* lado *m.*
sideboard *n* aparador *m;* alacena *f.*
sidewalk *n* calzada *f.*
siege *n (mil)* sitio *m.*
sieve *n* tamiz *m.*
sift *vt* cerner.
sigh *vi* suspirar.
sight *n* vista *f.*
sightseeing *n* excursionismo, turismo *m.*
sign *n* senal *f.*
signal *n* senal *f.*
signature *n* firma *f.*
significance *n* importancia *f.*

signify *vt* significar.
signpost *n* indicador *m*.
silence *n* silencio *m*.
silk *n* seda *f*.
silky *adj* hecho de seda; sedeno.
shower *n* nubada *f*; llovizna *f*; ducha *f*. **sill** *n* repisa *f*.
silly *adj* tonto.
silver *n* plata *f*.
similar *adj* similar; semejante.
similarity *n* semejanza *f*.
simile *n* simil *m*.
simmer *vi* hervir a fuego lento.
simple *adj* simple.
simplicity *n* sencillez *ff*.
simulate *vt* simular.
simulation *n* simulacion *f*.
sin *n* pecado *m*.
since *adv* desde.
sincerity *n* sinceridad *f*.
sinew *n* tendon *m*; nervio *m*.
sing *vi, vt* cantar.
singe *vt* chamuscar.
singer *n* cantor *m*; cantora *f*.
single *adj* solo; soltero, soltera.
singly *adv* separadamente.
singular *adj* singular.
sinister *adj* siniestro.
sink *vi* hundirse.
sinner *n* pecador *m*; pecadora *f*.
sinus *n* seno *m*.
sip *vt* sorber: —*n* sorbo *m*.
siphon *n* sifon *m*.
sir *n* senor *m*.
siren *n* sirena *f*.
sister *n* hermana *f*.
sister-in-law *n* cunada *f*.
sisterly *adj* con hermandad.
sit *vi* sentarse.
site *n* sitio *m*; situacion *f*.
sit-in *n* ocupacion *f*.
sitting room *n* sala de estar *f*.
situation *n* situacion *f*.
six *adj* , *n* seis.
sixteen *adj* , *n* diez y seis, dieciseis.
sixteenth *adj* , *n* decimosexto.
sixth *adj* , *n* sexto.
sixtieth *adj* , *n* sexagesimo.
sixty *adj* , *n* sesenta.
size *n* tamano *m*.
skate *n* patin *m*: —*vi* patinar.
skeleton *n* esqueleto *m*.
skeptic *n* esceptico.
skepticism *n* escepticismo *m*.
sketch *n* esbozo *m*.
ski *n* esqui *m*: —*vi* esquiar.
skid *n* patinazo *m*.
skill *n* destreza *f*.
skim *vt* espumar.
skin *n* piel *f*; cutis *m/f* .
skip *vi* saltar, brincar.
skirt *n* falda.
skittle *n* bolo *m*.
skulk *vi* escuchar, acechar.
skull *n* craneo *m*.
sky *n* cielo *m*.
skyscraper *n* rascacielos *m invar*.
slab *n* losa *f*.

slack *adj* flojo.
slag *n* escoria *f*.
slander *vt* calumniar *f*.
slang *n* argot *m f*.
slap *n* manotada *f*.
slate *n* pizarra *f*.
slave *n* esclavo *m*.
slaver *n* baba *f*: —*vi* babosear.
slay *vt* matar.
sled, sleigh *n* trineo *m*.
sleek *adj* liso.
sleep *vi* dormir.
sleeping bag *n* saco de dormir *m*.
sleeping pill *n* somnifero *m*.
sleepwalking *n* sonambulismo *m*.
sleet *n* aguanieve *f*.
sleeve *n* manga *f*.
slender *adj* delgado.
slice *n* rebanada *f*.
slide *vi* resbalar, deslizarse.
slight *adj* ligero.
slim *adj* delgado.
slime *n* lodo *m/f*.
slimy *adj* viscoso, pegajoso.
sling *n* honda *f*; cabestrillo *m*.
slingshot *n* catapulta *f*.
slip *vi* resbalar; escapar.
slipper *n* zapatilla *f*.
slogan *n* eslogan, lema *m*.
slope *n* cuesta *f*.
slow *adj* tardio, lento, torpe.
slum *n* tugurio *m*.
slump *n* depresion *f*.
slur *vt* ensuciar; calumniar.
slut *n* marrana *f*.
sly *adj* astuto.
smack *n* sabor, gusto *m*; chasquido delatigo *m*.
small *adj* pequeno.
smallpox *n* viruelas *fpl*.
smalltalk *n* charla, prosa *f*.
smart *adj* elegante; listo.
smash *vt* romper, quebrantar
smell *vt* , *vi* oler.
smile *vi* sonreirse: —*n* sonrisa *f*.
smoke *n* humo *m*; fumar.
smoker *n* fumador, ra *m/f* .
smooth *adj* liso.
smug *adj* presumido.
smut *n* tiznon *m*.
snack *n* bocadom.
snag *n* problema *m*.
snail *n* caracol *m*.
snake *n* culebra *f*.
snap *vt* , *vi* romper.
snapdragon *n (bot)* antirrino *m*.
snatch *vt* arrebatar.
sneeze *vi* estornudar.
sniff *vt* oler: —*vi* resollar con fuerza.
snob *n* (e)snob *m/f* .
snore *vi* roncar.
snow *n* nieve *f*.
snowdrop *n (bot)* campanilla blanca *f*.
snowman *n* figura de nieve *f*.
snub *vt* reprender.
snuff *n* rape *m*.
so *adv* asi; de este modo; tan.
soap *n* jabon *m*.

soap opera *n* telenovela *f.*
soar *vi* remontarse.
sob *n* sollozo *m;* —*vi* sollozar.
soccer *n* balón *m;* fútbol *m.*
soccer player *n* futbolista *m/f .*
sociable *adj* sociable.
social *adj* social.
socialism *n* socialismo *m.*
society *n* sociedad *f.*
sociologist *n* sociologo, ga *m/f .*
sociology *n* sociologia *f.*
sock *n* calcetin *m.*
sod *n* cesped *m.*
soda *n* sosa *f.*
sofa *n* sofa *m.*
soft *adj* blando.
soil *vt* ensuciar, tierra *f.*
solar *adj* solar.
soldier *n* soldado *m.*
sole *n* planta del pie *f.*
solemn *adj ,* **~ly** *adv* solemne(mente).
solicitor *n* representante, agente *m/ f.*
solid *adj* solido.
solitaire *n* solitario *m;* grueso diamante *m.*
solitude *n* soledad *f.*
solo *n (mus)* solo *m.*
solstice *n* solsticio *m.*
soluble *adj* soluble.
solution *n* solucion *f.*
solve *vt* resolver.
some *adj* algo de, un poco, algun, alguno, alguna, unos, pocos, ciertos.
somebody *n* alguien *m.*
something *n* alguna cosa, algo.
sometimes *adv* a veces.
somnambulism *n* somnambulismo *m.*
somnambulist *n* somnambulo *m.*
somnolence *n* somnolencia *f.*
son *n* hijo *m.*
sonata *n (mus)* sonata *f.*
song *n* cancion.
son-in-law *n* yerno *m.*
sonnet *n* soneto *m.*
soon *adv* pronto.
soot *n* hollin *m.*
soothe *vt* adular; calmar.
sop *n* sopa *f.*
sophisticate *vt* sofisticar.
sophisticated *adj* sofisticado.
sorcerer *n* hechicero *m.*
sorcery *n* hechizom.
sordid *adj* sordido.
sore *n* llaga, ulcera *f.*
sorrow *n* pesar *m;* tristeza *f.*
sorry *adj* triste.
soul *n* alma *f.*
sound *adj* sano; sonido, *vi* sonar.
soup *n* sopa *f.*
sour *adj* agrio.
souvenir *n* recuerdo *m.*
south *n* sur *m.*
sovereign *adj , n* soberano, na *(m/f).*
sovereignty *n* soberania *f.*
sow *n* puerca *f.*
sow *vt* sembrar.
space *n* espacio *m.*
spacious *adj* espacioso.

spade *n* laya.
spaghetti *n* espaguetis *mpl .*
span *n* palmo *m.*
spangle *n* lentejuela *f.*
spaniel *n* perro de aguas *m.*
Spanish *adj* espanol(a) **spar** *n* palo *m.*
spark *n* chispa *f.*
sparkle *n* centella.
sparrow *n* gorrion *m.*
sparse *adj* delgado.
spasm *n* espasmo *m.*
spatula *n* espatula *f.*
spawn *n* freza *f.*
speak *vt , vi* hablar.
spear *n* lanza *f.*
special *adj* especial.
species *n* especie *f.*
specific *adj* especifico *m.*
specimen *n* muestra *f.*
spectacle *n* espectaculo *m.*
spectator *n* espectador, ra *m/f .*
specter *n* espectro *m.*
speculate *vi* especular.
speculation *n* especulacion *f.*
speed *n* prisa *f;* velocidad *f.*
spell *n* hechizom.
spelling *n* ortografia *f.*
spend *vt* gastar.
sperm *n* esperma *f.*
spew *vi (sl)* vomitar.
sphere *n* esfera *f.*
spherical *adj* esferico.
spice *n* especia *f.*
spicy *adj* aromatico.
spider *n* arana *f.*
spike *n* espigon *m.*
spill *vt* derramar.
spin *vt* hilar.
spinach *n* espinaca *f.*
spinal *adj* espinal.
spine *n* espinazo *m.*
spinster *n* soltera *f.*
spiral *adj* espiral.
spire *n* espira *f.*
spirit *n* aliento *m;* espiritu *m.*
spiritual *adj ,* **~ly** *adv* espiritual(mente).
spiritualist *n* espiritualista *m.*
spit *n* asador *m;* saliva *f.*
spite *n* rencor *m.*
splash *vt* salpicar.
spleen *n* bazo *m.*
splendid *adj* esplendido.
splendor *n* esplendor *m.*
splint *n* tablilla *f.*
splinter *n* cacho *m.*
split *n* hendedura *f.*
spoil *vt* despojar.
spoke *n* rayo de la rueda *m.*
spokesman *n* portavoz *m.*
sponge *n* esponja *f.*
sponsor *n* fiador *m.*
spontaneity *n* espontaneidad *f.*
spool *n* carrete *m.*
spoon *n* cuchara *f.*
spoonful *n* cucharada *f.*
sport *n* deporte *m***spot** *n* mancha *f.*
spouse *n* esposo *m;* esposa *f.*

sprain *adj* descoyuntar.
sprat *n* meleta, nuesa *f* (pez).
sprawl *vi* revolcarse.
spray *n* rociada *f;* espray *m.*
spread *vt* extender
spree *n* fiesta *f;* juerga *f.*
sprig *n* ramito *m.*
sprinkle *vt* rociar.
spur *n* espuela *f.*
spurn *vt* despreciar.
spy *n* espia *m.*
squad *n* escuadra *f.*
squadron *n (mil)* escuadron *m.*
squalid *adj* sucio.
squall *n* rafaga *f.*
squalor *n* porqueria *f.*
squander *vt* malgastar.
square *adj* cuadrado *m;* plaza *f.*
squash *vt* aplastar.
squaw *n* hembra de un indiano *f.*
squeak *vi* planir.
squeamish *adj* fastidioso.
squeeze *vt* apretar.
squid *n* calamar *m.*
squint *adj* bizco.
squirrel *n* ardilla *f.*
stable *n* establo *m.*
stack *n* pila *f.*
staff *n* personal *m.*
stag *n* ciervo *m.*
stage *n* etapa *f;* escena *f.*
stagnate *vi* estancarse.
stain *vt* manchar.
stair *n* escalon *m.*
staircase *n* escalera *f.*
stale *adj* anejo.
stalk, tronco *m.*
stall *n* pesebre *m;* tienda portatil *f.*
stallion *n* semental *m.*
stamina *n* resistencia *f.*
stammer *vi* tartamudear.
stamp estampar, imprimir; sello *m.*
stampede *n* estampida *f.*
stand *vi* estar de pie o derecho; stand *m.*
standard *n* estandarte *m.*
staple *n* grapa *f.*
star *n* estrella *f.*
starch *n* almidon *m.*
stark *adj* fuerte, aspero.
starling *n* estornino *m.*
start *vi* empezar.
startle *vt* sobresaltar.
starvation *n* hambre *f.*
state *n* estado *m;* condicion *f.*
statement *n* afirmacion *f.*
static *adj* estatico.
station *n* estacion *f.*
stationary *adj* estacionario, fijo.
stationery *n* papeleria *f.*
statistics *npl* estadistica *f.*
statuary *n* estatuario *m.*
statue *n* estatua *f.*
stature *n* estatura *f.*
statute *n* estatuto *m.*
stay *n* estancia *f.*
steak *n* filete *m;* bistec *m.*
steal *vt , vi* robar.

stealth *n* hurto *m.*
steam *n* vapor *m.*
steel *n* acero *m.*
steep *adj* escarpado.
steeple *n* torre *f;* campanario *m.*
steer *n* novillo *m: —vt* manejar, conducir.
steering wheel *n* volante *m.*
stem *n* vastago.
stench *n* hedor *m.*
stencil *n* cliche *m.*
stenographer *n* taquigrafo, fa *m/f .*
stenography *n* taquigrafia *f.*
step *n* paso, escalon *m.*
stepbrother *n* hermanastro *m.*
stepdaughter *n* hijastra *f.*
stepfather *n* padrastro *m.*
stepmother *n* madrastra *f.*
stepsister *n* hermanastra *f.*
stepson *n* hijastro *m.*
stereo *n* estereo *m.*
stereotype *n* estereotipo *m.*
sterile *adj* esteril.
sterling *n* libras esterlinas *fpl.*
stethoscope *n (med)* estetoscopio *m.*
stew *vt* estofar *f.*
steward *n* mayordomo *m*
stick *n* palo, pegarse.
stiff *adj* tieso.
stifle *vt* sufocar.
stigma *n* estigma *m.*
stigmatize *vt* infamar.
stiletto *n* estilete *m***still** tranquilo; *adv* todavia.
stillborn *adj* nacido muerto.
stilts *npl* zancos *mpl .*
stimulant *n* estimulante *m.*
stimulate *vt* estimular.
stimulus *n* estimulo *m.*
sting *vt* picar o morder (un insecto).
stingy *adj* mezquino.
stink *vi* heder.
stint *n* tarea *f.*
stipulate *vt* estipular.
stipulation *n* estipulacion *f.*
stir *vt* agitar.
stirrup *n* estribo *m.*
stitch *vt* coser.
stoat *n* comadreja *f.*
stock *n* ganado *m;* caldo *m.*
stockbroker *n* agente de bolsa *m/f .*
stock exchange *n* bolsa *f.*
stocking *n* media *f.*
stock market *n* bolsa *f.*
stoic *n* estoico *m.*
stoical *adj* estoico.
stole *n* estola *f.*
stomach *n* estomago *m.*
stone *n* piedra *f.*
stop *vt* detener, parar.
stopwatch *n* cronometro *m.*
store *n* provision *f;* almacen *m.*
stork *n* ciguena *f.*
storm *n* tempestad.
story *n* historia *f.*
stout *adj* robusto.
stove *n* estufa *f.*
straight *adj* derecho.
strain *vt* colar, filtrar; *n* tension *f.*

strainer *n* colador *m*.
strange *adj* raro/a, extranjero.
stranger *n* desconocido *m*; extranjero, ra *m/f*.
strangle *vt* ahogar.
strap *n* correa.
strapping *adj* abultado.
stratagem *n* estratagema *f*; astucia *f*.
strategic *adj* estrategico *m*.
strategy *n* estrategia *f*.
stratum *n* estrato *m*.
straw *n* paja *m*; pajita *f*.
strawberry *n* fresa *f*.
stray *vi* extraviarse.
streak *n* raya.
street *n* calle *f*.
streetcar *n* tranvia *f*.
strength *n* fuerza.
strenuous *adj* arduo.
stress *n* presion *f*; estres *m*.
stretch *vt*, *vi* extender.
stretcher *n* camilla *f*.
strew *vt* esparcir.
strict *adj* estricto.
stride *n* tranco *m*.
string *n* cordon *m*.
stringent *adj* astringente.
strip *vt* desnudar.
stripe *n* raya.
strive *vi* esforzarse.
stroll *n* paseo.
strong *adj* fuerte.
strongbox *n* cofre fuerte *m*.
structure *n* estructura *f*.
struggle *vi* esforzarse.
strum *vt (mus)* rasguear.
strut *vi* pavonearse.
stubborn *adj* obstinado.
stucco *n* estuco *m*.
stud *n* corchete *m*.
student *n* estudiante *m/f*.
studio *n* estudio de un artista *m*.
studious *adj* estudioso.
study *n* estudio *m*.
stuff *n* materia *f*.
stuffing *n* relleno *m*.
stumble *vi* tropezar
stump *n* tronco *m*.
stun *vt* aturdir.
stunt *n* vuelo acrobático *m*; trucopublicitario *m*.
stuntman *n* especialista *m*.
stupid *adj* estupido.
sturdy *adj* fuerte.
sturgeon *n* esturion *m*.
stutter *vi* tartamudear.
sty *n* zahurda *f*.
stye *n* orzuelo *m*.
style *n* estilo *m*.
stylish *adj* elegante.
suave *adj* afable.
subdivide *vt* subdividir.
subdue *vt* sojuzgar, sujetar.
subject *adj* sujeto.
subjunctive *n* subjuntivo *m*.
sublime *adj* sublime
submarine *adj* submarino.
submerge *vt* sumergir.
submit *vt*, *(vi)* someter(se).

subordinate *adj* subordinado, inferior: —*vt* subordinar.
subscribe *vt*, *vi* suscribir.
subsequent *adj*, ~**ly** *adv* subsiguien-te(mente).
subservient *adj* subordinado.
subside *vi* sumergirse.
subsidence *n* derrumbamiento *m*.
subsidiary *adj* subsidiario.
subsidize *vt* subvencionar.
subsidy *n* subvencion *f*.
substance *n* substancia *f*.
substitute *vt* sustituir.
substratum *n* lecho *m*.
subterranean *adj* subterraneo.
subtitle *n* subtitulo *m*.
subtle *adj* sutil.
suburb *n* suburbio *m*.
subversion *n* subversion *f*.
subway *n* metro *m*.
succeed *vt*, *vi* seguir; conseguir, lograr, tener exito.
success *n* exito *m*.
succumb *vi* sucumbir.
such *adj* tal.
suck *vt*, *vi* chupar.
sudden *adj* repentino, no previsto.
sue *vt* poner por justicia; suplicar.
suede *n* ante *m*.
suffer *vt*, *vi* sufrir, padecer.
sufficient *adj* suficiente.
suffocate *vt* sufocar.
suffrage *n* sufragio.
sugar *n* azucar *m*.
sugar cane *n* cana de azucar *f*.
suggest *vt* sugerir.
suggestion *n* sugestion *f*.
suicide *n* suicidio *m*.
suit *n* conjunto *m*; traje *m*.
suitcase *n* maleta *f*.
suitor *n* suplicante *m*.
sultan *n* sultan *m*.
sultana *n* sultana *f*.
sum *n* suma *f*.
summary *adj*, *n* sumario *(m)*.
summer *n* verano *m*.
summit *n* apice *m*.
summon *vt* citar.
summons *n* citacion *f*.
sumptuous *adj* suntuoso.
sun *n* sol *m*.
sunbathe *vi* tomar el sol.
Sunday *n* domingo *m*.
sundial *n* reloj de sol *m*.
sundry *adj* varios.
sunflower *n* girasol *m*.
sunglasses *npl* gafas o antojos de sol *mpl*.
sunlight *n* luz del sol *f*.
sunrise *n* salida del sol *f*.
sunset *n* puesta del sol *f*.
sunshade *n* quitasol *m*.
sunstroke *n* insolacion *f*.
suntan *n* bronceado *m*.
suntan oil *n* aceite bronceador *m*.
superb *adj* magnifico.
superficial *adj* superficial.
superfluity *n* superfluidad *f*.
superior *adj*, *n* superior *(m)*.
supermarket *n* supermercado *m*.

supernatural *n* sobrenatural.
superpower *n* superpotencia *f.*
superstition *n* supersticion *f.*
supertanker *n* superpetrolero *m.*
supervise *vt* inspeccionar.
supper *n* cena *f.*
supple *adj* flexible.
supplement *n* suplemento *m.*
supplementary *adj* adicional.
suppleness *n* flexibilidad *f.*
suppli(c)ant *n* suplicante *m.*
supplicate *vt* suplicar.
supplication *n* suplica, suplicacion *f.*
supplier *n* distribuidor, ra *m/f.*
supply *vt* suministrar; suplir, completar; surtir: —*n* provision *f;* suministro *m.*
support *vt* sostener; soportar, asistir: —*n* apoyo *m.*
supportable *adj* soportable.
supporter *n* partidario, ria; aficionado, da *m/f.*
suppose *vt , vi* suponer.
supposition *n* suposicion *f.*
suppress *vt* suprimir.
suppression *n* supresion *f.*
supremacy *n* supremacia *f.*
supreme *adj* supremo: —**ly** *adv* supremamente.
surcharge *vt* sobrecargar: —*n* sobretasa *f.*
sure *adj* seguro, cierto; firme; estable: —**to be ~** sin duda; ya se ve: —**ly** *adv* ciertamente, seguramente, sin duda.
sureness *n* certeza, seguridad *f.*
surety *n* seguridad *f;* fiador *m.*
surf *n (mar)* resaca *f.*
surface *n* superficie *f:* —*vt* revestir: —*vi* salir a la superficie.
surfboard *n* plancha (de surf) *f.*
surfeit *n* exceso *m.*
surge *n* ola, onda *f:* —*vi* avanzar entropel.
surgeon *n* cirujano, na *m/f.*
surgery *n* cirujia *m.*
surgical *adj* quirurgico.
surliness *n* mal humor *m.*
surly *adj* aspero de genio.
surmise *vt* sospechar: —*n* sospecha *f.*
surmount *vt* sobrepujar.
surmountable *adj* superable.
surname *n* apellido, sobrenombre *m.*
surpass *vt* sobresalir, sobrepujar, exceder, aventajar.
surpassing *adj* sobresaliente.
surplice *n* sobrepelliz *f.*
surplus *n* excedente *m;* sobrante *m:* —*adj* sobrante.
surprise *vt* sorprender: —*n* sorpresa *f.*
surprising *adj* sorprendente.
surrender *vt , vi* rendir; ceder; ren-dirse: —*n* rendicion *f.*
surreptitious *adj* subrepticio: —**ly** *adv* subrepticiamente.
surrogate *vt* subrogar: —*n* subrogado *m.*
surrogate mother *n* madre porta-dora *f.*
surround *vt* circundar, cercar, rodear.
survey *vt* inspeccionar, examinar; apear: —*n* inspeccion *f;* apeo (de tierras) *m.*
survive *vi* sobrevivir: —*vt* sobrevivir a.
survivor *n* sobreviviente *m/f.*
susceptibility *n* susceptibilidad *f.*
susceptible *adj* susceptible.
suspect *vt , vi* sospechar: —*n* sospechoso, sa *m/f.*
suspend *vt* suspender.

suspense *n* suspense *m;* detencion *f;* incertidumbre *f.*
suspension *n* suspension *f.*
suspension bridge *n* puente colgante o colgado *m.*
suspicion *n* sospecha *f.*
suspicious *adj* suspicaz: —**ly** *adv* sospechosamente.
suspiciousness *n* suspicacia *f.*
sustain *vt* sostener, sustentar, mante-ner; apoyar; sufrir.
sustenance *n* sostenimiento, sus-tento *m.*
suture *n* sutura, costura *f.*
swab *n* algodon *m;* frotis *m* invar.
swaddle *vt* fajar.
swaddling-clothes *npl* panales *mpl .*
swagger *vi* baladronear.
swallow *n* golondrina *f:* —*vt* tragar, engullir.
swamp *n* pantano *m.*
swampy *adj* pantanoso.
swan *n* cisne *m.*
swap *vt* canjear: —*n* intercambio *m.*
swarm *n* enjambre *m;* gentio *m;* hormiguero *m:* —*vi* enjam brar; hormiguear de gente; abundar.
swarthy *adj* atezado.
swarthiness *n* tez morena *f.*
swashbuckling *adj* fanfarron.
swath *n* tranco *m.*
swathe *vt* fajar: —*n* faja *f.*
sway *vt* mover: —*vi* ladearse, inclinarse: —*n* balanceo *m;* poder, imperio, influjo *m.*
swear *vt , vi* jurar; hacer jurar; juramentar.
sweat *n* sudor *m:* —*vi* sudar; trabajar con fatiga.
sweater, sweatshirt *n* sueter *m.*
sweep *vt , vi* barrer; arrebatar; deshollinar; pasar o tocar liger amente; oscilar: —*n* barredura *f;* vuelta *f;* giro *m.*
sweeping *adj* rapido: —**s** *pl* barreduras *fpl.*
sweepstake *n* loteria *f.*
sweet *adj* dulce, grato, gustoso; suave; oloroso; melodioso; hermoso; amable: —*adv* dulcemente, suavemente.
sweetbread *n* mellejas de ternera *fpl.*
sweeten *vt* endulzar; suavizar; aplacar; perfumar.
sweetener *n* edulcorante *m.*
sweetheart *n* novio, via *m/f ;* querida *f.*
sweetmeats *npl* dulces secos *mpl .*
sweetness *n* dulzura, suavidad *f.*
swell *vi* hincharse; ensoberbecerse; embravecerse: —*vt* hin char, inflar, agravar: —*n* marejada *f:* —*adj (fam)* estupendo, fenomenal.
swelling *n* hinchazon *f;* tumor *m.*
swelter *vi* ahogarse de calor.
swerve *vi* vagar; desviarse.
swift *adj* veloz, ligero, rapido: —*n* vencejo, *m.*
swiftly *adv* velozmente.
swiftness *n* velocidad, rapidez *f.*
swill *vt* beber con exceso: —*n* bazo-fia *f.*
swim *vi* nadar; abundar en: —*vt* pasar a nado: —*n* nadada *f.*
swimming *n* natacion *f;* vertigo *m.*
swimming pool *n* piscina *f.*
swimsuit *n* traje de bano *m.*
swindle *vt* estafar.
swindler *n* trampista *m.*
swine *n* puerco, cochino *m.*
swing *vi* balancear, columpiarse; vibrar; agitarse: —*vt* colum piar; balancear; girar: —*n* vibracion *f;* balanceo *m.*

swinging *adj (fam)* alegre.
swinging door *n* puerta giratoria *f.*
swirl *n* hacer remolinos (en el agua).
switch *n* varilla *f;* interruptor *m; (rail)*aguja *f:* —*vt* cambiar de: —**to ~ off**apagar; parar: —**to ~ on** encender, prender.
switchboard *n* centralita (de telé-fonos) *f.*
swivel *vt* girar.
swoon *vi* desmayarse: —*n* desmayo, deliquio, pasmo *m.*
swoop *vi* calarse: —*n* calada; redada *f:* — **in one ~** de un golpe.
sword *n* espada *f.*
swordfish *n* pez espada *f.*
swordsman *n* guerrero *m.*
sycamore *n* sicomoro *m* (arbol).
sycophant *n* sicofante *m.*
syllabic *adj* silabico.
syllable *n* silaba *f.*
syllabus *n* programa de estudios *m.*
syllogism *n* silogismo *m.*
sylph *n* silfio *m;* silfida *f.*
symbol *n* simbolo *m.*
symbolic(al) *adj* simbolico.
symbolize *vt* simbolizar.
symmetrical *adj* simetrico: —**~ly** *adv* con simetria.

symmetry *n* simetria *f.*
sympathetic *adj* simpatico: —**~ally**adv simpati- camente.
sympathize *vi* compadecerse.
sympathy *n* simpatia *f.*
symphony *n* sinfonia *f.*
symposium *n* simposio *m.*
symptom *n* sintoma *m.*
synagogue *n* sinagoga *f.*
synchronism *n* sincronismo *m.*
syndicate *n* sindicato *m.*
syndrome *n* sindrome *m.*
synod *n* sinodo *m.*
synonym *n* sinonimo *m.*
synonymous *adj* sinonimo: —**~ly** *adv* con sino- nimia.
synopsis *n* sinopsis *f;* sumario *m.*
synoptical *adj* sinoptico.
syntax *n* sintaxis *f.*
synthesis *n* sintesis *f.*
syringe *n* jeringa, lavativa *f:* —*vt* jeringar.
system *n* sistema *m.*
systematic *adj* sistematico: —**~ally**adv sistemati- camente.
systems analyst *n* analista de sistemas *m/f* .

T

table *n* mesa *f m.*
tablecloth *n* mantel *m.*
tablespoon *n* cuchara para comer *f.*
tablet *n* tableta *f m.*
table tennis *n* ping-pong *m.*
taboo *adj* tabu.
tacit *adj* tacito.
taciturn *adj* taciturno.
tack *n* tachuela *f.*
tact *n* tacto *m.*
tactician *n* tactico *m.*
tactics *npl* tactica *f.*
tadpole *n* ranilla *f.*
taffeta *n* tafetan *m.*
tag *n* herrete *m.*
tail *n* cola *f.*
tailor *n* sastre *m.*
tailor-made *adj* hecho a la medida.
taint *vt* tachar.
take *vt* tomar, coger.
takeoff *n* despegue *m.*
takings *npl* ingresos *mpl* .
talc *n* talco *m.*
talent *n* talento *m.*
talisman *n* talisman *m.*
talk *vi* hablar.
talkative *adj* locuaz.
tall *adj* alto.
talon *n* garra de ave de rapina *f.*
tambourine *n* pandereta *f.*
tame *adj* amansado.
tamper *vi* tocar.
tampon *n* tampon *m.*
tan *vt* broncear.
tang *n* sabor fuerte *m.*

tangerine *n* mandarina *f.*
tangle *vt* enredar.
tank *n* cisterna *f;* aljibe *m.*
tanned *adj* bronceado.
tantrum *n* rabieta *f.*
tape *n* cinta *f.*
tape measure *n* metro *m.*
tapestry *n* tapiz *mf.*
tar *n* brea *f.*
target *n* blanco *m* (para tirar).
tariff *n* tarifa *f.*
tarmac *n* pista *f.*
tarnish *vt* deslustrar.
tarpaulin *n* alquitranado *m.*
tarragon *n (bot)* estragon *m.*
tartan *n* tela escocesa *f.*
tartar *n* tartaro *m.*
task *n* tarea *f.*
tassel *n* borlita *f.*
taste *n* gusto *m;* sabor *m.*
tasty *adj* sabroso.
tattoo *n* tatuaje *m.*
taunt *vt* mofar.
Taurus *n* Tauro *m.*
tax *n* impuesto *m.*
taxi *n* taxi *m.*
tea *n* te *m.*
teach *vt* ensenar.
teacher *n* profesor, ra *m/f* .
teak *n* teca *f* (arbol).
team *n* equipo *m.*
teamster *n* camionero *m.*
teapot *n* tetera *f.*
tear *vt* despedazar, rasgar.
tear *n* lagrima *f.*

tease *vt* tomar el pelo.
teaspoon *n* cucharita *f.*
teat *n* ubre, teta *f.*
technical *adj* tecnico.
technician *n* tecnico *m.*
technique *n* tecnica *f.*
technology *n* tecnologia *f.*
teddy (bear) *n* osito de felpa *m.*
tedious *adj* tedioso.
tedium *n* tedio *m.*
tee-shirt *n* camiseta *f.*
teeth *npl* de tooth.
telegraph *n* telegrafo *m.*
telegraphic *adj* telegrafico.
telepathy *n* telepatia *f.*
telephone *n* telefono *m.*
telescope *n* telescopio *m.*
telescopic *adj* telescopico.
television *n* television *f.*
tell *vi* decir.
teller *n* cajero *m.*
temper *vt* templar: —*n* mal genio *m.*
temperament *n* temperamento *m.*
temperate *adj* templado.
temperature *n* temperatura *f.*
template *n* plantilla *f.*
temple *n* templo *m.*
temporary *adj* temporal.
tempt *vt* tentar.
temptation *n* tentacion *f.*
ten *adj* , *n* diez.
tenacity *n* tenacidad *f.*
tenancy *n* tenencia *f.*
tenant *n* arrendador *m.*
tend *vt* guardar.
tendency *n* tendencia *f.*
tender *adj* tierno, estimar.
tendon *n* tendon *m.*
tennis *n* tenis *m.*
tense *adj* tieso, tenso.
tension *n* tension *f.*
tent *n* tienda de campana *f.*
tentacle *n* tentaculo *m.*
tenth *adj* , *n* decimo.
tenure *n* tenencia *f.*
tepid *adj* tibio.
term *n* termino *m.*
terminal *adj* mortal.
termination *n* terminacion *f.*
terminus *n* terminal *f.*
terrace *n* terraza *f.*
terrain *n* terreno *m.*
terrestrial *adj* terrestre.
terrible *adj* terrible.
terrier *n* terrier *m.*
terrific *adj* fantastico.
terrify *vt* aterrar.
territorial *adj* territorial.
territory *n* territorio, distrito *m.*
terror *n* terror *m.*
terrorism *n* terrorismo *m.*
test *n* examen *m.*
testament *n* testamento *m.*
testicles *npl* testiculos *mpl* .
testify *vt* testificar.
testimony *n* testimonio *m.*
tetanus *n* tetano *m.*

tether *vt* atar.
text *n* texto *m.*
textiles *npl* textiles *mpl* .
texture *n* textura *f.*
than *adv* que, de.
thank *vt* agradecer.
thanks *npl* gracias *fpl.*
that *pn* aquel, aquello, aquella; que; este.
thaw *n* deshielo *m.*
the *art* el, la, lo; los, las.
theater *n* teatro *m.*
theft *n* robo *m.*
their *pn* su, suyo, suya; de ellos, deellas: —**s** el suyo, la suya, los suyos, las suyas; de ellos, de ellas.
them *pn* los, las, les; ellos, ellas.
theme *n* tema *m.*
themselves *pn pl* ellos mismos, ellasmismas; si mismos; se.
then *adv* entonces, despues.
theology *n* teologia *f.*
theory *n* teoria *f.*
therapist *n* terapeuta *m.*
therapy *n* terapia *f.*
there *adv* alli, alla.
thermal *adj* termal.
thermometer *n* termometro *m.*
thesaurus *n* tesoro *m.*
these *pn pl* estos, estas.
thesis *n* tesis *f.*
they *pn pl* ellos, ellas.
thick *adj* espeso.
thicken *vi* espesar.
thief *n* ladron *m.*
thigh *n* muslo *m.*
thimble *n* dedal *m.*
thin *adj* delgado.
thing *n* cosa *f.*
think *vi* pensar.
third *adj* tercero.
thirst *n* sed *f.*
thirteen *adj* , *n* trece.
thirteenth *adj* , *n* decimotercio.
thirtieth *adj* , *n* trigesimo.
thirty *adj* , *n* treinta.
this *adj* este, esta, esto: —*pn* este, esta, esto.
thorn *n* espino *m;* espina *f.*
those *pn pl* esos, esas; aquellos, aquellas: —*adj* esos, esas; aquellos, aquellas.
thought *n* pensamiento *m.*
thousand *adj* , *n* mil.
thousandth *adj* , *n* milesimo.
thrash *vt* golpear.
thread *n* hilo *m.*
threat *n* amenaza *f.*
threaten *vt* amenazar.
three *adj* , *n* tres.
threshold *n* umbral *m.*
thrifty *adj* economico.
thrill *vt* emocionar.
thrive *vi* prosperar.
throat *n* garganta *f.*
throb *vi* palpitar.
throne *n* trono *m.*
through *prep* por; durante; mediante.
throw *vt* echar.
thrush *n* tordo *m* (ave).

thrust *vt* empujar.
thug *n* gamberro *m.*
thumb *n* pulgar *m.*
thump *n* golpe *m.*
thunder *n* trueno *m.*
Thursday *n* jueves *m.*
thus *adv* asi, de este modo.
thyme *n (bot)* tomillo *m.*
thyroid *n* tiroides *m.*
tiara *n* tiara *f.*
tic *n* tic *m.*
ticket *n* billete *m* .
tickle *vt* hacer cosquillas.
tidal *adj (mar)* de marea.
tide *n* marea *f.*
tidy *adj* ordenado.
tie *vt* anudar, atar
tiger *n* tigre *m.*
tight *adj* tirante, apretado/a.
tile *n* azulejo *m.*
till *n* caja *f: —vt* cultivar.
time *n* tiempo; epoca *f.*
timer *n* interruptor *m.*
timid *adj* timido.
timidity *n* timidez *f.*
tin *n* estano *m.*
tinfoil *n* papel de estano *m.*
tinsel *n* oropel *m.*
tint *n* tinte *m.*
tiny *adj* pequeno, chico.
tip *n* punta, extremidad *f;* propina *f.*
tire *vt* cansar, fatigar: —*n* neumático *m.*
tissue *n* tejido *m.*
title *n* titulo *m.*
titular *adj* titular.
to *prep* a; para; por; de; hasta; en; con; que.
toad *n* sapo *m.*
toadstool *n (bot)* hongovejin *m.*
toast *vt* tostar; brindar.
toaster *n* tostadora *f.*
tobacco *n* tabaco *m.*
tobacco shop *n* tabaqueria *f.*
today *adv* hoy.
toe *n* dedo del pie *m.*
together *adv* juntamente.
toilet paper *n* papel higienico *m.*
token *n* senal *f.*
tolerate *vt* tolerar.
tomato *n* tomate *m.*
tomb *n* tumba *f.*
tomboy *n* muchachota *f.*
tombstone *n* piedra sepulcral *f.*
tomcat *n* gato *m.*
tomorrow *adv* , *n* manana *f.*
ton *n* tonelada *f.*
tongs *npl* tenacillas *fpl.*
tongue *n* lengua *f.*
tonic *n (med)* tonico *m.*
tonight *adv* , *n* esta tarde (*f*).
tonsil *n* amigdala *f.*
too *adv* demasiado; tambien.
tool *n* herramienta *f.*
tooth *n* diente *m.*
toothache *n* dolor de muelas *m.*
top *n* cima.
topaz *n* topacio *m.*
topic *n* tema *m.*

topless *adj* topless.
topographic(al) *adj* topografico.
topography *n* topografia *f.*
torment *vt* atormentar.
tornado *n* tornado *m.*
torrent *n* torrente *m.*
torrid *adj* apasionado.
tortoise *n* tortuga *f.*
tortoiseshell *adj* de carey.
tortuous *adj* tortuoso.
torture *n* tortura *f.*
toss *vt* tirar, lanzar.
total *adj* total.
totalitarian *adj* totalitario.
totality *n* totalidad *f.*
totter *vi* vacilar.
touch *vt* tocar.
touchdown *n* aterrizaje *m.*
touching *adj* patetico, conmovedor.
tough *adj* duro.
toupee *n* tupe *m.*
tour *n* viaje *m.*
touring *n* viajes turisticos *mpl* .
tourism *n* turismo *m.*
tourist *n* turista *m/f* .
tourist office *n* oficina de turismo *f.*
tournament *n* torneo *m.*
tow *n* remolque *m.*
toward(s) *prep, adv* hacia.
towel *n* toalla *f.*
tower *n* torre *m.*
town *n* ciudad *f.*
town hall *n* ayuntamiento *m.*
toy *n* juguete *m.*
toy store *n* jugueteria *f.*
trace *n* huella *f: —vt* trazar.
trade *n* comercio *m;* ocupacion *f.*
trade(s) union *n* sindicato *m.*
tradition *n* tradicion *f* .
traditional *adj* tradicional.
traffic *n* trafico *m.*
traffic lights *npl* semaforo *m.*
tragedy *n* tragedia *f.*
tragic *adj* tragico.
trail *vt , vi* rastrear: — *n* senda *f.*
trailer *n* caravana *f.*
train *vt* entrenar * *n* tren *m.*
trainee *n* aprendiz *m.*
trainer *n* entrenador *m.*
trait *n* rasgo *m.*
traitor *n* traidor *m.*
tramp *n* vagabundo *m.*
trample *vt* pisotear.
trampoline *n* trampolin *m.*
trance *n* rapto *m.*
tranquil *adj* tranquilo.
tranquillizer *n* tranquilizante *m.*
transact *vt* negociar.
transaction *n* transaccion *f.*
transatlantic *adj* transatlántico.
transcription *n* traslado *m.*
transfer *vt* transferir.
transform *vt* transformar.
transformation *n* transformacion *f.*
transfusion *n* transfusion *f.*
transit *n* transito *m.*
transition *n* transito *m;* transicion *f.*

translate vt traducir.
translation n traduccion f.
translator n traductor, ra m/f.
transmit vt transmitir.
transparent adj transparente.
transpire vi resultar.
transplant vt trasplantar.
transport vt transportar.
trap n trampa f.
trapeze n trapecio m.
trappings npl adornos mpl.
trash n pacotilla f; basura f.
travel vi viajar.
trawler n pesquero de arrastre m.
tray n bandeja f
treachery n traicion f.
tread vi pisar.
treason n traicion n.
treasure n tesoro m.
treasurer n tesorero m.
treat vt tratar.
treatise n tratado m.
treatment n trato m.
treaty n tratado m.
treble adj triple.
treble clef n clave de sol f.
tree n arbol m.
trellis n enrejado m.
tremble vi temblar.
tremendous adj tremendo.
tremor n temblor m.
trench n foso m.
trend n tendencia f.
trendy adj de moda.
trespass vt transpasar.
tress n trenza f.
trestle n caballete de serrador m.
trial n proceso m.
triangle n triangulo m.
triangular adj triangular.
tribal adj tribal.
tribe n tribu f.
tribunal n tribunal m.
tributary adj, n tributario m.
tribute n tributo m.
trice n momento, tris m.
trick n engano m.
trickle vi gotear.
tricky adj dificil.
tricycle n triciclo m.
trifle n bagatela.
trigger n gatillo m.
trigonometry n trigonometria f.
trim adj aseado.
Trinity n Trinidad f.
trinket n joya.
trio n (mus) trio m.
trip vt hacer caer; viaje corto m.
tripe n callos mpl.
triple adj triple.
triplets npl trillizos mpl.
triplicate n triplicado m.
tripod n tripode m.
triumph n triunfo m.
triumphal adj triunfal.
triumphant adj triunfante.
trivia npl trivialidades fpl.

trivial adj trivial.
trolley n carrito m.
trombone n trombon m.
trophy n trofeo m.
tropical adj tropico.
trot n trote m.
trouble vt afligir.
trough n abrevadero m.
trout n trucha f.
trowel n paleta f.
truce n tregua f.
truck n camion m.
true adj verdadero.
truffle n trufa f.
truly adv en verdad.
trumpet n trompeta f.
trunk n baul, cofre m; trompa f.
trust n confianza f.
truth n verdad f.
try vt examinar, tentar.
tub n balde, cubo m.
tuba n tuba f.
tube n tubo m.
tuberculosis n tuberculosis f.
Tuesday n martes m.
tuition n enseñanza f.
tulip n tulipan m.
tumble vi caer.
tumbler n vaso m.
tummy n barriga f.
tumor n tumor m.
tumultuous adj tumultuoso.
tuna n atun m.
tune n tono m.
tunic n tunica f.
tunnel n tunel m.
turban n turbante m.
turbine n turbina f.
turbulence n turbulencia f.
tureen n sopera f.
turf n cesped m.
turgid adj pesado.
turkey n pavo m.
turmoil n disturbio m.
turn vi volver.
turncoat n desertor m.
turnip n nabo m.
turnover n facturacion f.
turnstile n torniquete m.
turpentine n trementina f.
turquoise n turquesa f.
turret n torrecilla f.
turtle n galapago m.
turtledove n tortola f.
tusk n colmillo m.
tussle n pelea f.
tutor n tutor m.
tuxedo n smoking m.
twang n gangueo m.
tweezers npl tenacillas fpl.
twelfth adj, n duodecimo.
twelve adj, n doce.
twentieth adj, n vigesimo.
twenty adj, n veinte.
twice adv dos veces.
twig n ramita f: —vi caer en lacuenta.
twilight n crepusculo m.

twin *n* gemelo *m.*
twist *vt* torcer.
twit *n (col)* tonto *m.*
twitch *vi* moverse nerviosamente.
two *adj , n* dos.
two-faced *adj* falso.
tycoon *n* magnate *m.*

type *n* tipo *m;* letra *f;* modelo *m:* —*vt* escribir a
maquina.
typewriter *n* maquina de escribir *f.*
typical *adj* tipico.
tyrannical *adj* tiranico.
tyranny *n* tirania *f.*
tyrant *n* tirano *m.*

U

ubiquitous *adj* ubicuo.
udder *n* ubre *f.*
ugh *excl* ¡uf!
ugliness *n* fealdad *f.*
ugly *adj* feo; peligroso.
ulcer *n* ulcera *f.*
ulterior *adj* ulterior.
ultimate *adj* ultimo.
ultimatum *n* ultimatum *m.*
umbrella *n* paraguas *m invar.*
umpire *n* arbitro *m.*
unable *adj* incapaz.
unaccompanied *adj* solo.
unaccustomed *adj* desacostum-brado.
unanimity *n* unanimidad *f.*
unanimous *adj* unanime.
unanswerable *adj* incontro-vertible.
unapproachable *adj* inaccesible.
unbearable *adj* intolerable.
unbecoming *adj* indecente.
unbutton *vt* desabotonar.
uncanny *adj* extraordinario.
unchanged *adj* no alterado.
uncharitable *adj* nada caritativo.
uncle *n* tio.
uncomfortable *adj* incomodo.
uncommon *adj* raro.
uncompromising *adj* irrecon-ciliable.
unconscious *adj* inconsciente.
unconventional *adj* poco conven-cional.
uncork *vt* destapar.
uncouth *adj* grosero.
uncover *vt* descubrir.
undaunted *adj* intrepido.
under *prep* debajo de.
under-age *adj* menor de edad.
underclothing *n* ropa intima *f.*
underdeveloped *adj* subdesarrollado.
underdog *n* desvalido *m.*
underestimate *vt* subestimar.
undergo *vt* sufrir.
undergraduate *n* estudiante *m.*
underground *n* movimiento clandestino *m.*
underline *vt* subrayar.
underpaid *adj* mal pagado.
undershirt *n* camiseta *f.*
understand *vt* entender, comprender.
understatement *n* subestimacion *f.*
underwear *n* ropa intima *f.*
underworld *n* hampa *f.*
undetermined *adj* indeterminado, indeciso.
undigested *adj* indigesto.
undisciplined *adj* indisciplinado.
undismayed *adj* intrepido.

undisputed *adj* incontestable.
undisturbed *adj* quieto, tranquilo.
undivided *adj* indiviso, entero.
undo *vt* deshacer, destar.
undoubted *adj* indudable.
undress *vi* desnudarse.
undue *adj* indebido.
undulating *adj* ondulante.
unduly *adv* indebidamente.
undying *adj* inmortal.
unearth *vt* desenterrar.
uneasy *adj* inquieto.
uneducated *adj* ignorante.
unemployed *adj* parado.
unemployment *n* paro *m.*
unenlightened *adj* no iluminado.
unenviable *adj* poco envidiable.
unequal *adj* desigual.
unequaled *adj* incomparable.
uneven *adj* desigual.
unexpected *adj* inesperado.
unexplored *adj* inexplorado.
unfair *adj* injusto.
unfaithful *adj* infiel.
unfamiliar *adj* desacostumbrado.
unfashionable *adj* pasado de moda.
unfasten *vt* desatar.
unfavorable *adj* desfavorable.
unfeeling *adj* insensible.
unfit *adj* indispuesto.
unfold *vt* desplegar.
unforeseen *adj* imprevisto.
unforgettable *adj* inolvidable.
unforgivable *adj* imperdonable.
unforgiving *adj* implacable.
unfortunate *adj* desafortunado.
unfounded *adj* sin fundamento.
unfriendly *adj* antipatico.
unfruitful *adj* esteril; infructuoso.
unfurnished *adj* sin muebles.
ungrateful *adj* ingrato.
unhappily *adv* infelizmente.
unhappy *adj* infeliz.
unhealthy *adj* malsano.
unhook *vt* desenganchar; descolgar; desabrochar.
unhoped(-for) *adj* inesperado.
unhurt *adj* ileso.
unicorn *n* unicornio *m.*
uniform *adj* uniforme: —*n* uniforme *m.*
uniformity *adj* uniformidad *f.*
unify *vt* unificar.
unimaginable *adj* inimaginable.
unimportant *adj* nada importante.
uninformed *adj* ignorante.

uninhabitable *adj* inhabitable.
uninhabited *adj* inhabitado, desierto.
uninjured *adj* ileso, no danado.
unintelligible *adj* ininteligible.
unintentional *adj* involuntario.
uninterested *adj* desinteresado.
uninteresting *adj* poco interesante.
uninvited *adj* no convidado.
union *n* union *f;* sindicato *m.*
unionist *n* unitario *m.*
unique *adj* unico, uno, singular.
unit *n* unidad *f.*
unite *vt vi* unir(se), juntarse.
United States (of America) *npl* Estados Unidos (de América) *mpl* .
unity *n* unidad *f.*
universal *adj* universal.
universe *n* universo *m.*
university *n* universidad *f.*
unjust *adj* injusto.
unkind *adj* poco amable.
unknown *adj* incognito.
unlawful *adj* ilícito/a.
unless *conj* a menos que, si no.
unload *vt* descargar.
unluckily *adv* desafortunadamente.
unlucky *adj* desafortunado.
unmarried *adj* soltero; soltera.
unmerited *adj* desmerecido.
unmistakable *adj* evidente.
unmoved *adj* inmoto, firme.
unnatural *adj* antinatural.
unnecessary *adj* inutil, innecesario.
unnoticed *adj* no observado.
unobserved *adj* invertido/a.
unobtainable *adj* inconseguible.
unobtrusive *adj* modesto.
unoccupied *adj* desocupado.
unofficial *adj* no oficial.
unpack *vt* desempacar; desenvol-ver.
unpaid *adj* no pagado.
unpleasant *adj* desagradable.
unpopular *adj* no popular.
unpracticed *adj* inexperto.
unprecedented *adj* sin ejemplo.
unpredictable *adj* imprevisible.
unprepared *adj* no preparado.
unprofitable *adj* inútil, vano; pocolucrativo.
unpunished *adj* impune.
unqualified *adj* sin titulos; to tal.
unquestionable *adj* indubitable.
unravel *vt* desenredar.
unrealistic *adj* poco realista.
unreasonable *adv* irracionalmente.
unrelated *adj* sin relacion; inconexo.
unrelenting *adj* incompasivo, inflex-ible.
unreliable *adj* poco fiable.
unrestrained *adj* desenfrenado; ilimi-tado.
unripe *adj* inmaduro.
unrivaled *adj* sin rival.
unroll *vt* desenrollar.
unsafe *adj* inseguro.
unsatisfactory *adj* insatisfactorio.
unscrew *vt* destornillar.
unscrupulous *adj* sin escrupulos.
unseemly *adj* indecente.
unseen *adj* invisible.

unselfish *adj* desinteresado.
unsettle *vt* perturbar.
unshaken *adj* firme, estable.
unskilled *adj* inhabil.
unsociable *adj* insociable.
unspeakable *adj* inefable.
unstable *adj* instable, inconstante.
unsteady *adj* inestable.
unsuccessful *adj* infeliz, desafortunado.
unsuitable *adj* inapropiado; inoportuno.
unsure *adj* inseguro.
unsympathetic *adj* inompasivo.
untapped *adj* sin explotar.
untenable *adj* insostenible.
unthinkable *adj* inconcebible.
unthinking *adj* desatento, irreflexivo.
untidiness *n* desalino *m.*
untidy *adj* desordenado; sucio.
untie *vt* desatar, deshacer, soltar.
until *prep* hasta: —*conj* hasta que.
untimely *adj* intempestivo.
untiring *adj* incansable.
untold *adj* nunca dicho; indecible; incalculable.
untouched *adj* intacto.
untoward *adj* impropio; adverso.
untried *adj* no ensayado o probado.
untroubled *adj* no perturbado, tranquilo.
untrue *adj* falso.
untrustworthy *adj* indigno de confianza.
untruth *n* falsedad, mentira *f.*
unused *adj* isin usar, no usado.
unusual *adj* inusitado, raro: —~ly *adv* inusitadamen-te, raramente.
unveil *vt* quitar el velo, descubrir.
unwavering *adj* inquebrantable.
unwelcome *adj* desagradable, inoportuno.
unwell *adj* enfermizo, malo.
unwieldy *adj* pesado.
unwilling *adj* desinclinado: —~ly *adv* de mala gana.
unwillingness *n* mala gana, repugnancia *f.*
unwind *vt* desenredar, desenmaranar: —*vi* relajarse.
unwise *adj* imprudente.
unwitting *adj* inconsciente.
unworkable *adj* poco practico.
unworthy *adj* indigno.
unwrap *vt* desenvolver.
unwritten *adj* no escrito.
up *adv* arriba, en lo alto; levantado: — *prep* hacia; hasta.
upbringing *n* educacion *f.*
update *vt* poner al dia.
upheaval *n* agitacion *f.*
uphill *adj* dificil, penoso: —*adv* cuesta arriba.
uphold *vt* sos tener, apoyar.
upholstery *n* tapiceria *f.*
upkeep *n* manteniniento *m.*
uplift *vt* levantar.
upon *prep* sobre, encima.
upper *adj* superior; mas elevado.
upper-class *adj* de la clase alta.
upper-hand *n* (*fig*) superioridad *f.*
uppermost *adj* mas alto, supremo: —**to be** ~ pre-dominar.
upright *adj* derecho, perpendicu-lar, recto; puesto en pie; hon rado.
uprising *n* sublevacion *f.*
uproar *n* tumulto, alboroto *m.*

uproot *vt* desarraigar.
upset *vt* trastornar; derramar, vol-car: —*n* reves *m;* trastorno *m:* —*adj* molesto; revuelto.
upshot *n* remate *m;* fin *m;* conclusion *f.*
upside-down *adv* de arriba abajo.
upstairs *adv* de arriba.
upstart *n* advenedizo *m.*
uptight *adj* nervioso.
up-to-date *adj* al dia.
upturn *n* mejora *f.*
upward *adj* ascendente: —**s** *adv* hacia arriba.
urban *adj* urbano.
urbane *adj* cortes.
urchin *n* golfillo *m.*
urge *vt* animar: —*n* impulso *m;* deseo *m.*
urgency *n* urgencia *f.*
urgent *adj* urgente.
urinal *n* orinal *m.*
urinate *vi* orinar.
urine *n* orina *f.*
urn *n* urna *f.*
us *pn* nos; nosotros.
usage *n* tratamiento *m;* uso *m.*

use *n* uso *m;* utilidad, practica *f:* —*vt* usar, emplear.
used *adj* usado.
useful *adj* , **~ly** *adv* util(mente).
usefulness *n* utilidad *f.*
useless *adj* inútil: —**~ly** *adv* inútilmente.
uselessness *n* inutilidad *f.*
user-friendly *adj* amistoso.
usher *n* ujier *m;* acomodador *m.*
usherette *n* acomodadora *f.*
usual *adj* usual, comun, normal: —**~ly** *adv* normalmente.
usurer *n* usurero *m.*
usurp *vt* usurpar.
usury *n* usura *f.*
utensil *n* utensilio *m.*
uterus *n* utero *m.*
utilize *vt* utilizar.
utility *n* utilidad *f.*
utmost *adj* extremo, sumo; ultimo.
utter *adj* total; to do; entero: —*vt* proferir; expresar; publicar.
utterance *n* expresion *f.*
utterly *adv* enteramente, del todo.

V

vacancy *n* cuarto libre *m.*
vacant *adj* vacio; desocupado.
vacate *vt* desocupar.
vacation *n* vacaciones *fpl.*
vaccinate *vt* vacunar.
vaccination *n* vacunacion *f.*
vaccine *n* vacuna *f.*
vacuous *adj* necio/a, bobo/a.
vacuum *n* vacio *m.*
vagina *n* vagina *f.*
vagrant *n* vagabundo.
vague *adj* vago.
vain *adj* vano.
valet *n* criado *m.*
valiant *adj* valiente.
valid *adj* valido.
valley *n* valle *m.*
valor *n* valor *m.*
valuable *adj* precioso.
valuation *n* tasa, valuacion *f.*
value *n* valor.
valued *adj* apreciado.
valve *n* valvula *f.*
vampire *n* vampiro *m.*
vandal *n* gamberro *m.*
vandalize *vt* danar.
vandalism *n* vandalismo *m.*
vanguard *n* vanguardia *f.*
vanilla *n* vainilla *f.*
vanish *vi* desvanecerse.
vanity *n* vanidad *f.*
vanquish *vt* vencer.
vantage point *n* punto panoramico *m.*
vapor *n* vapor *m.*
variable *adj* variable.
variance *n* discordia *f.*
variation *n* variacion *f.*
varicose vein *n* variz *f.*

varied *adj* variado.
variety *n* variedad *f.*
various *adj* vario.
varnish *n* barniz *m.*
vary *vt* , *vi* variar.
vase *n* florero *m.*
vast *adj* vasto.
vat *n* tina *f.*
vault *n* boveda *f.*
veal *n* ternera *f.*
veer *vi (mar)* virar.
vegetable *adj* vegetal, *n* **~s** *pl* legumbres *fpl.*
vegetable garden *n* huerta *f.*
vegetarian *n* vegetariano, na *m/f .*
vegetate *vi* vegetar.
vegetation *n* vegetacion *f.*
vehemence *n* vehemencia *f.*
vehement *adj* vehemente.
vehicle *n* vehiculo *m.*
veil *n* velo *m.*
vein *n* vena *f.*
velocity *n* velocidad *f.*
velvet *n* terciopelo *m.*
vendor *n* vendedor *m.*
veneer *n* chapa *f.*
venerable *adj* venerable.
venerate *vt* venerar.
veneration *n* veneracion *f.*
venereal *adj* venereo.
vengeance *n* venganza *f.*
venial *adj* venial.
venison *n* (carne de) venado *f.*
venom *n* veneno *m.*
venomous *adj* venenoso.
vent *n* respiradero *m;* salida *f.*
ventilate *vt* ventilar.
ventilation *n* ventilacion *f.*
ventilator *n* ventilador *m.*

ventriloquist *n* ventrilocuo *m.*
venture *n* empresa *f:* —*vi* aventurarse.
venue *n* lugar de reunion *m.*
veranda(h) *n* terraza *f.*
verb *n (gr)* verbo *m.*
verbal *adj* verbal.
verdict *n* (law) veredicto *m.*
verification *n* verificacion *f.*
verify *vt* verificar.
veritable *adj* verdadero.
vermin *n* bichos *mpl .*
vermouth *n* vermut *m.*
versatile *adj* versatil.
verse *n* verso *m.*
versed *adj* versado.
version *n* version *f.*
versus *prep* contra.
vertebra *n* vertebra *f.*
vertebral, vertebrate *adj* vertebral.
vertical *adj ,* **~ly** *adv* vertical(mente).
vertigo *n* vertigo *m.*
very *adj adv* muy, mucho.
vessel *n* vasija *f.*
vest *n* chaleco *m.*
vestibule *n* vestibulo *m.*
vestige *n* vestigio *m.*
vestry *n* sacristia *f.*
veteran *adj , n* veterano *(m).*
veterinary *adj* veterinario.
veto *n* veto *m.*
vex *vt* molestar.
via *prep* por.
viaduct *n* viaducto *m.*
vial *n* redoma *f.*
vibrate *vi* vibrar.
vibration *n* vibracion *f.*
vicarious *adj* sustituto.
vice *n* vicio *m.*
vice versa *adv* viceversa.
vicinity *n* vecindad *f.*
vicious *adj* vicioso.
victim *n* victima *f.*
victimize *vt* victimizar.
victor *n* vencedor *m.*
victorious *adj* victorioso.
victory *n* victoria *f.*
video *n* videofilm *m;* video cassette *f;* videograba-
dora *f.*
video tape *n* cinta de video *f.*
vie *vi* competir.
view *n* vista *f.*
viewpoint *n* punto de vista *m.*
vigilance *n* vigilancia *f.*
vigilant *adj* vigilante.
vigorous *adj* vigoroso.
vigor *n* vigor *m.*
vile *adj* vil.
vilify *vt* envilecer.
villa *n* chalet *m.*
village *n* aldea *f.*
villain *n* malvado *m.*
vindicate *vt* vindicar.
vindication *n* vindicacion *f.*
vindictive *adj* vengativo.
vine *n* vid *f.*
vinegar *n* vinagre *m.*
vineyard *n* vina *f.*

vintage *n* vendimia *f.*
vinyl *n* vinilo *m.*
viola *n (mus)* viola *f.*
violate *vt* violar.
violation *n* violacion *f.*
violence *n* violencia *f.*
violent *adj* violento.
violet *n (bot)* violeta *f.*
violin *n (mus)* violin *m.*
viper *n* vibora *f.*
virgin *n* virgen *f.*
virginity *n* virginidad *f.*
Virgo *n* Virgo *f* (signo del zodiaco).
virile *adj* viril.
virility *n* virilidad *f.*
virtual *adj ,* **~ly** *adv* virtual(mente).
virtue *n* virtud *f.*
virtuous *adj* virtuoso.
virulent *adj* virulento.
virus *n* virus *m.*
visa *n* visado *m,* visa *f.*
vis-a-vis *prep* con respecto a.
visibility *n* visibilidad *f.*
visible *adj* visible.
vision *n* vista *f.*
visit *vt* visitar: —*n* visita *f.*
visitor *n* visitante *m/f .*
visor *n* visera *f.*
vista *n* vista, perspectiva *f.*
visual *adj* visual.
visualize *vt* imaginarse.
vital *adj* vital.
vitality *n* vitalidad *f.*
vitamin *n* vitamina *f.*
vitiate *vt* viciar.
vivacious *adj* vivaz.
vivid *adj* vivo.
vivisection *n* viviseccion *f.*
vocabulary *n* vocabulario *m.*
vocal *adj* vocal.
vocation *n* vocacion *f.*
vociferous *adj* vocinglero.
vodka *n* vodka *m.*
vogue *n* moda *f;* boga *f.*
voice *n* voz *f:* —*vt* expresar.
void *adj* nulo: —*n* vacio *m.*
volatile *adj* volatil; voluble.
volcanic *adj* volcanico.
volcano *n* volcan *m.*
volition *n* voluntad *f.*
volley *n* descarga *f;* salva *f;* rociada *f;* volea *f.*
volleyball *n* voleibol *m.*
volt *n* voltio *m.*
voltage *n* voltaje *m.*
voluble *adj* locuaz.
volume *n* volumen *m.*
voluntarily *adv* voluntariamente.
voluntary *adj* voluntario.
volunteer *n* voluntario *m.*
voluptuous *adj* voluptuoso.
vomit *vt , vi* vomitar.
vortex *n* remolino *m.*
vote *n* voto.
voter *n* votante *m/f .*
voting *n* votacion *f.*
voucher *n* vale *m.*
vow *n* voto *m.*

vowel *n* vocal *f.*
voyage *n* viaje *m.*
vulgar *adj* ordinario.

vulgarity *n* groseria.
vulnerable *adj* vulnerable.
vulture *n* buitre *m.*

W

wad *n* fajo *m.*
waddle *vi* anadear.
wade *vi* vadear.
wafer *n* galleta *f.*
waffle *n* gofre *m.*
wag *vt* menear.
wage *n* salario *m.*
waggon *n* carro *m.*
wail *n* lamento *m.*
waist *n* cintura *f.*
wait *vi* esperar.
waiter *n* camarero *m.*
waiting list *n* lista de espera *f.*
waiting room *n* sala de espera *f.*
waive *vt* suspender.
wake *vi* despertarse.
waken *vt , (vi)* despertar(se).
walk *vt , vi* pasear; andar.
walking stick *n* baston *m.*
wall *n* pared *f;* muralla *f;* muro *m.*
wallflower *n (bot)* aleli *m.*
wallpaper *n* papel pintado *m.*
walnut *n* nogal *m;* nuez *f.*
walrus *n* morsa *f.*
waltz *n* vals *m* (baile).
wan *adj* palido.
wand *n* varita magica *f.*
wane *vi* menguar.
want *vt* querer.
wanton *adj* lascivo.
war *n* guerra *f.*
ward *n* sala *f*
wardrobe *n* guardarropa *f.*
warehouse *n* almacen *m.*
warm *adj* calido; caliente.
warm-hearted *adj* afectuoso.
warmth *n* calor *m.*
warn *vt* avisar.
warning *n* aviso *m.*
warp *vi* torcerse.
warrant *n* orden judicial *f.*
warranty *n* garantia *f.*
warren *n* conejero *m.*
warrior *n* guerrero *m.*
wart *n* verruga *f.*
wary *adj* cauto.
wash *vt* lavar.
washbowl *n* lavabo *m.*
washing machine *n* lavadora *f.*
washing-up *n* fregado *m.*
washroom *n* servicios *mpl .*
wasp *n* avispa *f.*
waste *vt* malgastar.
watch *n* reloj *m;* vigilar.
watchdog *n* perro guardian *m.*
water *n* agua *f.*
watercolor *n* acuarela *f.*
waterfall *n* cascada *f.*

watering-can *n* regadera *f.*
waterlily *n* ninfea *f.*
water melon *n* sandia *f.*
watertight *adj* impermeable.
watt *n* vatio *m.*
wave *n* ola, onda *f.*
waver *vi* vacilar.
wax *n* cera *f.*
way *n* camino *m;* via *f.*
we *pn* nosotros, nosotras.
weak *adj , ~ly* *adv* debil(mente).
wealth *n* riqueza *f.*
wealthy *adj* rico.
weapon *n* arma *f.*
wear *vt* gastar, consumir; usar, llevar.
weary *adj* cansado.
weasel *n* comadreja *f.*
weather *n* tiempo *m.*
weave *vt* tejer; trenzar.
weaving *n* tejido *m.*
web *n* telarana *f.*
wed *vt , vi* casar(se).
wedge *n* cuna *f.*
Wednesday *n* miercoles *m.*
wee *adj* pequenito.
weed *n* mala hierba *f.*
week *n* semana *f.*
weekend *n* fin de semana *m.*
weekly *adj* semanal.
weep *vt , vi* llorar.
weeping willow *n* sauce lloron *m.*
weigh *vt , vi* pesar.
weight *n* peso *m.*
welcome *adj* recibido con agrado: — ~! ¡bienve-
nido!.
weld *vt* soldar.
welfare *n* prosperidad *f*
well *n* fuente *f adv* bien.
wench *n* mozuela *f.*
west *n* oeste, occidente *m.*
wet *adj* humedo, mojado.
whale *n* ballena *f.*
wharf *n* muelle *m.*
what *pn* que, qué?, el que, la que, lo que.
whatever *pn* cualquier o cualquiera cosa que.
wheat *n* trigo *m.*
wheel *n* rueda *f.*
wheelbarrow *n* carretilla *f.*
wheelchair *n* sillita de ruedas *f.*
wheeze *vi* jadear.
when *adv* cuando.
whenever *adv* cuando; cada vez que.
where *adv* dónde? *conj* donde.
whether *conj* si.
which *pn* que; lo que; el que, el cual; cual: —*adj*
qué?; cuyo.
while *n* rato *m;* vez *f: —conj* durante; mientras;
aunque.

whim *n* antojo *m.*
whine *vi* llorar, lamentar
whinny *vi* relinchar.
whip *n* azote *m;* latigo *m.*
whirlpool *n* vortice *m.*
whirlwind *n* torbellino *m.*
whiskey *n* whisky *m.*
whisper *vi* cuchichear.
whistle *vi* silbar.
white *adj* blanco.
who *pn* quién?, que.
whoever *pn* quienquiera, cualquiera.
whole *adj* todo.
wholemeal *adj* integral.
wholly *adv* enteramente.
whom *pn* quién? que.
whooping cough *n* tos ferina *f.*
whore *n* puta *f.*
why *n* por qué?
wick *n* mecha *f.*
wicked *adj* malvado.
wide *adj* ancho.
widen *vt* ensanchar.
widow *n* viuda *f.*
widower *n* viudo *m.*
width *n* anchura *f.*
wield *vt* manejar.
wife *n* esposa *f.*
wig *n* peluca *f.*
wild *adj* silvestre.
wilderness *n* desierto *m.*
wild life *n* fauna *f.*
will *n* voluntad *f.*
willful *adj* deliberado; testarudo.
willow *n* sauce *m* (arbol).
willpower *n* fuerza de voluntad *f.*
wilt *vi* marchitarse.
wily *adj* astuto.
win *vt* ganar.
wince *vi* encogerse, estremecerse.
winch *n* torno *m.*
wind *n* viento *m.*
wind *vt* enrollar.
windfall *n* golpe de suerte *m.*
winding *adj* tortuoso.
windmill *n* molino de viento *m.*
window *n* ventana *f.*
window box *n* jardinera de ventana *f.*
window ledge *n* repisa *f.*
window pane *n* cristal *m.*
window sill *n* repisa *f.*
windpipe *n* traquea *f.*
windshield *n* parabrisas *m* invar.
windy *adj* de mucho viento.
wine *n* vino *m.*
wine cellar *n* bodega *f.*
wine glass *n* copa *f.*
wing *n* ala *f.*
winged *adj* alado.
wink *vi* guinar.
winner *n* ganador.
winter *n* invierno *m.*
wintry *adj* invernal.
wipe *vt* limpiar.
wire *n* telegrama *m.*
wisdom *n* sabiduria *f.*
wisdom teeth *npl* muelas de juicio*fpl.*

wise *adj* sabio.
wisecrack *n* broma *f.*
wish *vt* querer.
wishful *adj* deseoso.
wit *n* entendimiento *m.*
witch *n* bruja *f.*
witchcraft *n* brujeria *f.*
with *prep* con; por, de, a.
withdraw *vt* quitar.
withdrawal *n* retirada *f.*
withdrawn *adj* reservado.
withhold *vt* detener.
within *prep* dentro de.
without *prep* sin.
withstand *vt* resistir.
witless *adj* necio.
witness *n* testigo *m.*
witticism *n* ocurrencia *f.*
wittily *adv* ingeniosamente.
witty *adj* ingenioso.
wizard *n* brujo *m.*
woe *n* dolor *m;* miseria *f.*
woeful *adj* triste.
wolf *n* lobo *m.*
woman *n* mujer *f.*
womb *n* utero *m.*
wonder *n* milagro *m.*
wonderful *adj* maravilloso.
won't *abrev* de will not.
woo *vt* cortejar.
wood *n* bosque *m;* selva *f;* madera *f;* lena *f.*
woodland *n* arbolado *m.*
woodlouse *n* cochinilla *f.*
woodpecker *n* picamaderos *m*invar.
woodworm *n* carcoma *f.*
wool *n* lana *f.*
woolen *adj* de lana.
word *n* palabra *f.*
wordy *adj* verboso.
work *vi* trabajar; obrar.
world *n* mundo *m.*
worm *n* gusano *m.*
worn-out *adj* gastado.
worried *adj* preocupado.
worry *vt* preocupar.
worse *adj , adv* peor.
worship *n* culto *m;* adoracion *f.*
worst *adj* el/la peor.
worth *n* valor *m.*
worthwhile *adj* que vale la pena; valioso.
worthy *adj* digno.
wound *n* herida *f.*
wrangle *vi* renir *f.*
wrap *vt* envolver.
wrath *n* ira *f.*
wreath *n* corona *f.*
wreck *n* naufragio *m;* ruina *f.*
wreckage *n* restos *mpl .*
wren *n* reyezuelo *m* (avecilla).
wrestle *vi* luchar; disputar.
wrestling *n* lucha *f.*
wretched *adj* infeliz, miserable.
wring *vt* torcer.
wrinkle *n* arruga *f.*
wrist *n* muneca *f.*
wristband *n* puno de camisa *m.*
wristwatch *n* reloj de pulsera *m.*

writ *n* escrito *m;* escritura *f.*
write *vt* escribir.
write-off *n* perdida total *f.*
writer *n* escritor, ra, *m/f ;* autor, ra *m/ f.*
writhe *vi* retorcerse.
writing *n* escritura *f*

writing desk *n* escritorio *m.*
writing paper *n* papel para escribir *m.*
wrong *n* injuria *f;* injusticia *f.*
wrongful *adj* injusto.
wrongly *adv* injustamente.
wry *adj* ironico.

XYZ

Xmas *n* Navidad *f.*
X-ray *n* radiografia *f.*
xylophone *n* xilofano *m.*
yacht *n* yate *m.*
yachting *n* balandrismo *m.*
Yankee *n* yanqui *m.*
yard *n* corral *m;* yarda *f.*
yardstick *n* criterio *m.*
yarn *n* estambre *m;* hilo de lino *m.*
yawn *vi* bostezar **yeah** *adv* si.
year *n* ano *m.*
yearling *n* primal *m,* ala *f.*
yearly *adj* anual.
yearn *vi* anorar.
yearning *n* anoranza *f.*
yeast *n* levadura *f.*
yell *vi* aullar.
yellow *adj* amarillo.
yelp *vi* latir, ganir.
yes *adv ,* *n* si *(m).*
yesterday *adv , n* ayer *(m).*
yet *conj* sin embargo; pero: —*adv* todavia.
yew *n* tejo *m.*
yield *vt* dar, producir.
yoga *n* yoga *m.*
yog(h)urt *n* yogur *m.*
yoke *n* yugo *m.*
yolk *n* yema de huevo *f.*
yonder *adv* alla.
you *pn* vosotros, tu, usted, ustedes.

young *adj* joven.
youngster *n* jovencito, ta *m/f .*
your(s) *pn* tuyo, vuestro, suyo: —**sincerely ~s** su
     seguro ser vidor.
yourself *pn* tu mismo, usted mismo, vosotros mis-
     mos, ustedes mismos.
youth *n* juventud *f.*
youthful *adj* juvenil.
youthfulness *n* juventud *f.*
yuppie *adj , n* yuppie *m/f .*
zany *adj* estrafalario.
zap *vt* borrar.
zeal *n* celo *m;* ardor *m.*
zealous *adj* celoso.
zebra *n* cebra *f.*
zenith *n* cenit *m.*
zero *n* zero, cero *m.*
zest *n* animo *m.*
zigzag *n* zigzag *m.*
zinc *n* zinc *m.*
zip, zipper *n* cremallera *f.*
zodiac *n* zodiaco *m.*
zone *n* banda, faja *f;* zona *f.*
zoo *n* zoo *m.*
zoological *adj* zoologico.
zoologist *n* zoologo, ga *m/f .*
zoology *n* zoologia *f.*
zoom *vi* zumbar.
zoom lens *n* zoom *m*